MW01598851

Children, Politics, and Medicare

EXPERIENCES IN A CANADIAN PROVINCE

by

Geoffrey C. Robinson and George R. F. Elliot

with chapters by

John Doughty and James R. Miller

University of Calgary Press

University of Calgary Press
2500 University Drive N.W.
Calgary, Alberta, Canada T2N 1N4

Canadian Cataloguing in Publication Data

Robinson, Geoffrey C.
  Children, politics, and medicare

  Includes bibliographical references and index.
  ISBN 1-895176-31-X

  1. Child health services—British Columbia. 2. Medical
care—Government policy—British Columbia. 3. Medicine,
State—Canada. I. Elliot, George R. F., 1912– II. Title.

RJ103.C2R62 1993   362.1'9892'0009711   C93-091700-6

COMMITTED TO THE DEVELOPMENT OF CULTURE AND THE ARTS

Cover design by Jon Paine
Printed in Canada by Hignell Printing Limited

♾ This book is printed on acid-free paper.

Contents

Preface

This book describes the influence of national health insurance upon the development of population-based programs for children in British Columbia, the third largest province in Canada. Both authors have spent their working professional lives in British Columbia and have witnessed the development of health services before and after the introduction of health insurance. One of the authors, George R.F. Elliot, joined the provincial Department of Health and Welfare in 1946, when the annual health budget was $5 million. Today it is $5.4 billion.

During the course of countless interviews in the preparation of the book, we were impressed by two circumstances. First, even senior administrators knew little about the evolution of the program they were managing, let alone the larger organization of which they were an important part. Perhaps of more importance was the interest these individuals showed in learning about the earlier history of their departments. Second, we were struck by the very real difficulty of obtaining comparable information from other Canadian provinces and other countries with similar systems of health care organization.

The book is dedicated to Dr. Jack McCreary, first professor and head of the Department of Paediatrics in the Medical Faculty at the University of British Columbia. He left a secure practice in the Hospital for Sick Children in Toronto to start his new career in Vancouver. A special tribute to him follows.

MEMOIR: JOHN FERGUSON MCCREARY

On 14 October 1979, the University of British Columbia lost one of its most beloved when Jack McCreary died suddenly at his home in Gibsons, British Columbia. In a lifetime spanning nearly seventy years, the contributions he made to health care, education, and human welfare were prodigious.

Born in 1910 in Eganville in the upper Ottawa Valley, he graduated from the University of Toronto in 1934 with the degree Doctor of Medicine, before undertaking an internship and residencies in medicine, pathology, and paediatrics at Toronto General Hospital and Sick Children's Hospital. He spent two years as a Milbank Research Fellow at Harvard.

During World War II, he was a member of the RCAF and was seconded in 1944 to Supreme Allied Headquarters in Europe, where he conducted a clinical survey of children in the concentration camps in the occupied areas of Europe. For this work he was made an officer of the Royal Orange Order of Nassau by the Government of the Netherlands.

He practised in Toronto when he returned to civilian life in 1945. He arrived in British Columbia in 1951, accepting the position of professor and head of the Department of Paediatrics and Paediatrician in Chief of the Vancouver General Hospital Health Centre for Children.

In 1959, he was appointed Dean of Medicine, a position he held until 1972. He became the creator of and driving force behind the concept of the Health Sciences Centre. Some of his ideas swept across the country, due primarily to his vision and energy. He was an extremely popular lecturer and a superb teacher, loved and respected by his colleagues, students, and the public in general.

His leadership in the realm of medical education was not confined to his own community and university. He served with distinction as president of the Association of Medical Colleges and of two federal Royal Commissions, and as director or trustee of many other institutions and foundations at the community, provincial, and national levels.

His many contributions did not go unrecognized, and he was the recipient of numerous honours and awards. He received the Centennial Medal Award of the Government of Canada, and he was honoured as Knight of Grace of the Order of St. John and as an Officer of the Order of Canada.

He was granted honorary D.Sc. degrees by Memorial University and the University of British Columbia and an honorary LL.D. by the University of Toronto.

Jack was a very kind person, and those of us who were associated with him gained in stature and wisdom. He had many opportunities to leave British Columbia for both the national and international levels. He underwent a great deal of pressure from the federal government, which sought him for the position of Deputy Minister of Health.

As a practising paediatrician coming from a very large practice in Toronto, he continued to see patients when he arrived in Vancouver, where many of his former RCAF colleagues sought his paediatric expertise. Sick children were all smiles and giggles once they were on the road to recovery; Jack's happiness and smiles were infectious to all he was in contact with.

Jack was very much an outdoor man, and his wife Dorothy recalls a typical instance. When relaxing, Jack liked nothing better than to go fishing. Dorothy and Jack had great weekends at their cottage on Pitt Lake and were preparing to leave one Sunday evening. They had a journey ahead of them of approximately eighteen miles to the boathouse. They stepped off the wharf into the seventeen-foot motor boat and settled down for their usual pleasant trip. Jack started the engine with no trouble (a great relief . . . there are many other stories of its refusing to start!). However, when he tried forward gear, it wouldn't move. The gear shift had stuck. It would only go in reverse gear. So there was no choice; they started down the lake in reverse. They hadn't gone far when Jack decided that they might as well put out a couple of fishing rods and try their luck! Have you ever seen a boat travel eighteen miles backwards with two people fishing in it? As Dorothy remembers, they didn't catch a thing but did attract a lot of attention!

To have a Canadian flag at the top of a flag pole was always a must with Jack. who was very patriotic and proud to be Canadian. Of all his honours and awards, he was most proud of his Officer of the Order of Canada.

Jack was a truly extraordinary man, characterized by an unshakable optimism. At times he encountered frustration and opposition but he never gave in to obstacles that might seem insurmountable to others. He had many interests in life, including a great love of nature and the outdoors. He was a vital, enthusiastic, and happy man. If he ever felt sad or depressed, he rarely showed it.

The Health Sciences Centre at the University of British Columbia will stand as one of his monuments. The affection and esteem of his colleagues, his former students, and his patients will be another enduring memory.

He is survived by his wife Dorothy and son James.

There is no way back for Jack McCreary now. We can never regain the help, advice, and direction he gave to so many, so willingly and so generously, and for which his host of friends and colleagues will remain eternally grateful.

Acknowledgements

During the course of writing this book, the authors interviewed many individuals who were involved in the evolution of the health care programs in British Columbia. They gave freely of their recollections and insights and often provided us with reference material to document their experiences. We want to thank them all for their cooperation. They are noted by chapter below. We are especially grateful to John Doughty and James Miller, two consummate professionals, for contributing their chapters.

Chapters 2 and 3: Jim Mainguy, June Wick, Basil Boulton, Paul Pallen, Sharon Bearpark, Heather Clarke, Morris Barer, Nancy Hall, and Sam Sheps.

Chapter 6: Nancy Scott and Bob Evans.

Chapter 7: David Hardwick, Derek Applegarth, and Margaret Norman.

Chapter 8: David Boyes, Mavis Teasdale, Paul Rogers, George Goodman, Chris Fryer, Cindy Stutzer, and David Chan.

Chapter 9: Bill Arnold, Rob Hill, George Davidson, Mike Stephenson, David Lirenman, Eric Hassall, Sharon Connaughty, Jim Jan, and Barbara McKenzie.

Chapter 10: Peter Ransford, Tony Williams, and Carson Smith.

Chapter 11: Glen Moir, Jake Hlynka, Gillian Willis, and Derek Dawes.

Chapter 12: Archie Hardyment, Sydney Segal, Margaret Pendray, Sharon Staseson, and Ellen McNeill.

Chapter 13: Alan Gray and Malcolm Williamson.

Chapter 14: Dana Brynelson, Wanda Justice, Kay and Alan Cashmore, John Watson, Hamish Nichol, Terry Russell, Keith Sigmundson, Fred Bannon, Jo Dickie, Jackie Maniago, Al Edmanski, Phil Russell, John Russell, Susan Poulos, Roberta McQueen, Carl Rothschild, Derryck Smith, Cathy Crouse, Paula Grant, and Charles Watson.

Chapter 15: Ed Desjardins, Anne Martin, Beth Laurence, and Mary Pack.

Chapter 16: Margaret Clemons, Elizabeth McMahon, Joyce Edwards, Hilda Gregory, John Gilbert, Cliff Carbin, Claudia McMillan, Richard Fitzzaland, Ken Cambon, Dunella MacLean, and Jim Hingston.

Chapter 17: David Gilbert, Douglas Graham, Ed McRae, Art Steinmann, Lorena Green, Carole Legg, Bert Hoskin, Frank Johnston, Ron Hyde, Colin Mangham, Carl Strohl, Lorraine Brave, Rob Axsen, Bill Hansen, and Heather Macedo.

Chapter 18: Jim Miller, Patricia Baird, Brian Lowry, Dagmar Kahousek, and Barbara McGillvray.

Chapter 19: Peter van Rheenan and Florence Kane.

Chapter 20: Helen Parkyn.

We thank Bill Webber, former Dean of Medicine at the University of British Columbia and Judith Hall, current Professor and Head, Department of Paediatrics, University of British Columbia, for their concern, interest, and support, when needed.

Finally, we thank members of our "workshop" to paraphrase Dr. Amyot (see Chapter 4). We are especially grateful to Margaret Francis and Sherry Miyamoto for their skilled secretarial assistance and patience during the five years we worked on the book. Barbara Parker, Medical Library Service of the College of Physicians and Surgeons of British Columbia, for her assistance with the bibliography; Sheila Norton from the British Columbia Archives and Resource Services for her on-going support; Chris Munro, Department of Biomedical Communications, University of British Columbia, for the medical illustrations; Iris Brendle-Moczuk for her assistance with the tables in Chapter 12; Robert Keziere for his cover photograph of the group of children; Alan Soroka, U.B.C. Law Library and Barb Smith, Order in Council Administration, Ministry of the Attorney General, British Columbia, both of whom went out of their way to provide legal references; Annette Lorek for preparation of the index, and finally John King, Production Editor, University of Calgary Press for his careful supervision of the manuscript.

We acknowledge with thanks grants from the Hospital for Sick Children Foundation to assist with the preparation of the manuscript and the Vancouver Foundation towards the publication costs.

Part I
Population-based Health Care in Canada

1

Personal and Population Medicine

INTRODUCTION

Medicare to most people implies prepaid medical care (personal medicine). A glance at the index of this book shows that it also implies a variety of services to meet the needs of a community (population medicine). This is the unknown side of medicare. Personal and population medicine are separate disciplines, the one concerned with patient care (individual-based) and the other with the organization of health services to meet certain needs of a defined community (population-based). They are not mutually exclusive, however, as personal medicine plays an important role in many population-based programs. Strangely, the concept of population medicine is poorly understood by most physicians and even viewed by some as a threat to their existing mode of practice. Whereas personal medicine involves a similar content and form throughout the western world, population medicine varies greatly in scope from one jurisdiction to another. As a result, the potential benefits of population medicine are often unrecognized and, which is more important, are denied to the population.

Many countries have sought to provide health care to their populations with national health services, and maternal and child services have been important components of these programs (1). Similar services have not been developed in North America, but Canada has introduced national health insurance (medicare), comprising universal prepaid hospital and medical care insurance to the population. As a result, the majority of Canadians have either forgotten or never known the burden of hospital and medical bills. While hospital and medical services are funded by national health insurance, they do not comprise a national health service because patients enjoy freedom of choice of physician; the latter are self-employed and most are paid a fee for service. In this book, the authors, using the case study method, review population-based services for children and youth that have evolved since World War II in the third largest province of Canada, British Columbia. It is noteworthy in itself that little has been written in Canada about population-based programs since the introduction of medicare over thirty years ago. The province of British Columbia was chosen because the authors have worked in that setting in the post-war era, but unquestionably other provinces have also employed a population-based approach to provide health care services. Therefore the programs are local but the problem is national and international.

Health programs organized to serve a defined population of children and youth were identified and the origins of each one examined, their current status and scope were then reviewed, and, finally, the change in health status as a consequence of the introduction of the program was examined. In this exercise, special attention was directed to legislation, and politics was evaluated (the latter being defined as the science dealing with the form, organization, and administration of a state or part of one and with the regulation of its relations with other states), as were other factors influencing population medicine. Programs for children with health-related components (e.g., infant development and child abuse programs), which are funded by other ministries, were not included.

TERMINOLOGY

The terms used in describing population-based care are reviewed below.

Social Medicine

The scientific study of human populations is usually associated with the first half of this century, although several earlier prescient contributions exist (2). In the 1930s, clinicians and others began to study the effects of social and environmental conditions on disease prevalence, and the benefits of improving the social environment upon disease control and the promotion of health. Initially two studies, the *Infant Mortality Study* and the *Infant Morbidity Study*, in Newcastle-upon-Tyne (3), addressed the health needs of the population of infants as distinct from the care of the sick infant. These led to the publication *A Thousand Families in Newcastle-upon-Tyne* (4), and two follow-up reports, *Growing Up in Newcastle-upon-Tyne* (5) and *The School Years in Newcastle-upon-Tyne* (6). Spence (3) commented that it was fashionable to speak of these field studies as social medicine, but he took exception to the implication that the studies were distinct and apart from clinical and laboratory medicine. His interpretation of social medicine was (7):

> Rather than an aspect or segment of a subject, it is a way of thinking and an approach to a discipline; an approach which can be acquired and

used by anyone working with children. It can be applied to any type of activity at a local, regional, national or international level.

Miller (8), who worked closely with Spence in the study *A Thousand Families in Newcastle-upon-Tyne*, and completed the work after Spence's death, described how the study taught them to think of a child in a family in a community rather than a child in a hospital.

The study of populations gained credence in 1943 with the opening of the Institute of Social Medicine at Oxford University (9). The purpose of the institute was to study the relationship of social, genetic, environmental, and domestic factors on the incidence of human disease and disability, to seek and promote measures to protect the individual and the community against forces that interfered with the full development of humanity's mental and physical capacity, and to undertake teaching and research in the subject. John Ryle, formerly Regius Professor of Physics at Cambridge and a renowned internist, was the first director of the Institute of Social Medicine and professor of Social Medicine at Oxford University. In 1948, he wrote (10):

> The training of the doctor, which began with observations on and the care of the sick individual, is due now for a great forward stride. Observations on whole communities, whether great or small (or on appropriate samples), and improved health provisions for them, must henceforward become the prior objective. The individual is not likely to suffer neglect in the process, for all communities are composed of individuals. (p. 23)

He suggested that social medicine and social pathology be considered as the medicine and pathology of families, groups, societies, or larger populations. Reflecting on his career shift from clinical medicine to social medicine, he commented (10):

> Some of my friends rebuked me for leaving the clinical fold. I reply in effect that I have merely taken the necessary steps . . . to increase my opportunities for aetiological study. My allegiance to human medicine is in no whit broken. (p. 19)

Kerr White referred to the founding of the Institute of Social Medicine as the beginning of the post-Flexner era of medicine and its distinguishing characteristic as the focus on the health problems of populations (11). In contrast to traditional public health, it was concerned with "all personal health services which impinge on populations." He noted that the shift from a denominator of individual patients seen in an office practice or admitted to a hospital to a denominator composed of all residents of a defined population or a community—the epidemiological shift—was central to the field of medical care research (12).

During the 1950s, epidemiology and health care gained increasing recognition in university programs and in schools of public health and medicine in many countries. The old term "public health" was often replaced by various new titles such as "social medicine," "community health sciences," "health care and epidemiology," etc. One department head noted that one of the attractions of the term "social medicine" was that each chairman of the department could interpret it in his own way. White commented that the hope of these new departments was in the development of sound traditions of epidemiologic research and teaching in the problems of general populations (13). The epidemiological methods are applicable not only to the study of communicable and non-communicable diseases but also to the study of medical care and health services.

Community and Population Medicine

The term "community paediatrics" appeared in the medical literature in the 1960s to define the problems of the population as distinct from the individual (14). A concern for the gap between the level of prevention and curative services to children from different social classes initiated the Rochester Child Health Studies (15). The term "community paediatrics" was chosen to show concern for the health and medical care of all children. During the late 1960s and early 1970s, these authors undertook a series of studies in a specific community in Rochester, New York. The studies dealt with the medical and perceived needs of the base population, the facilities, manpower, and utilization of services, and changes in health services and their effects during the period of the study.

In the United Kingdom, Mitchell (16) reviewed the health of infants and children in the community and described the background to the maintenance of health in childhood, the work undertaken in a child health service, and the resources and organization required. Mitchell, like Spence, commented that social paediatrics was not a separate branch of medicine but a concept that focuses on the social and cultural background of the child as well as genetic and environmental characteristics. This concern for the population of children in the United Kingdom is further illustrated by two reports dealing with the organization of child health services in Scotland and England (17, 18).

In the 1970s in the United Kingdom, community medicine specialists replaced public health officers (19, 20). Their job was to investigate, assess, and plan for the needs of their populations in order to establish priorities for the promotion of health, the prevention of disease, and the provision of medical care.

An editorial in *Lancet* (21) introduced the term "population medicine" in a discussion of the place of departments of general practice in medical schools. The editorial made the distinction between "personal and population (or social) medicine" and questioned the placement of general practice in "departments of population or social medicine." It was argued that personal and population medicine are largely separate disciplines, the one concerned with personal patient care and the other with the organization of health care to a defined population.

Population-based Medicine

The concept of population-based medicine has long been a cornerstone of the practice of public health and preventive medicine. Dietary deficiencies, such as rickets and scurvy, and infectious diseases, such as smallpox and poliomyelitis, were controlled by organizing the widespread distribution and use of technologies for the benefit of the aggregate population.

The Rockefeller Foundation and the Institute of Medicine convened a conference of world leaders in health in 1980 and published the proceedings under the title, *Population-based Medicine* (22). This concept envisaged a health care system, including both public health and personal care, that addressed the needs of the entire population within which the patient resided. Its scope included identification of needs, followed by policy decisions, planning, and (re)allocation of resources. The principal conclusions of the conference were that a population-based approach was needed, that the tasks of measurement, management, and monitoring should be given high priority by the medical establishment, and that new educational and institutional arrangements are needed to accommodate these innovations.

In summary, the terms social, community, population medicine and population-based medicine are often used interchangeably. This may not be entirely appropriate or acceptable to everyone; however, the terms do share a number of common features. They imply a concern for all the health care needs and services of a defined human population. They promote the concept of a health system for the population with its characteristic biological, social, and environmental problems. In essence, they signify a new paradigm of care, one based on the needs of populations and individuals rather than the biological information of diseases (22).

The introduction of health insurance in Canada extended this population-based approach to acute and chronic medical care first in institutional and later other community settings. The provincial Ministries of Health thereby became involved not only in public health and preventive medicine, but also in the private practice of medicine (personal medicine) and in the organization of medical care to the population (population medicine).

WHY POPULATION MEDICINE?

Some examples of contemporary child health issues will illustrate the need for both personal and population medicine.

1. The perinatal mortality rate in one region of Canada is higher than in the others. Who is responsible for initiating action to examine this question and to attempt to reduce the high perinatal mortality rate?
2. There is a greater risk of chromosomal abnormalities and resultant congenital abnormalities in the offspring of pregnant women over thirty-five years of age. Amniocentesis can identify the existence of an abnormal karyotype in the offspring and therapeutic abortion can be considered by the parents. Who is responsible for organizing these services for all women at risk?
3. Alcohol embryopathy is recognized as an important cause of birth defects and mental retardation and in some regions of the country is the most common cause of this condition. Who is responsible for initiating action to prevent and control this problem?
4. The rising morbidity and mortality from accidents, particularly motor vehicle accidents, is a major concern. It is the commonest cause of death in the one to nineteen year age group and accounts for a rising number of head and spinal cord injuries. Who is responsible for providing the network of improved pre-hospital and hospital emergency services?

These examples demonstrate the need for both personal medicine (represented by obstetrical and neonatal care in the first three and the expertise of surgical specialties in the fourth) and population medicine, the former to provide individual patient care, and the latter to develop policy, plan health care and health promotion programs, and allocate resources for the specific population groups. Answering the questions posed in the above examples is clearly outside the limits of the private practice of medicine and traditional public health practice.

THE CHANGING DISABILITY PATTERN IN CHILDREN

A rational child health system begins with an understanding of the community disability pattern and load in childhood and youth.

Child health mortality has been divided into biogenic and sociogenic problems (23, 24). The biogenic include diseases peculiar to the newborn period, congenital malformations, infections, neoplasms, and genetic diseases; the sociogenic suicide, homicide, and motor vehicle and other accidents. The diseases peculiar to the newborn and congenital malformations remain a major cause of mortality, but after the first year of life, biogenic causes have declined steadily during the last several decades. Sociogenic causes, however, have gradually increased and outnumber the former three to one in the 1–19 year age group.

Likewise, the changing profile of disease is reflected in morbidity. Morbidity data are not easy to obtain because a survey of the population is required. It is important information, however, because it provides numbers of various chronic disabilities, thereby serving as a basis for planning programs of care and outcome data to measure the effectiveness of preventive strategies. Immunization and chemotherapeutic agents have blunted acute and chronic infections, and there is a new emphasis on the care of children with chronic mental and physical disabilities. An important classification of handicapped children proposed three groupings: physical, mental, and social (25). The estimated prevalence of the three groups and their components is shown in Table 1. While obviously related to time and place, it provides a useful overview of the pattern of disability in children. Furthermore, a new term, the "new morbidity," entered the paediatric lexicon in the mid–1970s (26) and expanded the constituency of paediatrics to include behavioural and developmental disorders, learning disabilities, adolescent adjustment problems, abuse and neglect, and chronic disorders and illnesses. Accurate data is difficult to obtain, but prevalence rates of chronic disabilities of 5–10 percent are generally accepted (27). Many of these children and adolescents have problems which interfere with their physical, psychological, and social functioning and their care often places impossible pressures on their family. Pless (28) has recently introduced the "newer morbidity," in which he includes AIDS, iatrogenic problems that arise from the new technology in medicine, and still unknown long-term effects of "old" therapies such as blood transfusions, cytotoxic drugs, etc.

Further progress in reducing mortality and morbidity in childhood is closely correlated with the resolution of sociogenic problems, which are rooted in the social or ecological problems.

HEALTH CARE STRATEGIES

Traditional approaches to prevention involve three levels, primary, secondary, and tertiary. Starfield has identified the diseases which benefit from medical care, each assigned to one of these three categories (29).

TABLE 1. CLASSIFICATION OF HANDICAPPED CHILDREN*

Handicap	Prevalence per 1000 Related Population	
Physical		
Blind (including partially sighted)	1.2	
Deaf (including partially hearing)	1.2	
Epileptic	7.2	
Speech defects	27.0	
Cerebral palsy	3.1	
Heart disease	2.4	
Orthopaedic condition	3.4	
Asthma	23.2	
Eczema	10.4	
Diabetes	1.2	
Other physical handicap	6.7	
Total		87.0
Mental		
Subnormal	20.0	
Severely subnormal	3.5	
Psychiatric disorder		
Moderate	46.0	
Severe	22.0	
Total		91.5
Social		
Illegitimate	58.0	
In family broken by death, divorce, or separation	120.0	
In intact family in poverty	60.0	
Total		238.0

* This table was assembled from Tables 1, 2, and 3(a) in Appendix Q of the *Report of the Committee on Local Authority and Allied Personal Social Services* (25).

Primary prevention: The prevention of, or the reduction in, the frequency of occurrence, e.g., neonatal mortality, post-neonatal mortality, low birthweight, teenage childbearing, communicable diseases and inadequate immunization, acute rheumatic fever, and child battering.[1]

---

1 Child battering was moved from the third category because of the evidence on effectiveness of care.

Secondary prevention: The detection of the condition in its early (pre-morbid) stage, e.g., congenital hypothyroidism, phenylketonuria, lead poisoning, and iron deficiency anaemia.

Tertiary prevention: The prevention of the complications of the condition, e.g., diabetes, bacterial meningitis, epilepsy, acute appendicitis, asthma, and gastroenteritis.

Starfield also emphasized that modes of prevention or treatment that are efficacious under optimal conditions are dependent for their success on the availability of health services at the community level. Improvements in health status are due not only to technological interventions but also to approaches which improve access to medical care. Access depends on availability of resources (doctors, nurses, hospitals, diagnostic equipment, drugs, etc.) and on a system to finance the services (30). Furthermore, full access to services does not guarantee their receipt. At least in the case of children, someone has to take the patient for care. In essence, the effectiveness of a health care system is determined by the proportion of the population receiving the services.

HEALTH PROMOTION

Thirty years ago (31) child health was defined as:

> [a] term to indicate the broadening scope of paediatrics, to encompass preventive and social aspects as well as the medicine of childhood. It includes the positive concept of the promotion of health as well as the more orthodox one of the treatment of disease and its consequences. Health is taken to mean the state in which the child achieves the best use of his genetic endowment and accomplishes the most satisfying adjustment to the environment into which he must mature. Thus it includes the study of the normal child and his development from conception and his mental and emotional as well as his physical well-being and of the family and social environment in which he lives.

This statement clearly recognized the distinction between the delivery of health care (the medicine of childhood) and the promotion of health, and the importance of both in the quest for improved health status.

In 1977, the World Health Assembly, the central authority in the World Health Organization (WHO), resolved that "the main social target of WHO should be the attainment by all citizens of the world by the year 2000 of a level of health that would permit them to lead a socially and economically productive life" (32). In 1980, the WHO Regional Committee for Europe approved a regional strategy for health for all by the year 2000 (33), and, in 1981, the "Global Strategy of Health For All by the Year 2000" was accepted as WHO policy by the thirty-fourth World Health Assembly (34). The strategy envisaged a new public health movement involving effective community participation and collaboration between policy makers and the private sector. WHO identified three main objectives for health for all, namely, the promotion of life styles conducive to health, the prevention of preventable conditions, and rehabilitation and health services. In essence, this strategy is aimed at "the elimination of inequalities in health based on a broad public health concept of primary care" (35). The underlying intention of the "Health for All" strategy is that each country and region within countries should develop its own health for all strategy.

These WHO initiatives have given rise to the concept of health promotion which, like primary prevention, seeks to prevent the occurrence of disease. This implies a recognition of the importance of underlying social causes of ill health and confrontation of the latter by public policy and legislation. The basic strategies for health promotion are empowerment, skill development, building self-esteem, and improving the physical and social environment. The community, through its policy makers and the private sector, must accept the responsibility of developing healthy communities with affordable housing, nutrition, recreation, and employment opportunities. This process of empowerment implies new relationships between the health professions and the consumers, and the redistribution of power leading to social action and the development of healthy communities.

In 1986, the federal government released *Achieving Health for All: A Framework for Health Promotion* (36). It followed discussions with the WHO regional office in Europe and endorsed the notion of health as a positive resource, rather than something resulting from the prevention or treatment of illness (37).

At the 1986 Ottawa Conference on Health Promotion, Health and Welfare Canada, the European Region of WHO, and the Canadian Public Health Association endorsed the principles of health promotion as the Ottawa Charter for Health Promotion (38). The charter, subtitled "The move towards a new public health," proposed five principles of health promotion:

1. Building public policies that support health.
2. Creating supportive environments.
3. Strengthening community action.
4. Developing personal skills.
5. Reorienting health services.

These principles acknowledged that many of the underlying causes of ill-health lie outside the direct influence of medicine and will not be resolved by health care and health insurance. The large differences in health status across socio-economic groups, despite the presence of universal health insurance, have led to the suggestion that over-emphasis on health care intervention may absorb attention and resources that could make a greater contribution to health if used outside the health care system (39).

In essence, while some problems may yield to a definitive technology such as chemotherapy, others do not. They are multicausal in nature and their reduction is dependent on social, economic, and ecological change. The management of these problems calls for new and imaginative public health strategies of prevention and health promotion to improve the health of a defined population.[2]

IMPLICATIONS

The responsibility for health rests with the individual, the health providers, and society (40). Change can be mediated by any one of the three. There is a good deal of subjective evidence that individuals, and parents in the case of young children, are beginning to assume more responsibility for their personal behaviour (e.g., increased use of seat belts and bicycle helmets, less smoking and alcohol use). The bulk of personal health care is provided by personal medicine (and increasingly other health professionals), and few would tamper with the present programs funded by government health insurance. There are, however, health problems that the personal care system cannot resolve alone. The practising physician cannot implement the preventive and health promotion strategies that require a population-based approach. This is the responsibility of society, represented by the government. This approach is illustrated by interventions during prenatal life to reduce preterm births and low birthweight infants (41, 42, 43); the regionalization of perinatal and neonatal intensive care to reduce neonatal morbidity and mortality (44) and early enrichment programs to benefit deprived children (45, 46); community-based programs to reduce accidents (47, 48); programs for the prevention of alcohol and drug abuse (49) and anti-social behaviour in children (50); and a concern for child ecology, including the involvement of children in urban government (51).

The introduction of these population-based programs requires leadership from the top down, just as the abolition and control of infectious

---

2 The Canadian Institute for Advanced Research has identified population health as one of its initial projects for study. It seeks to advance understanding of the factors influencing health status and function, including social, economic, cultural, genetic, and health care factors and their complex inter-relationships, in order to generate information relevant to designing strategies for improving health both within and outside the health care system (30). It is involved in studies of the determinants of human health and the assessment of the value of interventions to improve the human health status in a given population, taking into account social values and ethics.

disease did in a previous era. It is the responsibility of these programs to foster healthy communities and to deploy the health resources in a rational way, giving priority to those problems that are frequent and severe rather than responding to entrepreneurial demands. Does national health insurance accommodate population medicine? Are its benefits confined to personal medicine?

The federal government has provided a universal framework for examining health problems and for suggesting courses of action needed for the solution (52). In Canada, the delivery of health services, however, is the responsibility of each provincial government; hence, the provincial experience must be examined to study the influence of universal health insurance upon population-based approaches to contemporary problems of children and youth.

In subsequent chapters, the origins, scope, and effectiveness, where measured, of twenty-four population-based programs that have been introduced in British Columbia are reviewed. But first the organization of the Canadian and British Columbia health care systems is described, followed by a description of the Division of Vital Statistics—the "statistical workshop" of public health.

REFERENCES

1. WALLACE, H. M. (ed.). *Health Care of Mothers and Children in National Health Services: Implication for the United States*. Cambridge, MA: Ballinger, 1975.
2. ROTHMAN, K. J. The rise and fall of epidemiology, 1950–2000 A.D. *New England Journal of Medicine* 304 (1981): 600–602.
3. SPENCE, J.. Family studies in preventive paediatrics. In *The Purpose and Practice of Medicine*, ed. J. Spence. London: Oxford University Press, 1960.
4. SPENCE, J., WALTON, W. S., MILLER, F.J.W., and COURT, S.D.M. *A Thousand Families in Newcastle-upon-Tyne: An Approach to the Study of Health and Illness in Children*. London: Oxford University Press, 1954.
5. MILLER, F.J.W., COURT, S.D.M., WALTON, W. S., and KNOX, E. G. *Growing Up in Newcastle-upon-Tyne*. London: Oxford University Press, 1960.
6. MILLER, F.J.W., COURT, S.D.M., KNOX, E. G., and BRANDON, S. *The School Years in Newcastle-upon-Tyne, 1952–62*. London: Oxford University Press, 1974.
7. MILLER, F.J.W. Social paediatrics: Aspect or attitude? In *Health Care of Mothers and Children in National Health Services: Implications for the United States*, ed. H. M. WALLACE. Cambridge, MA: Ballinger, 1975.
8. MILLER, F.J.W. Childhood morbidity and mortality in Newcastle-upon-Tyne. Further Report on the Thousand Family Study. *New England Journal of Medicine* 275 (1966): 683–90.
9. RYLE, J. A. Teaching and research in social medicine: An account of the Oxford experiment. In *Changing Disciplines. Lectures on the History Method*

and Motives of Social Pathology, ed. John A. Ryle. London: Oxford University Press, 1948.

10. RYLE, J. A. Social pathology and the new age in medicine. In *Changing Disciplines. Lectures on the History Method and Motives of Social Pathology*, ed. John A. Ryle. London: Oxford University Press, 1948, pp. 1–24.

11. WHITE, K. L. Clinical scholars and health services. *New England Journal of Medicine* 283 (1970): 929–30.

12. WHITE, K. L. Commentary. *American Journal of Public Health* 59 (1969): 66–68.

13. WHITE, K. L. The medical school and the community. *Yale Journal of Biology and Medicine* 39 (1967): 383–94.

14. HAGGERTY, R. J. Community pediatrics. *New England Journal of Medicine* 278 (1968): 15–21.

15. HAGGERTY, R. J., ROGHMANN, K. J., and PLESS, I. B., *Child Health and the Community*. New York: John Wiley & Sons, 1975.

16. MITCHELL, R. G. (ed.) *Child Health in the Community*, 2d ed. Edinburgh: Churchill Livingstone, 1980.

17. SCOTTISH HOME AND HEALTH DEPARTMENT. *Towards an Integrated Child Health Service*. Joint Working Party on the Integration of Medical Work. Report of a Sub-Group on the Child Health Service. Edinburgh: Her Majesty's Stationery Office, 1973.

18. COURT, S.D.M. (Chairman) *Fit for the Future*, 2 vols. Report of the Committee on Child Health Services. London: Her Majesty's Stationery Office, December 1976.

19. BROTHERSTON, J. Population-based medicine: The need for specialists. In *Population-Based Medicine*, ed. M. Lipkin, Jr. and W. A. Lybrand. New York: Praeger, 1982, pp. 42–46.

20. ACHESON, R. M. Epidemiology: The training of community physicians in Great Britain. In *Epidemiology as a Fundamental Science: Its Uses in Health Services Planning, Administration, and Evaluation*, ed. K. L. White and M. M. Henderson. New York: Oxford University Press, 1976, pp. 103–13.

21. Editorial. Personal and population medicine. *Lancet* 2 (12 October 1968): 815–16.

22. LIPKIN, M., JR. and LYBRAND, W. A. Introduction. In *Population-Based Medicine*, ed. Mack Lipkin, Jr. and William A. Lybrand. New York: Praeger, 1982, pp. vii–xiv.

23. TONKIN, R. S. *Child Health Profile*. British Columbia, 1981.

24. TONKIN, R. S. *Child Health Profile: Violence in Adolescence*. British Columbia, 1981.

25. Report of the Committee on Local Authority and Allied Personal Social Services, 1968. Appendix Q, pp. 349–51. Frederic Seebohm, Chairman. London: Her Majesty's Stationery Office.

26. PLESS, I. B. and SATTERWHITE, B. B. The new morbidity. In *Child Health and the Community*, ed. Robert J. Haggerty, Klaus J. Roghmann, and Ivan B. Pless. New York: John Wiley & Sons, 1975, pp. 94–95.

27. CADMAN, D., BOYLE, M. H., OFFORD, D. R., SZATMARI, P., RAE-GRANT, N. I., CRAWFORD, J., and BYLES, J. Chronic illness and functional limitation in Ontario children: Findings of the Ontario Child Health Study. *Canadian Medical Association Journal* 135 (1986): 761–67.

28. PLESS, B. Redesigning the health care encounter for youth. In *Redesigning Relationships in Child Health Care*, ed. R. S. Tonkin and J. R. Wright. B.C. Childrens Hospital, 1987.

29. STARFIELD, B. *The Effectiveness of Medical Care: Validating Clinical Wisdom*. Baltimore: Johns Hopkins University Press, 1985.

30. EVANS, R. G. and STODDART, G. L. Producing Health, Consuming Health Care. Canadian Institute for Advanced Research, Population Health Program. CIAR Population Health Working Paper, No. 6, April 1990.

31. JANEWAY, C.A. and WATKINS, A. G. A definition of child health. *Bulletin of the International Paediatric Association* 2 (1962): 7.

32. Targets for Health for All: Targets in Support of the European Regional Strategy for Health for All. WHO Regional Office for Europe, Copenhagen, p. 1.

33. WHO EUROPE (1982). Regional Strategy for Attaining Health for All by the Year 2000. EUR/RC 30/8, Rev. 2, 0425D, 2 September 1982, WHO Copenhagen, p. 2.

34. WHO EUROPE (1981). Global Strategy for Health for All by the Year 2000. WHO, Geneva.

35. ASHTON, J. and SEYMOUR, H. The setting for a new public health. In *The New Public Health: The Liverpool Experience*, Milton Keynes: Open University Press, 1988, p. 23.

36. EPP, J. *Achieving Health for All: A Framework for Health Promotion*. Ottawa: Health and Welfare Canada, November 1986.

37. LAW, M. *Health Promotion: A Dynamic for Change*. Proceedings of the National Symposium on Health Promotion and Disease Prevention, 12–15 March 1989, Victoria, B.C.: 61–67.

38. WORLD HEALTH ORGANIZATION, Health and Welfare Canada, Canadian Public Health Association (1986). Ottawa Charter for Health Promotion, WHO Copenhagen.

39. The Health of Populations and the Program in Population Health. Canadian Institute for Advanced Research. Population Health Program, CIAR. Population Health Publication, No. 1, January 1989, Toronto.

40. MCKEOWN, T. Whose responsibility? In *The Child in the World of Tomorrow: A Window into the Future*, ed. S. Doxiadis, J. Tyrwhitt, and S. Nakou. Oxford: Pergamon Press, 1979.

41. PAPIERNIK, E., BOUYER, J., DREYFUS, J., COLLIN, D., WINISDORFFER, G., GUEGEN, S., LECOMTE, M., and LAZAR, P. Prevention of preterm births: A perinatal study in Haguenau, France. *Pediatrics* 76:2 (1985): 154–58.

42. WYNN, M. and WYNN, A. *The Prevention of Preterm Birth: An Introduction to Some European Developments Aimed at the Prevention of Handicap*. London: Foundation for Education and Research in Childbearing, 1977.

43. BONHAM, G. H. The measurement of birth outcome. *Canadian Journal of Public Health* 79 (1988): 385.

44. Editorial. Perinatal care: Organization and outcome. *Lancet* 1 (5 April 1986): 777–78.

45. BERRUETA-CLEMENT, J. R., SCHWEINHART, L. J., BARNETT, W. S., EPSTEIN, A. S., and WEIKART, D. P. *Changed Lives: The Effects of the Perry Preschool Program on Youths Through Age 19*. Monograph of the High/Scope Educa-

tional Research Foundation, No. 8. Ypsilanti, Michigan: High/Scope Press, 1984.

46. JORDON, T. J., GRALLO, R., DEUTSCH, M., and DEUTSCH, C. P. Long-term effects of early enrichment: A 20-year perspective on persistence and change. *American Journal of Community Psychology* 13:4 (1985): 393–415.

47. GUSTAFSSON, L. H., HAMMARSTROM, A., LINDER, K., STJERNBERG, E., SUNDELIN, C., and THULIN, C. Child-environment supervisors—A new strategy for prevention of childhood accidents. *Acta Paediatrica Scandinavia* Suppl. 275 (1979): 102–107.

48. BERFENSTAM, R. The work of the Swedish Joint Committee for Childhood Accident Prevention. In *Children the Environment and Accidents*, ed. H. Jackson. Tunbridge, Kent: Pitman Medical Publ., 1977, pp. 133–53.

49. PENTZ, M. A., DWYER, J. H., MACKINNON, D. P., FLAY, B. R., HANSEN, W. B., WANG, E. YU I., and JOHNSON, C. A. A multi-community trial for primary prevention of adolescent drug abuse: Effects on drug use prevalence. *J.A.M.A.* 261 (1989): 3259–66.

50. JONES, M. B. and OFFORD, D. R. Reduction of antisocial behaviour in poor children by non-school skill-development. *Journal of Child Psychiatry* 30 (1989): 737–50.

51. ALDRICH, R. A. Children and youth in cities: The story of Seattle's Kidspace. In *Issues and Trends in Health*, ed. R. J. Carlson and B. Newman. St. Louis: C.V. Mosby, 1987, pp. 63–69.

52. LALONDE, M. *A New Perspective on the Health of Canadians: A Working Document*. Ottawa: Health and Welfare Canada, 1974.

2

The Canadian Health Care System: The Role of the Federal Government

This chapter outlines the evolution of the Canadian health care system and the linkages between the evolving federal health care policies and the provincial health care programs. The current services of the federal government are then briefly described.

EVOLUTION OF THE FEDERAL HEALTH INSURANCE PROGRAM

Canada's federal system of government provides for a division of powers between two levels of government, in contrast to a unitary system, in which all state powers are concentrated in a central government. Ten provinces and two territories share sovereign powers with the federal government. In a federal system, the powers of federal and provincial governments are autonomous, and the citizens participate, through their elected representatives, in both federal and provincial government affairs. In the modern industrial world, the two administrations are highly interdependent and must work together. This is particularly true of the fiscal relations between the two levels.

Canada's written constitution is contained in the *British North America Act*, an Act of the British parliament of 1867 that defined the separate powers of the federal and provincial governments. The power to amend the Act and hence the constitution was transferred to Canada in 1983. Education, health, and welfare services have emerged as provincial responsibilities (1). There were few references to health in the *British North America Act* aside from quarantine and the establishment of marine hospitals, which were designed to control epidemics of communicable diseases such as smallpox and cholera. The federal government created the Department of Health in 1919, and its responsibilities included maritime quarantine, health of potential immigrants, environmental health services on federal projects and interprovincial carriers, food, drug, and narcotics control, national vital statistics, and direct health services to Indians, Inuit, veterans, the armed forces, and sick mariners. The Department of National Health and Welfare was formed in 1944.

The inequality of health care in different social classes increased during the depression of the 1930s, particularly for low income groups, including the elderly. Commercial and non-profit hospital and medical insurance schemes emerged across the country. The federal government was not empowered to introduce a national health program because the primary responsibility for health care lay with the provinces; however, it sought to achieve this objective by offering to share the cost with the provinces. The concept of federal aid to the provinces for a comprehensive health insurance system was first proposed in 1945 at the Dominion-Provincial Conference on Post War Reconstruction (2), but provincial agreement was not obtained. Shah (3) has recently reviewed the evolution of the federal role in the Canadian health care system.

Federal Health Grants

The program of federal health grants was offered by the federal government and accepted by the provinces in 1948 (4). It included the following grant categories: crippled children, professional training, hospital construction, venereal disease control, mental health, tuberculosis control, public health research, health survey, general public health, and cancer control. All but the health survey recurred annually and, except for hospital construction, were cumulative. Only the cancer control and hospital construction grants were non-matching. These grants had a significant effect on the availability of health care and led to improved public and mental health services, a standard hospital accounting and reporting system, upgrading of diagnostic services and, through the Hospital Construction Grant, an upgrading of physical facilities. Federal matching grants were also offered to municipalities for hospital construction. The Public Health Research Grant (PHRG) was introduced in 1969 to fund health services research. The federal health grants were terminated in 1972, with the exception of the PHRG and the Professional Training Grant. In 1975, the PHRG was amalgamated with the new health services research grant to form the National Health Research and Development Program (5).

Hospital Insurance and Diagnostic Services Act

Provincial hospital insurance programs were started in Saskatchewan in 1947 and in British Columbia in 1949. In the 1950s, the federal government proposed sharing the cost of provincial hospital programs on condition the provinces agreed to five basic requirements. These were universal coverage; comprehensiveness (participation by all hospitals designated for acute, convalescent, or chronic care, and excluding mental hospitals, tuberculosis sanatoria, nursing homes, and institutions for custodial care), and specified insured services, including medical services by radiology and laboratory departments; accessibility with services available on uniform terms and conditions; portability; and public administration. In 1957, the federal *Hospital Insurance and Diagnostic Services Act* (6) was enacted and, in 1961, all provinces were participating. The cost-sharing formula gave equal attention to the per capita cost in each province and the per capita cost in the country as a whole. Provinces with high costs received less than 50 percent and those with low costs more than 50 percent of the cost of insured services. The hospital insurance services provided inpatient care in acute hospitals, but, at the option of the provinces, the care could be provided as insured outpatient services.

Medical Care Act

The success of the hospital insurance program was followed by pressure for a government medical care insurance system. In 1961, the federal government appointed the Royal Commission on Health Services, chaired by Justice Emmett M. Hall, and the report (7) proposed that the federal government assist the provinces to introduce and operate comprehensive, universal provincial programs of personal health services, with similar arrangements for the Yukon and Northwest Territories. The following programs were recommended, with the provinces determining the order of priority and the timing of introduction: medical services; dental services for children, expectant mothers, and public assistance recipients; prescription drugs; optical services for children and public assistance recipients; prosthetic services; home care services; and, finally, a re-organization and re-orientation of the Mental Health Services and changes in the Hospital Insurance Program. The commission reinforced the guidelines from the 1957 hospital insurance and diagnostic services legislation to the effect that "all personal health services should be universally available on uniform terms and conditions for all residents."

In 1966, the federal *Medical Care Act* (8) was enacted and extended cost sharing to include medical services to each province, on condition that the provinces agreed to ensure the same five basic requirements noted above. By 1971, all provinces had joined the system. The cost-sharing formula differed from that of the *Hospital Insurance and Diagnostic Services Act* and was based on the national average per capita cost. This resulted in a greater penalty for high cost provinces than the hospital insurance policy.

In 1966, the federal Health Resources Fund was instituted, providing for a federal cost-sharing program to support the provinces in construction of research establishments, teaching hospitals, medical schools, and training facilities for other health professionals. This terminated in December 1980.

A New Perspective on the Health of Canadians

In 1974, the federal government working document (9), *A New Perspective on the Health of Canadians* (the Lalonde Report), assessed the health status of Canadians and provided a universal framework for examining health problems and for suggesting courses of action needed for the solution. The factors influencing sickness and health were divided into four categories—human biology, environment, lifestyle, and health care organization. The report noted that the bulk of health expenditures was focused on the health care organization, the result being that vast sums of money were being spent treating diseases that could have been prevented in the first place. Two of the determining categories were outside the traditional sphere of influence of medicine. Shortly afterwards, in 1978, the federal government established the Health Promotion Directorate within the Health Services and Promotion Branch.

While cost containment has occurred in Canada, Evans (10) concluded that the redeployment of resources from the health care system to environmental and lifestyle problems has been much less apparent. The economic conflicts between governments and providers were reviewed, with the conclusion that the number and range of economic interests threatened by a major effort to improve health care status, either by an attack on the sources of unhealthy lifestyles or environment, or by redeployment of resources from health care systems for this purpose, were such that not much can be done in the short run, i.e., within a decade or so. Nevertheless, gains in health status, which may be attributable to lifestyle or environmental improvement, have occurred, i.e., toleration of public smoking has declined, legislation regarding seat belt use has been extended, and alcohol consumption is declining. He concluded that the underlying philosophy of the Lalonde Report was of great importance because it confirmed the concept of the health care system as a collective enterprise, as a set of social institutions intended to promote the health of the population.

The new emphasis on lifestyle and individual responsibility for health, exemplified by the wellness campaign (Participaction), was also criticized as a non-human, non-social concept of health. "What is the likely impact of a fitness campaign on the health of an isolated single mother trying to raise children on mean spirited, often humiliating, public assistance?" (11) Initially, the emphasis on individual lifestyle change tended to eclipse some of the other ideas proposed in *A New Perspective on the Health of Canadians*. In the early 1980s, this imbalance began to be redressed, and the influence of social, psychological, and physical environmental conditions such as economic and gender inequality, pollutants, and occupational hazards was acknowledged. These conditions were beyond the control of individuals, but their contribution to ill health was significant (12). In spite of criticism, the publication was an important policy pronouncement by a national government accepting responsibility for promoting the health of its population and acknowledging that other issues besides health care contributed to population health. Others have suggested that the report ushered in the "New Public Health," "which brings together environmental change and personal preventive measures with appropriate therapeutic interventions especially for the elderly and disabled" (13).

Established Programs Financing Act

In the early 1970s, the rising cost of health services led to an interest in alternative and, it is hoped, less expensive ways of producing health in the population. The existing cost-sharing formulae between provincial and federal governments forced the federal government to match all health expenditures incurred by provincial governments. Faced with alarming increases in health care costs in the mid-1970s, and recognizing that there was a limit to what a treatment-oriented health care system contributes to health status, the federal government, without consultation with the provinces, announced that ceilings would be placed on the sharing of medical insurance program costs (14). In 1976, the federal government proposed a new sharing arrangement. The *Federal-Provincial Fiscal Arrangements and Established Programs Financing (EPF) Act* (15) was introduced in 1977, substituting block funding for the cost-sharing formulae for the established programs of hospital and medical care insurance. The terms of the Act permitted the federal government to terminate the arrangements with three years' warning. The final formula provided for 50 percent of the funds to be on a cash basis and 50 percent from transfer of tax revenue potential. The cash payments were to parallel the national economy and would escalate with growth of the economy. The amount of tax revenue allocated to a province would depend upon the state of its own economy, not the costs of the provincial health programs. There was also a per capita contribution to the provinces for the Extended Health Care Services, which provided the incentive to develop less costly alternative services to hospitals, such as nursing homes, home care and ambulatory care. There were no explicit requirements or limitations with respect to provincial expenditures, so long as the provinces respected the five principles of medicare: universal coverage, comprehensiveness, accessibility, portability, and public administration. Failure to comply with statutory requirements of the other Acts resulted in the reduction or withholding of federal financial contributions.

Canada Health Act

There were charges that some provinces were introducing extra billing by physicians and user fees by hospitals and that the federal government was not fulfilling its obligations to ensure that standards were maintained. The federal government then commissioned Justice Hall to review the extent to which goals of the Royal Commission on Health Services were being achieved, whether there should be other basic principles underlying health insurance delivery, the nature and extent of necessary revision to the *Hospital Insurance and Diagnostic Services Act* and the *Medical Care Act*, and other means by which public authorities may best comply with the above principles. The report (17) recommended that the "user pay" concept was contrary to the principle and spirit of the National Health Program advocated by the Royal Commission (1964). Furthermore, the report advocated that the *Medical Care Act* be revised to eliminate extra billing by physicians because it inhibited reasonable access to physicians and was contrary to the intent and purposes of the Act, and that the provinces develop a mechanism to ensure reasonable compensation to physicians. Unfortunately, lack of time and money limited the extent of this report and led to the formation of an all-party task force to examine the whole field of federal-provincial fiscal relations, including the impact of the *EPF Act*. The report (18) addressed the delivery system, program conditions (universality, comprehensiveness, portability, accessibility, and public administration), and the national commitment to health care as follows:

The delivery system: Five issues were examined: first, increased extended health care resources for the aging population; second, alternative health care resources to shift from a medical and hospital to a prevention and health promotion approach; third, geographical imbalances in medical manpower services and facilities; fourth, under-utilization of non-physician health workers; and fifth, more effective co-ordination between government providers and consumers.

Program conditions: There was concern that the change in federal transfer of funds had reduced provincial compliance with program conditions and that erosion of national program conditions might follow. There was also concern about accessibility because of the increase in the practices of hospital user fees and extra billing. The task force concluded that user fees for hospital services should be discouraged and that extra billing by physicians be banned.

The national commitment to health care: The appropriate proportion of national resources required to meet essential health needs was reviewed, together with the charge that the system was underfunded. The task force concluded that the evidence was not sufficient to show that the system was underfunded, and that further advances in health care would be related to better nutrition, improved lifestyles, improved environment, and safety measures in the workplace and on the highway.

Following these two reports, the *Canada Health Act* (19) was introduced in 1984, replacing the *Hospital Insurance and Diagnostic Services Act* and the *Medical Care Act*. Its purpose was to advance the objectives of Canadian health care policy, while recognizing the primary responsibility of the provinces for the provision of health care services. Criteria and conditions were defined, including deletion of hospital user fees and physician extra billing, that were to be met before full payment under the *EPF Act*. Conditions for cash contributions from federal to provincial governments and defaults were dependent on evidence of user fees or extra billing (3). It is noteworthy that none of the provinces have confirmed the five principles of medicare by enacting them in legislation.

Achieving Health For All

In 1986, the federal government released *Achieving Health for All: A Framework for Health Promotion* (20). This was the culmination of on-going discussions with the WHO regional office in Europe and endorsed the notion of health proposed by WHO as a positive resource, rather than as something resulting from the prevention or treatment of illness. The links between health and the social environment, including poverty and environmental disadvantage, were acknowledged, along with the limits of medical interventions. The framework emphasized three health challenges: reducing inequities, increasing prevention, and enhancing coping; proposed health promotion mechanisms (self care, mutual aid, and healthy environments); and three implementation strategies. These included fostering public participation in issues that affect health; strengthening community health services by improving links between services and the communities they serve; and co-ordinating public policy so that professionals involved in policy matters are aware of health-related responsibilities in their communities (e.g., hunger, homelessness, unemployment, poverty, and illiteracy) and the co-ordination of public policy to support them. While the third strategy focuses on professionals, the first two recognize that health must be socially created by a "healthy community" (11). These ideas led to the Canadian Healthy Communities Project (12), whose counterpart, the Healthy Cities Project, thrives in many European communities. The concept behind these projects encourages municipalities to weigh the health implications of their actions at every stage of policy planning and formation. In a spirited discussion of Canadian health promotion, so unusual in official publications, Law (12) concluded, "We have high hopes that health promotion will take its proper place beside health care as a cornerstone of Canada's system for health."

In 1988, the Canadian Institute of Planners, the Canadian Public Health Association, and the Federation of Canadian Municipalities initiated the Canadian Healthy Communities Project, funded by Health and Welfare Canada. This process reflects a shift in focus from healthy lifestyles and personal responsibility to community-based action with improvement of the social and physical environments of home and workplace. The Healthy Communities movement is "about achieving health for all" by recognizing our collective responsibility for the health of the community in which we live (21). It is the practical application of the goals set out in *Achieving Health for All* (20): "to create a healthy environment you need other people to help you." The process taps the talent of the community to address the problems at the local level, involving the municipal government, the community, and the private sector in decisions about health. The Canadian Healthy Communities Project has a secretariat in Ottawa, and any Canadian municipality may become a member upon agreement from the local council to endorse five criteria:

1. A broad public policy approach to health.
2. An inter-departmental and inter-sectoral strategy.
3. Full community participation.
4. Sharing information derived from the project with other participating municipalities.
5. Evaluation of local projects.

Government Expenditures Restraint Act

The *Government Expenditures Restraint Act* (22), enacted in June 1990, amends the *Federal-Provincial Fiscal Arrangements and Federal Post-Secondary Education and Health Contributions Act* (15) and reduces federal cash transfers to the provinces for health and education. The passage of this Act has raised concerns that the cash transfers may be eliminated. The 1991 federal budget stabilized federal support for health care and social services for three years (23). There is concern that the less affluent provinces will not be able to pick up the slack and that health care will suffer.

CONCERN FOR CHILDREN

In defiance of the second law of epidemiology (broken down by age and sex), the federal government, however, had confined its policies to the aggregate population (9, 20). Aside from one federal health grant (crippled children), there was limited concern for the special needs of children and youth until the formation of the Health Promotion Directorate in 1978. In 1982, the federal cabinet approved a health promotion policy program to address six issues (tobacco, alcohol, drugs, nutrition, safety, and mental health) and targeted four population groups: children and youth, women, the elderly, and the disabled.

Thereafter, the federal government has supported programs for children and parents such as the Nobody's Perfect Program, the Post Partum Parent Support Program, the Community Support Program in the substance abuse field and the publication *You and Your Baby. Foundations for the Future, a Report of the Working Group on Child and Youth Mental Health Services* is a further example (24).

The Canadian Institute of Child Health (CICH), a non-government agency, was founded in 1977, its mission to improve the health and the quality of life for Canadian children and youth and to serve as their advocate. The institute called for an integrated child health system in Canada, with national policies to promote the health of children and standards for personnel and facilities providing care for children (25). It has collaborated with the Health Services Directorate, Health Services and Health Promotion Branch, and has published a series of guidelines (26) for establishing standards for special services in hospital. Recently, the institute published a report dealing with national health data on children (27). The Canadian Association of Paediatric Hospitals has published reviews of paediatric services (28, 29).

The United Nations adopted the Declaration on the Rights of Children in 1959 and in 1989 ratified the Convention on the Rights of the Child. In 1990, the United Nations Children's Summit resulted in the issuing of a declaration and plan of action for the survival, protection, and development of children adopted by all members based on a new ethic, the ethic of giving "first call to children" in each and every nation (30). The Canadian ratification[1] process was complicated by the split federal/provincial jurisdiction in many areas covered by the convention. This required each province to support the convention prior to ratification. Following the summit, the Minister of National Health and Welfare announced the formation of the Children's Bureau to assist in co-ordination of child/youth programs, and encourage support from all provinces for commitments stemming from the Convention on the Rights of the Child and from the summit declaration. The bureau's main role is to ensure the effectiveness of federal policies and programs relating to the health, welfare, and development of children and families (31).

---

1 United Nations declarations carry no legislative obligations, but once the conventions have been ratified by a country there is an obligation to comply with the document's provisions.

A national child care strategy was a prominent election promise of the Conservative government of Canada in 1984. This involved doubling the capacity of the day-care system, but it was abandoned in 1988 and replaced by another program called Brighter Futures, Canada's Children's Initiatives in 1992 (32). Brighter Futures included four initiatives:

1. Ratification by Canada on 11 December 1991 of the United Nations Convention on the Rights of the Child.
2. The child benefit for middle and low income families, which combines the existing family allowances, tax credits and refunds into one monthly payment generally to the mother; a new federal earned-income supplement, which increased the new benefit by up to $500 for low income working families with children, all children under eighteen years being eligible.
3. Canada's Action Plan for Children to provide the government's response to the 1990 World Summit for Children and the framework to address the long-term needs of Canadian families and children.
4. The Child Development Initiative, comprising a group of long-term programs designed to address conditions of risk during the earliest years in a child's life. The initial emphasis will focus on children living in low-income circumstances and on preventing conditions of risk to children. The Child Development Initiative will be developed in partnership with the provinces, territories, first nations and Inuit communities, and non-government organizations. A five-year initiative, it will provide ongoing support for programs in the areas of prevention, promotion, protection, and partnership through community action.

ORGANIZATION OF HEALTH SERVICES

The general organization and the different responsibilities of the federal government are described in this section.

The mandate of Health and Welfare Canada is to promote and preserve the health and to ensure the social security of life of all Canadians. A brief description of some of the major health branches of the Department of National Health and Welfare follows (33).

Health Protection Branch

This branch regulates the safety and nutritional quality of foods, the safety and effectiveness of drugs and medical devices, and programs to reduce the presence of dangerous chemicals in our environment, to monitor exposure to radioactivity, and to improve capability to diagnose diseases. The branch also monitors exposure to communicable and non-communicable diseases, including the spread of AIDS in Canada.

Medical Services Branch

This branch provides a variety of health services to a number of client groups, including registered Indians and Inuit, all residents of the Yukon and Northwest Territories, immigrants and temporary residents, international travellers, federal public servants, civil aviation personnel, the physically handicapped, and disaster victims.

Although the provincial government is responsible for the provision of health services to the residents of the province, the federal government has traditionally assumed responsibility for the registered on-reserve Indian population. Off-reserve native people are the responsibility of the province.

The Indian and Northern Health Services Directorate provide primary health care services to Canada's native people on reserves. During recent years a number of tribal councils have taken over the responsibility for the health care of their people. The provincial and territorial medical and hospital programs are used in the same manner as by the non-native population.

The National Native Advisory on Drug and Alcohol Program (NNADAP) is a community-based approach to prevention and treatment of the problems of on-reserve status Indians and Inuit (Chapter 17).

The Public Service Health Directorate addresses occupational medicine and hazards' investigation.

Health Services and Promotion Branch

This branch develops, promotes, and supports measures designed to preserve and improve the health and well-being of Canadians.

The Health Promotion Directorate develops and implements programs that promote health and encourage the avoidance of health risks. Its focus includes risk reduction issues (alcohol, drug, and tobacco use, nutrition, and cardiovascular health), population groups (family, children and youth, women, seniors, and the disabled), and delivery settings (schools and the workplace). Programs are implemented in co-operation with provincial and territorial governments, professional and voluntary organizations, and community groups. The directorate administers the Health Promotion Contribution Program, which supports voluntary organizations for community-based activities that enable Canadians to achieve greater control over, and thereby improve, their health. The directorate introduced the National Drug Strategy, Action on Drug Abuse, in 1987 (see Chapter 17).

Community-based projects also receive funding through community action components of the National Drug Strategy and the Long-Term National Program on Impaired Driving. Projects advancing health promotion include Strengthening Community Health, Canadian Healthy Communities, and Sustainable Development and Health.

The Health Insurance Directorate is responsible for the administration of the *Canada Health Act* and payments concerning provincial and territorial programs providing insured health care services and certain extended health care services as provided by legislation, and for monitoring provincial compliance with the program conditions associated with the federal payments.

The Extramural Research Programs Directorate operates the National Health Research and Development Program, which supports health care research and related scientific activities in university and hospital settings.

The Health Services Directorate collaborates with provincial governments, professional and national organizations, and others to address priority issues in health. The Community Health Division focuses on issues that include teen pregnancy, home care, and child sexual abuse. Sustaining grants are awarded to voluntary organizations in support of community services. The publication *Mental Health for Canadians: Striking a Balance* was also issued. The Preventive Health Division focuses on heart health, prevention of breast cancer, and organ donor awareness.

The Medical Research Council

This council reports directly to Parliament through the Minister of National Health and Welfare. Its function is to "promote, assist and undertake basic, applied, and clinical research in Canada in the health sciences, other than public health research." The council provides grants and scholarships in aid of operating and equipment needs for research projects, supporting investigators and trainees.

COMMENT

The federal government has played the leadership role in the introduction of universal health insurance in Canada. Initially its financial contributions gave rise to hospital and medical insurance in all provinces and territories. The rising costs of health care have been a concern from the early seventies, and federal efforts to control the costs have taken two approaches. The first approach involved the publication of two landmark reports, *A New Perspective on the Health of Canadians* (9) and *Achieving*

Health for All: A Framework for Health Promotion (20), both of which attempted to shift the emphasis from treatment to prevention of disease and health promotion. The former also gave rise to the federal Health Promotion Directorate, and the latter to the conceptualization of a framework for health promotion that identified contemporary health challenges, health promotion mechanisms, and implementation strategies. The application of these implementation strategies is a provincial responsibility, and prevention programs and "healthy communities" are gradually being introduced in Canada.

The second approach was the introduction of the *EPF Act*, which removed the link between federal contributions and provincial health costs. This Act was also designed to encourage the use of less costly alternative facilities to hospitals for the care of the population with chronic disability and illness. From the late 1950s to the 1970s, federal health care legislation encouraged inpatient hospital care and resulted in an expensive inpatient treatment centred service. *A New Perspective on the Health of Canadians*, the *EPF Act*, the formation of the Health Promotion Directorate, and *Achieving Health For All*, all contributed to a reorientation of health services.

A special concern for the health of children and youth has been apparent during the past decade, culminating in the World Summit for Children, held in 1990 with Canada a co-host. The summit set out seven major goals for the survival, protection, and development of children by the year 2000. The federal government has stated that children matter.

REFERENCES

1. HATCHER, G. H., HATCHER, P. R., and HATCHER, E. C. Health services in Canada. In *Comparative Health Systems: Descriptive Analyses of Fourteen National Health Systems*, ed. Marshall W. Raffel. University Park: Pennsylvania State University Press, 1984, pp. 86–132.
2. TAYLOR, M. G. The Canadian health care system 1974–1984. In *Medicare at Maturity: Achievements, Lessons and Challenges*, ed. R. G. Evans and G. L. Stoddart. Proceedings of the Health Policy Conference on Canada's National Health Care System, Management Studies Programs. Calgary: The Banff Centre for Continuing Education, 1986, pp. 3–39.
3. SHAH, C. P. *Public Health and Preventive Medicine in Canada*. Toronto: University of Toronto Press, 1989. Chapter 6: The Evolution of the Health Care System in Canada, pp. 76–84.
4. BRITISH COLUMBIA. *Third Report of the Department of Health and Welfare (Health Branch)*. Fifty-second Annual Report of Public Health Services, Year Ended December 31, 1948, Victoria, 1948.
5. HEACOCK, R. A., Director General, Extra-Mural Research Programs Directorate Health Services and Promotion Branch, Health and Welfare Canada, 1987, personal communication.

6. *Hospital Insurance and Diagnostic Services Act*, S.C. 1957, c. 28.
7. *Royal Commission on Health Services*, Vols. I and II. Ottawa: Queen's Printer, 1964.
8. *Medical Care Act*, S.C. 1966–67, c. 64.
9. LALONDE, M. *A New Perspective on the Health of Canadians: A Working Document*. Ottawa: Health and Welfare Canada, 1974.
10. EVANS, R. G. A Retrospective on the "New Perspective." *Journal of Health Policy and Law* 7 (1982): 325–44.
11. BOOTHROYD, P. and EBERLE, M. Healthy communities: What they are, how they're made. *CHS Research Bulletin, B.C. Centre for Human Settlements*, July 1990, pp. 1–13.
12. LAW, M. *Health Promotion: A Dynamic for Change*. Proceedings of the National Symposium on Health Promotion and Disease Prevention, 12–15 March 1989, Victoria, B.C., pp. 61–67.
13. ASHTON, J. and SEYMOUR, H. The setting for a new public health. In *The New Public Health: The Liverpool Experience*. Milton Keynes: Open University Press, 1988, pp. 15–40.
14. MAINGUY, J.W., personal communication, 1990.
15. *Federal–Provincial Fiscal Arrangements and Established Programs Financing Act*, S.C. 1976–77, c. 10, Subsequently renamed *Federal–Provincial Fiscal Arrangements and Federal Post-Secondary Education and Health Contributions Act*, R.S.C. 1985, c. F-8.
16. MOYES, E. A., personal communication, 1992.
17. HALL, E. M. Canada's National-Provincial Health Program for the 1980's: 'A Commitment for Renewal,' 1980.
18. CANADA. Minister of Supply and Services. Fiscal Federalism in Canada. Parliamentary Task Force on Federal-Provincial Fiscal Arrangements, House of Commons, August 1981.
19. *Canada Health Act*, S.C. 1984, c. 6.
20. CANADA. *Achieving Health for All: A Framework for Health Promotion*. Jake Epp, Minister of National Health and Welfare Canada, 1986.
21. BRITISH COLUMBIA. *Health Promotion in Action*. B.C. Office of Health Promotion. Vol. 1, No. 3, November, 1990.
22. *Government Expenditures Restraint Act*, S.C. 1991, c. 9.
23. CMA criticizes federal budget for freezing health care transfer payments to provinces. *Canadian Medical Association Journal* 144 (April 1991): 891.
24. CANADA. *Foundations for the Future, A Report of the Working Group on Child and Youth Mental Health Services*. Health Services and Promotion Branch, Health and Welfare Canada, 1991.
25. LAW, J. T. and POST, S. E. A Look Toward the Future of the Canadian Institute of Child Health, October 1977. Mimeographed document.
26. CANADA. *Child and Adolescent Services in General Hospital Guidelines*. Ministry of National Health and Welfare, 1983, Appendix IV, p. 103.
27. AVARD, D. and HARVEY, L. Message from the chairperson. *The Health of Canada's Children: A CICH Profile*. Canadian Institute of Child Health, Ottawa, 1989.
28. McLEAN, D. C. (ed.). *Report of the CAPH Advisory Group on Paediatric Ambulatory Care*. Ottawa: Canadian Association of Paediatric Hospitals, 1989.

29. MACGREGOR, D. (ed.). *Paediatric Long-Term Care in Canada*. Report of a Task Force Convened by the Canadian Association of Paediatric Hospitals. Ottawa: Canadian Association of Paediatric Hospitals, 1990.

30. DUNCAN, H. Point of view. *American Academy of Pediatrics News* (July 1991), p. 13.

31. Children's Bureau, Ministry of Health and Welfare, 1990. Mimeographed document.

32. CANADA. *Brighter Futures, Canada's Action Plan for Children*. Ministry of Supply and Services, 1992.

33. CANADA. *Annual Report, 1988–89*. Ministry of National Health and Welfare Canada. Minister of Supply and Services, 1989.

3

The Provincial Health Care System in British Columbia

There are ten provinces and two territories in Canada, and, within the federal guidelines described in Chapter 2, each province and territory is responsible for the development of its health care services. In this chapter, the evolution of the public health and other population-based health services in British Columbia is reviewed, followed by an outline of the current health care system.

HISTORICAL CONSIDERATIONS

Public Health Services

In 1869, *An Ordinance for Promoting the Public Health in the Colony of British Columbia* was enacted, which "empowered the Governor-in-Council to create Health Districts, establish local Boards of Health, and define the duties and jurisdictions of these Boards, with the proper method of enforcing their rules by fines and imprisonment" (1). There was also special provision for the appointment of a health officer to act during extraordinary crises, such as serious epidemics, and "Whose duties it shall be to provide that the Local Boards carry out the orders in Council." Aside from this, there was no organized health service when British Columbia became a province in 1871.

The need for better legislation was recognized and the *Health Act, 1893*, was proclaimed in 1895, providing a provincial board of health that was "to concern itself with all things affecting or likely to affect the public health" (2). In 1899, the *Health Act* was amended to provide a permanent board and the Lieutenant Governor-in-Council, consisting of the premier and his ministers (cabinet), became the provincial board of health. The Act also provided that there should be a local board of health in each municipality. In 1899, Dr. Charles J. Fagan was appointed secretary to the provincial board of health, which was under the jurisdiction of the Attorney-General until 1906, when it was transferred to the Agriculture Department, and, less than a year later, to the Department of the Provincial Secretary. In 1920, three of the principal branches of the Department of the Provincial Secretary were "the Board of Health, Mental (Insane) Hospitals and Hospitals" (3), which remained until 1946, when a separate Department of Health and Welfare was established.

Dr. Henry Esson Young, who had been a member of the legislative assembly and Provincial Secretary, succeeded Dr. Fagan in 1924. His appointment was officially changed from Secretary to the Provincial Board of Health to that of Provincial Health Officer. He remained in that position until his death in 1939 (4). The public health branch was the informal name for the staff of the Provincial Health Officer. Dr. Young organized a public health nursing course at the University of British Columbia, and the Canadian Red Cross agreed to sponsor the course for a three-year period and to set up eight nursing stations in remote areas in the province, where the graduates were employed (5). In 1919, the Department of Nursing and Public Health was established at the University of British Columbia, along with the first public health nursing course for registered nurses in Canada. The diploma required one year of study, and the first class graduated in 1920, helping to form the nucleus of the public health nursing service. The demand for public health nurses increased, the Bachelor of Applied Science in Nursing was added, and the first three nurses graduated in 1923.

The first health unit was opened in Saanich, adjoining Victoria on Vancouver Island, in 1919, marking the beginning of the provincial public health nursing services.

Dr. Gregoire F. Amyot, the son of Dr. John Amyot, Canada's first Deputy Minister of National Health, was appointed the director of the North Vancouver Health Unit in 1930. Then he accepted an appointment at the School of Public Health, University of Minnesota, but returned briefly to British Columbia in 1936 to undertake a number of studies at the request of Dr. Young. In 1940, he returned to the position of Provincial Health Officer. He supervised the division of the province into eighteen semi-autonomous health units, each under the direction of a medical officer of health. The health departments of Greater Victoria and Greater Vancouver are separate administrations.

Reorganization of Health Services

The *Department of Health and Welfare Act* (6) was enacted in 1946 by the provincial legislature, and the new department was divided into the Health and Welfare Branches. The Provincial Health Officer became the Deputy Minister of Health in charge of the Health Branch, and Dr. Amyot was appointed to that position.

The Health Branch of the provincial Department of Health and Welfare comprised a central office of health consultants in Victoria, a provincial laboratory in Vancouver, and regional health units, that provided local public health services, including well child care and school health programs. Until the 1940s, the provincial government's role in child health included supervision of well child care, including immunization, school health, the prevention and management of infectious diseases, including tuberculosis, and the provision of services for the mentally handicapped and mentally ill. Most medical services were purchased by the consumer. The advent of provincial hospital insurance in 1948, followed by national health insurance, first hospital and subsequently medical, placed major new and unprecedented responsibilities upon the health department. This was reflected in a series of further organizational changes.

The provincial *Hospital Insurance Act* (7) was proclaimed in 1948 and Hospital Insurance Service (HIS)[1] became a third branch of the Department of Health and Welfare. The department was renamed the Department of Health Services and Hospital Insurance in 1959, and the Welfare Branch became a separate department, the Social Welfare Department. Dr. Amyot was appointed deputy minister of the Health Branch[2] and remained in that capacity until he retired in 1961. The Mental Health Services were transferred from the Department of the Provincial Secretary to the new department and named the Mental Health Branch in 1959.

Further reorganization created the Department of Health in 1975, changed to the Ministry of Health in November 1977. The department was extensively reorganized into Medical and Hospital Programs and Community Health Programs, which included Mental Health and Public Health. The two main programs each had a deputy minister who reported to the Deputy Minister of Health. A single annual report was published by the ministry, in contrast to the prior pattern of separate reports from the Health Branch, Mental Health Branch, and Hospital Insurance Service. The Office of Health Promotion was added in 1989.

Health Insurance Services

Provincial: An Act to Regulate Public Aid to Hospitals (Hospital Act) was proclaimed in 1902 (8). This Act defined "hospital" and "days' treatment," and specified the rate the government paid per patient day, the data to be recorded on all admissions, and inspection of all hospitals receiving aid. Hospital services in public hospitals charged patients a per

---

1 The name was changed to Hospital Programs in 1975.

2 The Provincial Health Officer became a separate position with this reorganization.

diem rate. Hospitals complying with the requirements of the *Hospital Act* also received public monies based on the number of treatment days provided per year. Municipalities were responsible for their indigent persons who were admitted to a public hospital (9). The Act was amended many times to include private, chronic, and convalescent hospitals, and the requirements pertaining to their management and inspection to monitor the performance of all hospitals and to enforce the Act.

British Columbia has a long history of interest in health insurance. The concept and initial studies of the hospital and medical insurance were initiated within the Department of the Provincial Secretary.

In 1921, a royal commission recommended that health insurance be adopted and, in 1932, a second royal commission recommended legislation (10). A preliminary plan was presented to the legislature in 1935 that included, on a compulsory basis, wage earners earning less than $200 per month and their dependents, as well as all indigent persons. The insured persons were to receive the services of doctors and hospitals. The scheme was to be financed by employers and employees and the care of indigents by the provincial government. In 1936, a *Health Insurance Act* was passed in the legislature, but the Act was never proclaimed (11, 12). A commission was appointed after adoption of the Act and, by the beginning of 1937, was ready to "put in motion the machinery of health insurance." However, after protracted negotiations, the physicians of the province would not accept the terms they were offered, and the start was postponed indefinitely (10). Turnbull (13) has recently described some serious deficiencies in the Act. It did not include old-age pensioners, the indigent, part-time labourers, domestic servants, or those receiving less than ten dollars per week. The proposed hospital service was impossible to attain under existing circumstances. Furthermore, remuneration proposed for the doctors was insufficient. Senior accountants worried that the total fund proposed to support the Act was inadequate by a considerable amount.

While these negotiations were under way, in 1936, Dr. G. F. Amyot was appointed Advisor on Hospital Services and assistant to the Provincial Health Officer and was asked to survey the public and private hospitals as a preliminary to the formulation of a new hospital policy (10). His research assistant in the hospital survey, Miss Nancy Scott (14) (later to be Dr. Donald Paterson's associate in the Registry for Crippled Children; see Chapter 5), remembered a hostile relationship between the staff of different hospitals and the researchers. The survey disclosed that there was much use of acute hospital beds for social problem cases not suffering acute illnesses, and there was a lack of uniformity in administrative procedures and records, particularly in accounting, in the various public hospitals. The researchers also found that the hospital records were composed of nurses' notes with no medical notations. They introduced a face sheet, in duplicate, to the hospital record to record demographic and diagnostic information, with one copy sent to the government to enable the compilation of an annual report.

The *Hospital Act* was subsequently amended to unify the administrative control of public hospitals, to organize medical staffs in hospitals and thereby provide advice to hospital management, to mitigate overhospitalization, and to inaugurate a standard system of hospital accounting.

The introduction of provincial hospital insurance in British Columbia in 1948 provided acute hospital care to all residents (see Chapter 6). It soon became apparent, however, that there was an important need for other patterns of care for those who had chronic disabilities. In 1960 and 1966, rehabilitation and extended care inpatient services became available in designated long-stay hospitals (see Chapter 6), but hospital-based ambulatory clinics and community-based services did not qualify for provincial insurance benefits. A few ambulatory programs were introduced (Speech and Hearing at the Health Centre for Children of the Vancouver General Hospital, and Arthritis and Cerebral Palsy at the G. F. Strong Rehabilitation Centre, with funding from federal health grants and voluntary societies.

In 1967, the provincial *Medical Services Act* was enacted (15) and, in 1968, the Medical Services Plan was established in British Columbia, under the supervision of the Medical Services Commission. Medical services were provided by physicians chosen by patients on a fee-for-service basis. It was now possible to employ physicians in hospital and community-based ambulatory programs for different populations of children with chronic disabilities, although salaries for other health professions and administration were dependent on other funding.

The *Medical Services Act* was replaced in July 1992 by the *Medical and Health Care Services Act* (16), which imposed a fixed global cap for physician service payments. This decision ignored the *Canada Health Act*, which requires provinces to negotiate fees with the medical profession and to go to conciliation or binding arbitration if those talks fail.

Federal: The introduction of the *Hospital Insurance and Diagnostic Services Act* (17) in 1957 provided cost sharing for inpatient services in acute hospitals and, at the option of the provinces, care could be provided as insured outpatient programs. In British Columbia in the 1960s, this option was adopted only for outpatient cancer therapy, psychiatric outpatients, and day surgery in acute hospitals. Although the ambulatory programs served the same populations of children as the acute and long-stay hospitals and reduced inpatient utilization, only inpatient services qualified for insured benefits. As a result of this bizarre administrative arrangement, children with chronic disease and disabilities were rendered the poor relations of the health care family.

The *Established Programs Financing Act* (18) in 1977 (Chapter 7), designed to promote community services and to replace hospital services, put an end to this irrational approach. The Extended Health Care Services were provided as an incentive to stimulate use of less costly community services. It was ironic that the provincial government elected to use the Extended Health Care Services funds in 1978 to develop the Long-Term Care Program for seniors, children under eighteen years being excluded.

Health Security for British Columbians

During the tenure of the New Democratic Party, the government commissioned a special consultant, Dr. R. G. Foulkes, to undertake a study of health care in British Columbia. The report, entitled *Health Security for British Columbians* (19), recommended major changes in the organization of health care for the local community, for regions, and for the Ministry of Health. It also proposed amalgamation of the Departments of Health and Human Resources into one Department of Social Affairs. While a few community human resource and health centres were established to provide a full range of health and social services, the government was defeated before any further changes were introduced.

Inter-Ministerial Children's Committees

In 1977, Inter-Ministry Children's Committees (IMCCs) were established by the Social Services Committee of cabinet in an effort to provide co-ordinated responses to case management issues at the local, regional, and provincial levels (20). The purpose of the IMCCs was identified as facilitating the provision of services to children and youth whose needs could not be met by a single ministry or through the normal procedures of the ministries involved. The Ministries of the Attorney General, Education, Health and Human Resources (now Social Services) appointed representatives to the committees. When the provincial IMCC was later dissolved, the activities of the local and regional IMCCs became inconsistent across the province and dependent on the skills, strength, and commitment of individual members.

In 1989, a task force on inter-ministry issues was established by the Deputy Ministers' Committee on Social Policy (DMCSP) to develop recommendations to improve the operation of the IMCCs in a number of areas, including the delivery of services to children (21). The importance of local and regional IMCCs to achieve co-ordinated care, policy development, and planning between agencies and ministries was recognized. Likewise, the need for integration between ministries was emphasized by the Ombudsman's report (22). A new body, the Child and Youth Secretariat, was created to focus responsibility for co-ordination, integration, and implementation of inter-ministry policies and programs for children and youth.

One of the secretariat's major tasks is supporting the revitalization and refocusing of local and regional committees throughout the provinces. In addition, the IMCCs have been renamed the Child and Youth Committees (CYC) to reflect the fact that some members are not ministry staff.

Provincial Study of Handicapped Children

In 1979, the Ministry of Health commissioned the Provincial Study of Severely Handicapped Children (23). The main objectives of the study were to describe the numbers of severely handicapped[3] children and adolescents in the province by their physical, mental, and sensory disabilities, to identify the services required to maintain severely handicapped children in their own communities, and to recommend the role, responsibilities and interrelationships of the three ministries (Education, Human Resources and Health), voluntary agencies, and parents in regard to services for severely handicapped children.

The report included 116 recommendations pertaining to monitoring and surveillance, assessment and diagnosis, special needs of children up to six years old, school age children, young adults, the four types of therapies (physiotherapy, occupational therapy, speech therapy, and audiology), family support services, and residential care. The final chapters dealt with allocation of funding by the three ministries and their proposed responsibilities.

The need for a surveillance function for handicapped children was emphasized "to identify, refer and assist in planning services for these children." Although the Health Surveillance Registry (see Chapter 5) was initially intended to function as a data resource for planning services for disabled and chronically ill children, this role had been discontinued.

Three major functions at the provincial, regional, and local levels were identified that required particular attention, namely, continuity and co-ordination of services, resource development and planning, and information services. The report noted that "no single branch or ministry has the responsibility to provide services to children to ensure that there is a 'continuum of care' for handicapped children." The existing IMCCs, while designed to facilitate co-ordination of services across ministries,

---

3 Definition of severely handicapped: children and adolescents (up to nineteen years of age) who suffer either permanently or for a period of time greater than one year from a disability that interferes to a significant degree with their capacity to function in one or more of the following important life activities: mobility, self care, speech and communication, learning, and self direction (independent living).

gave committees little authority and responsibility to plan, co-ordinate, or fund services at the regional or local level. It is disconcerting that the need for integration of services within and across ministries remains ten years later (22).

The report recommended a new Local Children's Special Service Team (comprising a community health nurse, a co-ordinator of special services for each school district, and a social worker to co-ordinate special services for young adults) to be responsible for all special needs children, including "the handicapped, emotionally disturbed, learning disabled and delinquents." It also recommended the addition of a planning and research officer, a vocational and rehabilitation counsellor, and a resource planner to the Regional Inter-ministry Children's Committee with responsibility to co-ordinate regional and local services. The Local Children's Special Service Team would be responsible for diagnosis, assessment, and follow-up for all handicapped children, assisting in the development and review of individual programs involving child and parent, and developing community support services to allow children to return from institutions to their own homes.

The report was received with conditional approval by the government, doubtless because it reflected poorly on the existing services for handicapped children, and was never published, though a summary was made available upon request. It was, however, a thought-provoking and comprehensive report by a knowledgeable team, which advocated a population-based approach to identify and then provide for integrated and continuing care for disabled children. In essence, the public health model for the control of infectious disease was proposed for chronic disabilities.

British Columbia Royal Commission on Health Care and Costs

Introduction: In 1991, *Closer to Home*, the report of the British Columbia Royal Commission on Health Care and Costs, was published (24). The report recommended that the five principles of medicare become an integral part of British Columbian law and presented a further set of guidelines. These included providing services in or as near to the patient's residence as was consistent with quality and cost-effective health care; measurement of outcomes and funding only for those services shown to improve health care; community involvement; recognition that annual funding for health needs to be less variable than in other sectors of the provincial budget; development of an integrated system; fostering volunteer help in governance, patient service, and advocacy, but not by replacing paid staff; and making information on health and health care collected by the public service available to the public and researchers.

The report noted that the provincial government spending on health care has varied between 30.6 and 33.2 percent of the provincial budget during the past decade. The components, physicians (medical service plan), hospitals, continuing care, and community and family services—while fluctuating from year to year—even out over the decade.

The report emphasized that there never has been an overall plan in British Columbia, and the present structure lacks the ability to evaluate its effectiveness in providing health care. It proposed a permanent provincial health council to oversee the health care system and to review the plans, policies, and programs of the Ministry of Health and other public or private bodies that affect the health of the population. The council would enunciate specific goals for the health care system, evaluate information to determine the degree of progress in reaching these goals, and review and comment on health policies and plans of the Ministry of Health or other ministries. It must be completely independent of government and the health care industry and accountable to the legislative assembly, not the Ministry of Health.

The report advocated a shift in focus from curative medicine to improved health status of the population by the prevention of illness or injury and by protecting health. Strategies for change were identified and included increased involvement of the Provincial Health Officer and the medical officers of health in the pursuit of the public's health, and the establishment of measurable health indices, with which to plan and evaluate public policies for health. This implies determination and collection of data needed by the province and a periodic health survey to provide information on health status.

The report recommended regionalization of the province to improve management of health services with funding containing all health dollars assigned to each region. The planning of province-wide standards and programs and the funding of province-wide services (tertiary care) should be undertaken by the central office in Victoria.

Children and Youth: One chapter was devoted to children and youth, and further input was included in the chapters on native health, disabilities, substance abuse, and mental health. It began with a review of the changing structure and role of the family, with the reasons for this and their consequences, and recommended that the Ministry of Education institute a province-wide program in the schools to implement the Nobody's Perfect program (a parenting program developed by the Health Promotion Directorate of Health and Welfare Canada). The profound effect of poverty on the mortality and morbidity of children was noted and increased welfare rates for these families recommended. The importance of child abuse and neglect and family violence was then discussed, and targets and strategies to reduce the consequences of family violence were defined. The Commission recommended that the province request the Canadian Radio-Television and Telecommunications Commission to reduce violence in television programs and develop information programs encouraging parents to control children's choice of television programs.

The report then turned to the vulnerability of children during the first year of life and recommended that the Division of Vital Statistics improve the quality and quantity of information recorded on the Physician's Notice of Live Birth and Registration of Live Birth and develop the capacity to track and evaluate the quality of prenatal care. The very real hazards of low birthweight and the long-term consequences for the child, the family, and society of saving very low birthweight infants (less than 1,000 grams birthweight) and infants with severe congenital anomalies prompted the commission to recommend that hospital ethics committees develop programs based on the long-term consequences for children, families, and society of severely disabling conditions. Furthermore, it proposed that this information be used to provide counselling when diagnostic screening establishes that a severely disabling condition exists.

The commission then recommended improving antenatal care and developing prenatal education packages and videos in the major language groups in British Columbia. It also supported expansion of prenatal nutrition programs, including outreach projects for high-risk clients.

A number of other strategies were reviewed and some are briefly summarized below. The provision of services to disabled children is often the responsibility of several ministries, and the commission recommended assigning the responsibility of continuing care to one ministry or agency. Injuries are the leading cause of death in children and youth in British Columbia, and the commission recommended further education and research to reduce the number and severity of injuries. The sexual activity of teenagers, leading to pregnancies and sexually acquired diseases and sequelae thereof, indicates the failure of our social, educational, and health policies. The commission recommended that the Ministries of Health, Social Services, and Education jointly fund youth health clinics throughout the province and ensure that condom vending machines are available in all high schools. Finally, the commission observed that mental health services have not been a priority and the needs of many children have been unattended. Appropriate services were recommended for children with multiple problems, young offenders, sexual abuse victims, and young sexual offenders, along with travelling consultants for those living in remote and rural communities.

Additional child and youth concerns were discussed in subsequent chapters and are briefly reviewed below.

Native Health: The commission noted the need for special programs for native children and youth and recommended that all ministries address the health, social, and economic concerns of native people, and that government consult and involve native people in the design, development, and implementation of programs, services, and policies intended for them. The commission recommended that an office of the Chief Native Advisor be made into a separate branch within the Ministry of Health, and that the ministry support the development of native-controlled health services, including services to urban natives.

Services to People with Disabilities: The commission recommended that program development be directed toward conditions for which there is the greatest probability of cure. A Registry of Individuals with Disabilities was proposed to organize assessment and treatment services using a multidisciplinary team approach to plan for each person on an annual basis.

Substance Abuse: The commission recommended that the priority for prevention, planning, program development, and services must be, in order, children and youth for tobacco and alcohol, natives for alcohol and drugs, and seniors for prescription drugs and alcohol. The commission recommended that at least one-third of the resources of the Alcohol and Drug Commission be devoted to prevention and the outcome of alcohol and drug treatment programs be evaluated. It also recommended enforcement and strengthening rules that limit access, including a ban on all alcohol advertising and the use of health warnings on liquor labels, with particular attention directed at the effects of alcohol on pregnancy, and increasing the legal age for buying and using tobacco products to nineteen.

CURRENT ORGANIZATION OF HEALTH SERVICES

The pace of development and the organizational framework of health care varied from one provincial area to another, but the overall responses have been similar. The Ministry of Health in British Columbia is organized into four functional divisions: Management Operations, which includes Vital Statistics and the Office of Health Promotion, Community and Family Health, Institutional Services, and Medical Services (25).

Management Operations

This division includes Human Resources, Policy Planning and Legislation, Financial Services, Ministry Support Services, Staff Development and Safety Programs, Systems Division, Legal Services, Vital Statistics, and the Office of Health Promotion.

Office of Health Promotion: An advisory committee on health promotion was given the mandate to recommend new approaches that will produce sustained change in the health status of citizens (26). An office of health promotion was proposed in 1989 and initiated in 1990. Four regions, each with a manager, have been introduced to promote development of community programs.

The office is a resource unit that collaborates with all parts of the Ministry of Health in relation to health promotion strategies (27). Current programs include Healthy Communities; Healthy Schools, involving school age children and youth in learning and practising skills for decision making for health; Population Health Strategy, including information on health determinants, as well as health status data as a tool for planning and implementing actions to improve health; Healthy Public Policy to teach that health and government policy are interlinked; Tobacco Reduction Strategy; Professional Liaison/Knowledge Development within the major health sectors; Workplace Health; Choosing Wellness, supporting seniors' health promotion programs; and Active Living Concept.

Four priorities for children and youth (up to and including nineteen years of age) were identified (28). These were special needs groups (native, poor, and disabled), prevention of low birthweight and prematurity, prevention of injury and poisoning, and promotion of mental health and family functioning. Recommendations to promote the health of children included intra- and interministerial committees to set priorities and policies, a focus on the above four priority areas, and family focus for health programming, with recognition that family resources vary greatly from one unit to another. The school and community were cited as the primary foci for action in promoting awareness and adoption of healthy lifestyle choices for children and youth and for the creation of environments to support health,

Community and Family Health[4]

This division includes the following services:

Provincial Health Officer: The provincial *Health Act* defines certain regulations for the prevention of disease, which are carried out by local health units. The Provincial Health Officer is responsible for monitoring the regulations throughout the province.

The British Columbia Centre for Disease Control: The Centre administers and supervises a variety of special services. These include:

---

4 Alcohol and Drug Programs, responsible for planning, funding, and co-ordinating treatment and prevention programs related to abuse of alcohol and other drugs, were the responsibility of the Ministry of Health from 1975 to 1988, when they were transferred to the Ministry of Labour and Consumer Affairs (see Chapter 17). They were transferred back to the Ministry of Health in 1991.

Provincial Laboratories provide medical advice and laboratory tests for diseases caused by disease agents and related immunology, serology, and environmental biology. The services are available to physicians, hospitals, health units, and health-related agencies at no direct cost to the users.

Sexually Transmitted Disease Control is responsible for controlling the spread of sexually transmitted diseases and provides training and consultation to public health nurses. Treatment for these diseases is provided at no cost to the patient through physicians, health units, and the Sexually Transmitted Disease Control Clinic in Vancouver.

Tuberculosis Control directs all phases of tuberculosis prevention and treatment. Services include outpatient care, consultation to private physicians, advice regarding tracing active cases, supervision of cases under treatment, screening, and surveillance.

Medical Supplies/Kidney Dialysis Services provide a range of services, therapy, supplies, and medication to patients with end-stage renal disease, haemophilia, cystic fibrosis, leprosy, rheumatic fever, and those receiving parenteral and enteral nutrition. These services are provided on a home care basis or at limited care facilities at no cost to the patient. Biologicals for immunizations, botulism, snake bites, and black widow spider venom are also provided.

Government Employee Health Services are responsible for promoting the occupational health of public servants, and controlling hazards of the working environment.

Radiation Protection Services Branch is responsible for the policy and inspection of radiation issues and the investigation of unexpected events.

Family Health: The following services are included:

Child and Youth Mental Health Services: This program is described in Mental Health Services (Chapter 14).

Public Health Nursing and Community Supports: The core programs are health prevention and promotion and include family/child health, adult health, community care facilities licensing, staff development, and community development. The in-home nursing respite program (Chapter 19) cares for persons with traumatic head injury. School health programs are also included.

Speech Services and Audiology Services: These are described in Chapter 16.

Services to the Handicapped: This program is described in Chapter 19.

Dental Programs: This program is described in Chapter 13.

Mental Health Services: This program is responsible for ensuring that the mental health system provides effective care to residents with mental disorders. This is accomplished through direct services or by the co-ordination of the mental health system, including services by other government divisions, ministries, and private and voluntary agencies. A separate mental health service for children and youth is within Family Health.

Forensic Psychiatric Services provides assessment of individuals remanded by the court for psychiatric examination, diagnosis, and treatment of individuals found "unfit to stand trial" or "not guilty by reason of insanity," and diagnosis and treatment of persons who become mentally ill while in custody. It is also responsible for providing consultation to agencies and institutions in the correctional system. A special program for children and adolescents, Juvenile Services to the Courts, is described in Chapter 14.

Institutional Services

This division includes three programs: British Columbia Ambulance Service, Continuing Care, and Hospital Programs.

The British Columbia Ambulance Service provides pre-hospital ground and air ambulance services and medical aspects of disaster planning. A permanent Air Evac crew, consisting of the Advanced Life Support and the Infant Transport Team members, is stationed in Vancouver. This service is described in Chapter 10.

Continuing Care Division includes the Long-Term Care, Home Nursing Care, and Community Physiotherapy Programs. These programs integrate health care services for acutely ill, handicapped, and infirm persons, especially the elderly, into a single, comprehensive range of services. The overall policy direction and control derive from the central office, and the programs are delivered through the provincial and municipal health units.

The Long-Term Care Program assists adults with long-term health-related problems to retain independence in their own homes, the community, or a residential care setting. These services are directed to adults in British Columbia and are not provided to children and youth.

The Home Care Nursing Program provides nursing care to patients who are discharged early from hospital (e.g., day-care surgery), who require home nursing services as an alternative to admission to hospital, who are terminally ill, or who require in-home nursing services on a long-term basis.

The Community Physiotherapy Program provides direct treatment, consultative, and preventive services to clients in their homes, arranges provision of equipment to cope with physical disabilities, and trains family members to assist clients.

Hospital Programs Division is responsible for the operation of acute care, rehabilitation, and extended care hospitals. The role of Hospital Programs is that of a funding agency, with the responsibility for facility operations remaining with the institutions. The ultimate responsibility remains with the Ministry of Health, but an arm's-length relationship is maintained with the facilities.

The division also monitors quality of care, develops long-range capital plans, monitors, reviews, and adjusts facility funding allocations, and provides an investigative service when concerns arise about the delivery system. The division works with hospitals to encourage the introduction of innovative management and staffing techniques. Continuing Advisory Task Force Subcommittees (CASC), with membership from the practising profession and the Ministry of Health, are appointed to examine and make recommendations on a variety of clinical and technological issues.

Acute and long-stay hospital services are described in Chapter 6 and maternal and newborn services are described in Chapter 12.

Medical Services

The Medical Services Plan is administered in accordance with the *Medical Services Act* under the supervision of the Medical Services Commission and provides payment for all medically required services of physicians and surgeons and for specially defined dental surgery. The provincial government, at its own expense, provides partial coverage of extra health benefits, including chiropractic, podiatry, optometry, physiotherapy, massage treatments, and naturopathic medicine.

The plan registers all subscribers, collects premiums, provides premium assistance for low income groups, and provides reimbursement for qualified practitioners for insured services to eligible subscribers. Payment is made on a fee-for-service basis according to a schedule approved by the commission, or on a salaried, sessional, or contract basis at levels approved by the commission.

Each province has a fee schedule that sets a province-wide fee for office or hospital visits, consultations, surgical procedures, laboratory tests, and radiological procedures. Each year or two, negotiations between the Ministry of Health and the Medical Association are held to revise the fee schedule to reflect current overhead costs, new procedures, etc.

Pharmacare was introduced in 1974 by the Ministry of Human Resources and initially covered prescribed drugs to seniors, low income earners, and those on social assistance. In 1987, Pharmacare was transferred to the Ministry of Health, and it currently covers entirely those on social assistance, all persons in designated long-term care facilities, and three-quarters of the dispensing fees of seniors.

Other Services

The Professional Advisory Committee to the Ministry of Health initiates studies in health care that are referred to it by the ministry or the British Columbia Medical Association. To carry out this function, temporary or continuing advisory subcommittees (TASC and CASC) are appointed to provide advice on either a short-term or an ongoing basis. Occasional reference is made to the work of these subcommittees in the text.

The Centre for Health Services and Policy Research: The Health Manpower Resources Unit was founded in 1973 and staffed by the Department of Health Care and Epidemiology in the Faculty of Medicine and the Division of Health Services Research and Development in the multischool Health Sciences Centre in Vancouver (29). The purpose of the unit was to assist decision makers in health care planning and the allocation of resources. The director of the unit reported to an inter-ministerial health manpower working group, chaired by a representative of the Ministry of Health, and produced a variety of reports for the provincial Health Manpower Working Group, the Federal-Provincial Health Manpower Committee, and for professional groups over the years. A basic commitment was the collation of information by region on physicians, dentists, dental hygienists, pharmacists, and registered nurses.

In the early 1980s, the data base was broadened to include health services data—hospital utilization, medical plan, long-term care utilization, and Pharmacare—expanding the scope of the service. The concept of a health policy unit was endorsed by the co-ordinator of the Health Sciences Centre, and the Health Policy Research Unit was formally established in 1988. In 1990, the name was changed to the Centre for Health Services and Policy Research, and an autonomous unit of the University of British Columbia, accountable to a committee of deans, was born. It comprises four units, the Health and Human Resources Research Unit, the Health Policy Research Unit, the British Columbia Office of Health Technology Assessment, and the Health Information Development Unit. The Research Unit is funded by grants and the other units by the Ministry of Health.

The British Columbia Health Research Foundation[5] was established in 1977 to act as an agency for the allocation of lottery fund proceeds to health research and scholarship in the province (30). The purpose of the foundation is to assist and collaborate with organizations conducting research in the field of health care in British Columbia and, without limiting the generality of the foregoing, to assist basic research, clinical research, and applied research in the field of health care. Community

---

5 Previously the British Columbia Health Care Foundation.

health care delivery and clinical studies are priorities. The current annual budget is $13 million.

COMMENT

The present resources reflect the provincial response to federal legislation in the 1950s and 1960s, which was dominated by support for acute care hospital services and the proliferation of professional manpower. Voluntary societies (e.g., Cerebral Palsy Association, British Columbia Association for Community Living, Canadian Arthritis and Rheumatism Society, etc.) initiated many community-based services for the disabled population during this time.

Further provincial responses in the 1970s and 1980s, associated with rising health costs, emphasized alternatives to inpatient hospital beds, including ambulatory community programs, long-term care services, and new emphasis on the health of the public.

The federal publications, *A New Perspective on the Health of Canadians* (1974) and *Achieving Health for All* (1986), together gave rise to new preventive health and health promotion initiatives, which are beginning to show results. Likewise, the *Federal-Provincial Fiscal Arrangements and Established Programs Financing (EPF) Act* shifted the emphasis away from the hospital to less costly alternative patterns of care. The worth of children (as voters) is emphasized by the government's decision to use the Extended Health Care Services funds for seniors exclusively.

The need for a population-based approach to many contemporary child-health problems has been emphasized in Chapter 1. There are many small populations of children, low birthweight infants being a prime example, whose care requires both the traditional one-to-one medical and nursing care (personal medicine) and the organization of a provincial network of perinatal and neonatal services (population medicine) to improve the outcomes of care. Other examples requiring the dual approach are children with chronic diseases and disabilities, and the diseases associated with the physical environment (accidents and poisonings), the social environment (developmental and behavioural problems), and lifestyle (substance abuse and child abuse). The following chapters examine the origins and outcomes of health services for these different populations of children, as well as related questions: What special programs have evolved to deal with contemporary child health problems? How did the programs begin? What was the source of funds? Did they originate from the top down, or from the bottom up? What data is being collected and examined to measure the outcomes of these new programs?

The recent British Columbia Royal Commission on Health Care and Costs has given special attention to contemporary child and youth problems, stressing family problems, antenatal and postnatal care, accidents, native health, substance abuse, mental health, and disabilities. It has emphasized the need to shift to health promotion and prevention strategies, the greater use of community resources, and the importance of outcome measures that check the effectiveness of programs. It will be interesting to follow the government's response to the recommendations and particularly to the selection of policy priorities. Doubtless much will depend upon, on the one hand, the strength of the provincial economy and, on the other, the impact of the *Government Expenditures Restraint Act* (31).

Before examining the population-based programs, the data systems, i.e., the Division of Vital Statistics, are described. This provides us with data to monitor mortality and morbidity trends, and the incidence and prevalence rates of chronic disabilities.

REFERENCES

1. MONRO, A. S. The medical history of British Columbia. *Canadian Medical Journal* 26 (1932): 725–32.
2. AMYOT, G. F. and DEFRIES, R. D. The British Columbia Department of Health and Welfare. In *British Columbia: Patterns in Economic, Political and Cultural Development*, ed. Dickson M. Falconer. Victoria, B.C.: Camosun College, 1982.
3. Four Years of Progressive Administration in the Department of the Honourable Dr. J. D. MacLean, Provincial Secretary and Minister of Education, 1920. Mimeographed document.
4. *Seventieth Annual Report of the Public Health Services of British Columbia.* Health Branch, Department of Health Services and Hospital Insurance. Year ended 31 December 1966, p. 20.
5. GREEN, M. M. *Through the Years with Public Health Nursing—A History of Public Health Nursing in the Provincial Government Jurisdiction British Columbia.* Canadian Public Health Nursing Association, 1984. Monograph Series, Public Health in Canada, scientific editor, J. M. Last.
6. *Department of Health and Welfare Act*, S.B.C. 1946, c. 31.
7. *Hospital Insurance Act*, S.B.C. 1948, c. 28.
8. *Hospital Act*, S.B.C. 1902, c. 33.
9. *Hospital Act*, R.S.B.C. 1911, c. 102.
10. BRITISH COLUMBIA. *New Developments in Health and Welfare, 1933–1937.* Department of Provincial Secretary, Health and Welfare Service, pp. 6–9. Victoria, B.C., 1 May 1937. Mimeographed document.
11. BRITISH COLUMBIA. *First Annual Report, B.C. Hospital Insurance Service*, 1 January 1949–31, December 1949.
12. ELLIOT, G.R.F. and MCDONNELL, C. E. Profile: Dr. T. H. "Harry" Milburn. *B.C. Medical Journal* 26 (1984): 687–89.
13. TURNBULL, F. The introduction of medicare to B.C. *B.C. Medical Journal* 32 (1990): 514.
14. SCOTT, A. E., personal communication, 1989.
15. *Medical Services Act*, S.B.C. 1967, c. 24.

16. *Medical and Health Care Services Act*, S.B.C. 1992, c. 76.
17. *Hospital Insurance and Diagnostic Services Act*, S.C. 1957, c. 28
18. *Federal-Provincial Fiscal Arrangements and Established Programs Financing Act*, S.C. 1976–77, c. 10. Subsequently renamed *Federal–Provincial Fiscal Arrangements and Federal Post-Secondary Education and Health Contributions Act*, R.S.C. 1985, c. F–8.
19. FOULKES, R. G. *Health Security for British Columbians*. Report to the Minister of Health, British Columbia. Victoria, B.C.: Queen's Printer, December 1974.
20. BRITISH COLUMBIA. *Annual Report, 1977*. Ministry of Health.
21. *Revised Child and Youth Services: Integrated Approaches*. Child and Youth Secretariat, February 1992. Mimeographed document.
22. *Public Services to Children, Youth and their Families in British Columbia: The Need for Integration*. Office of the Ombudsman. Public Report No. 22, November 1990.
23. TALBOT, J., DUNBAR, P. B., STULL, S., and SHEPS, S. *Provincial Study of Severely Handicapped Children*, 1981 (unpublished).
24. BRITISH COLUMBIA. *Closer to Home*. The Report of the British Columbia Royal Commission on Health Care and Costs, 1991.
25. BRITISH COLUMBIA. *Organization Chart*, Ministry of Health, 1 November 1989.
26. WOLCZUK, P. *Proceedings of the National Symposium on Health Promotion and Disease Prevention*, Provincial Reports, British Columbia, pp. 41–43, 12–15 March 1989, Victoria, B.C.
27. BRITISH COLUMBIA. *Program Update, April 1992*. Office of Health Promotion, Ministry of Health and Minister Responsible for Seniors, 1991/92.
28. BEARPARK, S. The Health of Children and Youth in British Columbia: Issues for Health Promotion. Discussion Paper, Mimeographed document. The Office of Health Promotion, B.C. Ministry of Health, 1 April 1990.
29. ANDERSON, D. O. Canada: Epidemiology in the planning process in British Columbia: Description of an experience with a new model. In *Epidemiology as a Fundamental Science. Its Uses in Health Services Planning, Administration and Evaluation*, ed. K. White and M. Henderson. New York: Oxford University Press, 1976.
30. *Annual Report*. British Columbia Health Care Research Foundation, 1989–90.
31. *Government Expenditures Restraint Act*, S.C. 1991, c. 9.

The Division of Vital Statistics

by John Doughty

INTRODUCTION

Vital statistics have long played an important role in the field of medicine and health, serving to identify health problems, quantify their severity, and evaluate remedial measures. In British Columbia, the vital statistics and related services of the province's Division of Vital Statistics have been of distinct consequence to the development of the child health services described in this book. A brief overview of the history of that division, including its civil registration data base and its extensive bio-statistical activities, is therefore presented in this chapter. The account focuses on developments that significantly affected the quality of the vital statistics data and on those divisional pursuits that have had especial relevance to the child health field.

EARLY RECORDS

The collection of vital statistics in British Columbia dates back virtually to the birth of the province when, on 11 April 1872, the first session of the new parliament passed *An Act Respecting the Registration of Births, Deaths and Marriages in British Columbia* (1). However, even earlier recordings of vital events occurring in the former colonies on Vancouver Island and the mainland had in fact been made from 1837 onward, in parish registers maintained in accordance with ecclesiastical custom. Additionally, marriages had been entered in official marriage registers provided by the colonial administrations. Many years later, with the concurrence of the ecclesiastical authorities, the early parish entries were copied into the province's official vital statistic records, thereby ensuring their survival and accessibility.

ADMINISTRATIVE FRAMEWORK

The legal requirements for the registration of births, deaths, and marriages, and the collection and preservation of the vital records, were set forth in the 1872 Act. The basic features of the vital statistics system as laid down at that time remain substantially the same to this day. The Act was to be administered by a Registrar-General, who was also to be responsible for the custody of the vital records. The province was divided into registration districts, each under an appointee known as the "District Registrar of Births, Deaths and Marriages" and responsible to the Registrar-General. Events were to be registered with the local district registrar, who was required to retain a copy of each registration and transmit the original to the Registrar-General.

As a matter of policy, district registrar appointments were vested, wherever possible, in existing government officials, such as gold commissioners and mining recorders in the early years and subsequently government agents and sub-agents. Over the years, this policy of utilizing officials already trained and experienced in government procedures proved to be an important factor in the efficiency and stability of the registration system. As the province developed and the need arose to provide vital statistics service in communities not having ready access to a government agent's office, additional appointments were made of municipal employees, police, and even private individuals.

RESPONSIBILITY TO REGISTER VITAL EVENTS

The responsibility for registering births was placed initially upon the father, with contingent responsibility resting respectively upon the mother, a person standing in place of the parents, the occupier of the premises wherein the birth took place, and finally upon the attending nurse. From 1917 onward, both parents shared the prime duty to register. The responsibility for registering marriages fell to the officiating clergyman or civil marriage commissioner. The duty to register deaths was laid upon "the occupier of the house or tenement wherein the death took place" or upon a resident of the house. For deaths not occurring in a house, it fell upon any person who had knowledge of the circumstances, or upon the coroner. Over the years, the statutory responsibility for registering deaths has been progressively changed to meet changed circumstances. It now rests upon the undertaker, with "undertaker" being broadly defined as "any person having charge of a dead body for the purpose of burial or other disposition." The 1872 Act also required the attending physician to provide to the district registrar a certificate stating the cause of death, a requirement still in effect today.

LIMITATIONS OF EARLY VITAL STATISTICS

Although the Act of 1872 made the registration of births, deaths, and marriages mandatory, compliance with its provisions remained far from complete for several decades. Many factors contributed to the shortfall, including an inadequate number of district registrar offices for such a vast and rugged geographic area, lack of public awareness of the law and of the importance of registration, and the impracticability of enforcing punitive measures. It was not until 1913 that compliance had improved to the point where the Registrar-General saw fit to compile some of the raw data in his annual report into percentages.

A further limitation of the province's early vital statistics was that Indians and Chinese were excluded from registration up to 1888, while Indians as defined by the federal *Indian Act* were excluded between 1899 and 1917. In 1917, the federal Indian agents were appointed as district registrars for their respective agencies and were encouraged to register Indian events, but it was not until 1937 that the registration of all Indian births, deaths, and marriages became mandatory under British Columbia law.

VITAL STATISTICS TRANSFERRED TO HEALTH JURISDICTIONS

During those early decades of grossly incomplete vital statistics registration, strong and persistent demands for improvement came from the health field. The provincial Board of Health, soon after coming into existence in 1895, lost no time in drawing attention to the inadequacies of the vital statistics and in presenting eloquent testimony to the health and social benefits which would ensue from full registration. The board kept this matter constantly to the fore by formal resolutions, letters to appropriate government officials and bodies, and recommendations for statutory and administrative improvements.(2) These efforts were not in vain. In 1911, the administration of the *Registration of Births, Deaths and Marriages Act* was transferred from the jurisdiction of the Registrar-General of Titles to that of the provincial Board of Health.

STRENGTHENING THE REGISTRATION SYSTEM

In the decade between 1911 and 1921, the vital statistics system was progressively strengthened through a series of statutory amendments and orders-in-council. In 1911, as a means of detecting unregistered births, the physician in attendance was made responsible for submitting a notice of birth to the district registrar, an obligation which formerly rested only upon the attending nurse. From 1 January 1912, the regulations relating to certification of death were changed to elicit greater specificity respecting the cause of death. Prior to that date, physicians and coroners had been required to state the cause of death simply in terms of one of the following broad categories:[1]

Zymotic	Organs of Generation
Diseases, Uncertain Seat	Organs of Locomotion
Tubercular	Skin Diseases
Brain and Nervous System	Malformation
Organs of Circulation	Atrophy
Respiratory Organs	Old Age
Organs of Digestion	Sudden Death
Urinary Organs	Violent Death

Under the revised regulations, the medical certificate called for both the "immediate or final determining cause" and any "remote or earlier pathological or morbid condition," for the duration of each, and for information indicating whether an operation had been performed within one month of death. A further amendment in 1913 required physicians to certify deaths in terms of the International Statistical Classification of Causes of Death.

Other improvement measures taken in 1913 included increasing the number of district offices from twenty to forty-nine and defining in legislation the duties of the district registrar, making him responsible for aggressively pursuing registration for every event occurring in his jurisdiction. In the same year, the position of Inspector of Vital Statistics was created to provide for the ongoing inspection of district offices, although no appointment was made until 1929. Commencing in 1917, as a means of providing a further check on unregistered events, hospitals were required to submit monthly lists of births to the local district registrar, an obligation which remained in effect for over thirty-five years.

IMPROVEMENTS DURING INTER-WAR YEARS

The task of further upgrading the registration system through both legislative refinements and operational improvements was pursued vigorously in the two decades following World War I. In 1921, a major change affecting the presentation of statistical data was implemented, the details of which are described later in this chapter. In 1927, the field organization was greatly strengthened when arrangements were made for the Provin-

---

1 These categories were prescribed by the Registrar General for use on the medical certificate of death (2).

cial Police to serve as deputy district registrars in twenty-six smaller communities throughout the province. Over the next five decades, the Provincial Police and their successors, the Royal Canadian Mounted Police, provided a quality and a continuity of service that would otherwise have been difficult or impossible to obtain in the rural areas. In 1929, the first Inspector of Vital Statistics was appointed, enabling direct instruction to the district registrars and more adequate monitoring of their work. In 1930, a comprehensive manual for district registrars was prepared and issued, adding an additional element of quality control to the vital statistics system.

Other steps taken around the same time to secure a higher level of registration also bore fruit. Permission was obtained from the Postmaster General for displaying in the 840 post offices throughout the province a poster promoting birth registration. This measure yielded results that far exceeded expectations. Commencing in 1933, school teachers were charged with submitting annual lists of children entering school for the first time. These lists were checked against the central birth indexes and unregistered births were followed up. The lists provided, incidentally, an estimate of the under-registration that existed approximately six years earlier and also a measure of the progress being made in overcoming that problem. For example, the returns for the school year 1933–34 revealed that fully 16 percent of new enrollees born in the province had escaped birth registration. The lists for 1936–37 revealed 8.9 percent unregistered, while those for 1944–45 indicated only a 5.2 percent shortfall. The problem of non-registration was further reduced sharply in 1946 with the inauguration of the federal family allowance program, which mandated birth registration as *prima facie* evidence of eligibility.

FEDERAL GOVERNMENT INVOLVEMENT

Although it had been established, after some initial uncertainty, that under the *British North America Act* the registration of births, deaths, and marriages was a provincial responsibility, the vital statistics of most provinces remained rudimentary for several decades. The federal government was acutely aware of the lack of adequate vital statistics data on a national level and made several attempts to alleviate the situation. Between 1882 and 1893, it sought to obtain mortuary statistics through a subsidy arrangement with cities of over 25,000 population and subsequently tried to collect mortality data through the censuses of 1901 and 1911. These measures did not prove to be satisfactory.

In 1918, with the passage of the federal *Statistics Act* (3) and the creation of the Dominion Bureau of Statistics, the federal government made renewed efforts to provide for comprehensive, Canada-wide vital statistics. Dominion-provincial conferences on vital statistics were convened in

June and December of 1918, resulting in collaborative agreements with the provinces that enabled the federal government to become an active participant in the vital statistics field. Under these agreements, the provinces undertook to base their vital statistics legislation on a model *Vital Statistics Act*, which had been ratified at the 1918 conferences, to adopt birth, marriage, and death registration forms as also approved at the conferences, and routinely to provide transcripts of all registrations to the Dominion Bureau of Statistics. The federal government in turn agreed to furnish each province, without cost, with all the vital statistics registration forms it might need to compile and supply its detailed vital statistics tabulations and to prepare and distribute free to all physicians a "Physician's Pocket Reference to the International List of Causes of Death."

ADVENT OF CANADA-WIDE VITAL STATISTICS

The collaborative agreements arrived at in 1918 were implemented in all provinces except Quebec on 1 January 1921, and in Quebec on 1 January 1926, and brought about an immediate upgrading of vital statistics in Canada. For most practical purposes, the year 1921 marks the beginning of comprehensive, reasonably reliable Canadian vital statistics, comparable across the entire country. The Dominion Bureau of Statistics, in addition to producing the uniform tabulations for provincial use, began publishing a comprehensive annual report containing both national and provincial data. Thus, for the first time, detailed comparable vital statistics became available for all of Canada, notwithstanding the lack of adequate statistical resources in certain provinces.

PREPARATION OF BRITISH COLUMBIA VITAL STATISTICS AFTER 1921

British Columbia, which had been expanding its published vital statistics even prior to 1921, chose not to abandon its incipient statistical activities by relying solely on the availability of federally prepared data. The Division of Vital Statistics, or Vital Statistics Branch as it was then termed, continued to prepare its own statistics on a preliminary basis but withheld publication of its annual vital statistics report until the agreed upon "official" tabulations provided by the Dominion Bureau of Statistics had been received and incorporated into it. As time went on, the Division supplemented the standard tables provided by Ottawa with locally prepared time series, summary data, additional classifications of special interest, and narrative comments. It is significant that, by thus maintaining its independent statistical capability, the Division was ultimately in a position to embark on the many major statistical undertakings in the health field described below.

INFLUENCE OF FAMILY ALLOWANCES PROGRAM

The collaborative arrangements with the Dominion Bureau of Statistics, implemented in 1921, proved to be mutually advantageous and continued in effect for the next twenty-five years. However, developments in the social and political fields spurred by World War II were to bring about change. A number of sweeping social measures, foremost of which was a program of universal family allowances, came under active consideration at the federal level. Technical planning discussions quickly focused on the important role vital statistics registrations might play in the administrative control of any such schemes, provided that certain standardizations in registration practice and record identification could be achieved. These considerations led to the convening of dominion-provincial conferences on vital statistics in 1943 and 1944, from which emerged new formal agreements respecting the processing of Canadian vital statistics.

NEW FEDERAL-PROVINCIAL AGREEMENTS

Changes agreed upon at the 1944 conference included the adoption of a single, ten-digit numbering system applicable to all registrations filed anywhere in Canada, the use of microfilm for the prompt transmission of registration copies to Ottawa, and the preparation by the Dominion Bureau of Statistics of uniform registration indexes for each province. The indexes were to be the property of the province concerned but accessible to the federal government for verification of program eligibility only. This reliance on birth registration as the preferred means of establishing eligibility for family allowances had a salutary effect on the completeness of birth registration, virtually ensuring the accuracy of this important baseline component of Canadian health statistics.

VITAL STATISTICS COUNCIL FOR CANADA

The new agreements also established a formal body, the Vital Statistics Council for Canada, to promote close liaison between the provincial and federal governments in matters relating to vital statistics. The council was to be composed of the provincial Directors of Vital Statistics, or Registrars-General as they were titled in some provinces, the Dominion Statistician, and the chiefs of the Vital Statistics and Census Branches of the Dominion Bureau of Statistics. It was required to meet at least once a year "for the purpose of discussing and advising on problems arising out of the administration of the Vital Records system and related statistics." The council has functioned most effectively ever since its inception in 1946, and, while its decisions are advisory only insofar as each participating government is concerned, its impact on the improvement of Canadian vital statistics has been great. It has provided a forum for the exploration of problems arising in the administration of vital statistics legislation, for the examination of registration policies and procedures, and for the development of improved standards of registration practice and statistical presentation. It has also provided the mechanism for determining Canadian responses to vital statistics issues at the international level, including morbidity and mortality classifications and standardized definitions of vital statistics events, such as births, stillbirths, neonatal deaths, and perinatal deaths.

EXPANSION OF STATISTICAL ACTIVITIES

By the middle of the present century, the British Columbia vital statistics registration system had essentially matured, providing a secure foundation for the statistical data derived therefrom. Many refinements and operating efficiencies continued to be made over the succeeding years and, while these tended to improve further the quality of the statistical output, they did not significantly alter the basic data collection mechanisms and hence are not discussed here. On the other hand, the statistical and research activities of the division underwent a rapid and exciting growth, commencing soon after the end of World War II. The remainder of this chapter is devoted to a brief account of those developments.

GROWTH OF THE DIVISION'S STATISTICAL ROLE

There was always, of course, a statistical component to the division's work, even in the earliest years, when only rudimentary classifications of the data were required. The statistical responsibility gradually grew with the increasing demand from the health field for vital statistics data until, in the decade prior to 1921, a significant amount of statistical information was being produced. The statistical role assumed further importance upon the implementation of the historic federal-provincial collaborative agreements respecting vital statistics in 1921 and continued to increase over the next two decades.

INTRODUCTION OF MECHANICAL DATA PROCESSING

The statistical activities of the division might well have remained limited to the preparation and analysis of conventional vital statistics data, as had been the case in many other jurisdictions in North America, had it not been for the exceptional drive and enterprise of Mr. J. T. Marshall, who had been appointed Inspector of Vital Statistics in 1929. The innovative measures he promoted over the new few years set the stage for the eventual expansion of the division's small statistical unit into a full biostatistical section, providing service to the entire public health organization and to certain other health agencies as well. Marshall was quick to foresee the advantages of applying to vital statistics work the relatively new mechanical means of processing data using Hollerith punch cards, and began promoting that objective as early as 1932. Approval to proceed with mechanical data processing was obtained in 1934, and the first manual punch card equipment was installed in February 1935.

The division's mechanical tabulation unit was the first such installation in the provincial government and aroused great interest. The increased efficiency and flexibility it offered soon prompted other departments to request assistance with their data requirements. By the end of 1936, the division was carrying out major assignments for the Departments of Labour, Mines, Public Works, Attorney General and Provincial Secretary, and for the Health Insurance Commission and the provincial police.

In 1938, a central Bureau of Economics and Statistics was set up in the Department of Trade and Industry, relieving the Division of Vital Statistics of its undertakings for the other departments. Initially, there was concern that the division would have to relinquish all its statistical processing activities to the new bureau, but that move was successfully opposed by the Board of Health on the grounds that medical records and medical statistics are of a very specialized nature, requiring the direct supervision of the health administration.

STATISTICAL WORKSHOP FOR PUBLIC HEALTH

During the mid-1930s, the Division of Vital Statistics was increasingly called upon to provide statistical service outside its own immediate sphere, and the concept took root that it should become the statistical workshop for the entire Health Branch. It is not clear when or by whom the idea was first proposed, although precedent existed in certain health jurisdictions in the United States. The division's early success with mechanical data processing undoubtedly contributed to this concept being adopted as Health Branch policy. The annual report of Vital Statistics for 1936 referred to the division as "rendering service to the other Divisions, not only with the preparation of their statistics, but also as a clearing house for all the record systems and forms." An order-in-council (4) dated 12 September 1938, which dealt with the distribution of responsibilities between the division and the new Bureau of Economics and Statistics, specified, among other things, that the Vital Statistics Branch be authorized to supervise the medical records, and shall be responsible, inter alia,

(a) for the collection, collation and correlation of material, information and data from medical records (record system) within the Provincial Board of Health in consultation with the Directors of the Divisions of the Board of Health.

The mandate for the division to be the "statistical workshop" for the public health service was thus made clear and official.

GROWTH OF THE "WORKSHOP"

The first major assignment undertaken by the division in its broader "workshop" role was to develop a system for mechanically processing the extensive inpatient and outpatient records of the Division of Tuberculosis Control and routinely to prepare all the statistical material required by that division. The new system was brought into operation in 1936. In the following year, the division similarly adapted the records of the Division of Venereal Disease Control to mechanical processing. In 1938, a Statistical Services Section, later to be known as the Research Section, was set up within the Division of Vital Statistics, headed by a professional statistician.

POST-WAR EXPANSION OF RESEARCH SERVICES

World War II placed heavy demands on the registration and certification services of the division, bringing about a hiatus in the development of its biostatistical capabilities. However, immediately upon the end of the war, priority was again given to the research arm. The division's mechanical tabulation equipment was updated and the staff of the research section increased. In 1948, with financial assistance from the newly announced federal health grants, a program of postgraduate training in biostatistics for the research officers was commenced. In 1949, a suboffice of the research section was established in Vancouver to provide liaison with and service to those divisions of the Health Branch located in that city.

RELEASE OF VITAL STATISTICS DATA

Notwithstanding its greatly augmented service to other sections of the Health Branch, the division's core statistical responsibility continued to be the preparation and analysis of conventional vital statistics. Demand for such data grew rapidly with expanding health and social programs and the accelerated research in those fields. Many requests came from research workers and students in academic institutions in Canada and the

United States. It was the division's policy to try to satisfy all such requests, even those requiring special machine tabulations. The division also gave high priority to ensuring that the province's vital statistics were made readily accessible and presented in a form that would encourage and facilitate reference to them. To that end, it published extensive detail in its annual reports, including municipal and regional distributions and mortality statistics classified according to the Detailed List of the International Statistical Classification of Causes of Death. It also published a special reports series covering a wide range of vital and health statistics, not otherwise available in printed form. For circulation within the Health Branch only, it issued weekly or biweekly a one-page bulletin containing an item of statistical information designed to draw attention to the availability of such data or to precipitate further enquiry.

SERVICE TO OTHER DIVISIONS

Within a relatively few short years after the mid-century, the Division of Vital Statistics was providing service to virtually all divisions and units of the Health Branch. As well as the large scale statistical programs for the divisions of Tuberculosis Control and Venereal Disease Control, the division was carrying out extensive ongoing assignments for the Divisions of Public Health Nursing, Public Health Inspection, Epidemiology, Dental Health Services, and Speech and Hearing. It was also participating in numerous ad hoc projects for these and other units of the Health Branch. In addition, it was operating the Notifiable Disease Reporting System, the Rheumatic Fever Registry, and the Cancer Notification Registry. Throughout 1950 and 1951, it administered the British Columbia component of the Canada Sickness Survey, which relied on public health nurses as enumerators. The "statistical workshop" concept envisaged in the early 1930s had indeed become a reality.

HEALTH SURVEILLANCE REGISTRY

In 1952, the division launched what was destined to be one of its most extensive and productive undertakings, the Crippled Children's Registry, the forerunner of the present Health Surveillance Registry. An account of this registry and of the circumstances leading to its establishment form the next chapter of this book.

SERVICE TO OTHER HEALTH AGENCIES

As the activities of the division's research section became more widely known, it began receiving requests from health organizations outside the department for consultative advice, for assistance in establishing or reorganizing statistical systems, and for routine data processing service. While the division did not have the resources to accede to all calls for help, it attempted to be as accommodating as possible, realizing that its experience in the health statistics field was unique in the province at that time. It therefore accepted a number of major ongoing assignments where the need was urgent and the anticipated benefits judged to be substantial. Most notable of these undertakings were the development and operation of mechanized statistical systems for the medical treatment and follow-up records of the British Columbia Cancer Institute, the Cytology Laboratory, the provincial Mental Health Service, and the G. F. Strong Rehabilitation Centre, and the medical claims records of the British Columbia Government Employees' Medical Service.

CO-OPERATION WITH THE FACULTY OF MEDICINE, UNIVERSITY OF BRITISH COLUMBIA

The establishment of the Faculty of Medicine at the University of British Columbia in 1950 had a significant impact on the Division of Vital Statistics. Requests for vital statistics and demographic data made by both students and staff very quickly brought virtually all departments of the faculty into contact with the division. Frequently these requests necessitated special tabulations or research in the original registrations on file. The interchange that developed through these requests led to a considerable number of scientific papers and articles being co-authored by members of the faculty and of the division. A particularly close liaison developed between the division's Health Surveillance Registry and the Departments of Paediatrics and Medical Genetics, with members from these departments serving for many years as consultants to the registry. Over the years, the division became a significant data source for the Faculty of Medicine, while the faculty, in turn, constituted a valuable technical advisory resource for the division.

CHILD-ORIENTED STATISTICS

Most of the statistical programs referred to in the foregoing account, while encompassing children, covered the entire age spectrum. However, the division also engaged in a number of other projects targeted exclusively toward children or having child health as a major concern. These are outlined below.

Infant Mortality Statistics

Infant mortality was one of the first special concerns addressed by the research section in the immediate post-war years. At that time, most infant mortality statistics were derived solely from the limited information on death registrations and hence were inadequate for identifying underlying factors that may have contributed to death. Information such as parental age and occupation, birth order, legitimacy status, hospitalization, and place of birth were not available from death registrations but did appear on birth registrations. To exploit these additional items, in 1946, the division began manually matching all infant death registrations with their corresponding birth registrations and subjecting the combined information to statistical analysis.

Statistics derived from the two-way matching project provided information on certain aspects of infant mortality not previously measured for this province. These augmented local data were made available to medical personnel who had previously expressed an interest in infant mortality. They stimulated renewed discussion of the infant mortality problem and focused attention on the relatively high infant mortality rate still prevailing in British Columbia (37.7 per 1,000 live births in 1946). They also provoked many questions that could not be answered with data derived only from birth and death registrations, and by that very limitation helped pave the way for the introduction in 1952 of a radically new physician's notice of birth.

Statistics from Physician's Notice of Live Birth or Stillbirth

Submission of a "physician's notice of birth" had been mandatory in this province since 1913, but the notice contained no medical information whatsoever, since its sole purpose was to provide a check for unregistered births. In 1931, a single medical item was added, namely, "Were drops used to prevent blindness and if so, what?" Around the year 1950, several needs converged to make the division seriously consider adding additional items of a medical nature to the physician's notice. In the first place, increased emphasis on infant care programs and on the reduction of infant mortality had underscored the need for more statistical information that could be gleaned from birth and death registrations. The medical circumstances surrounding birth also needed to be known. A second consideration was that preliminary data from the Survey of Crippling Diseases of Children (discussed in the next chapter) were pointing up the need for early identification of infants born with congenital anomalies or birth injuries. Finally, the public health field staff required a mechanism by which they could be promptly informed of every birth in order that they might initiate their postnatal programs. A committee, which included representatives from paediatrics, obstetrics, anaesthesiology, general practice, public health, and the Division of Vital Statistics, was therefore established to determine what information was most urgently needed and might reasonably be obtained through an expanded physician's notice.

As a result of the committee's work, a new "Physician's Notice of a Live Birth or Stillbirth" was introduced on 1 February 1951. With minor modifications, it has remained in use to the present day. In addition to the usual identifying items, the form elicited information on birthweight, gestation period, maturity status, need for measures to promote respiration, number of pregnancies, number of live births, Rh factor, operative procedures, birth injuries, congenital anomalies, and complications of pregnancy or delivery. The form was printed in duplicate in order that the copy could be sent to the appropriate public health unit immediately upon receipt by the district registrar.

Since its introduction in 1951, the new physician's notice has yielded a wealth of statistics on newborns, which have been widely used. Some of these data were published in the Special Reports Series of the Division of Vital Statistics (5). The revised notice has also fulfilled its other objectives of providing current birth information to public health units and prompt notification to the Health Surveillance Registry of infants having congenital anomalies or other handicapping conditions.

With the advent of the new physician's notice, the infant mortality study based on the matching of birth and death registrations was immediately expanded into a three-way linkage project by incorporating information from this new source. The scope and utility of the resultant statistics was thus greatly increased, enabling perinatal mortality to be studied in much greater depth. Certain of these data were also published in the division's Special Reports Series (6), while considerably more have been made available to researchers in response to specific requests.

Obstetrical Discharge Study

In 1956, the division agreed to collaborate with the Departments of Obstetrics and Public Health of the Faculty of Medicine of the University of British Columbia in an ongoing study of all obstetrical discharges in the Vancouver General Hospital. The statistics from the physician's notice of birth had played an important role in kindling this project by pointing up problem areas in maternal and infant care and in obstetrical practice for which more detailed statistical information was required. The stated aims of the project were two-fold: first, to provide data for research and study by the Faculty of Medicine, and second, to provide educational material for the teaching of medical students.

An "Obstetrical Discharge Summary," containing pertinent information respecting both the mother and the infant, and including details of pregnancy, labour, and delivery, was developed as a supplementary hospital medical record. The Division of Vital Statistics carried out the editing, processing, and statistical analysis of this record. It also published selected data from the study in its Special Reports Series (7).

The Vancouver General Hospital participated in the study from 1956 to 1981, Grace Hospital from 1959 to 1977, St. Paul's Hospital from 1961 to 1977, and St. Vincent's Hospital from 1961 to 1966. The project was terminated when its initial purposes had largely been served and when improvements in hospital record systems made it redundant.

Dental Health of Children Surveys

In 1957, the Division of Preventive Dentistry initiated an ambitious project to assess the dental health status of school children, using a sampling technique originated at the University of Toronto. The Division of Vital Statistics assisted in developing a methodology suitable for application in this province and in devising a sampling plan. The division also undertook to process the examination returns and to carry out the statistical analyses. This ongoing project has been highly successful and has yielded information not only on the current dental health status of children at various ages, but also on changes in dental health status over time (8). Data of this type are available elsewhere in Canada.

Congenital Anomaly Surveillance

The much publicized "thalidomide episode" of 1962 dramatically focused attention on the problem of congenital anomalies and precipitated a clamour for statistical information on the occurrence of these conditions. Fortunately the division had certain data available from the physician's notice of a live birth or stillbirth and from its Registry for Handicapped Children. However, these were minimal counts only, since not all anomalies are detected at birth and not all are severe enough to fall within the registry's definition of a handicapping condition. The need for a reporting mechanism that would provide early detection of any abnormal incidence of congenital anomalies, both major and minor, became apparent.

The federal government moved quickly to determine what could be done to provide the necessary early warning system by establishing the Expert Committee on the Occurrence of Congenital Anomalies, on which the division was asked to serve. From the early meetings of the committee it was clear that a considerable amount of ground work was required in most provinces, before a national monitoring system could be implemented. It was also evident that, to achieve reasonably complete reporting, it would be necessary to meld information from a number of different sources.

In British Columbia, because of the data systems it already had in place, the Division of Vital Statistics was in a position to move more rapidly and hence took immediate steps to set up its own monitoring system for this province. Using the mechanisms and techniques of the

Registry for Handicapped Children, it established a subregistry of congenital anomalies, incorporating information from the registry, the physician's notice of birth and registrations of births, stillbirths, and deaths. In addition, the British Columbia Hospital Insurance Service agreed to report all hospital discharges for which any congenital anomaly had been recorded.

By utilizing the existing registry organization, which was well experienced in dealing with multiple sources of registration, non-duplicated counts of congenital anomalies occurring in British Columbia were obtained routinely. The Department of Medical Genetics of the University of British Columbia Faculty of Medicine, through its consultant to the registry, monitored the incoming anomaly reports and provided technical advice. Any apparent aberrations in the normal incidence patterns were investigated by obtaining epidemiological information respecting the suspicious occurrences through the local health unit directors. In 1966, the federal government inaugurated a national Congenital Anomaly Surveillance System. The division co-operated fully in this system by supplying the input data from British Columbia and acting as the focal point for any follow-up enquiries. However, the division's own system, which later became known as the Birth Defects Monitor, was continued as the first line of surveillance for this province.

SUMMARY AND CONCLUSION

The brief outline of British Columbia's civil registration system included in the foregoing account does not purport to cover all important events in the history of the Division of Vital Statistics. Rather, it directs attention to factors underlying the vital statistics data base and to developments affecting the quality of the resultant vital statistics. It also reflects the gradual accommodation of the civil registration system to the needs of the medical field.

The review of the division's biostatistical activities portrays an unusually wide and varied range of services. It reveals that, as well as fulfilling its statutory obligation to collect and publish vital statistics, the division functioned as a valuable resource and service centre for demographic and health statistics, accessible to health administrators, students, research workers, and the medical community alike. This was at a time when no other such facility was available within the province to meet the needs of rapidly expanding health programs and emerging health research projects.

In terms of resources, the division's research section was only modestly equipped and staffed, but it enjoyed the great advantage of being self-contained, having its own mechanical tabulation equipment, clerical staff, medical coding staff, and professional staff with biostatistical training. It thus had the capability not only to design new statistical projects but also to implement them and carry them through to the final production and analysis of data. This total control over all stages of the statistical operation enabled the division to be flexible and to undertake, at minimal additional cost, such major new commitments as the Health Surveillance Registry, the Obstetrical Discharge Study, the Dental Health of Children Surveys, and the Birth Defects Monitor, as well as numerous smaller ad hoc statistical projects, studies, and special assignments.

Perhaps the greatest single factor contributing to the division's success in the biostatistical area was the inspiration and sense of purpose given to it by Dr. G. F. Amyot, who had been appointed Provincial Health Officer in 1940, and who served as the province's first Deputy Minister of Health from 1946 to his retirement in 1961. Dr. Amyot was acutely aware of the serious limitations the virtual absence of morbidity statistics and program evaluation statistics imposed on the planning and administration of health programs. He held an almost passionate conviction that the key to the efficient provision of health services lay in comprehensive statistical information flowing from a strong biostatistical unit. Likewise, he was convinced that in British Columbia the biostatistical unit belonged in the Division of Vital Statistics in the Department of Health. So strongly did Dr. Amyot hold to this view that on one

Dr. G. F. Amyot

occasion, when, in spite of his vehement protests, the government appeared determined to proceed with a plan to relocate the Division of Vital Statistics in another department, he offered his resignation. The plan was abandoned.

In line with the great importance he attached to statistics, Dr. Amyot gave the division strong support, involving it to the fullest possible extent in departmental matters and expediting the postgraduate biostatistical training of its professional staff. At the same time, he impatiently called for results, never hesitating to rail against what he considered to be inadequate or "useless" statistics. His unceasing demands for morbidity statistics and for a broader range of health statistics, invariably accompanied by a dissertation on the benefits that would accrue therefrom, encouraged the division to attempt many of its ambitious and innovative undertakings.

The division also profited from the salutary working environment which existed within the public health service, due in no small measure to Dr. Amyot's inspired leadership. The professional staff of the department was highly motivated, and a remarkable team spirit prevailed. New programs were being developed in response to rapidly expanding vistas in public health, while established programs were constantly being improved, reassessed, and refined. Opportunities for statistical consultation and involvement abounded. These factors had a profound effect, widening the division's horizons and stimulating it to exploit its full research potential.

As a result of administrative reorganizations within the Ministry of Health in the 1980s, and the centralization of data processing, which began in the mid-1970s, the division has lost much of its statistical self-sufficiency. While the net effect of these changes cannot yet be appraised, it is clear that the advantages to be gained through computer technology alone are enormous and offer exciting prospects for further advances in vital and health statistics.

The reorganization of the Department of Health in 1975 divided services into Medical and Hospital Programs and Community Health Programs (Public Health and Mental Health) under a single Deputy Minister of Health. The Division of Vital Statistics remained within Public Health and then moved to Management Operations (formed in 1981) in 1989. The format and content of the annual report was changed in the 1980s, and the 1981–82 and 1985–86 reports were combined into single volumes. Furthermore, the annual report of the Health Surveillance Registry, which had been produced since its origin in 1952 to 1981 inclusive, was replaced by a one-page summary of activities in the annual report of the Division of Vital Statistics.

In 1988, the latter introduced a new format with improved illustrations, though again the activities of the Health Surveillance Registry were described briefly on one page.

During this period, there was a breakdown in communication between the Division of Vital Statistics and the paediatric community. In the 1950s and 1960s, neonatal mortality was a major interest of the division. This concern was not sustained during the 1970s, when perinatal medicine became a specialized field, as evidenced by the absence of birthweight specific morbidity and mortality rates during these early years of the specialty. These data would be invaluable to provide trend patterns before and after the introduction of the regional neonatal care program.

The previous interest in providing regional population-based data concerning chronic disabilities diminished. The epidemiological activity did not extend to chronic disability and health care issues. The lack of health statistics for community-based programs is reflected in a lack of evaluation data for these programs (Chapter 21).

The close collaboration between the Division of Vital Statistics and the Health Surveillance Registry, the medical profession, and the Department of Paediatrics at the University of British Columbia diminished in the 1970s and 1980s, probably in association with the retirement or promotion of several of the key actors on both sides. Dr. Amyot's obsession for data was not shared by his successors. As a result, the potential value of both vital and health statistical data was unused, particularly in the recently developing perinatal field and in related prevalence data of chronic disabilities. As noted in the next chapter, there is reason to believe that the Health Surveillance Registry will be reactivated and its role in policy and planning in child health restored.

REFERENCES

1. *An Act Respecting the Registration of Births, Deaths and Marriages in British Columbia*, S.B.C. 1872, c. 26.
2. MARSHAL, J. T. *Vital Statistics in British Columbia*. Provincial Board of Health, British Columbia, 1932.
3. *Statistics Act*, S.C. 1918, c. 43.
4. British Columbia Order-in-Council 1213, 1938.
5. Division of Vital Statistics, *Special Reports* Nos. 7, 8, 9, 11, 89, 126.
6. Division of Vital Statistics, *Special Reports* Nos. 110, 113, 124.
7. Division of Vital Statistics, *Special Reports* No. 110.
8. Division of Vital Statistics, *Special Reports* Nos. 52, 100, 145; Ministry of Health, *British Columbia Children's Dental Health Survey*.

The British Columbia
Health Surveillance Registry

by James. R. Miller

HISTORICAL CONSIDERATIONS

Donald Hugh Paterson[1] probably never received formal training in statistics or epidemiology, but one of the outstanding traits characterizing that singular man was an ability to assess, often after little exposure, the contribution some hitherto unknown discipline could make to paediatrics, the passion of his professional life. Consequently, it is not surprising that, when he arrived in Vancouver in 1947, he recognized that establishing adequate province-wide paediatric services required detailed statistics on handicapped children: numbers, distribution, extent of disability, and needs. Such statistics are the key elements in any descriptive epidemiologic study, and he realized that their acquisition was essential if appropriate services were to be organized for the children of British Columbia.

Paterson's task was made easier than it might have been had he attempted it elsewhere or at a different time by the existence within the provincial Division of Vital Statistics of a superb research section, and by

---

1 Donald Paterson was born in Portage La Prairie in May 1890. After graduating from Manitoba College with Honours in 1912, he attended the University of Edinburgh, where he obtained the M.B. and Ch.B. degrees in 1916. He served in France as a medical officer between 1916 and 1918. During the period 1919–23, he trained in paediatrics at the Hospital for Sick Children in Great Ormond Street, London. Then, for twenty-four years (1923–47), he had a distinguished career in British paediatrics as a private consultant, as paediatrician to Westminster Hospital, and as a senior physician at Great Ormond Street. He played a key role in the founding of the British Paediatric Association in 1928 and served for seven years as its first secretary and subsequently as its president. He moved to Vancouver in 1947 and became active in establishing a paediatric unit at Vancouver General Hospital. In later years, he was a respected elder statesman in the medical community of the city and province. He died in December 1968.

the establishment of the federal health grants (1) in May 1948, when the federal government announced that it would provide each province with grants to assist in promoting public health services. Among ten separate grants was a recurring one for "crippled children" whose purpose was:

> to assist the Provinces in the establishment of a program for the prevention, control and treatment of crippling conditions in children. To assist the Province [sic] in the development of a rehabilitation and training program for crippled children.

British Columbia's annual share of this grant was $42,574. The responsibility for supervising each grant was assigned to a subcommittee that reported to a director of health studies and a health survey committee, both of which reported in turn to the Minister and Deputy Minister of Health. Donald Paterson, who was physician-in-charge of the Health Centre for Children, the children's outpatient service at the Vancouver General Hospital, was appointed chairman of the crippled children's grant subcommittee.

Through Paterson's initiative, part of the crippled children's grant was used to conduct a survey of handicapped children in the province. Extensive statistical surveys of this type were not common forty-five years ago, because collecting, recording, and extracting data were cumbersome and expensive. However, the research section of the Division of Vital Statistics was experienced in demographic studies and had its own IBM machines to process records and compile statistics. Thus, the equipment and expertise for conducting the survey were available. The survey was approved by the executive of the British Columbia Medical Association (BCMA), and all physicians in the province were requested "to cooperate to the fullest extent to ensure a complete and accurate picture being obtained." However, a small pilot survey indicated that the response from private physicians would not be great, and it was realized that if the survey were to be successful, it would have to be conducted by public health nurses and doctors through schools and well baby clinics, and would have to involve a large scale examination of hospital records, preferably by a nurse who would report directly to Paterson's subcommittee. The questionnaire used was drawn up by a group of paediatricians, surgeons, and disease specialists, with the advice of the provincial Division of Vital Statistics. The survey was conducted from late 1949 to late 1950.

In May 1950, a preliminary analysis was made of 7,000 cards and, although no definite conclusions could be made, certain points were quite clear. For example, it appeared that children were not being treated early enough to achieve the most satisfactory repair of their malformations. Diseases and deformities present at birth were not reported or treated until much later. This preliminary information indicated that the optimum time to report congenital disorders was at birth and, before the survey was even completed, the Division of Vital Statistics began working with the sub-committee to review the provincial physician's notice of birth form to determine whether information relevant to congenital disabilities could be placed on it.

In the summer of 1950, as data accumulated, the subcommittee began to consider the question of establishing a voluntary provincial Register of Crippling Diseases of Children. The survey, which included over 19,000 children, was completed in October, and the subcommittee formally recommended to the Deputy Minister of Health that such a Register be set up. At about the same time, the ad hoc committee working on the revised physician's notice of birth recommended changes to permit recording on the form morbidity of pregnancy, operative procedures at birth, birth injuries, and congenital malformations. The new physician's notice of birth was put into use in

Dr. Donald Paterson

February 1951 and, when the Crippled Children's Registry began operating in January 1952, the new forms provided the first sources of registration.

Early Years

The Deputy Minister of Health established the registry under the supervision of the medical statistics section of the Division of Vital Statistics. A. E. (Nancy) Scott, a research assistant from the Vancouver office of the division, who had been the liaison to the survey, was seconded to the registry for this purpose. Donald Paterson served as medical advisor and chaired the Medical Advisory Board, consisting of sixteen representatives of the BCMA from the sections of otolaryngology, ophthalmology, obstetrics, neurology, paediatrics, surgery, and psychiatry, and a representative of the provincial Department of Health. In addition to providing individual consultation about special problem cases, these representatives met together several times a year to review the work of the registry. A small policy committee, comprising Paterson, Scott, the Assistant Provincial Health Officer of the Department of Health (G.R.F. Elliot) and the Professor of Paediatrics (John F. McCreary) in the newly established Faculty of

Medicine of the University of British Columbia, met frequently in the formative stages.

The efforts of George Elliot must be singled out for comment. Throughout his career in the health service, he made enormous and largely unrecognized contributions to improving the public health of the province. Among these was his steadfast support of the registry throughout its existence. As Director of Health Studies, he was directly responsible in a way that no one else was for determining that the federal health grants were used most effectively. In particular, he advocated the initial survey of handicapped children and the subsequent establishment and operation of the registry at the top levels of the Department of Health and Welfare in Victoria. He also spent a great deal of time selling the concept of the registry to other government departments, the health unit directors, the BCMA, and private physicians. It is not an exaggeration to state that without his strong backing and understanding, the registry would not have been established nor would it have thrived.

The coding and statistical aspects of the registry operations were handled by Nancy Scott, who was ideal for the task. She had joined the civil service in 1936 in a temporary position as research assistant to G. F. Amyot, who had been appointed special assistant to the Provincial Health Officer to carry out a survey of British Columbian hospitals with particular reference to records and length of stay. This survey resulted in the establishment of the Division of Hospital Services, to which Miss Scott was appointed in 1938. Her task was to improve hospital records and to develop hospital statistics. In 1950, she transferred to the Division of Vital Statistics. In addition to her considerable knowledge of health statistics, she had a strong personality—a definite asset when working with Donald Paterson. Together they made a forceful team that established the registry on a firm footing and nursed it through the early years. Both maintained their ties with the registry for many years, he until his death in December 1968, and she until her retirement in 1974. Although the registry evolved over the years in response to new challenges, its essential philosophy and operating methods remained as they were established by this remarkable pair.

The registry always managed to operate with a small, efficient, and often heavily overworked staff. In the early years, Donald Paterson personally reviewed all new registrations, especially those based on the physician's notice of birth; he would then suggest a program for each child. He recommended that infants born with clubfoot, pyloric stenosis, cleft lip and palate, heart defects, etc., should be referred to specialists in Vancouver or Victoria as quickly as possible. He advised that certain other children be referred for more accurate diagnosis and treatment. A clerical staff of two, paid from a federal health grant, did the office work, supervised by Nancy Scott. At first, the registry was located in a rented house but soon moved to the Provincial Health Building at 828 West 10th Avenue, where it remained for twenty-five years.

The survey had indicated that there were many handicapped children with unmet needs; hence, the first criterion for registration was "any child under 21 years of age who has a disability severe enough to interfere with normal living, obtaining an education, and later earning a livelihood."

The second annual report (1953) listed the goals of the registry as:

1. to obtain accurate knowledge of the magnitude of the problem of crippling diseases of children in British Columbia;
2. with this knowledge, to aid in developing facilities and organizations that will assist in the rehabilitation of these children; and
3. to develop the Registry as an organization that will assist the physicians of the province in disposing of their cases of crippling diseases of childhood.

It was also mentioned that the registry provided liaison with the various institutions for child care throughout the province and disseminated information about facilities for the care of handicapped children.

In the early years, most registrations came from the provincial and metropolitan health nursing staffs, with the approval of the family physician in each instance. These registrations quickly confirmed the unmet needs that had emerged from the survey. Outside Vancouver and Victoria, there were few specialists in paediatrics or any of its subspecialties. A travelling clinic from Children's Hospital in Vancouver visited certain areas of the province at least once a year. The staff of these clinics followed up patients discharged from Children's Hospital and saw new patients referred by local private physicians. The service provided by the registry augmented that given by these clinics and brought many other children to various clinics in Vancouver.

Paediatric services in Vancouver and Victoria were not used by families living in regions remote from these cities, because physicians in more distant parts of the province were unaware of what was available, transportation was difficult and expensive, and living costs in the cities were too high for many families. The registry worked with hospitals, service clubs, and private agencies to overcome these problems.

The registry, through the statistics it compiled and disseminated, was instrumental in establishing special provincial services (e.g., audiology and speech therapy) and even large associations such as the Association of Retarded Children of British Columbia. By the mid-1950s, the registry regularly provided statistics to this and other voluntary organizations for use in planning, providing services, appealing for funds, etc. In a report given to the Public Health Workers of British Columbia in April 1957, Donald Paterson listed a formidable array of organizations with which "a representative of the Registry" (probably Donald Paterson himself) had at least monthly contact, and others with which meetings were held "often."

From the outset, the registry published an annual report that was full of detailed information on the caseload, analyzed from different points of view. For seventeen years, beginning with the 1958 report, it contained a section (IV) devoted to special topics. Usually these related to new developments or to research underway, but the 1961 report contained the most detailed overview available of the first decade of the registry and the names of members of its advisory committees (2). The annual reports were used extensively by health units throughout the province and were often quoted by individuals planning resources for handicapped children throughout North America and elsewhere; each year about 400 reports were sent outside Canada. Unfortunately, the annual report was discontinued in the early 1980s, and now the only published annual data on the registry appear as a few tables reporting birth incidence rates of selected congenital anomalies and the frequency by age groups of selected disabilities at the end of the annual report of the Division of Vital Statistics.

Middle Years

By the late 1950s, conditions had changed. As special services developed throughout the province, and as better roads enabled patients and their families to travel to Vancouver to attend special clinics, the registry's service role, in the form of direct intervention, was no longer as important as it had been seven or eight years before.

The registry's historical file contains a 1958 report, produced internally, that summarized the history, organization, and achievements of the registry. The report then pointed out that, although the registry's success to date had been a consequence of its service role, a registry had other functions and "the outstanding point to be remembered is that a Registry must be kept as a useful tool or else it should be discontinued." The potential uses of the registry data listed include determining incidence and trends in incidence, determining prevalence, evaluating case findings, analyzing geographical distribution to serve as a basis for epidemiological studies, performing retrospective studies that might yield information on aetiology and subsequently lead to prevention in some instances, and developing an adult chronic disease program.

The report emphasized that, although the direct service role should be maintained where necessary, these other aspects of the registry should be developed. It made several recommendations, two of which were that more statistical staff be added to the Vancouver office and "that the age limit of 21 years be discontinued and that the registry in collaboration with the Rehabilitation Division of the Health Department develop a program for the registration and follow-up of adult chronic cases."

It is not clear to whom this report was addressed but, about that time or shortly thereafter, another research officer, Guy Renwick, was added to the Vancouver office, and Nancy Scott became administrator. In 1960, the name was changed to the Registry for Handicapped Children and Adults, and the criteria for registration were extended to include "a person who possesses a long term physical, mental and/or emotional problem which is likely to be permanently disabling, interfere with his/her education or prevent full and open employment." In 1962, these were modified to include "any person with a familial condition or congenital malformation which is not disabling." Guy Renwick, an unassuming man whose statistical standards were meticulous, did much of the routine but essential statistical analyses contained in the annual reports and undertook some splendid studies during his twenty-three years with the registry.

By the early 1970s, the registry maintained a number of sub-registers on genetic defects, congenital anomalies, disabling and handicapping conditions and specific "at risk" populations. In 1975, it became the British Columbia Health Surveillance Registry.

CASE FINDING, REGISTRATION, AND OUTPUT

To obtain as complete an ascertainment as possible, multiple sources were used from the outset (Table 2). Over the years the vast majority of registrations have come from the provincial and metropolitan health units but, as Table 2 indicates, the sources of registration were diverse, and this diversity provided the registry with a wealth of supplementary information in many cases.

In general, the number of individuals registered increased steadily, although periodic bursts in registrations occurred when a new source of registration was introduced or when an old source that was negligent for a period suddenly reawakened. Registered live cases increased in a relatively uniform linear fashion from around 1,000 in 1952 to about 64,000 in 1975; then the rate of increase changed sharply and, by the end of 1984, over 133,000 live cases were registered.

The first registration form, a sheet, was replaced after three years by a simple 8×5 inch card with space for a maximum amount of essential information, personal data to identify unambiguously the individual, physicians, treatment centres attended, medical diagnosis, and disabilities. The back of the card was blank, and those who registered were encouraged to provide additional information there, aetiological clues, special

TABLE 2. MAJOR SOURCES OF ASCERTAINMENT IN THE BRITISH COLUMBIA HEALTH SURVEILLANCE REGISTRY

From the Beginning
1. Physician's Notice of Birth—must be completed within forty-eight hours of birth; a useful source of data on major surface defects present at birth.
2. Public Health Units—generalized public health program including schools and special institutions for the handicapped.
3. Special Treatment Centres—details have changed over the years, but a steady core of paediatric outpatient and diagnostic clinics, genetic counselling units, specialty clinics for mental retardation, rehabilitation units, etc., have registered cases.
4. Voluntary Health Agencies—Canadian Arthritis and Rheumatism Society, Canadian National Institute for the Blind, Cerebral Palsy Association, Diabetes Association, Cystic Fibrosis Foundation, Multiple Sclerosis Society.

Since 1964
5. Stillbirth Registration—rapid access to valuable data for incidence rates on major congenital defects.

Since 1975
6. Specialty Clinics for Disabled Adults—stroke, spinal cord injuries, etc.

Since 1982–83
7. British Columbia's Children's Hospital (the major paediatric unit in the province)—all discharge summary sheets provide information on children and young adults up to age nineteen years.
8. Grace Hospital (the major obstetrical-gynaecological unit in the province)—provides data, when relevant, on mother or child.
9. Newborn Screening Laboratory—all cases with a positive result.

needs, relevant socioeconomic data, etc. Incoming notifications were checked against the current caseload to avoid duplication and to add information to cards already on file. Registerable disorders were coded according to the current International Classification of Diseases (ICD). Although the information on the card changed over the years, the goal of a simple record with an optimum amount of essential information was retained.

In 1983, the card was revised when the computer system of data storage and retrieval was updated. The information contained on the new version was essentially the same as that on earlier ones, but the card was enlarged to allow for the registration of up to twenty diagnostic codes and aetiologies, the date of each registration, and the date of onset or of

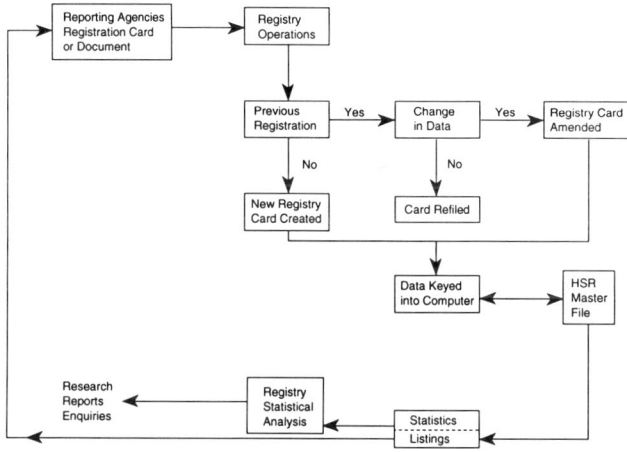

Figure 1 Flowchart showing the processing of registry data.

diagnosis for each registered disorder. In addition, the use of certain "status codes" (to record, for example, that the registered person has a prosthesis) further increased the staff's capability of responding to enquiries related to status and the planning of facilities.

For many years the data on the cards were coded and transferred to eighty-column IBM punch cards for mechanical tabulation. In the early 1970s, data storage and retrieval were transferred to a computer system; this was updated in 1982, and a new system was introduced in January 1983. The data on the cards are coded and entered directly onto tape. This taped data can be transferred to a master registry file as often as desired. The general procedures used are outlined in the flow chart presented in Figure 1.

Annually, each provincial and metropolitan health unit was provided with an alphabetical and diagnostic listing of individuals originally registered by the unit and still residing within it. The same type of listing can be provided to any registering source. The registry maintains a numeric and a statistical index of the total caseload; the latter contains the number of cases by ICD code, age group, and gender. These functions have been temporarily discontinued while the future role of the registry is under review (see Concluding Comments).

USES OF REGISTRY DATA

The data on the registry have been used in many ways, some of which have already been alluded to; a partial listing of some of the published studies based on registry data is given in the Bibliography at the end of this chapter. Here I will confine myself to five topics: a profile of a disability load in children and young adults, some incidence and prevalence data, follow-up studies, genetic studies, and record linkage.

Profile of a Disability Load

Each annual report contained a table listing the most frequent disabilities. Each year's profile was probably a reasonably accurate representation of the situation in the province at that time. The profile at the end of 1976 is presented in Table 3.

Incidence and Prevalence

Although absolute numbers are important for assessing immediate needs, incidence and prevalence rates are critical for evaluating trends and changes and for developing practical long-term planning. Over the years, the registry staff and consultants and their students published a series of reports (see Bibliography, section B) dealing with broad issues related to incidence and prevalence rates based on registry data (3, 4), or rates of specific entities such as cleft lip and palate (5, 6), Down syndrome (7, 8), mental retardation (9), and pyloric stenosis (10).

Follow-Up

The ability to follow-up cases has made the registry vital and contributed significantly to its success. Many disease registers have foundered on this issue. A register that is unable to follow up on its caseload becomes, in time, full of files on individuals whose whereabouts and current health status are unknown. For this reason, many public health administrators have shunned all types of registers as well intentioned and theoretically sound but of little practical use. The hazard of stagnation was recognized from the outset by those who administered the British Columbia registry; consequently, follow-up procedures were always actively pursued. The use of multiple sources of ascertainment without age restriction automatically assures some degree of follow-up, because information on the second and subsequent registrations of the same individual provide opportunities for assessing the original diagnosis, adding or changing diagnoses, and following the natural history of certain diseases. Registry personnel routinely followed up cases on which additional information is desired. Again, this function has been discontinued pending classification of the role of the registry. Because the registry is located within the Division of Vital Statistics, it was possible to cross-check its registrations with death registrations. The data on the death registration was entered on the registry record, which remained on file.

TABLE 3. THE TEN MOST FREQUENT DISABILITIES OF CHILDREN (UNDER TWENTY YEARS) AMONG LIVE CASES ON THE REGISTER AT YEAR END 1976*

Disability Category (in descending order) with ICD Code Number	Number of Children	Percent of Total $N = 35,717$
Strabismus (373)	5,581	15.6
Mental retardation (310–315)	3,509	9.8
Congenital cardiovascular disease (746, 747)	3,243	9.1
Clubfoot (754)	2,832	7.9
Epilepsy (345)	1,957	5.5
Cerebral paralysis (343, 344)	1,465 **	4.1
Congenital dislocation of hip (755.6)	1,720	4.8
Impaired hearing and deafness (389)	1,350	3.8
Cleft lip and/or palate (749)	1,306	3.7
Speech disturbance (781.5)	1,242	3.5

* Adapted from Table 1 (p. 16) in M. H. Colls, *The British Columbia Health Surveillance Registry: Outline of Development, Organization, and Operation.* Victoria: Province of British Columbia Ministry of Health, 1978.

** Includes 1,251 children with cerebral spastic infantile paralysis (code 343).

In 1965, to ensure a more comprehensive follow-up of all cases and to ascertain to some degree the level of residual handicap in the caseload, a systematic follow-up of all registered individuals who became seven or fourteen years of age in a given year was begun. These ages were chosen because the seven-year-olds had been in school for two years and learning disabilities would probably have become manifest, and the fourteen-year-olds were one year away from the legal school leaving age. The public health units throughout the province collected the data. Each unit was sent forms on the seven- and fourteen-year-old registry cohort known to it. The form was shocking pink to attract attention and was made brief and simple to maximize returns.

The results of the first five years of this follow-up, published in 1975 (11), revealed several striking points. First, the co-operation of the public health personnel was amazing: over 97 percent of the forms were returned. Second, over 80 percent of the forms were completed. Third, the returns gave a consistent pattern within and between the age groups: about 66 percent of cases in both had some residual handicap and, among the 14-year-olds, over 50 percent with residual handicaps were estimated to need some special job placement when they completed schooling.

The lesson seemed, and still seems, clear: the consistency from year to year and age group to age group indicates that long-term planning for the minimal needs of a cohort can be determined when that cohort is seven years old. To my knowledge, no attempt was ever made to use this information for health planning in the province, although the registry worked closely with Rehabilitation Services, beginning in the late 1950s. Unfortunately the seven- and fourteen-year survey was discontinued in the early 1980s.

GENETIC STUDIES

Potentially useful genetic data began to appear in the registry files at a very early date. The minutes of a "statistical meeting" held on 12 April 1956 contained the item "Familial Pattern," under which it was noted that "information on the incidence of congenital malformation and certain other conditions occurring in members of the same family may prove someday to be of great importance. . . . Therefore, it was agreed that this data would be kept." This was the first small beginning of genetic studies in the registry. Shortly after I joined the Faculty of Medicine in the autumn of 1958, Jack McCreary, then head of the Department of Paediatrics at the University of British Columbia, introduced me to Nancy Scott. After several years of informal association, I joined the registry in 1961 as genetic consultant, a position I held for nineteen years. I was subsequently joined by Brian Lowry, who became medical consultant in the late 1960s, and Patricia Baird, in 1976.

Through these consultancies, the three of us and our students and fellows extracted and published a wealth of genetic research data (see listings in the Bibliography, sections B and C). Now that no annual report is published, it is not easy to obtain listings of these publications, but the research based on registry data continues. Patricia Baird and her colleagues have recently published reports on hypospadias, mental retardation, pyloric stenosis, and imperforate anus.

Record Linkage

The registry also became involved in genetic studies by another route. In the mid-1950s, John Doughty, as Director of Vital Statistics, became aware of the work of Howard Newcombe, a geneticist at Atomic Energy of Canada Limited (a Crown corporation), who had developed computer techniques for linking files of marriages, births, and deaths. It says much for both men that they were compatible spirits, but Doughty deserves the accolade, for he had the foresight to recognize that Newcombe's ideas on record linkage would have profound implications for health care; he also had the mettle to venture into an agreement shunned by his counterparts in other provinces. Although Newcombe did not include registry data in his linkage studies for some time, he made use of them to publish a series of important reports in the late 1960s and throughout the 1970s (12, 13). Ben Trimble, a student of Newcombe's, joined the Department of Medical Genetics at the University of British Columbia and became record linkage consultant to the registry for a few years in the mid-1970s; he died at the tragically early age of thirty in November 1977. In 1974, Trimble and Doughty published a study based on registry data on the amount of hereditary disease in human populations. Despite serious shortcomings, which caused adverse criticism, the study represented the only major attempt to that date to obtain some measure of the load of genetic disease in a defined population, and the data were used extensively by the United Nations Scientific Committee on the Effects of Atomic Radiation and by other international agencies. The study has recently been repeated with a more refined methodology to obtain a more accurate estimate of the load of genetic disease in a population of children and young adults (see Baird et al., 1988, Bibliography, section C).

CONTROVERSIES, CRITICISMS, AND PROBLEMS

The registry has experienced its share of difficulties. I do not intend to catalogue the many internal problems related to inadequate financing and policy or personnel changes within the government, the Health Branch, or the Division of Vital Statistics; rather, I will deal with some broad issues of registry policy and function.

Voluntary versus Compulsory Registration

The registry was conceived as voluntary rather than compulsory. At the outset this seemed wise; to have attempted to enforce compulsory registration would probably have ensured failure. However, in later years, as the reputation of the registry became established, and the quality of the statistics improved, visitors often asked why the administration did not build upon the substantial base already established to develop a system of compulsory registration. The answer was, and still is, that the gain would be minimal, whereas the expense in terms of trying to enforce compulsion would be great. Even the legal requirement of registering severe infectious diseases, enforced by many legal jurisdictions, failed to elicit complete ascertainment.

Incompleteness of Registration

This issue relates, in a way, to the one just discussed. The registry was often accused of having incomplete data; someone or other always knew of cases that were not registered, and visitors to the registry, who were concerned about the inadequacies of their own statistics, were often shocked to learn that the British Columbia registry could not claim complete ascertainment. Realistically, no system, unless it deals with a small population in a very restricted geographical area, can claim complete ascertainment of "handicapping illnesses"—an ill-defined health problem at best. The most that could be hoped for, and the goal the registry tried to achieve, was to obtain minimal estimates that were reasonable approximations of true incidence and prevalence rates.

Inadequacies of ICD Codes

The criticism was often expressed that the ICD codes do not provide a sufficiently detailed classification of congenital malformations and other handicapping illnesses. It was recognized within the registry that these codes were imperfect; however, if the registry's statistics were to be used to compare British Columbia incidence and prevalence rates with those derived for other populations, an internationally recognized classification had to be used. Over the years, the registry produced special codes for internal use and, in the late 1970s, developed an aetiology code, which, in conjunction with the ICD codes, allowed the caseload to be broken down into a variety of manageable groups.

Security and Confidentiality

Administrators and personnel of any health register must constantly be aware of the need to maintain the security and confidentiality of records in their trust. Two features of the operation of the British Columbia registry guarantee the confidentiality of the files. First, since the registry is part of the Division of Vital Statistics, all personnel are trained to respect the information they handle daily. No one has routine access to the registry files other than the staff of the Division of Vital Statistics and the consultants (before the latter positions were terminated). Health units, other departments of government, and private agencies are not given names and addresses of individuals unknown to them. Individuals who use the records for special projects are sworn to an oath of secrecy. In themselves, these procedures do not guarantee confidentiality, but they do impress upon those who use the records the importance of maintaining it. Second, the registry personnel never make direct contact with any registered person. Follow-up, regardless of the purpose, is carried out through the person or agency that registered the case. If direct contact is required, permission is obtained through that person or agency. For a period of about eighteen years, beginning in 1967, there was a third guarantee: the provincial *Evidence Act* (14) specifically protected those who registered, those who were registered, and those who used the data on the register. All information on the register was "declared to be privileged communications which may not be used, offered or received in evidence in any legal proceeding at any time." The most recent version of the Act lacks this wording.

WHY THE REGISTRY DEVELOPED SUCCESSFULLY IN BRITISH COLUMBIA

The successful development of the British Columbia registry resulted from a confluence of several persons and circumstances. Donald Paterson was the principal driving force; his enthusiasm, his passionate concern for the welfare of handicapped children, and his dynamic personality were unquestionably the elements that created interest in the survey that led to the registry being established. However, his compelling personality and his grand vision would have been for naught if other persons and agencies had not been in place. Although private physicians as a group did not hinder data being collected, they did not contribute enthusiastically to the survey or, subsequently, to the registry. Under these circumstances, the key to success was the generalized public health service that functioned in Vancouver and Victoria as metropolitan health units and extended throughout the province as provincial health units. The staffs of these units provided the bulk of the data and maintained liaison with the practising physicians. This was particularly true outside the metropolitan regions.

In itself, a compilation of medical diagnoses possesses little value; meaningful analyses are required to produce statistics usable for planning services or for research purposes. Fortunately, in the early 1950s, British Columbia had a superb Director of Vital Statistics, John Doughty, who was aware of what was required to make the registry function effectively and who was able to obtain the services of someone with the knowledge and practical talents of Nancy Scott to manage the registry.

Finally, the newly formed Department of Paediatrics at the University of British Columbia, under the chairmanship of John F. McCreary, provided a pool of consultants who were available to provide expert advice when it was required.

The coming together of these several elements in the early 1950s, in a province with a manageable population of about 1.5 million, created a unique situation that probably explains why the registry was conceived and flourished in British Columbia.

CONCLUDING COMMENTS

The registry's survival for over forty years is a certain measure of its success, but survival alone does not necessarily guarantee or prove success. A stagnant register full of useless files cannot be deemed a success; success requires constant use, critical evaluation, and response to new demands. Anyone who knew Donald Paterson and Nancy Scott in 1952 would have predicted the success of the new registry. Those two individuals were determined to provide the required use, evaluation, and responses. Under their direction and that of those whom they trained and who succeeded them, the registry flourished and evolved. Flexibility, the ability to respond to new challenges, guaranteed success.

Although the wealth of data on the registry files has been used productively until recent years, as can be judged by the references to the current studies of Professor Baird and her colleagues cited in the bibliography, the future of the registry as a vital public health entity is uncertain. This uncertainty arises from a number of factors, among which are administrative and policy changes within the Division of Vital Statistics, severe budgetary restraints that affected the entire Ministry of Health, and the death of Helen Colls, the able administrator who succeeded Nancy Scott and who has never been replaced.

In the previous chapter, mention was made of the changed relationship between the Division of Vital Statistics and the paediatric and medical community. The earlier collaborative epidemiological studies designed to measure paediatric needs and plan services were set aside, and the genetic studies only continued with funding obtained from outside sources. In 1989, the position of medical consultant was terminated and, in 1990, the registry files were moved to Victoria. While reporting from the field continues, the function provided by the consultant has been omitted, with resultant loss of quality control of the data.

It is encouraging to note, however, that an advisory committee has recently been appointed to determine the future role of the Health Surveillance Registry in British Columbia.

ACKNOWLEDGEMENTS

When I first arrived in Vancouver in September 1958, I was fortunate to meet quickly several individuals who, in one way or another, provided sound advice and guidance throughout the twenty-two years I remained at the University of British Columbia. Two of those individuals are the editors of this volume and two others, Nancy Scott and John Doughty, characteristically responded generously when I needed help with this chapter. I thank them all for their wise counsel and warm friendship during the years we worked together. I also thank Professors P. A. Baird and R. B. Lowry for their constructive criticism of an early draft, and I acknowledge with pleasure the help of Betty MacDonald, former manager of the registry, who kindly gave me access to its historical files and provided detailed information about current developments.

REFERENCES

1. AMYOT, G. F. *Third Report of the Department of Health and Welfare (Health Branch, Province of British Columbia. Year Ended December 31st 1948)*. Victoria: The King's Printer, 11–19.

2. *Division of Vital Statistics Special Reports No. 70—Registry for Handicapped Children and Adults. Annual Report 1961*. Victoria: Health Branch, Department of Health Services and Hospital Insurance of British Columbia 1963.

3. RENWICK, D.H.G. Estimating prevalence of certain chronic childhood conditions by use of a central registry. *Public Health Reports* 82 (1967): 261–69.

4. RENWICK, D.H.G. The combined use of a central registry and vital records for incidence studies of congenital defects. *British Journal of Preventive and Social Medicine* 22 (1968): 61–67.

5. LOWRY, R. B. and RENWICK, D.H.G. Incidence of cleft lip and palate in British Columbia Indians. *Journal of Medical Genetics* 6 (1969): 67–69.

6. LOWRY, R. B. and TRIMBLE, B. K. Incidence rates for cleft lip and palate in British Columbia 1952–71 for North American Indian, Japanese, Chinese and total populations: Secular trends over 20 years. *Teratology* 16 (1977): 277–84.

7. LOWRY, R. B., JONES, D. C., RENWICK, D.G.H., and TRIMBLE, B. K. Down syndrome in British Columbia, 1952–73: Incidence and mean maternal age. *Teratology* 14 (1976): 29–34.

8. TRIMBLE, B. K. and BAIRD, P. A. Maternal age and Down syndrome: Age-specific incidence rates by single year intervals. *American Journal of Medical Genetics* 2 (1978): 1–5.

9. HERBST, D. S. and MILLER, J. R. Non-specific X linked mental retardation. II. The frequency in British Columbia. *American Journal of Medical Genetics* 7 (1980): 461–69.

10. WALPOLE, I. R. Some epidemiological aspects of pyloric stenosis in British Columbia. *American Journal of Medical Genetics* 10 (1981): 237–44.

11. MILLER, J. R. and GALLAGHER, R. P. The use of a registry case load survey in predicting trends in rehabilitative needs for the handicapped. *Journal of Mental Deficiency Research* 19 (1975): 101–106.

12. NEWCOMBE, H. B. Screening for effects of maternal age and birth order in a register of handicapped children. *Annals of Human Genetics* 27 (1964): 367.

13. NEWCOMBE, H. B. Familial tendencies in diseases of children. *British Journal of Preventive and Social Medicine* 20 (1966): 49.

14. *Evidence Act*, S.B.C. 1979, c. 116.

BIBLIOGRAPHY. SELECTED PUBLICATIONS RELATED TO THE BRITISH COLUMBIA REGISTRY AND STUDIES DERIVED FROM ITS DATA BASE.

A. General Overviews

1. *Division of Vital Statistics Special Reports No. 70—Registry for Handicapped Children and Adults. Annual Report 1961.* Victoria: Health Branch, Department of Health Services and Hospital Insurance of British Columbia, 1963.
2. MILLER, J. R. The use of registries and vital statistics in the study of congenital malformations. In *Second International Conference on Congenital Malformations*, ed. M. Fishbein. New York: International Medical Congress 1964, pp. 334–40.
3. MILLER, J. R. Human genetics in public health research and programming. *Canadian Journal of Public Health* 57 (1966): 1–8.
4. LOWRY, R. B., MILLER, J. R., SCOTT, A. E., and RENWICK, D.H.G. The British Columbia Registry for Handicapped Children and Adults: evolutionary changes over twenty years. *Canadian Journal of Public Health* 66 (1975): 322–26.
5. MILLER, J. R. and GALLAGHER, R. P. The use of a registry case load survey in predicting trends in rehabilitative needs for the handicapped. *Journal of Mental Deficiency Research* 19 (1975): 101–106.
6. EMERY, A.E.H. and MILLER, J. R. (eds.). *Registers for the Detection and Prevention of Genetic Disease.* Miami: Symposium Specialists, 1976.
7. MILLER, J. R. Description of a handicapped population: The British Columbia Health Surveillance Registry. *Birth Defects: Original Article Series* 12(4) (1976): 1–11.
8. LOWRY, R. B., ROCHELEAU, J., and KEILLOR, L. Comparison of existing classifications for coding congenital malformations and genetic syndromes. *Birth Defects: Original Article Series* 13:3A (1977): 53–59.
9. MILLER, J. R. and LOWRY, R. B. Birth defects registries and surveillance. In *Handbook of Teratology*, vol. 3, ed. J. G. Wilson and F. C. Fraser. New York: Plenum Press, 1977, pp. 227–42.
10. COLLS, M. H. A method for converting a disease registry's case-load to a new classification of diagnostic codes. *Medical Information* 5 (1980): 121–30.
11. COLLS, M. H., BAIRD, P. A., and GIBSON, D. L. Measuring morbidity in a population: the British Columbia Health Surveillance Registry. *Canadian Journal of Public Health* 73 (1982): 313–18.
12. BAIRD, P. A. Measuring birth defects and handicapping disorders in the population: the British Columbia Health Surveillance Registry. *Canadian Medical Association Journal* 136 (1987): 109–111.

B. Incidence and Prevalence

1. RENWICK, D.H.G., MILLER, J. R., and PATERSON, D. Estimates of incidence and prevalence of mongolism and of congenital heart disease in British Columbia. *Canadian Medical Association Journal* 91 (1964): 365–71.
2. RENWICK, D.H.G. Estimating prevalence of certain chronic childhood conditions by use of a central registry. *Public Health Reports* 82 (1967): 261–69.
3. RENWICK, D.H.G. The combined use of a central registry and vital records for incidence studies of congenital defects. *British Journal of Preventive and Social Medicine* 22 (1968): 61–67.
4. LOWRY, R. B. and RENWICK, D.H.G. Incidence of cleft lip and palate in British Columbia Indians. *Journal of Medical Genetics* 6 (1969): 67–69.
5. GRAY, I. M., LOWRY, R. B., and RENWICK, D.G.H. Incidence and genetics of Legg-Perthes disease (osteochondritis deformans) in British Columbia: Evidence of polygenic determination. *Journal of Medical Genetics* 9 (1972): 197–202.
6. LOWRY, R. B., TISCHLER, B., COCKCROFT, W. H., and RENWICK, D.H.G. Incidence of phenylketonuria in British Columbia, 1950–1971. *Canadian Medical Association Journal* 106 (1972): 1299–1302.
7. LOWRY, R. B., JONES, D. C., RENWICK, D.G.H., and TRIMBLE, B. K. Down syndrome in British Columbia, 1952–73: Incidence and mean maternal age. *Teratology* 14 (1976): 29–34.
8. MCLEOD, R. and LOWRY, R. B. Incidence of albinism in British Columbia. Separation by hairbulb test. *Clinical Genetics* 9 (1976): 77–80.
9. MCGILLIVRAY, B. C. and LOWRY, R. B. Poland syndrome in British Columbia: Incidence and reproductive experience of affected persons. *American Journal of Medical Genetics* 1 (1977): 65–74.
10. LOWRY, R. B. and TRIMBLE, B. K. Incidence rates for cleft lip and palate in British Columbia 1952–71 for North American Indian, Japanese, Chinese and total populations: Secular trends over 20 years. *Teratology* 16 (1977): 277–84.
11. TRIMBLE, B. K. and BAIRD, P. A. Congenital anomalies of the central nervous system: Incidence in British Columbia, 1952–72. *Teratology* 17 (1978): 43–49.
12. TRIMBLE, B. K. and BAIRD, P. A. Maternal age and Down syndrome: Age-specific incidence rates by single year intervals. *American Journal of Medical Genetics* 2 (1978): 1–5.
13. HERBST, D. S. and MILLER, J. R. Non-specific X-linked mental retardation. II. The frequency in British Columbia. *American Journal of Medical Genetics* 7 (1980): 461–69.
14. BAIRD, P. A. and MACDONALD, E. C. An epidemiological study of congenital malformations of the anterior abdominal wall in more than half a million consecutive livebirths. *American Journal of Medical Genetics* 33 (1981): 470–78.
15. WALPOLE, I. R. Some epidemiological aspects of pyloric stenosis in British Columbia. *American Journal of Medical Genetics* 10 (1981): 237–44.

16. HERBST, D. S. and BAIRD, P. A. Nonspecific mental retardation in British Columbia as ascertained through a registry. *American Journal of Mental Deficiency* 87 (1983): 506–13.

17. BAIRD, P. A. and SADOVNICK, A. D. Mental retardation in over half-a-million consecutive livebirths—an epidemiological study. *American Journal of Mental Deficiency* 89 (1985): 323–30.

18. SPOUGE, D. and BAIRD, P. A. Hirschsprung disease in a large birth cohort. *Teratology* 32 (1985): 171–77.

19. LEUNG, T. J., BAIRD, P. A., and McGILLIVRAY, B. Hypospadias in British Columbia. *American Journal of Medical Genetics* 21 (1985): 43–52.

20. WILSON, R. D. and BAIRD, P. A. Renal agenesis in British Columbia. *American Journal of Medical Genetics* 21 (1985): 153–65.

21. SPOUGE, D. and BAIRD, P. A. Imperforate anus in 700,000 consecutive liveborn infants. *American Journal of Medical Genetics*, Suppl. 2 (1986): 151–61.

22. FROSTER-ISKENIUS, U. and BAIRD, P. A. Limb reduction defects in over a million consecutive livebirths. *Teratology* 39 (1989): 127–35.

23. BAMFORTH, S. and BAIRD, P. A. Spina bifida and hydrocephalus: a population study over a 35 year period. *American Journal of Human Genetics* 44 (1989): 225–32.

24. FROSTER-ISKENIUS, U. and BAIRD, P. A. Amelia: Incidence and associated defects in a large population. *Teratology* 41 (1990): 23–31.

C. Genetics

1. LOWRY, R. B. Sex-linked cleft palate in British Columbia Indian family. *Pediatrics* 46 (1970): 123–28.

2. LOWRY, R. B. X-linked cleft palate. *Birth Defects Original Article Series* 7 (1971): 76–79.

3. TRIMBLE, B. K. and DOUGHTY, J. H. The amount of hereditary disease in human populations. *Annals of Human Genetics* 38 (1974): 199–233.

4. TRIMBLE, B. K. and SMITH, M. E. The incidence of genetic disease and the impact on man of an altered mutation rate. *Canadian Journal of Genetics and Cytology* 19 (1977): 375–85.

5. HOOK, E. B., CROSS, P. K., LAMSON, S. H., REGAL, R. R., BAIRD, P. A., and UH, S. H. Paternal age and Down syndrome in British Columbia. *American Journal of Human Genetics* 33 (1981): 123–28.

6. HERBST, D. S. Non-specific X-linked mental retardation. I. A review with information from 24 new families. *American Journal of Medical Genetics* 7 (1980): 443–60.

7. BAIRD, P. A., ANDERSON, T. W., NEWCOMBE, H. B., and LOWRY, R. B. Genetic disorders in children and young adults: a population study. *American Journal of Human Genetics* 42 (1988): 677–93.

D. Record Linkage

1. NEWCOMBE, H. B. Screening for effects of maternal age and birth order in a register of handicapped children. *Annals of Human Genetics* 27 (1964): 367–82.
2. NEWCOMBE, H. B. Familial tendencies in diseases of children. *British Journal of Preventive and Social Medicine* 20 (1966): 49–57.

E. Miscellaneous

1. GALLAGHER, R. P. and LOWRY, R. B. Longevity in Down's syndrome in British Columbia. *Journal of Mental Deficiency Research* 19 (1975): 157–63.
2. MCBRIDE, M.L. Sib risks of anencephaly and spina bifida in British Columbia. *American Journal of Medical Genetics* 3 (1979): 377–89.
3. LOWRY, R. B., THUNEM, N. Y., and SILVER, M. Congenital anomalies in American Indians of British Columbia. *Genetic Epidemiology* 3 (1986): 455–67.
4. BAIRD, P. A., SADOVNICK, A. D., and YEE, I.M.L. Maternal age and birth defects: A population study. *Lancet* 337 (1991): 527–30.

Part II
Population-based Institutional Services

Acute and Long-stay Hospital Services

HISTORICAL CONSIDERATIONS

Hospital Insurance Service

In the late 1940s, the municipalities and hospitals in British Columbia were having financial problems and sought help from the provincial government. In 1948, the provincial *Hospital Insurance Act* (1) was enacted, and the British Columbia Hospital Insurance Service (BCHIS) was established to administer the Act. A Commissioner or Deputy Minister of the Hospital Insurance Service was appointed, who reported directly to the Minister of Health and Welfare. In addition to administrating the *Hospital Insurance Act*, the Deputy Minister of Hospital Insurance was responsible for the administration of the *Hospital Act* (2). This Act also appointed the deputy minister the Chief Inspector of Hospitals and controlled the organization and operation of hospitals. All hospitals are owned by non-profit hospital societies and are required to appoint boards of trustees, some of the trustees being appointed by government and some elected from the hospital society. An administrator is responsible to the board of directors for the operation of the hospital. Admitting privileges are granted to physicians to admit patients. The number of physicians enrolled can be limited by the hospital and hence some control of the size of the medical staff is maintained.

The funding of hospitals is provided in accordance with the *Hospital Insurance Act*, and, since 1982, is allocated on a global basis, whereby hospitals do not receive adjustments for either deficits or surpluses. There are charges for private rooms, but added hospital charges or user fees are illegal (Chapter 2). Initially, the hospital insurance expenditures were funded by annual premiums and all residents of the province were required to participate. Registration started in September 1948, and sixty-one district offices were opened. Simultaneously, arrangements were made with hospitals for services to be rendered to insured persons, and financial procedures were developed by which hospitals would be reimbursed for services. The benefits consisted of public ward treatment in an acute general hospital, payment for emergency treatments (short-stay benefits), and payment for treatment by hospitals outside of British Columbia.

Grants for hospital construction and equipment were also introduced and comprised 50 percent of approved hospital construction costs and one third of equipment purchases and building improvements and renovations.

The problems of the early years of hospital insurance have been described by Turnbull (3), who was Minister of Health and Welfare from 1949–52, and included a "large gap between receipts from premiums and payments to hospitals." Undoubtedly, there was insufficient time to fully prepare for the plan by the starting date of 1 January 1949. Rescue efforts included visits to Saskatchewan to study their hospital insurance system, discussions with consultants from Minneapolis, and the resignation of the commissioner, followed by a board of enquiry. Finally, the legislature was prorogued and an election called in June 1952. The new government, the Social Credit Party, with W.A.C. Bennett as leader, cancelled all arrears of BCHIS premiums and made participation in the plan voluntary. Premiums were reduced and co-insurance was retained on a dollar a day basis.[1] Financial problems continued, and in 1954 the *Hospital Insurance Act* was amended and premiums were abolished (4). Benefits were funded from consolidated revenue, augmented by increasing the social services sales tax from 3 to 5 percent. The elimination of the premium billing and collection operation resulted in considerable savings.

After the federal *Hospital Insurance and Diagnostic Services Act* (see Chapter 2) was passed in 1957, British Columbia joined the Federal-Provincial Hospital Insurance Plan in July 1958, and the federal government assumed approximately 50 percent of the cost of acute hospital care.

In September 1960, a new hospital program (Rehabilitation, Chronic Treatment, and Convalescent Care Plan) was introduced for rehabilitation and convalescent patients (5). Participation was limited to approved chronic hospitals or chronic units of acute hospitals. Insurance coverage was for inpatient care of rehabilitation and convalescent patients who no longer required intensive diagnostic and treatment services in an acute hospital, who were deemed likely to benefit from rehabilitation services, and who were to be returned to community living and, in the case of adults, to useful employment. Benefits did not include treatment of tuberculosis, mental disease, and alcoholism, or the provision of outpatient services, "take home" drugs, prescriptions, or appliances. The coverage

---

1 This charge was increased to $4.00 in 1976 and discontinued in 1984, when the *Canada Health Act* outlawed user fees.

was designed to fit within the Federal-Provincial Hospital Insurance Program.

In December 1965, the Extended Hospital Care Program (6) was introduced for patients requiring a lower level of care but still requiring skilled nursing services and continuing medical supervision. The services were limited to non-profit extended care hospitals or units in acute hospitals.

In 1966, biochemical screening of all newborn infants became an additional benefit (7). Outpatient cancer therapy benefits at facilities in Vancouver and Victoria were introduced in 1966 (8). In 1967, regional hospital districts were established for financing hospital construction. The *Regional Hospital Districts Act* (9) and the *British Columbia Regional Hospital Districts Financial Authority Act* (10) were passed, enabling individual hospital districts to plan, develop, and finance hospital projects in collaboration with the Ministry of Health.

Day care surgery became an insurance benefit in February 1968. The definition was based on the assumption that day care surgical services are a compact form of inpatient care requiring the operating room services available to inpatients (11).

The services are divided into four main groups:

(a) Those elective or non-elective diagnostic and/or treatment procedures requiring the use of hospital facilities and a general anaesthesia.

(b) Those procedures which would normally be carried out under general anaesthetic but where the attending physician has elected to use local anaesthesia (e.g., biopsy, closed reduction of fracture).

(c) Endoscopic procedures carried out under local or general anaesthesia, including bronchoscopy, oesophagoscopy, gastroscopy, and colonoscopy.

(d) Certain cosmetic and plastic surgical procedures that may be done under local anaesthesia. These include certain plastic surgical, ophthalmological, and other procedures on the face that require full operating room and hospital facilities.

Outpatient psychiatric services in designated hospitals, including a paediatric unit in the Health Centre for Children, were introduced in December 1968 (8). Ambulatory medical programs for children with chronic disabilities (arthritis, cerebral palsy, visual and hearing impairment, spina bifida, cleft palate, fibrocystic disease, etc.) were included as insurance benefits in designated hospitals following the federal *Medical Care Act* (1966) and after the Medical Service Plan (1968) was introduced in British Columbia. Prior to that, the salaries of medical and allied health professionals derived from federal health grants, provincial health grants, and voluntary organizations. These ambulatory medical programs expanded extensively in the 1970s.

In 1977, the federal *Established Programs Financing Act* (Chapter 2) was designed to assist provinces to develop low cost alternatives to inpatient hospital care, including long-term and ambulatory care. The long-term care program funded nursing homes, intermediate care, and adult residential care homes in the community. These services were introduced in British Columbia in January 1978; however, children under eighteen years were excluded.

The Vancouver General Hospital was named the provincial Neonatal Tertiary Care Centre in 1975. A regional perinatal and neonatal program was introduced in 1978, with one tertiary hospital (type III), four secondary hospitals (type II), and all the remaining hospitals classified as type I (12). This program is described in Chapter 12.

The impact of the health insurance programs upon acute and long-stay hospital utilization is now described.

Paediatric Utilization Response of Acute Care Hospitals

The inpatient hospital utilization rates per 1,000 population by age group and year are displayed in Table 4 (13). There is a remarkable decline in paediatric use.[2] In sixteen years, utilization per 1,000 population fell by nearly 60 percent among the age group from 28 days to 14 years. The data for the 0–14 year group show a smaller decline because of the rapid increase in utilization among sick newborns and other paediatric cases under 28 days of age. Among these latter groups, use by infants diagnosed as sick has nearly doubled. The drop for the rest of the first year of life has been as great as that for children over one year of age.

As a result of the progressive increase in utilization by sick newborns and other paediatric cases under 28 days of age, paediatric hospital utilization has become more and more concentrated in the first month of life. Paediatric utilization has always been higher in children under one year of age than for older children, and this pattern has been accentuated by the increases in the first month. This phenomenon appears to be due in part to the increase in numbers of newborns designated as sick. The routine hospital utilization data, however, for sick infants under 28 days

---

2 These data apply up to 1982/83, because in 1983/84 the Ministry of Health ceased coding separation discharges in-house and began to rely instead on the services of an external agency, the Hospital Medical Records Institute (HMRI). This change in procedure imparts a potential discrepancy of unknown magnitude to comparisons between these two years, and it makes longitudinal comparisons across that boundary questionable.

TABLE 4. BRITISH COLUMBIA PAEDIATRIC UTILIZATION, BY AGE GROUP, 1966–1982/83*

Annualized Patient Days per 1,000 Population	1966	1971	1976	1981/82	1982/83	Population 1982/83
0–27 days	20,817	28,274	34,501	36,631	35,177	3,067
28 days–1 year	3,295	2,871	2,080	1,392	1,314	38,393
All 0–1 year	4,637	4,818	4,566	4,098	3,914	41,460
1–4 years	1,136	1,056	746	486	389	153,869
5–9 years	578	453	358	259	223	189,906
10–14 years	438	358	339	272	257	205,800
All 0–14	918	816	694	581	537	591,033
All 1–14	691	567	445	326	282	549,573
All 28 days +	830	692	537	393	349	587,966

* All figures are rounded to the nearest whole number.

are underestimated by the method of recording data, in that only sick infants transferred from one hospital to another are included. As many sick infants are treated in their hospital of birth and are not transferred, the system reports a minimal estimate of paediatric hospital utilization in the 0–27 day and the under one year age groups. In order to reflect the more accurate paediatric utilization in the first year of life, the rates for 0–27 day, 28 day–1 year, and all over 28 day age groups were calculated with denominators adjusted to reflect the reduced proportion of time of "exposure" during the study year. The reported population in the under one year age group has been divided in the proportions 27/365 and 338/365 to yield estimated denominators for the calculation of utilization rates in these age groups. The very high rates for the infants under 28 days are thus the rates they would have experienced had they continued to be hospitalized at the same rate for an entire year. They are the rates per child year for children 27 days or less.

The rapid growth in utilization among the very young may be in part attributed to the progress in neonatal intensive care and to the increase in numbers of low and very low birthweight babies, but this cannot be the dominant factor, because the average length of stay for children admitted in the first twenty-seven days of life during this time period has fallen from 16.66 days to 6.51 days (14). An increasing proportion of transfers could lead to reduced lengths of stay; however, the falling proportion of newborns reported as healthy—with no diagnosis—suggests that the increase in patient days is primarily the result of the rapid increase in newborns designated as ill. In 1966, over 90 percent of newborns were discharged without a diagnosis; by the early 1980s, this ratio was down to two-thirds. The proportion of low birthweight infants is not nearly enough to account for a shift of this magnitude.

The decline in utilization rates has been more rapid after 1976 than before and showed no sign of slowing down, at least in the early 1980s. The decline in the birth rates after 1965 reduced the relative proportion of children in the under one year and 1–4 year age groups and exerted downward pressure on crude utilization rates. But the rates of utilization fell by about 60 percent in each of the age groups; 28 days–1 year, 1–4 years, 5–9 years, and 10–14 years, with the largest decline in the 1–4 year group. Clearly the aggregate effect is not just a demographic effect.

The significance of this decline in utilization is emphasized by calculating the additional patient days that would have been used in 1982/83 if the 1966 utilization rates had persisted. In round figures, the shift in paediatric utilization saved approximately 300,000 days annually or the equivalent of a 1,000 bed paediatric hospital at 80 percent occupancy. Total separations are divided into medical and surgical categories, the latter defined as all those with a surgical procedure performed. The decline in medical patient days is 57.2 percent and in surgical days 59.4 percent (Table 5). Since the surgical utilization rate is almost half the medical rate, this implies that two-thirds of the total patient days saved are attributable to changes in the utilization patterns among medical cases. Just over half the reduction in medical use is accounted for by reduced utilization—both separations and length of stay—for respiratory conditions. One-third of the decline in surgical utilization is the result of reduced rates of separation for tonsils and adenoids (T & A). Thus, changes in patterns of treatment of respiratory diseases, both medical and surgical, have accounted for just under half of the whole decline in paediatric utilization.

Medical admissions for respiratory problems fell most sharply in the 28 day–1 year age group (72%) and, since the medical utilization rates are so much larger in the lower age groups, it is apparent that the really large changes for respiratory diseases were for very young children. Virtually all the T & A surgery in 1966 was in the 1–4 and 5–9 year age groups, and this is where the large reductions in utilization took place.

Finally, regional variation in paediatric hospital utilization showed marked differences in medical, but not surgical, cases. The rates were lower in the two metropolitan areas (Vancouver and Victoria) and much higher in non-metropolitan areas. In the medical cases, the variation in respiratory cases was most marked. While utilization rates have declined in the metro and non-metropolitan areas, the differential between areas has largely been preserved.

TABLE 5. BRITISH COLUMBIA PAEDIATRIC HOSPITAL UTILIZATION BY TYPE OF CASE: 28 DAYS–14 YEARS AGE GROUP, 1966 AND 1982/83*

	Separations/1,000		Length of Stay		Patient Days/1,000	
	1966	1982/83	1966	1982/83	1966	1982/83
Medical						
Respiratory	31.8	19.0	7.7	4.1	244.8	78.1
Other	41.0	31.4	7.8	5.2	319.0	163.1
Surgical						
T & A	30.0	6.8	2.3	1.9	69.1	13.1
Other	27.6	17.4	7.2	5.4	196.9	94.8
Total	130.4	74.6	6.4	4.7	830.0	349.3
T & A,						
respiratory	61.8	25.8	5.1	3.5	313.9	91.3
Other	68.6	48.8	7.5	5.3	515.9	257.9

* All figures are rounded to one decimal place.

In summary, a marked decline in paediatric utilization has occurred in British Columbia since 1966. This fall was associated with a rapid expansion of day care surgery. Are they related? We have shown above that two-thirds, or 200,000, "saved" days are due to a fall in medical utilization and cannot be attributed to the substitution effects of day care surgery. Of the remaining 100,000 saved days, about 35 percent are attributable to a fall in T & A rates, leaving only 65,000 days saved by non-T & A surgery. A further 30,000 days can be attributed to a reduction in the length of stay of non-T & A surgery, leaving 35,000 days due to reduced surgical admissions. Therefore the data suggests that substitution of day surgery probably accounted for 10 percent or less of the decline in paediatric utilization.

Accordingly, the major cause of the decline was probably changing professional criteria and attitudes toward inpatient care, doubtless aided or stimulated by parental pressures. In the absence of any corresponding changes in morbidity, physicians changed the way they treated children, and particularly young children, with respiratory disease. The reduction of T & A surgery was a factor, but of far less quantitative importance than the reduction in medical admissions.

Paediatric Utilization Response of Long-stay Hospitals

Children with physical disability due to chronic diseases (tuberculosis, chronic chest disease, osteomyelitis, rheumatic fever, and poliomyelitis) were cared for in two paediatric long-stay hospitals in British Columbia. These were the Queen Alexandra Solarium in Victoria (opened in 1926), renamed the Queen Alexandra Hospital for Children, and the Preventorium in Vancouver (opened in 1932) and renamed the Sunny Hill Hospital for Children. Smaller units attached to general hospitals were added at Pouce Coupe (1968) and Vernon (1974).

The changing pattern of paediatric morbidity in the 1950s and 1960s initially led to reduced utilization of the long-stay hospitals. The new hospital benefits for patients judged suitable for rehabilitation and extended care, however, resulted in children with multiple neurological handicaps moving to long-stay hospitals.

An interministerial (Health Education and Human Resources) review of services to severely handicapped children was carried out in 1980–81 in British Columbia (15). It noted that there was considerable confusion regarding the definition of paediatric extended care and that children were placed inappropriately, and recommended that evaluation of the paediatric extended care assessment process be undertaken to clarify and rationalize the criteria.

The care of the population of disabled children has undergone profound change during the past twenty years. This includes the location of care (institution versus community), and the type and extent of intervention (therapy, recreation, education) provided. The normalization and integration of both the mentally and physically handicapped population is a reflection of the salutary effects of community living upon behaviour and development and the effectiveness of early intervention on the course of significant developmental disability. The end result has been reduced utilization of long-stay hospitals. It is perhaps of some historical interest that one report (16) in the Greater Vancouver Regional District in the mid-1970s recommended twenty-five new extended care beds and emphasized that home care was practical when children were young (up to 5–7 years), but speculated that most will ultimately require institutional care! The paediatric facility was built but, because of lack of demand, was converted to adult use.

The first group home for physically handicapped children, Slocan House, was opened in 1975 by the Sunny Hill Hospital, and several others have opened since then (17). The drive to place children in the community has moved many children out of extended care units.

TABLE 6. BRITISH COLUMBIA PAEDIATRIC HOSPITAL
UTILIZATION BY MEDICAL AND SURGICAL DIAGNOSTIC
CATEGORY, 28 DAYS–14 YEARS AGE GROUP, 1982/1983

	Separations /1,000 pop.	Patient Days /1,000 pop.
(a) *Medical*		
Respiratory	19.04	78.12
Injuries and Accidents	7.71	29.55
Digestive	4.96	19.98
Nervous System and Sense Organs	2.95	19.49
Infectious and Parasitic Disease	3.46	15.50
Other	12.29	78.66
Subtotal	50.41	241.30
(b) *Surgical*		
Musculoskeletal	5.29	26.64
Digestive	4.01	21.11
Tonsils and Adenoids	6.78	13.13
Skin and Subcutaneous Tissue	1.40	8.49
Nervous System	0.46	5.81
Male Genitals	1.53	5.11
Other	4.75	27.69
Subtotal	24.22	107.98
Total	74.63	342.28

PRESENT SERVICES

Acute Care Hospitals

Inpatient Services: Calculation of the age distribution of children in acute
hospital beds in 1982/83 (18) reveals that 54 percent of patient days are
occupied by the 28 day–1 year and the 1–4 year age groups.

The mix of separations in the 28 day–14 year age group in the early
1980s in British Columbia was two-thirds medical and one-third surgical,
and the patient days showed a similar pattern (Table 6). Respiratory diseases utilized one-third of medical patient days and were highest in the
28 day–1 year group followed by the 1–4 year age groups. The next highest patient day rates are injuries and poisonings, followed by digestive,
nervous system, sense organs, and infectious and parasitic diseases. The
age group distribution consistently showed highest patient day rates in

the 28 day–1 year age group, followed by 1–4 year. The accidents and poisonings rates remain high in all age groups.

Turning to surgical utilization (Table 6), the highest patient day rates were musculoskeletal, followed by digestive, T & A's, skin and subcutaneous tissue, nervous system, and male genital. The age group distribution again showed highest rates for patient days in the 28 day–1 year age group, except for musculoskeletal, T & A's, and male genital, which showed higher rates in the 1–4, 5–9, and 10–14 years age groups.

Day Care Surgery: In 1987/88, 17,000 procedures or 46 percent of total paediatric surgical procedures in the 0–14 year age group were performed on a day care basis. The most common procedure categories in paediatric day care surgery in British Columbia were otorhino-laryngology, dental, orthopaedics, urology, plastic, diagnostic endoscopy, and ophthalmology. Myringotomy was by far the most common operative procedure, both in 1976 and 1982/83, followed by cystoscopy and restoration of tooth.

A recent study of day care surgery in Canada (19) obtained statistics from five paediatric hospitals, and the five commonest procedures were tympanostomy (tube) insertion/removal and/or adenoidectomy, removal/restoration of teeth, tonsillectomy and/or adenoidectomy, strabismus repair, and inguinal hernia repair.

Day Care Medicine: Day care medicine has been approved by Hospital Programs as a hospital benefit for selected investigative procedures that require general anaesthesia or sedatives. These include cardiac catheterization, fiberoptic bronchoscopy, endoscopy, electromyograms, and myelogram. The length of stay is less than six hours, and they are discharged before midnight of the day of admission. Not included in this category are the ambulatory preplanned diagnostic, educational, or therapeutic visits of children with chronic illness (leukaemia, diabetes, spina bifida, fibrocystic disease, etc.). These multidiscipline ambulatory visits avoid hospital admissions but have small impact on total paediatric utilization (20).

Long-stay Hospitals

As noted above, the long-stay hospitals developed activation and rehabilitation and extended care services in the 1960s. This was followed by an influx of multihandicapped children into long-stay hospitals, which provided an alternative to admission to the institutions for mentally retarded children. In 1985, children over eight years in long-stay hospitals were surveyed ($n = 99$) to obtain diagnostic information (21); every child had a diagnosis of mental retardation and 90 percent had multiple handicaps. Cerebral palsy was present in 74 percent of children, epilepsy in 55 percent, blindness in 20 percent, and sensorineural hearing loss in 7 percent. The institutions responded to that change with special therapy and educational services, the introduction of respite care, and the development of ambulatory services for the continuing care of children with chronic neuromuscular and other problems. These hospital departments now include medicine, dentistry, nursing, occupational/physical therapy, speech and language pathology, social services, psychology, recreation, and preschool. School programs are provided on site by the local school district.

The long-stay hospitals also responded to the general trend to integrate the population with chronic disabilities and have become actively involved in developing community living for this population since the mid-1970s. They have demonstrated that the majority of these children can be placed in private homes (own or foster) and group homes in the community, provided that appropriate resources are available, including family support therapy, education, recreation, and respite (see Chapter 19).

The roles of the long-stay hospital are changing to accept more children from acute care hospitals for convalescent and post-operative care, with a new mix of problems, including head injuries, narcotic addicted babies, technology dependent children, and near drowning victims, and to serve as a community resource for specialized programs (e.g., seating clinics, augmented communication, development clinics, etc.) and as a resource for respite care.

In the 1970s, the Sunny Hill Hospital began to provide respite care and, during the period 1975–79, one-third of admissions and 12 percent of patient days were for this cause. This was doubtless related to their active efforts to place children in community homes.

COMMENT

In 1949, the provincial government introduced legislation to provide a population-based hospital insurance program in British Columbia. The four main objectives of the plan (5) were: first, to protect the residents against the financial burden associated with hospitalization; second, to provide the hospitals with a regular source of income; third, to assist hospitals in developing and maintaining high standards of patient care, and fourth, to assist communities in providing adequate hospital facilities.

The federal *Hospital Insurance and Diagnostic Services Act* allowed cost sharing with the federal government. Subsequently, amendments to the provincial *Hospital Insurance Act* have provided rehabilitation, chronic treatment and convalescent care, an extended care program, and ambulatory services.

The organization of a universal hospital system is the quintessential example of population medicine. The patient's care in hospital is directed by the patient's physician (personal medicine) together with the hospital staff.

There has been an extraordinary reduction in paediatric utilization in acute care hospitals since 1966, which has been shown to be largely due to reduced respiratory admissions and to a lesser extent of T & A and non-T & A surgery. The consequences of separating young children from their families (22, 23) have become common knowledge and have changed professional and consumer attitudes regarding paediatric hospital utilization. It is important to note that over half of the paediatric hospital days are still used by the 28 day–1 year and 1–4 year age groups.

The development of ambulatory hospital-based care was a different story. Hospital outpatient care was traditionally provided to the medically indigent (public patients). The notion of providing ambulatory care to the "private patient" was an alien one, even if it represented an obvious means of reducing inpatient utilization. The introduction of insurance benefits for ambulatory patients began with cancer chemotherapy in 1966, and outpatient psychiatry services followed in 1968 in designated hospitals. Ambulatory surgery was introduced in 1968, and it was assumed that substitution for inpatient care would lead to important cost savings, but this did not prove to be the case. The unit cost of a surgical procedure was reduced, but the generation effect of more surgical cases cancelled the savings to the insurance service (24). Ambulatory medical services for children attending hospital-based clinics for chronic disease and disabilities in designated hospitals were introduced in the 1970s, when the *Medical Care Act* authorized payment for medical (but not other health professional) care.

The federal *Established Programs Financing Act* (1977) was designed to provide incentives to the provinces to develop alternatives to inpatient care, including ambulatory and long-term care, and to improve the integration and continuity of health services. This important Act gave rise to the further development of ambulatory hospital care and the Long-Term Care Program (see Chapter 3) for the population with chronic disability and disease. The decision, politically motivated, to exclude children and youth from the Long-Term Care Program in British Columbia was arguably the most ill-informed and regressive decision of the Ministry of Health of the past forty years.

This is not to suggest that there were no community services for children with chronic diseases and disabilities. Many services and facilities did emerge, thanks to voluntary societies, the Health Branch, and the directors of acute and long-stay hospitals for children. These services, however, lacked any over-all plan to meet the changing need as recorded by the Health Surveillance Registry, or to link hospital and community services, thereby establishing a degree of continuity of care. Coordination of hospital and community educational, health, and other services was nonexistent. It was a nightmare, however, for the parents of children with chronic disease and disabilities. The fact that these children had special needs, and that parents had problems in coping with their children, was given scant attention by the system. With one notable exception (25) there was no regional planning for children.

This exception was the Capital Regional District on Vancouver Island, which undertook a regional study, funded jointly by government and Queen Alexandra Hospital for Children. The study addressed the reproductive health of women and the health care of infants, children, and youth. The contemporary health care trends were first defined, including the importance of prenatal care for all pregnant women, the placement of obstetrical and neonatal care in one hospital, the changing pattern of paediatric morbidity, with the decreased need for hospital beds and the greater emphasis on ambulatory care, the follow-up of children with chronic disabilities, and greater family participation with improved integration of services. This report served as the basis for the development of services for children and youth during the subsequent decade.

REFERENCES

1. *Hospital Insurance Act*, S.B.C. 1948, c. 28.
2. *Hospital Act*, S.B.C. 1911, c. 102.
3. TURNBULL, A. D., Memoir: Early years of hospital insurance in British Columbia. *B.C. Studies* 76 (1987/88): 58–81.
4. BRITISH COLUMBIA. *Sixth Annual Report*. B.C. Hospital Insurance Service, January 1 to December 31, 1954.
5. BRITISH COLUMBIA. *Twelfth Annual Report*. B.C. Hospital Insurance Service, January 1 to December 31, 1960.
6. BRITISH COLUMBIA. *Seventeenth Annual Report*. B.C. Hospital Insurance Service, January 1 to December 31, 1965.
7. BRITISH COLUMBIA. *Eighteenth Annual Report*. B.C. Hospital Insurance Service, January 1 to December 31, 1966.
8. BRITISH COLUMBIA. *Twentieth Annual Report*. B.C. Hospital Insurance Service, January 1 to December 31, 1968.
9. *Regional Hospital Districts Act*, S.B.C. 1967, c. 43.
10. *British Columbia Regional Hospital District Financial Authority Act*, S.B.C. 1967, c. 5.
11. BRITISH COLUMBIA. *Report on Day Care Surgery 1985/86*, Ministry of Health.
12. BRITISH COLUMBIA. *Memorandum re: Provincial Program for the Regionalization of Obstetrical and Newborn Services*. Hospital Programs, Victoria, B.C., 30 November 1978. Ministry of Health.
13. EVANS, R. G., ROBINSON, G. C., and BARER, M. L. Where have all the children gone? Accounting for the pediatric hospital implosion. In *Redesigning Relationships in Child Health Care*, ed. R. S. TONKIN and J. R. WRIGHT, Vancouver: British Columbia Children's Hospital, 1987, pp. 63–76.

14. EVANS, R. G., ROBINSON, G. C., and BARER, M. L. *Final Report. The Impact of Paediatric Hospital-based Ambulatory Care Upon Paediatric Hospital Utilization in British Columbia.* Part I: Trends in paediatric utilization in British Columbia, 1966–1982/83. Ottawa Health and Welfare Canada, Grant No. 6610-1411-46, December 1987.

15. BRITISH COLUMBIA. *The Provincial Study of Severely Handicapped Children,* John Talbot, Coordinator, Ministry of Health, Victoria, B.C., 1981.

16. *Paediatric Extended Care*: An examination of the facilities and services required to meet the present and estimated future demands of the paediatric extended care population. Greater Vancouver Regional Hospital District, 1976.

17. MCNAUGHTON, D., personal communication, 1989.

18. ELO, J.A.I., EVANS, R. G., BARER, M. L., and ROBINSON, G. C. *Final Report. The Impact of Paediatric Hospital-based Ambulatory Care Upon Paediatric Hospital Utilization in British Columbia.* Part III. The impact of hospital-based surgical day care services on paediatric inpatient utilization in British Columbia, 1966–1983/84. Ottawa Health and Welfare Canada, Grant No. 6610-1411-46, December 1987.

19. NEWELL, C. Surgical Day Care in Canada: A national survey of programs in acute care hospitals 1987/1988. Summary. Research and Development Program, Canadian Hospital Association, 1989. Mimeographed document.

20. MORRIS, S. M., BARER, M. L., ROBINSON, G. C., and EVANS, R. G. *Final Report. The Impact of Paediatric Hospital-based Ambulatory Care Upon Paediatric Hospital Utilization in British Columbia.* Part II: The impact of hospital-based medical day care services on paediatric inpatient utilization in British Columbia, 1966–1983/84. Ottawa Health and Welfare Canada, Grant No. 6610-1411-46, December 1987.

21. ROBINSON, G. C., SHEPS, S. B., BULLOCK, M., TISCHLER, B., and HILL, R. H. *Final Report. A Survey of Severely Handicapped Children Residing in Long Stay Hospitals/Institutions in British Columbia.* Phase II. Ottawa, Health and Welfare Canada, Grant No. 6610-1284-46, March 1986.

22. VERNON, D.T.A., FOLEY, J. M., SIPOWICZ, R. R., and SCHULMAN, J. L. *The Psychological Responses of Children to Hospitalization and Illness. A Review of the Literature.* Springfield, Ill.: Charles C. Thomas, 1965.

23. ROBERTSON, J. *Young Children in Hospital.* London: Tavistock, 1970.

24. EVANS, R. G. and ROBINSON, G. C. Surgical day care: Measurements of the economic payoff. *Canadian Medical Association Journal* 123 (1980): 873–80.

25. MAINGUY, J. W. and BOULTON, B. C. *Report of the Capital Region Child Health Care Study, Victoria, B.C., 1980.* Victoria, 1980.

7

The Provincial Biochemical Disease Program

HISTORICAL CONSIDERATIONS

The recognition of the causal relationship between mental retardation and phenylketonuria (PKU), and the discovery of the therapeutic value of a diet low in phenylalanine, led to the widespread development of diagnostic and treatment services for this disorder. In British Columbia, a multidisciplinary team (paediatrician, dietician, psychologist, and laboratory staff) at the major institution for the mentally handicapped population (Woodlands School) during the late 1950s (1) provided diagnostic and treatment services for residents of the institution and outpatient services for newly diagnosed infants and children. Lofenlac, a low phenylalanine product, was supplied by the institution to all patients free of charge. Then the development of the simple bacterial-inhibition assay (2), which measured phenylalanine in blood, made possible the screening of all newborns and the diagnosis of PKU prior to the occurrence of irreversible brain damage.

The concept of a provincial Biochemical Disease Program consisting of a newborn screening program, a diagnostic laboratory, and an investigation treatment facility, was conceived by Dr. David Hardwick, an enlightened paediatric pathologist, and his colleague, Dr. D. Applegarth, in the mid-1960s (3), in response to the need for a coherent system to diagnose and treat children with rare metabolic diseases.

Newborn Biochemical Screening Program

The PKU screening program was started in the bacteriology laboratory at the Vancouver General Hospital in 1964 (4) with voluntary participation of British Columbia hospitals. Guthrie cards (blood dots) were mailed to the Department of Pathology at the Vancouver General Hospital. The direct costs of the program (5) were initially included in the latter hospital's budget, until PKU testing in all acute hospitals was funded by the Hospital Insurance Program in 1966 (6).

The neonatal screening program in Victoria was introduced in 1967 and, in addition to the Guthrie test (7), included blood and urine screening tests for other amino acids. A similar screening program was introduced in Vancouver (8), using the Guthrie blood dot to screen for other amino acidopathies. Further assessment of positive tests was undertaken in the Biochemical Disease Laboratory in Vancouver.

Between 1971 and 1977, the Metabolic Screening Program of the Children's Hospital, which screened urine for a number of amino acids and galactosaemia, was offered to the majority of hospitals in British Columbia (9). It was a voluntary program. The parents collected the urine at three to four weeks and specimens were sent to the Children's Hospital. The compliance rate was 46 percent of live births in the test hospitals, and 0.06 percent of newborns were shown to have an abnormality, mainly because of defective renal tubular transport, which was benign in nature. The need for a follow-up service was emphasized. In 1979, the provincial government announced the development of a comprehensive metabolic screening program encompassing the PKU program, testing for hypothyroidism, and the Metabolic Screening Program at the Children's Hospital (10), to serve the population of British Columbia (except for those in the Victoria area, which had its own program), to be housed in the Children's Hospital in Vancouver. In the latter program, a specimen of urine collected by the mother was shipped to the Children's Hospital.

The routine screening for congenital hypothyroidism was added in 1979 on the same specimen used for PKU and using a radioimmunoassay method, which identified the 10 percent of infants with the lowest thyroxine (T4) on whom thyroid stimulating hormone (TSH) was then measured. Finally, in 1984, the routine screening for galactosaemia was added, using the blood dot for PKU and T4 testing (11). The urine screening program was replaced because it identified galactosaemia at three to four weeks of age, by which time substantial brain damage had occurred. A primary TSH screen with immunofluorescent assay was recently introduced (12). In 1986, routine screening for biotinadase was introduced for a trial period, and no final decision of its value has been made as yet. In 1989, the Victoria Newborn Screening Program was discontinued (13).

Biochemical Disease Laboratory

A laboratory for inherited metabolic diseases had its origin in the Paediatric Microchemistry Laboratory at the Vancouver General Hospital in the early 1960s. It was directed by Dr. D. Applegarth, a clinical chemist working in collaboration with Dr. D. Hardwick. A working relationship was soon established with both the clinicians at the Woodlands School and in Victoria. In 1969, a biochemical disease laboratory was established at the old Vancouver Children's Hospital (14), funded by a grant of $120,000 from the directors of the hospital. This was the first of a series of innovative programs in child health services undertaken by the hospital.

Clinical Investigation Facility

This unit was opened at the Children's Hospital in 1971 (15) under the direction of Dr. George Davidson. It was funded by Hospital Programs and the Medical Services Commission. Seven beds were assigned for the investigation and treatment of children with rare metabolic diseases. A nurse and a dietician were assigned to co-ordinate investigation, specimen collection, and nutritional intake. An ambulatory clinic was also developed to supervise ongoing management of the children. Gradually, children attending the outpatient service at Woodlands School were transferred to the clinic at the Children's Hospital. In the new British Columbia Children's Hospital, the inpatient facility was increased to fourteen beds, eight of which have parent accommodation and facilities.

PRESENT SERVICES

Newborn Screening Program

Centralized screening of newborns for metabolic diseases occurs in each province in Canada. Screening for hyperphenylalanine and hypothyroidism are universal. Galactosaemia and other metabolic screens vary from province to province. In British Columbia, screening is performed for hyperphenylalanaemia, hypothyroidism, and galactosaemia. The rationale is based on the evidence that other metabolic diseases are extremely rare or there is no treatment for them; hence, screening is not justified. Decisions to change the screening program are placed before the Patient Care Committee of the Children's Hospital. The membership comprises professional and lay members, in an effort to reflect society's values.

The routine practised in British Columbia is as follows (16): first, the optimal time for the PKU/galactosaemia/TSH blood dot to be taken is when the infant is seventy-two hours of age or older; second, even if an infant is less than seventy-two hours of age, he or she should be tested on discharge from hospital; third, if the infant is less than twenty-four hours of age, this is noted on the requisition, as the screening laboratory requests a second test on all infants first tested at less than twenty-four hours of age; fourth, infants under thirty-seven weeks of age, sick infants, and those on parenteral alimentation should be tested on day seven. Second tests are not necessary unless requested by the screening laboratory. When the specimen is received in the screening laboratory, a receipt is mailed to the Medical Records Department of the hospital of origin. This is attached to the infant's chart, which is considered incomplete until the slip is attached. If the slip has not been attached to the front of the chart by two weeks of age, the medical records librarian advises the infant's physician, who is asked to arrange for the baby to be tested.

When parents refuse to have their infant tested, they are asked to sign a refusal of testing form, which is available in hospitals and public health units. The form is returned to the screening laboratory.

When the newborn screening program obtains an abnormal result, the infant's physician is telephoned and advised of the abnormality. When PKU and galactosaemia are suspected, infants are referred to the Biochemical Diseases Laboratory to confirm the diagnosis. Infants with congenital hypothyroidism are referred to local consultants or to the endocrine clinic at the Children's Hospital.

Biochemical Disease Laboratory

One of the major functions of this laboratory is the investigation of newborn infants with positive tests in the screening program. In 1987, the screening program (number of births = ±42,000) and the Biochemical Disease Laboratory identified the following diseases (11): congenital hypothyroidism 13, PKU 6, hyperphenylalanaemia 1, benign transient hyperphenylalanaemia 1, biotinadase deficiency 1, galactosaemia carrier 2, galactosaemia/variant enzyme 1, and galactosaemia 0.

In addition, it serves as a reference laboratory for specific diseases across the continent.

Clinical Investigation Facility

The newly diagnosed infants are admitted to the Clinical Investigation Facility at the British Columbia Children's Hospital, and the parents are taught about the disease, the treatment, future prospects, and the genetic implications.

The Clinical Investigation Facility carries out accurate biological sample collection and specialized testing in collaboration with the Biochemical Disease Laboratory. It also provides an ideal setting for clinical observation and dietary control. Children with other disorders, including fibrocystic disease, coeliac disease, and renal and endocrine diseases, also utilize this facility.

The clinical team includes a physician, a dietician, and a nurse. The dietician is involved in teaching the dietary prescription to the parents, assessing their ability to manage the diet, and ensuring that the dietary recommendations fall within the social, economic, and cultural boundaries of the families. The nurse assists in the planning of diagnostic tests and their interpretation to parents. Following the diagnostic phase, the nurse assists the family in establishing the treatment program, gradually transferring the care and treatment to the parents. The nurse serves as the co-ordinator of discharge plans and follow-up visits.

After the diagnosis is established and treatment instituted, the next concern is the genetic nature of the condition. The nature of the genetic transmission, its recurrence risk, and the implications for other family members are explained by the consultant geneticist. Approximately sixty inborn errors of metabolism can be diagnosed prenatally using amniocentesis and a biochemical measurement of the altered gene product in fibroblasts grown from the foetus. Therapeutic abortion is an option, which families may prefer, rather than having a second affected child, particularly when there is no effective therapy for the condition.

The distribution of the dietary products for treatment of metabolic disorders continued at Woodlands until 1988, when it was transferred to the British Columbia Children's Hospital and amalgamated with the existing Specialized Products Distribution Centre.

Retrospective studies of the offspring of women with PKU who were untreated during pregnancy have shown a high incidence of mental retardation and congenital anomalies (17). These defects have also been found less frequently in infants of treated mothers with normal intelligence or with mild hyperphenylalanaemia. It is important, therefore, to find and treat these women before conception. A register of all females with PKU is kept, and their family physicians are advised of the possibility of pregnancy resulting in increased phenylalanine blood levels and brain damage to the infant. Parents and their children are also advised that any females at risk must resume the low phenylalanine diet during the pregnancy.

COMMENT

The provincial Biochemical Disease Program, with associated screening, diagnostic, and treatment services, is a population-based program for newborn infants and a follow-up program for those with genetic metabolic diseases. The costs of the screening program, and later of the investigations in the Biochemical Disease Program and the ongoing treatment in the Clinical Investigation Facility, were accepted as insurance benefits by the Hospital Insurance Service in response to the recommendations of the paediatric community in Vancouver and Victoria. Further costs of additional screening programs were accepted later.

There is general acceptance of the cost effectiveness of neonatal screening programs for PKU, congenital hypothyroidism, and galactosaemia. The value of routine screening for other metabolic diseases, however, is controversial because of the low incidence of these diseases and the lack of effective treatment.

The PKU screening began in the mid-1960s, and a generation of early treated intelligent women with hyperphenylalanaemia has resulted. The ongoing collaborative study in Canada and the United States is designed to develop an appropriate approach to the management of maternal PKU that allows these women to have healthy children with normal intelligence. There are seventeen accredited centres for the treatment of PKU in Canada, and each centre can provide appropriate nutritional advice and monitoring to control serum levels of phenylalanine (17). The management of maternal PKU has recently been reviewed (18) and includes pre-pregnancy counselling, testing of father for carrier status, and restarting of diet. By the year 2000, all women with phenylalanaemia will have been born after the introduction of neonatal screening. It will then theoretically be possible to prevent this cause of mental retardation. The importance of advising patients with PKU and their parents of this issue is crucial.

REFERENCES

1. TISCHLER, B., GIBSON, W. C., MCGEER, E. G., and NUTALL, J. Degrees of mental retardation in phenylketonuria. *American Journal of Mental Deficiencies* 65 (1961): 726–38.
2. GUTHRIE, R. and SUSI, A. A simple phenylalanine method for the detection of phenylketonuria in large populations of newborn infants. *Pediatrics* 32 (1963): 338–43.
3. Children's Hospital Biochemical Diseases Program. *B.C.'s Children* 4:2 (1980).
4. LOWRY, R. B., TISCHLER, B., COCKCROFT, W. H., and RENWICK, D.H.G. Incidence of phenylketonuria in British Columbia, 1950–1971. *Canadian Medical Association Journal* 106 (1972): 1299–1302.
5. Report of the Task Force established to study the problem of screening for inborn errors of Metabolism in the Neonatal and Perinatal Periods, 1974. Mimeographed document.
6. BRITISH COLUMBIA. *Eighteenth Annual Report*, B.C. Hospital Insurance Service, January 1–December 31, 1966.
7. GILLESPIE, A. E. Letter to the Editor. *B.C.'s Children* 4:3 (1980).
8. APPLEGARTH, D. A., HARDWICK, D. F., ISRAELS, S., and ROSS, P. M. Results of a screening program for amino acidopathies in British Columbia. *B.C. Medical Journal* 12 (1970): 129–32.
9. WONG, L.T.R., HARDWICK, D. A., APPLEGARTH, D. A., and DAVIDSON, A.F.G. Review of Metabolic Screening Program of Children's Hospital, Vancouver, British Columbia, 1971–77. *Clinical Biochemistry* 12:5 (1979): 167–72.
10. HARDWICK, D. F. Current status of development of newborn screening programs in B.C. (letter to the editor). *B.C. Medical Journal* 21 (1979): 185.

11. KIRBY, L. T., NORMAN, M. G., APPLEGARTH, D. A., and HARDWICK, D. F. Screening of newborn infants for galactosaemia in British Columbia. *Canadian Medical Association Journal* 132 (1985): 1033–35.
12. NORMAN, M. G. Congenital hypothyroidism. *B.C. Medical Journal* 30:3 (March 1988): 201.
13. GELPKE, P. M. Newborn screening. *B.C. Medical Journal* 31 (1989): 386.
14. APPLEGARTH, D., personal communication, 1989.
15. DAVIDSON, A.G.F., personal communication, 1988.
16. NORMAN, M. G. Changes in neonatal screening programs. *B.C. Medical Journal* 24 (1982): 374.
17. HANLEY, W. B. and BELL, L. Maternal phenylketonuria: Finding and treating women before conception (editorial). *Canadian Medical Association Journal* 126 (1982): 1259–60.
18. CLARSON, C. L. and STRANGE, N. Maternal phenylketonuria. *Canadian Pediatric Quarterly* (Fall 1990): 219–21.

Services for Children with Cancer

HISTORICAL CONSIDERATIONS

Introduction

A recent review article by a respected Canadian physician (1) traces the development of the treatment of cancer. He noted that the limits of operative excision of cancer had been defined by 1940 and that further progress was related to refinement in techniques, improved assessment of the extent of disease, and better pre- and post-operative care. After the discovery of X-rays, radiotherapy was established, and its effectiveness against certain types of cancer was known by 1940. Since then, radiation methods have been perfected with the invention of the cobalt unit and linear accelerator. Thus surgery and radiotherapy made the initial important contributions to the treatment of cancer in the first half of this century.

The medical treatment of cancer began with the demonstration that nitrogen mustard gases and the leaves of the periwinkle (vinca rosea) were effective against some neoplasms. In 1948, Farber and colleagues (2) described the use of aminopterin, an antifolate drug, that produced temporary remissions in acute lymphatic leukaemia in children. Subsequent developments that have improved the overall results of treatment include the use of a combination of drugs (e.g., mustard, oncovine, prednisone, procarbazine [MOPP]), the integration of chemotherapy and radiotherapy, the advances in diagnostic technology, including computer tomography and magnetic resonance imaging (MRI), and coincidental improvements in surgical techniques. Finally, the first bone marrow transplants were performed in the 1950s and allogenic transplants were introduced in the 1960s (3). Doses of radiation and chemotherapy that eradicate the leukaemia or tumour also cause marrow aplasia unless new marrow cells are given to the patient.

There is relatively little overlap in the profile of cancer in adults and children, and a separate specialty of paediatric oncology has emerged. There have been dramatic advances in paediatric oncology during the past forty years (4). Even thirty years ago acute leukaemia was uniformly fatal and temporary remissions could not be maintained. Current treatment produces 70 percent survival rates seven years after the cessation of treatment. Progress in the treatment of solid tumours has been impressive with the introduction of chemotherapy after surgery and radiation.

Advances in paediatric radiotherapy in the last ten years (5) have been attributed to five factors: first, the improved localization of the tumour and the reduced damage to surrounding tissues; second, the recognition of the interplay between radiation and chemotherapy; third, the greater use of irradiation as systemic treatment for cancer; fourth, the use of co-operative group trials to define the role of irradiation; and fifth, the reduction in the late effects of irradiation.

There has also been a marked increase in the intensity of therapy exemplified by five new strategies (6). These are:

1. The Goldie Coldman theory, which postulates that multiple drug resistance can be prevented by "front loaded," first time treatment strategy with as many effective agents and in the highest dosage possible. This applies to a number of childhood tumours, including non-Hodgkin's lymphoma, Hodgkin's disease, brain tumours, and osteosarcoma.

2. Drug delivery devices: venous access devices greatly facilitate chemotherapy in children and infants and have made feasible continuous infusions and multidrug regimes.

3. Prolonged continuous infusions of high dose drugs have been shown to be more effective for several drugs (e.g., methotrexate). The toxicity has been found to be lessened in some drugs with the infusion approach (e.g., antiracyclines).

4. Duration of chemotherapy: many cancers in infants and children require chemotherapy for up to three years. The tumours that require less or more time are gradually being identified.

5. Measures of compliance: plasma drug profiles of different agents are correlated with therapeutic efficacy and toxicity. Problems with compliance have been noted in the adolescent age group.

Children tolerate the adverse effects of chemotherapy better than adults. The growing child, however, may be more vulnerable than the adult to long term sequelae of chemotherapy. There is concern about the effects on behavioural, psychological, and intellectual functions; growth;

endocrine states, and fertility; teratogenic effects in offspring; and second malignancies. Continuous surveillance is essential, but the benefits are well worth the potential risks.

Development of Services in British Columbia

In the early 1930s, the British Columbia Medical Association, concerned that "little was being done on a provincial level to counter the problem" formed a Cancer Committee, which took the lead in developing diagnostic and therapeutic services for cancer in British Columbia (7, 8, 9). Their concept was of a fully equipped central clinic and smaller diagnostic centres in British Columbia. The British Columbia Cancer Foundation[1] was formed as a fund-raising arm in 1935. The foundation conducted a successful fund-raising campaign, followed by the purchase of radium, and of therapeutic X-ray equipment and founded the British Columbia Cancer Institute (BCCI) in Vancouver in 1938. Dr. Max Evans was appointed director and a clinic was started. Full-time specialists were appointed, and services were available to all citizens upon referral by private physician. Patients were expected to pay if able to do so. In 1948, the foundation opened a diagnostic clinic at the Royal Jubilee Hospital in Victoria. This was expanded to include treatment facilities in 1951 and a cobalt unit in 1963 (10).

The British Columbia Division of the Canadian Cancer Society was formed in 1938 and provided funds for transportation and living expenses for needy patients. During the 1940s, the division worked closely with the British Columbia Cancer Foundation and BCCI in the development of education and research. Dr. H. F. Batho was appointed physicist to BCCI to initiate research.

In the late 1940s, a fourteen-bed boarding home was acquired adjacent to BCCI and consultation clinics were started in Penticton, Vernon, Kelowna, and Kamloops.

In the mid-1940s, Dr. Ralston Paterson, at the Holt Radium Institute, Manchester, was brought to Vancouver to advise on future expansion. Likewise, Dr. S. T. Cantril, director of the Tumour Clinic at Swedish Hospital in Seattle, was invited to British Columbia. In 1948, when federal health grants were introduced, the provincial government asked the foundation to outline a program for the diagnosis and treatment of cancer in the province. Dr. O. H. Warwick, executive director of the National Cancer Institute in Toronto, conducted a survey of all services and facilities in British Columbia (11). His report recommended that the British Columbia Cancer Foundation be made the agent of the Health Branch, Depart-

---

1 In 1967, the name was changed to the British Columbia Cancer Treatment and Research Foundation.

ment of Health and Welfare for the care of the cancer patients in this province. Other recommendations included professional and lay education, free diagnostic biopsy services, regional consultative services, specialization in cancer surgery, a central radiotherapy service, and coordination of records and follow-up of all centres interested in the diagnosis and treatment of cancer under the direction of the Division of Vital Statistics. The plan was approved by the Department of Health and Welfare and the foundation was officially designated the agency through which the cancer program for the province would be implemented (12).

With the growth of the clinic at BCCI, a tunnel was built to connect the clinic with the adjacent Vancouver General Hospital, and thirty hospital beds were set aside for patients attending BCCI. In 1952, the old clinic was redesigned, and, in 1955, a thirty-six-bed hospital was opened at BCCI. In 1965, a floor was added increasing capacity to fifty-four beds, and BCCI was designated a hospital facility by the Hospital Insurance Service, thereby providing hospital insurance coverage to inpatients. In 1966 (13), hospital benefits were extended to cover outpatient radiotherapy and chemotherapy at BCCI and the clinic at the Royal Jubilee Hospital in Victoria. In 1970, the British Columbia Cancer Treatment and Research Foundation operated BCCI and its adjoining hospital, the Victoria Cancer Clinic, and fifteen consultative cancer clinics throughout the province.

The rapid development of radiation technology and chemotherapy during the 1960s ushered in a new phase in cancer care. The Department of Health Services and Hospital Insurance appointed a review committee in 1969, chaired by Dr. D. H. Williams,[2] to study cancer care and control (14). The principal recommendation of the committee was the establishment of a comprehensive, co-ordinated, province-wide cancer control program, with the services to prevent, detect, and treat all forms of cancer.

In October 1974, BCCI was transferred to the province by the British Columbia Cancer Treatment and Research Foundation, and on the same day the institute property was leased for a nominal sum to the Cancer Control Agency of British Columbia (CCABC). The agency was a non-

---

2 The Minister of Health invited this remarkable physician to chair three other major committees as follows: (1) The Committee for the Review of Diagnostic and Surgical Facilities for Heart Surgery in British Columbia with Particular Reference to the City of Victoria. Chairman Dr. D. H. Williams. Submitted to Minister of Health Services and Hospital Insurance, province of British Columbia, 15 September 1962. (2) The Committee for the Review of Diagnostic and Surgical Facilities for Heart Surgery in British Columbia. Chairman Dr. D. H. Williams. Second report, submitted to the Minister of Health Services and Hospital Insurance, province of British Columbia, February 1966. (3) The Committee for the Review of Intensive Cardiac Care in British Columbia. Chairman Dr. D. H. Williams. Report submitted to the Minister of Health Services and Hospital Insurance, province of British Columbia, 31 January 1969.

profit society created to carry out an expanded province-wide program of cancer care and control (15). An agency board and a thirty-member lay provincial advisory council were established in 1974 (16, 17) to manage BCCI in Vancouver and its Victoria clinic. Dr. Thomas Hall was appointed director of the CCABC (18). A cancer clinic was opened in 1976 at the Royal Inland Hospital in Kamloops to provide regional chemotherapy services and closer co-operation between medical oncologists in the private sector in Vernon, Kelowna, Penticton, and Vancouver. The various aspects of the services have been described (19, 20, 21). In 1989, the name of the agency was changed to the British Columbia Cancer Agency (BCCA).

The Tri-University Meson Facility (TRIUMF) accelerator went into operation at the University of British Columbia in 1974, making available in Canada a beam of negative pimesons for nuclear physics research. A biomedical facility (the Batho Biomedical Laboratory) was sponsored jointly by the British Columbia Cancer Treatment and Research Foundation and the federal Health Resources Fund (22) to evaluate this new particle in radiation therapy of cancer. The preclinical and clinical studies have been described (23).

All radiotherapy is carried out in the BCCA clinics in Vancouver and Victoria plus the TRIUMF facility in Vancouver (24). The advantage of this is that the patient has the benefit of centralized, well equipped, multidisciplinary advice and care. Radiation oncologists advise on investigation and initial management of newly diagnosed cancers, working in teams with individual clinical subspecialty physicians.

The consultative clinics named Outreach (25) comprised twenty clinics in British Columbia and one in Yukon. They have been renamed the Community Oncology Program. They are conducted by staff physicians of BCCA together with regional oncologists in private practice providing service in local communities in line with defined treatment policies. In addition, a regional pharmacy service was established.

In 1984, a new facility was opened with full ambulatory and diagnostic services and 100 beds was opened. It was named the A. Maxwell Evans Clinic. The British Columbia Cancer Registry, formerly part of the Health Surveillance Registry, which was transferred to BCCA in 1979, attempts to document every cancer case diagnosed in the population of British Columbia. The uses of the registry have been described (26).

Development of Paediatric Services in British Columbia

The introduction of chemotherapy, and recognition of the fact that the combination of radiotherapy and chemotherapy enhanced survival, led to the discussions between Dr. J. F. McCreary, professor of paediatrics at the University of British Columbia and Dr. Max Evans, director of BCCI, regarding the care of children with cancer. Paediatric clinics were instituted in the late 1960s in the outpatient department of the Health Centre for Children of the Vancouver General Hospital by Dr. Mavis Teasdale in collaboration with the radiotherapy oncologists and chemotherapy nurses from BCCI. A satellite clinic was subsequently started in Victoria in 1976 with local paediatricians and a paediatric oncologist or radiotherapist from the British Columbia Children's Hospital in Vancouver attending every two months. The Paediatric Oncology Service was transferred to the new British Columbia Children's Hospital in 1982.

The low prevalence of cancer in children prompted participation in multicentre clinical trials with the Children's Cancer Study Group, and the treatment protocols of virtually all children have been determined in this way. The progress in paediatric management has been the result of successive controlled clinical trials, which have compared different combinations of surgery, radiotherapy, and chemotherapy. This implies uniform criteria for diagnosis, treatment, and evaluation of outcomes and expertise in all disciplines required for diagnosis, treatment and support to the child and family. This has been possible because the majority of children are referred to major treatment centres.

As a consequence, sophisticated pathology techniques developed rapidly. The paediatric pathologist is not only charged with making the diagnosis but also with recognizing favourable and unfavourable morphologic features in the neoplasm prior to instituting treatment. The prognostic parameters include histologic and cytologic features, chromosomal deletions and/or translocations, and oncogene expression. The paediatric oncologist and pathologist discuss the case before biopsy and resection. Delays may occur before a final diagnosis is possible. Studies such as MRI or computer tomography (CT) may be indicated before biopsy; or immunohistochemical staining or cytogenic study of fresh tumour tissue may be required to define risk groups of different tumours. These are all readily available at the British Columbia Children's Hospital. As chemotherapy was shown to actually cure children with leukaemia, the need for paediatric tertiary care became obvious and was instrumental in placing paediatric oncology services in the British Columbia Children's Hospital, rather than in BCCA. Finally, the psychosocial support services required for these children and their families was the other important determinant in placing the services in the British Columbia Children's Hospital.

PRESENT SERVICES

Policy

The British Columbia Children's Hospital is the tertiary referral centre for children in British Columbia and provides cancer care for children under the auspices of BCCA. The Division of Paediatric Oncology at BCCA has adopted the following policy (27):

1. It is recommended that all patients under the age of 16 who are suspected of having or are diagnosed with malignancy be referred to the British Columbia Children's Hospital for initial evaluation and therapy. All such patients are registered with BCCA.
2. Whenever possible these patients are entered into the Children's Cancer Study Group.
3. After initial evaluation and therapy most patients can be treated in their local community under the supervision of the paediatric oncologist with periodic reassessments at the British Columbia Children's Hospital.
4. A paediatric oncology clinic is operated in Victoria for continued supervision of children on Vancouver Island.
5. A long-term follow-up clinic is conducted weekly at the British Columbia Children's Hospital to evaluate current status and disease and any late sequelae.

Paediatric Services

All children with cancer are registered with BCCA and the British Columbia Children's Hospital. The clinical services, including assessment and treatment, are provided in either the dedicated Oncology Clinic or the inpatient ward. There are currently two beds set aside for bone marrow transplant patients in an area referred to as the third intensive care unit of the hospital. The children are admitted under the care of the paediatric oncologist during hospital stay. There are four paediatric oncologists and two radiation oncologists, together with nursing, social work, and psychology staff. The delegation of patient care to the clinical team, rather than to private paediatric consultants, opened the way for participation in multicentre clinical trials in a way that would not be possible in the private model of medical practice.

This program has given priority to linking the hospital with the community. A clinical nurse specialist has organized a patient/family and staff education program, a school re-entry program, a counselling support program for parents and staff, instruction of home care nurses and staff of the nursing respite program (Chapter 19), and palliative care; and a parent bereavement follow-up program.

An occasional child is admitted to the Vancouver Clinic for surgical removal of a skin lesion. Similarly, some children are transferred to the Vancouver General Hospital to attend the Head and Neck Clinic or admitted for a limb salvage procedure and then returned to the British Columbia Children's Hospital. All radiotherapy is done at BCCA.

The follow-up care, including chemotherapy, is managed either at a community hospital near the child's home in collaboration with a paediatric oncologist at the British Columbia Children's Hospital or at the Oncology Clinic of British Columbia Children's Hospital. The follow-up program is determined by the residence of the patient and the complexity of the treatment. When difficult procedures are required (such as intrathecal methotrexate), the follow-up care is at the Children's Hospital. After the seventeenth birthday, patients are followed in the adult clinic at BCCA. The paediatric team remains in contact until the patient is twenty-one years old.

COMMENT

The need for a population-based approach to cancer treatment was identified by the British Columbia Medical Association in the 1930s and led to the formation of the British Columbia Cancer Foundation and BCCI in Vancouver, a clinic in Victoria and, subsequently, the development of consultative cancer clinics across the province. In 1948, the provincial government asked the British Columbia Cancer Foundation to outline a provincial program for diagnosis and treatment. The consultant recommended that the foundation be made the agent to implement the plan, and this suggestion was officially approved. Again, in the early 1970s, the provincial government appointed a committee to review cancer care, and the report resulted in the transfer of BCCI to a non-profit society, BCCA with a mandate to carry out a provincial program of cancer care and control. This approach recognized the need for both personal and population medicine in the management of cancer. The inpatient and the ambulatory services at BCCA qualified as benefits of the national hospital and medical insurance programs.

The services for children were developed along with the adult program, but the low prevalence of cancer in this age group and the complexity and intensity of modern care have limited the development of regional clinics to Victoria. In contrast to all other age groups, paediatric care, with the exception of radiotherapy, is based at the British Columbia Children's Hospital rather than the Vancouver Clinic. It is noteworthy that the British Columbia Cancer Registry conducts an active follow-up of all patients. Further evaluation of outcomes is conducted by the Children's Cancer Study Group.

REFERENCES

1. WHITELAW, D. M. Cancer in this century. *B.C. Medical Journal* 30 (1988): 31–34.
2. FARBER, S., DIAMOND, K., MERCER, R. D., et al. Temporary remission in acute leukemia in children produced by folic acid antagonist and aminopterol-glutamic acid (aminopterin). *New England Journal of Medicine* 238 (1948): 787–93.
3. QUINN, J. J. Bone marrow transplantation in the management of childhood cancer. The Pediatric Clinics of North America. *Symposium on Pediatric Oncology* 32:3 (June 1985): 811–27.
4. HAMMOND, G. D. The cure of childhood cancers. *Supplement to Cancer* 58:2 (15 July 1986): 407–13.
5. FRYER, C.J.H. Advances in pediatric radiotherapy in the last ten years and future proposals. *Cancer* 58, Suppl. (15 July 1986): 554–60.
6. BLEYER, W. A. Cancer chemotherapy in infants and children. The Pediatric Clinics of North America. *Symposium on Pediatric Oncology* 32:3 (June 1985): 557–74.
7. STRONG, G. F. President's Annual Report of the Vancouver Medical Association. *Vancouver Medical Association Bulletin* 7 (1931): 197–202.
8. ELLIOT, G.R.F. and MCDONNELL, C. E. Profile: Dr. T.H. "Harry" Milburn. *B.C. Medical Journal* 26 (1984): 687–89.
9. MCDONNELL, C. E. Dr. G. F. Strong. *Annuals Royal College of Physicians and Surgeons Canada* 22:6 (1989): 411–14.
10. ROSE, T. F. *From Shaman to Modern Medicine. A Century of the Healing Arts in British Columbia.* Vancouver: Mitchell Press, 1972, Chapter 22, Cancer, pp. 141–2.
11. WARWICK, O. H. Care of the Cancer Patient, With Special Reference to the Province of British Columbia. Summarized in G.R.F. Elliot, *Survey of Health Services and Facilities in British Columbia in Existence on Dec. 31, 1948.* Health Branch, Department of Health and Welfare, British Columbia, 1952, pp. 34–5.
12. *Annual Report.* British Columbia Cancer Treatment and Research Foundation, 1969.
13. BRITISH COLUMBIA. Order-in-Council 2298, 1966.
14. Report of the Committee for the Review of Cancer Care in British Columbia, 1970. D. H. Williams, Chairman.
15. *Twenty-sixth Annual Report*, British Columbia Hospital Insurance Service, January 1–December 31, 1974.
16. June 1 target date for Cancer Agency. *B.C. Medical Journal* 16 (1974): 148.
17. Cancer Control Agency of B.C. *B.C. Medical Journal* 18 (1976): 370.
18. Doctors in the news. *B.C. Medical Journal* 17 (1975): 130.
19. CHRITCHLEY, J. H. Cancer services and the Cancer Control Agency of B.C. *B.C. Medical Journal* 29 (1987): 393.

20. BASCO, V. Plans and predictions for Cancer Control Agency of B.C. *B.C. Medical Journal* 30 (1988): 13.

21. NELEMS, W. Lung cancer: The ongoing challenge (guest editorial). *B.C. Medical Journal* 29 (1987): 589.

22. TRIUMF Accelerator scheduled for early 1974. *B.C. Medical Journal* 15 (1973): 169.

23. GOODMAN, G. B., BOWEN, J. L., DIXON, P., GAFFNEY, C., OGAWA, Y., POMEROY, M., RHEAUME, D., SAITO, T., SHIRATO, H., and VERNIMMEN, F. Pimeson Radiotherapy at TRIUMF. *J. Jpn. Soc. Ther. Radiol. Oncol.* 2:2 (June 1990): 85–99.

24. GOODMAN, G. B., SKARSGARD, L. D., and LaBROOY, M. TRIUMF Pion Therapy. *B.C. Medical Journal* 29 (1987): 394.

25. BECK, R. E. Outreach in B.C. *B.C. Medical Journal* 29 (1987): 403.

26. BOYES, D. A., BAIRD, P. R., and McBRIDE, N. Medical uses of a cancer registry (editorial). *B.C. Medical Journal* 29 (1987): 27.

27. *Cancer Treatment Policies. Cancer Control Agency of B.C.*, 3d ed. Cancer Control Agency of British Columbia, 1988, p. 385.

Children with Chronic Physical Illness

INTRODUCTION

In addition to the children with mental handicaps and developmental disabilities such as cerebral palsy, there is a third group with chronic physical illness whose needs challenge the health care system. This group includes a large number of relatively uncommon diseases such as juvenile diabetes, rheumatoid arthritis, asthma, spina bifida, cleft palate, craniofacial anomalies, congenital heart disease, leukaemia, haemophilia, cystic fibrosis, and muscular dystrophy, to list a few of the better known conditions. The authors of the *Vanderbilt University Study of Chronically Ill Children* (1) emphasized that many issues faced by these children and their families are similar and serve to separate them from their healthy contemporaries. Some of the similarities include the sustained burden on the child and family, the high cost of care, the uncertain course, often with premature death, treatments that are strenuous and often painful, the need for integration and continuity of medical care, and the importance of helping families cope with difficulties and uncertainties associated with chronic diseases. It has been suggested that these issues justify addressing severe chronic illness in childhood as a class for purposes of public policy formation.

In British Columbia, the majority of children with these chronic illnesses are managed by the private model of medical care (personal medicine) in either private offices or hospital outpatient clinics. In the hospital setting, other health professionals (e.g., nurses, social workers, psychologists, therapists, etc.) are usually available when needed for consultation. The link with the child's family and local community is through the final report to the family physician from the clinic physician, with additional reports from other staff members when they are involved.

In a minority of chronic illnesses, usually of low prevalence, often associated with several other disabilities and sometimes high technology, a more structured ambulatory program has evolved at the British

Columbia Children's Hospital, which provides a population-based service for the province. This approach has been adopted for children with cancer (Chapter 8), arthritis, haemophilia, diabetes and other endocrine diseases, chronic gastrointestinal diseases, chronic renal failure, biochemical diseases, fibrocystic disease, meningomyelocele, cleft palate and craniofacial anomalies, and visual impairment.

In these latter programs, the core staff either work together in dedicated space or gather in a multipurpose ambulatory clinic area once weekly. Hospital clerical staff handle clinic-related correspondence. When children are admitted to hospital, the program staff are involved in the inpatient care and in discharge planning. Nurse practitioners play a key role in planning and co-ordinating patient visits, in teaching patient and parent about the child's illness, including the preparation of written materials, and, when necessary, in providing advice and support by telephone between clinic visits.

These more structured programs began in the 1960s and expanded significantly following the enactment of the provincial *Medical Services Act* (2) in 1968, when sessional fees became available to employ physicians in the hospital-based programs.

In this chapter, the programs for this subgroup of children with chronic physical illness are described.

PRESENT SERVICES

Arthritis

A children's arthritis clinic was started in 1960 at the G. F. Strong Rehabilitation Centre in Vancouver and represented the paediatric program of the Canadian Arthritis and Rheumatism Society (3, 4). The clinic moved in 1969 to the Arthritis Centre, which was designated as a rehabilitation hospital and eligible for funding by the British Columbia Hospital Insurance Service. Outpatient services to patients with arthritis and rheumatism were funded in 1972 (5). With the opening of the British Columbia Children's Hospital in 1982, a weekly arthritis clinic was instituted in that setting.

Each child and family is assessed by a team comprised of a paediatrician, social worker, physiotherapist, and occupational therapist. The extent to which ongoing care is carried on by the family physician or the clinic is negotiable. The clinic, in contrast to private consultants, assumes the prerogative of recalling patients for follow-up.

Haemophilia

A clinic for children with haemophilia was started in 1968 and moved into the Arthritis Centre the following year. The introduction of this program coincided with the new technology (cryoprecipitated factor viii and other factor viii and factor ix concentrates) to prevent and arrest bleeding episodes. These replacement agents are administered at home under the general supervision of a nurse co-ordinator. The program provides education regarding home management for the prevention and treatment of bleeding episodes.

Trend analysis of inpatient hospital utilization by these children from 1966 to 1983 strongly suggested that the new technology, co-ordinated through the haemophilia program, accounted for reduced inpatient admissions (6).

Diabetes and Other Endocrine Illnesses

The Division of Endocrinology operates diabetic and other endocrine programs in a dedicated facility in the ambulatory area, where offices for physicians, nurses, dieticians, social workers, and clinical staff are located. The unit includes a testing room where various loading tests are conducted during the assessment process, thereby eliminating hospital admissions. The programs exist to assist the family physician or paediatrician in case management, and children are followed for review on a regular basis until sixteen years of age. The physicians provide twenty-four-hour coverage for patient care and, with other staff, attend patients in the outpatient area, the Emergency Department, or the inpatient ward as required.

The nursing role includes the pre-planning of patient visits, extensive teaching to the child and the parents about the nature and treatment of the child's illness, backed up by written information to take home, and discharge planning, including, when necessary, a letter for parents to give to the staff of the local hospital in case of emergency describing the child's problem and specifying required treatment (e.g., for hypoglycaemia). Formal or informal conferences conclude each visit, and a report of the visit is written by the physician, with copies going to the local health unit, school, etc.

Biochemical Disease Program/Fibrocystic and Liver Disease

The children identified by the Newborn Biochemical Screening Program are referred to the Biochemical Disease Program for diagnostic study and treatment (Chapter 7). The case load includes children with PKU, galactosaemia, and homocystinuria. In addition, the program, in collaboration with a clinic in Victoria, oversees the management of virtually all children with fibrocystic disease and liver disease. In 1975, an adult fibrocystic disease clinic was started, which follows over seventy-five adults.

Chronic Gastrointestinal Disease

There is a very limited number of children with chronic inflammatory bowel disease or other pathology who require total parenteral nutrition (TPN) on an indefinite basis. In contrast, there is a sizeable population of children (approximately thirty) who require TPN for one to several months before they are able to survive on enteral feeds. About half of these children are in the special care nursery (SCN); the remainder are either graduates of the SCN (post-surgical bowel loss) or acutely ill children including cardiac post-operative, oncology patients receiving bone marrow transplants, or chronic gastrointestinal disease. The former group is decreasing, the latter increasing. The neonatologists in the SCN care for the neonatal group, and another paediatrician supervises the remainder. Two nurses are employed to monitor nutritional input, bio-chemical status, infection hazards, etc., for all patients on TPN. The nutritional supplements are provided free of charge (Chapter 3). There is also a nurse for enteral feeds and the home care program.

Chronic Renal Disease

A program to provide treatment of children with end stage renal disease was initiated at the Vancouver General Hospital to provide dialysis (1966) and transplantation (1968). The program moved to the British Columbia Children's Hospital in 1982.

The staff includes two paediatricians, three surgeons (two urologists and one vascular surgeon), a clinical nurse specialist, a dialysis nurse, a dietician, and a social worker, in addition to the nursing staff of the in-patient ward (Clinical Investigation Facility).

The facilities include use of multipurpose offices in the ambulatory area, hospital beds in the Clinical Investigation Facility, and an adjacent haemodialysis unit.

The services include assessment in the outpatient or inpatient unit and dialysis and transplantation. Home peritoneal dialysis is used for younger children, including newborn infants. Haemodialysis is less com-mon than in earlier years, as transplantation procedures have increased.

Nursing staff educate parents in the basics of dialysis and train them in peritoneal dialysis at home. Likewise, they educate parents about transplantation and prepare them for the procedure, post-operative die-tary therapy, and the use of immunosuppressant drugs. A staff member also visits the child's school to explain the health-related issues to the teachers.

The children are followed up on a regular basis until twenty years of age, when they are transferred to an adult program either at Vancouver General or St. Paul's Hospital.

British Columbia Transplant Society: This society was formed by the provincial government in 1985 to integrate and supervise all solid organ transplant facilities in the province, and to ensure the subsequent care of these recipients. The multiorgan transplant program includes procedures for kidney, heart, lung, heart-lung, liver, and pancreas.

The organ retrieval program deals with organ procurement and donation. The Pacific Organ Retrieval and Transplantation (PORT) program is a provincially funded organization for organ donation in British Columbia. Transplant co-ordinators are on call twenty-four hours a day, seven days a week. The objectives of the PORT program are to increase the supply of kidneys and other organs for transplantation, to maximize the use of these organs through efficient co-ordination, and to increase both public and medical awareness.

In 1988, the British Columbia Transplant Society assumed funding responsibility for the distribution of immunosuppressant drugs to transplant patients throughout British Columbia. Drugs are provided to patients free of charge. The society has developed ambulatory care facilities for long-term follow-up in the major hospital regions of the province. In this setting, patients are followed conjointly by the transplant team and the medical director of the relevant regional transplant clinic. A common format for clinical and laboratory data is employed to facilitate rapid exchange of information throughout the transplant program and to permit computerization of all salient data.

Meningomyelocele

This provincial program was introduced in Vancouver Children's Hospital in 1971 to foster early identification and intervention and includes early assessment by a multidisciplinary team, early closure of the wound, and early insertion of a cerebrovascular shunt. The multidisciplinary team includes a full-time nurse co-ordinator, part-time secretary, social worker, and physio- and occupational therapists. The medical staff includes two paediatricians, a child psychiatrist, paediatric neurosurgeon, orthopaedist, and urologist. Parent education in bowel and bladder training are managed by short admission to the Care by Parent Unit at the British Columbia Children's Hospital.

A similar program was started in Victoria in 1978. The introduction of the programs has reduced utilization of hospital inpatient days, probably in large measure due to improved co-ordination of care (5). An adult program for graduates is under development.

Cleft Palate and Craniofacial Programs

The Cleft Palate Program was started in the outpatient department of the Health Centre for Children of the Vancouver General Hospital in the late 1960s and moved to the Children's Hospital in 1970. The program's mandate is to provide a multidisciplinary assessment and follow-up of children with clefts of the lip or palate. Related problems such as hypernasal speech without clefting are also seen. The Craniofacial Program (7) developed within the Cleft Palate Program and provides the same multidisciplinary assessment and follow-up for children with various facial anomalies and syndromes associated with craniostenosis (such as Apert, Crouzon, and Pfeiffer syndromes). Both teams operate from the British Columbia Children's Hospital.

The cleft palate team comprises a paediatrician, orthodontists, plastic surgeons, otologist, half-time community health nurse, part-time speech and language pathologist, social worker, and audiologist, all of whom are available to provide ongoing monitoring and support in their areas of skill and to discuss treatment needs with the full team. Consultations with other specialists (cardiology, genetics, etc.) are arranged at the Children's Hospital.

The cleft palate surgery is performed at the British Columbia Children's Hospital by a limited number of plastic surgeons associated with the program. Oral surgeons are not involved in this program, much to their displeasure. In contrast, orthodontic care is provided in the child's home community, and this service is paid for by the Medical Services Plan of British Columbia. Similarly, speech therapy is provided in the child's home community. A similar program is available at the Queen Alexandra Hospital for children in Victoria.

The craniofacial team draws on the above staff and is augmented by the addition of ophthalmic and neurosurgeons. These children experience cognitive and psychosocial developmental problems during the school years; hence, a psychologist forms part of the regular team. A parent support group, Parents of Children with Apert Syndrome, has been formed, as has a provincial chapter of the national program, About Face. The craniofacial surgery is performed by a surgical team at the British Columbia Children's Hospital.

These programs serve British Columbia and the Yukon. Children in the southern half of Vancouver Island are usually seen in the Cleft Palate Program in Victoria.

Visual Impairment

The sudden epidemic of retinopathy of prematurity in the late 1940s and early 1950s prompted the Canadian National Institute for the Blind (CNIB) to develop supportive services for young, visually impaired infants and children and their families. Miss Eileen Scott, a primary teacher and social worker, was employed and devoted her professional career to these children. She provided parent counselling and an infant development program twenty years before the Infant Development Program became generally available to children with developmental disabilities (Chapter 14). Dr. Howard Mallek, an ophthalmologist, and Dr. Peter Spohn, a paediatrician at St. Paul's Hospital, Vancouver, which housed the first premature nursery in British Columbia, were actively involved in the late 1940s and 1950s (8) and referred all affected neonates to the CNIB.

In the early 1960s, the staff at the CNIB and the Department of Paediatrics, Faculty of Medicine, University of British Columbia, began to work together in the care and management of visually impaired children, and in 1970 the Visually Impaired Program was established at the Children's Hospital in Vancouver to deal with the complex problems of blind children (9). A multidiscipline team, which included a social worker at the CNIB, was formed.

The program has been modified over the years and now accepts a wide array of visual problems, co-ordinates consultations with other experts, and plans habilitation in association with the CNIB and the teacher of the child. The method of operation of the Visually Impaired Program has recently been described (10).

In addition to the assessment and follow-up role, the Visually Impaired Program has been an active advocate on behalf of the children, improving community services, and parent education. The team has published a book for parents (11) and has also been active in research, both in the prevalence and aetiology of visual impairment and in the study of many ocular and visual cortical lesions.

The provincial residential school for the blind was closed in 1978, and the children were integrated into the school system near their homes. The Ministry of Education appointed a provincial co-ordinator for visually impaired children to assist school districts and agencies in the provision of services. A provincial resource centre is available to lend specialized equipment and instructional material. The regular classroom teacher is aided by an itinerant teacher. The provincial Infant Development Program, which serves the under three year age group, is also actively involved in the early development of these children, and, when multiple handicaps are present, the children may also attend the local child development centre.

COMMENT

The Hall Commission (12) recommended the development of outpatient services as one of the principal means of lowering or controlling health care and particularly hospital costs. This notion was very attractive to those involved in paediatric care because of the undesirable side effects of hospitalization on children. The federal *Hospital Insurance and Diagnostic Service Act* (13) (1957) provided inpatient services in acute hospitals and, at the option of the provinces, care could be provided in insured outpatient programs. In British Columbia, a few ambulatory hospital-based programs were in operation (e.g., Cerebral Palsy, at the G. F. Strong Rehabilitation Centre, and preschool deaf programs, at the Health Centre for Children) before 1960, subsidized by federal health grants and voluntary societies. The prevailing notion was that hospital outpatient services were designed for the sick poor (public patients). A paediatric arthritis clinic was started in 1960 and outpatient cancer therapy in 1966. The advent of the provincial Medical Services Plan in 1968 was the key that opened the door part way to hospital-based ambulatory care of children with chronic physical illness by providing payment of the physician or surgeon for services provided in the ambulatory setting. Both salaried and sessional fees were paid by the Medical Services Commission, and care in hospital-based clinics became available to all children regardless of family incomes. This put an end to the public clinic and ward for the "public" or medically indigent patients. Subsequently, the *Established Programs Financing Act* (14) (see Chapter 2) in 1977 promoted the utilization of ambulatory service in place of more costly inpatient facilities, and clerical and other health professional staff became eligible for hospital insurance benefits (see Chapter 3).

The introduction of population-based, structured, medical day-care programs for the different groups of children with chronic physical disease, though slow to show, has been one of the most successful outcomes in British Columbia of national health insurance. Furthermore, in a number of instances, it has been associated with reduced utilization of inpatient beds by the relevant child population (haemophilia and meningomyelorate), largely because of improved co-ordinating of services and compliance (15).

REFERENCES

1. HOBBS, N., PERRIN, J. M., and IREYS, H. T. *Chronically Ill Children and their Families. Problems, Prospects and Proposals from the Vanderbilt Study.* San Francisco: Jossey-Bass, 1985.
2. *Medical Services Act*, S.B.C. 1967, c. 24.
3. WALKER, P. F. and HILL, R. H. Children's arthritis programme. *Journal of the Canadian Physiotherapy Association* 20 (1968): 1–3.
4. HILL, R. H. Children's arthritis programme in British Columbia. *Arthritis and Rheumatism* 20 (1977): 602–603.
5. BRITISH COLUMBIA. Order-in-Council 4110, 1972.
6. MORRIS, S. M., BARER, M. L., ROBINSON, G. C., and EVANS, R. G. *Final Report.* The Impact of Paediatric Hospital-based Medical Day Care Services on Paediatric Hospital Utilization in British Columbia, 1966–1983/84, December 1987.
7. STEPHENSON, J. M. Congenital craniofacial deformities. *B.C. Medical Journal* 32 (1990): 534–35.
8. MALLEK, H. and SPOHN, P. Retrolental fibroplasia. *Canadian Medical Association Journal* 63 (1950): 586–88.
9. JAN, J. E., ROBINSON, G. C., and SCOTT, E. P. A multidisciplinary approach to the problems of the multi-handicapped blind child. *Canadian Medical Association Journal* 109 (1973): 705–707.
10. JAN, J. E. and ROBINSON, G. C. A multi-disciplinary program for visually impaired children and youths. *International Ophthalmology Clinics* 29:1 (1989): 33–36.
11. SCOTT, E. P., JAN, J. E., and FREEMAN, R. D. *Can't Your Child See?*, 2d ed Austin: Pro-Ed, 1985.
12. CANADA. *Royal Commission on Health Services*, Vol. 1. Ottawa: Queen's Printer, 1964, pp. 54–55.
13. *Hospital Insurance and Diagnostic Services Act*, S.C. 1957, c. 28.
14. *Federal-Provincial Fiscal Arrangements and Established Programs Financing Act*, S.C. 1976–77, c. 10. Subsequently renamed *Federal-Provincial Fiscal Arrangements and Federal Post-Secondary Education and Health Contributions Act*, R.S.C. 1985, c. F-8.
15. ROBINSON, G. C. and CLARKE, H. F. *The Hospital Care of Children*, New York: Oxford University Press, 1980, pp. 131–48.

10

British Columbia Ambulance Services

HISTORICAL CONSIDERATIONS

After World War II, there were five or six private ambulance services in the Greater Vancouver region. They were operated by funeral parlours, voluntary societies, the city of Vancouver (for communicable disease patients), and the fire department. There was no central dispatch system, and often more than one company would answer a call. The accident rate for ambulances was high, and there are reports of collisions between ambulances on the way to the same accident. As a public relations gesture, dinners and poker games were sponsored by one company to encourage physicians and other users to patronize the company. There was no training for ambulance staff. The driver was required to have a chauffeur's licence, but no qualifications were required of the attendant (called a swamper). In the early 1950s, a by-law in Vancouver required two persons per ambulance, each with an industrial first aid certificate.[1]

Carson Smith (2), formerly president of Metropolitan Ambulance Company in Vancouver, and later director of Ambulance Services of the Emergency Health Services Commission, recalls working up to 126 hours per week, with a staff of eight, to run three ambulances on a twenty-four hour a day basis. There is a story that one driver, a patient in the tuberculosis hospital in Vancouver, would sneak out at night to drive the ambulance!

---

1 In 1915, the *Ambulance Act*, 1915 (1), an Act for the protection of workmen engaged in industrial operations, was enacted in British Columbia. This Act required employers operating any mine, camp, construction work, or industry employing more than thirty persons and situated more than six miles from the office of a medical practitioner to provide a person possessing a certificate of competency in first aid to the injured. The Act was repealed as obsolete in 1922.

In the late 1950s, discussions were held to consider merging the companies, and the advantages of a central dispatch system were cited to encourage the smaller companies to participate.

In the 1960s, the need for minimum standards of competence and for training programs was recognized in Canada and the United States. The municipal fire departments began to attend accidents as rescue and safety experts, and the extrication kit (jaws of life) was introduced. In Vancouver, the Metropolitan Ambulance Company started a three-month training school.

In 1973, during the tenure of the New Democratic Party, Dr. R. G. Foulkes, director of the Health Security Program Project (Chapter 3) invited Dr. Peter Ransford, a paediatrician and chairman of the Traffic and Safety Committee, British Columbia Medical Association, to survey all aspects of emergency health services: hospital emergency departments, ambulance and other rescue vehicles, personnel and their training, communications, and capabilities. This also included advising the Department of Health Services and Hospital Insurance in the formulation of standards for emergency vehicles and their attendants, for incorporation into legislation. The report (3) advocated a division of Emergency Medical Services, with identification of regional referral centres and appropriate staff education; a provincially funded ambulance service with training of personnel and province-wide air service; change in the provincial *Medical Practitioners Act* (4) to legalize the tasks performed by the medical attendant staff, and a 911 centralized emergency reporting system throughout the province. This report formed the basis of the current Emergency Health Services Program in British Columbia.

The *Emergency Health Services Act* (5) was enacted in 1974, the Emergency Health Services Commission was appointed to administer the Act, and Ransford was appointed chairman (6). In 1974, the government took over the pre-existing private ambulance services, all of which were losing money, with the exception of the Vancouver Metropolitan Ambulance Company, which was heavily subsidized by the City of Vancouver. Carson Smith and his two partners sold Metropolitan Ambulance Company to the province for one dollar, and their continuing involvement in the service ensured the success of the new project. In 1976, the responsibility for air evacuation was moved from the Canadian Air Force's Air-Sea Rescue Service to the Emergency Health Services Commission (see Chapter 12).

The *Emergency Health Services Act* provided for training in cardiopulmonary resuscitation (CPR) for emergency room hospital staffs all over British Columbia, the development of community disaster planning, and the provision of ambulance services. When the New Democratic Party government was defeated in 1975, the newly elected Social Credit government considered dismantling the Emergency Health Services

Program, but this plan was abandoned when a senior member of the provincial cabinet collapsed at a public meeting and was resuscitated by the attending paramedics. Subsequently, the first two components were discontinued, but the ambulance services and the title, Emergency Health Services, were retained. As a result, a twenty-four hour ambulance service was formed throughout British Columbia. The government program was popular with the ambulance crews because it provided proper training and regular work.

In 1978, the training of police and firemen was moved to the Justice Institute in Vancouver, as was the training of emergency medical attendants with the formation of the Emergency Health Services Academy in 1980. This centralization of training enhanced the respect in which each service held the others.

This chapter describes the organization of the ambulance services and the services available for infants and children.

PRESENT PROGRAM

The Emergency Health Services Commission comprises the British Columbia Ambulance Service and the Registrar of Licences and is accountable to the Assistant Deputy Minister of Institutional Services (see Chapter 3). The Ambulance Service deals with employment conditions and the registrar with professional practice issues.

Five commissioners, including the chairman, comprise the Emergency Health Services Commission and oversee the program. The chairman of the commission is the Deputy Minister of Health.

The Services

The services include standard road ambulance and air evacuation (Air Evac) programs, and both provide pre-hospital and inter-hospital transport. In this way the acutely ill and severely injured receive initial stabilization at the local hospital and are then moved to the referral hospital for further diagnosis and treatment. The Air Evac service uses both government and commercial aircraft. Helicopter service in urban areas is in the planning stages. There are approximately 185 ambulance stations and 376 ambulances in the province, the majority of which are located in small communities. The ambulance chassis is purchased and modified at the Vehicle Modification Depot, which is maintained by the government.

There is one private ambulance company in Vancouver, which functions as a horizontal taxi. It is authorized to move stable patients from hospital to home and to stand by at athletic events. Unlike the British Columbia Ambulance Service, the staff are not authorized to perform any procedures on patients.

Medical Support: There are six medical regional consultants who oversee local medical standards. They monitor the quality of care provided to patients at the community level. There are also five program specific advisors: Emergency Medical Attendants 1 and 2 (EMA-1 and EMA-2); Infant Transport; Paediatric; Air Evac; and Advanced Life Support. A director of medical programs oversees all regional and program advisors.

Levels of Service: There are three levels of medical attendants, referred to as EMA-1, EMA-2, and EMA-3. The EMA-1 are part-time employees, and 2,400 are located throughout the province. The EMA-2 and EMA-3 are both full-time, and there are 550 and 150 in each category. The EMA-3, also referred to as paramedics, are of two types, adult and infant. The adult paramedics are referred to as the Advanced Life Support Team and infant and child paramedics as the Infant Transport Team.

Volume of Service: The transport of infants and children to the British Columbia Children's Hospital is organized in two ways. Preterm and acutely ill newborns are admitted to the Special Care Nursery (SCN), and newborns over 2,500 grams with congenital surgical or cardiac abnormalities, or older children with acute illness or injury, are admitted to either the paediatric Intensive Care Unit (ICU) or the paediatric wards. There are approximately 200 acute (mostly low birthweight [LBW] infants) and 400 reverse (returnees to hospital of origin) newborn transfers per year. There are also 200 high risk maternal transports to Grace Hospital in Vancouver, in which the infant may or may not have been delivered. Finally, there are approximately 300 sick newborns over 2,500 grams or older children with acute illness or injury admitted to the ICU or paediatric wards at the British Columbia Children's Hospital.

Charges: The Emergency Health Services Commission charges ambulance user fees.

Training

The training programs are under medical direction and are developed by the program advisors in co-operation with the anaesthetists, emergency physicians, and neonatologists in several major hospitals in the province. The training centre, the Emergency Health Services Academy, is located in the grounds of the Justice Institute of British Columbia in Vancouver.

EMA-1 and -2 Training: The EMA-1 attendants are recruited from their communities and are trained locally by distance education methods from the academy. In 1989, the academy began teaching part-time staff to the EMA-2 level. The applicants for the EMA-2 must have at least a grade twelve education, an Industrial First Aid Certificate, prior part-time employment in the Ambulance Service, and a clean criminal record. The EMA-2 training is offered at regional centres and at the academy. They receive approximately 350 hours of training in standard ambulance procedures, basic physiology, and emergency techniques. The use of medical anti-shock trousers (MAST), intravenous (IV) therapy, automatic external defibrillation (AED), and nitrous oxide analgesia is included in EMA-2 skills. They are licensed by the Emergency Health Services Commission and currently recertified every five years. After three years of experience, they can apply for the EMA-3 training.

EMA-3 Training: This includes the Advanced Life Support (ALS) and the Infant Transport Team (ITT) and is offered at the academy. The EMA-3 training is one year long for ALS and eighteen months for the ITT. EMA-3 staff use full advanced cardiac life support resuscitation skills, including endotracheal intubation, direct current (DC) defibrillation, and anti-arrythmic drugs. All delegated medical acts are covered under the Act and all staff are insured. A staff training manual for the Infant Transport Team (7) and Paediatric Emergency Transport Booklet (8) are available.

The advanced tactical driving training, which all attendants undertake, was developed in collaboration with the Royal Canadian Mounted Police. The Emergency Health Services Academy publishes a quarterly newsletter (*EHS Mirror*, reflecting British Columbia's Ambulance Service).

Referrals

There are three regional dispatch centres in the province, Vancouver, Victoria, and Kamloops. The Air Evac service is dispatched from a separate provincial dispatch centre in Victoria.

When there is a need for maternal, neonatal, or paediatric transport, the referring physician contacts the designated transport co-ordinator (maternal, neonatal, or paediatric) on call, who in turn co-ordinates all details of transport (7). In all cases, it must be decided whether the infant or child can be cared for at the local level or whether transport to another hospital is required. All hospitals are provided with a booklet that itemizes transport information requirements and the documents to accompany the child.

The transport co-ordinator supervises all inter-hospital transfers and coordinates planning with referring physicians, Provincial Dispatch, the Transport Team, and the British Columbia Children's Hospital. They determine the call priority, the optimal combination of necessary escort personnel, care needs en route, and the appropriate ward on arrival. They also advise on resuscitation needs and stabilization prior to transfer and management by the transport team en route. The complexities and responsibilities of the escort process have recently been reviewed (9).

When the transport team arrives at the referring hospital, the infant or child is reassessed, any appropriate additional tests or procedures are performed, and the transport co-ordinator is contacted and briefed before transfer to the ambulance or aircraft.

The majority of paediatric transports are done by Infant Transport Team personnel. In special situations, a physician, a respiratory therapist, and Air-Evac paramedics may be included. The team works under the supervision of the SCN neonatologist or ICU paediatrician and is in contact with this individual during the transport.

Every effort is made to include a parent on the transport, and, when this is not possible, they are taken aboard to see their child and the general plan of care is explained to them by the transport team. Furthermore, accommodation for parents close to the hospital is always available.

The medical and legal responsibility remains with the sending physician until another physician physically accepts the patient.

COMMENT

The provincial ambulance service is a classic example of a population-based program for all age groups. Special maternal, neonatal, and paediatric teams, including road and air transport, have been developed to provide pre-hospital and inter-hospital medical care.

The stimulus for planning the Emergency Health Services came from the provincial government. A concern for the need for a comprehensive emergency health service in British Columbia resulted in the invitation to the chairman of the Traffic and Safety Committee of the British Columbia Medical Association to produce a working paper of the new service. One year later, the *Emergency Health Services Act* was proclaimed, and the Emergency Health Services Commission was formed to administer the Act. The new service was accountable through the Emergency Services Commission to the Deputy Minister of Medical and Institutional Services in the organizational chart of the Ministry of Health.[2] A province-wide ambulance service with a vast improvement in staff training resulted. Undoubtedly the smaller communities, formerly devoid of such service, have benefitted the most.

The continuing success of the ambulance service has been attributed (10) to the legislation (*Health Emergency Act*) providing authority to medical attendants to perform emergency procedures, the take-over by government of all ambulance services in the province, the close working relationship with the medical community, and medical control over medical acts performed in the field.

The centralization of all ambulance training in the Emergency Health Services Academy on the grounds of the Justice Institute of British

---

2 Currently to the Assistant Deputy Minister, Institutional Services.

Columbia has had many benefits, notably the integration of ambulance personnel with other public services and the refinement of modern distance education techniques. The emergency physicians and anaesthesiologists at the Royal Columbian Hospital, and later at the Vancouver General Hospital, have been very co-operative in training all levels of medical attendants, particularly the EMA-3s.

The Infant Transport Team provides safe and consistent service and does not deplete the nursery of nursing staff. The team provides an invaluable medical service and in the process is an excellent ambassador for the British Columbia Children's Hospital and the Grace Salvation Army Maternity Hospital.

REFERENCES

1. *Ambulance Act*, S.B.C. 1915, c. 4. Repealed S.B.C. 1922, c. 71 Schedule.
2. SMITH, C., personal communication, 1990.
3. RANSFORD, P. M. *Working Paper XXXIX, Emergency Services in British Columbia*, 1973. Mimeographed document.
4. *Medical Practitioners Act*, R.S.B.C. 1979, c. 254.
5. *Emergency Health Services Act*, S.B.C. 1974, c. 30. Name changed to *Health Emergency Act*, R.S.B.C. 1979, c. 162.
6. British Columbia doctors in the news. *B.C. Medical Journal* 16 (1974): 149.
7. WILLIAMS, T., PENDRAY, M. R., IRWIN, S., and CHOW, F. J. *Infant Transport Team Training Manual*. Vancouver: Emergency Health Services Academy, 1989.
8. MACNAB, A. J. and LAURIENTE, C. *Paediatric Emergency Transport*, Vancouver: Biomedical Communications, University of British Columbia, 1988.
9. MACNAB, R. J. Inter-hospital transfer: Physician escorts. *Canadian Journal of Pediatrics* (December 1990): 6–13.
10. ASSAD, P., CHRISTENSON, J. M., and VERTESI, L. Ambulance service in B.C.: Prehospital and air transport. *B.C. Medical Journal* 29 (1987): 513–19.

11

British Columbia Drug and Poison Information Centre

HISTORICAL CONSIDERATIONS

Two independent poison information centres were established in British Columbia during the mid-1950s, one at the Royal Jubilee Hospital, Victoria (under the direction of J. E. Smith, former chief pharmacist) and the other at the Vancouver General Hospital. The British Columbia Poison Control Council was formed in the late 1950s with representation from the British Columbia Health Branch, the federal Food and Drug Department, and the Victoria and Vancouver Poison Control Centres. They were concerned with the development of regional information centres in hospitals to dispense product information and treatment. A modest grant was obtained from the British Columbia Child Care and Poliomyelitis Foundation, which funded a red phone in the Emergency Department at Vancouver General Hospital, a series of cartoons for television advertising, and a booklet *Poison and Your Child*. Subsequently, Dr. John Dean, a paediatrician, was employed as a part-time consultant.

In 1960, the British Columbia Poison Control Council and the Bureau of Local Health Services of the Health Branch had established regional poison control information centres in thirty-four hospitals (1). Information cards provided by the Food and Drug Directorate, Department of National Health and Welfare, were available, detailing the constituents of many poisons. An educational program, including home visits by public health nurses to victims of poisoning, was introduced, and a statistical record of all poisoning was also kept. The Health Branch took over the supervisory role and the Poison Control Council became an advisory body in 1961 (2).

Charles Burr, formerly staff pharmacist at the Royal Jubilee Hospital and subsequently pharmacist consultant to the Deputy Minster of Health Services and Hospital Insurance, proposed that the Faculty of Pharmaceutical Sciences at the University of British Columbia become involved in the Poison Control Program. In 1964, the Health Branch and the Faculty of Pharmaceutical Sciences jointly assumed responsibility for a province-wide poison control service with financial support from the General Public Health Grant, one of the ten federal health grants. Following the termination of these grants, the Poison Control Program was supported by the provincial Health Department until 1974. The Health Branch and the Faculty of Pharmaceutical Sciences collaborated in the production of new product information and treatment cards, replacing the cards previously supplied by the federal government. The cards were placed at the Royal Jubilee Hospital and the Vancouver General Hospital and subsequently in the majority of hospitals with more than seventy-five beds. The smaller hospitals contacted referral centres at the Royal Jubilee Hospital or the Vancouver General Hospital, both of which provided information on a twenty-four-hour basis. A review board, which included a paediatrician, a pharmacologist, and a pharmacist, was appointed in 1965 to review the content of the new cards. Health units were advised of accidental poisonings, and home visits were arranged in selected cases. Statistical data was also collected in the faculty office and tabulated by the Division of Vital Statistics. These data were then transmitted to the individual health units.

Two research projects, which were undertaken with J. Glen Moir of the Faculty of Pharmaceutical Sciences as the principal investigator, played an important role in combining drug and poison information and in utilizing contemporary data storage and retrieval. They were funded by the Public Health Research Grant, another of the ten components of the federal health grant programs introduced in 1948 to develop the health care system, and comprised:

1. A project to develop a drug information service for the University of British Columbia Health Sciences Centre and other hospitals in the province of British Columbia was initiated in 1966–67 and received term assistance for the subsequent two years (3). The objective was to devise a plan to supply drug information in depth to staff at the University of British Columbia Health Sciences Centre and to other hospitals and general practitioners of medicine and pharmacy. This study presented specific recommendations concerning the functions of the Drug and Poison Information Centre (DPIC) for the University of British Columbia Health Services Centre.

2. A project to develop a computerized poison control information system was obtained in 1966–67 (4). The objectives were: first, to study methods of data processing and the various essential categories of information regarding the toxicity of drugs and other commercially available products having toxic properties, symptomatology, and treatment regimes for overdosage and/or accidental poisonings by such drugs and

products; second, to develop a computerized poison control information system; and third, to provide a solution to current problems regarding inadequate poison control information.

The University of British Columbia Computing Centre wrote an information and storage program for poison information, which was stored in their computer. The generic and trade names of 1,500 poisonous substances, their toxicity, and the signs and symptoms of overdose, and treatment were included. These data were manipulated from an office in the Faculty of Pharmaceutical Science and provided the answers to requests for poisoning related information (5). The essential data elements for a computer-based poison control information system were determined and some of the major problems respecting data base maintenance were identified.

These studies developed the basic policies and procedures for the Drug and Poison Information Centre (DPIC) to be located in the Health Science Centre at the University of British Columbia. In 1969, however, the planning of the Health Sciences Centre was temporarily discontinued. The updating of product information cards was continued by the Faculty of Pharmaceutical Sciences, but the increasing demands for clinical information emphasized the need for a clinical base for the Poison Control Centre. This need was met in 1975 with the transfer of the Poison Control Information Centre to its present location at St. Paul's Hospital, Vancouver (6). Dr. J. Hlynka, professor, Faculty of Pharmaceutical Sciences, was appointed the director of the DPIC, and funding of the program was switched from the Health Branch to Hospital Programs (7).

At that time, two unrelated drug and poison information data sources existed, a drug formulary, which featured information on the safe and rational use of drugs, developed by the Pharmacy Department at the Lions Gate Hospital, North Vancouver, and the poison information and treatment cards prepared by the Faculty of Pharmaceutical Sciences at the University of British Columbia and the Health Branch. These sources were amalgamated at DPIC, and the new centre offered to undertake the regular updating of these data (8).

The representative of the Health Branch, Dr. A. A. Larsen, played an important role from the first meetings of the Poison Control Council until the formation of DPIC (9).

THE PRESENT SERVICES

The Drug and Poison Information Centre (DPIC)

A management committee, composed of representatives of the British Columbia Ministry of Health (one from Hospital Programs and one from Community and Family Health), the Faculty of Pharmaceutical Sciences at the University of British Columbia, St. Paul's Hospital, and the managing director of DPIC, is responsible for the programs and budgeting needs. The managing director of DPIC reports through the regional hospital district to Institutional Services. The budget largely derives from this source and is administered by the Department of Finance at the University of British Columbia. A professional advisory committee, with representatives from the pharmaceutical, medical, and nursing associations in British Columbia, advises the management committee with respect to user's information needs. A medical review board composed of several physicians reviews drug and poison information monographs produced at the centre from a clinical perspective prior to publication. There is also an ongoing quality assurance program, consisting of a peer review of responses to drug and poison information requests.

The staff consists of a managing director, medical director and medical consultants, staff pharmacists, nurses, and secretaries. The pharmacists hold cross appointments at the Faculty of Pharmaceutical Sciences at the University of British Columbia for teaching purposes.

Currently, four separate services are provided, Drug Information, Poison Information, Poison Control, and Education Services (10).

Drug Information: The original objective of the Drug Information Service was to devise an effective provincial system to promote the rational and safe use of drugs. The development of DPIC eliminated the cost of duplicating this function in individual hospitals.

There are two types of basic drug information services provided to health professionals in British Columbia. First, telephone consultation concerning drug information is provided to all health professionals in British Columbia from 9 a.m. to 5 p.m., Monday through Friday. Current information is available on such topics as drug usage in pregnancy, adverse reactions, therapeutic alternatives, and foreign drug identification. Public calls for information about drug use are referred back to their physicians or community pharmacy. Priority is given to the requests as follows:

1. of a toxicological or emergency nature;
2. from subscribers of Drug Information Reference (DIR);

3. for information not readily available in DIR or other references located at the site of practice;
4. patient specific for current therapy; and
5. communicated by the health professional directly responsible to the patient.

Second, three drug information publications are prepared by DPIC. These are the Drug Information Reference (DIR), the Drug Information Perspectives Newsletter, and the Master Drug List (MDL). The DIR includes approximately 300 monographs on commonly used drugs and lists the efficacy of each drug, potential side effects, drug interactions, guidelines for drug administration, nursing implications, and patient counselling. This material is available in book and computerized formats. The newsletter is prepared quarterly and provides an update on the information in the current DIR. It focuses on new drugs, current assessment of drug interactions, and patterns of drug utilization in the province. The MDL contains more than 4,000 drug product listings and is available in hard copy and computerized format. It can serve as a baseline for developing formulary, drug inventory control, and drug use review programs. Combined with the computerized DIR, the MDL can be used to provide alert notices on significant allergies, drug interactions, or other medical conditions that should be considered prior to initiating drug therapy.

The Drug Use Review (DUR) program was started in 1978 to assist physicians and pharmacies in improving the quality of drug use in this province. The study is conducted in collaboration with Pharmacare, which provides prescription drugs to those in the population who are sixty-five years and over and to patients on social assistance. The three components of DUR are the identification of exceptional patterns of target drug usage (receipt of medications in amounts or combinations that fall outside the recommended parameters), the reviewing of this usage by the practitioners involved, and the assessment of the effects of such efforts on subsequent patterns of use. The results of the DUR program are reported in an annual newsletter distributed to all physicians and pharmacists in the province. The value of education programs in reducing the exceptional usage of target drugs has been demonstrated, as well as the need for regular educational programs to ensure continuous effects.

Poison Information: Again, two services are provided concerning poison information. First, toll free telephone consultation services are available twenty-four hours a day and seven days a week to the public and to health professionals who reside in the Greater Vancouver Regional District (GVRD). This service is provided by nursing staff with support from staff pharmacists. Outside the GVRD, local emergency departments respond to requests for information from the public and provide treatment. Those patients requiring emergency treatment are referred to the nearest emergency unit. When ipecac syrup is recommended by DPIC, the family physician is advised in writing.

Second, poison information publications prepared by the centre are the Poison Management Manual (PMM) and the Poisoning Perspective newsletter. The former contains 250 monographs of guidelines on the toxicity, symptoms, and treatment of commonly encountered exposures and overdoses. The Canadian Pharmaceutical Association has published this book for national distribution. The newsletter is prepared quarterly and features topics such as seasonal hazards, principles of poison management, and poisoning statistics.

Data entry and statistical reports are produced at DPIC on an annual, quarterly, or *ad hoc* basis. There were 2,266 requests for drug information and 25,803 requests for poisoning information in 1989/90. The majority of requests for poisoning information derived from preschool age poisonings and non-pharmaceutical poisonings were more common in the preschool age group. Pharmacists, physicians, and nurses (25 percent) and the public (75 percent) are the major users.

Poison Control: This service is presently comprised of centralized (DPIC) and regional service (hospital emergency departments) components, distributes educational materials to pharmacies, hospital emergency departments, and public health units, and provides media presentations, health fairs, speakers' bureaux, and poison control week. The staff of DPIC visits the emergency departments of hospitals periodically and provides seminars on poison management, uses of DPIC services, and recording procedures. Hospital and public health nurses are also briefed in the poison control education services with a view to reducing the incidence and severity of poisonings in British Columbia.

Education: This involves participation in undergraduate teaching in the Faculty of Pharmaceutical Sciences at the University of British Columbia and supervision of hospital pharmacy residents rotating through the centre and residents in emergency medicine.

COMMENT

The DPIC is another classic example of a population-based approach to managing important medical and public health problems. It illustrates the separate roles of personal medicine and population or community medicine.

The initial stimulus for a population-based poison information and education program was mobilized by the Poison Control Council, comprised of a group of concerned individuals, which included a representative of the Health Branch. The early efforts of the Poison Control Council, followed by the collaboration of the Health Branch and the Faculty of

Pharmaceutical Sciences at the University of British Columbia, culminated in a provincial service, the Drug and Poison Information Centre, located in a metropolitan hospital in Vancouver. The Health Branch (later renamed Community and Family Services) involved the Faculty of Pharmaceutical Sciences, which provided the professional credibility to operate a program. The later move from the university to a hospital base and the inclusion of a drug information program were associated with the shift from Community and Family Services to Hospital Programs[1] and access to the latter's budget. It is probable that the addition of drug information to the centre provided the clinical acceptability to bring about this shift.

REFERENCES

1. *Annual Report of the Health Branch*. Department of Health Services and Hospital Insurance, 1960.
2. *Annual Report of the Health Branch*. Department of Health Services and Hospital Insurance, 1961.
3. MOIR, J. G. *Final Report. A Project to Develop a Drug Information Service for the University of British Columbia Health Sciences Centre and Other Hospitals in the Province of British Columbia*. National Health Grant 609-7-156, 1967–69.
4. MOIR, J. G. *Final Report. A Project to Develop a Computer Based Poison Control Information System*. National Health Grant 609-7-165, 1966–67.
5. CAMPBELL, J. and FOWLER, A.G. A computer-based poison control information system. *Clinical Toxicology* 2 (1969): 149-57.
6. BRITISH COLUMBIA, *Annual Report*, Department of Health, 1975, p. 18.
7. BRITISH COLUMBIA. Order-in-Council 2358, 1975.
8. HLYNKA, J., GOLIGHTLY, L.K., and WILLIS, G.A. The B.C. Drug and Poison Information Centre. *Canadian Journal of Hospital Pharmacy* (1978): 129–31.
9. LARSEN, A.A., personal communication.
10. B.C. expands drug and poison information services. *B.C. Medical Journal* 29 (1987): 420–22.

---

1 Formerly the Hospital Insurance Service.

12

British Columbia Maternal and Neonatal Program[1]

HISTORICAL CONSIDERATIONS

Introduction

This chapter traces the development of perinatal and neonatal services in British Columbia. Initially, concern was focused on individual-based care of the premature infant, but it soon widened to embrace the diseases of the newborn infant. Services began in individual hospitals in the late 1940s and progressed to a population-based provincial program for all pregnant women and newborn infants in 1978.

Dr. Peter Spohn, a practising paediatrician, undertook a survey (1) of mortality rates of premature infants in two hospitals in British Columbia and documented the beginning of professional concern for the problem of preterm birth. He noted that there was no official definition of prematurity in Canada and commented that inconsistencies in the use of the term "prematurity" made comparative studies of prematurity between hospitals impossible. He recommended that birthweight be included on both the notification of birth form and the death certificate, so that mortality could be reported by birthweight.

The second step in the evolution of neonatal care was triggered by an outbreak of pyogenic staphylococcal infection in the early 1950s in the newborn nursery at the Vancouver General Hospital. The Medical Officer of Health appointed a committee to study the problem, which recommended establishing a physician in charge of the newborn nursery. This recommendation was accepted, and Dr. A. F. Hardyment was appointed to this position (2). The epidemic was brought under control by introducing improved isolation techniques in the nursery. This event coincided with the emergence of a worldwide interest in perinatal and neonatal

---

1 Formerly the British Columbia Perinatal Care Programme.

care. The Professor of Paediatrics at the University of British Columbia, the physician in charge of the newborn nursery at the Vancouver General Hospital, and the Director of the Division of Vital Statistics, recognizing the need for improved neonatal mortality and morbidity statistics, introduced a new physician's notice of live birth or stillbirth form in 1951. This included birthweight, gestation, and morbidity data for mother and infant and significantly enhanced the value of the perinatal and neonatal mortality data provided by the Division of Vital Statistics and other data to the Health Surveillance Registry.

The third step in the evolution of neonatal care was the adaptation of medical technology to the needs of premature and sick newborn infants. Dr. Sydney Segal, a pioneer neonatologist, was appointed as physician in charge of the newborn nursery at the Vancouver General Hospital in 1958 and introduced improved incubators, blood pressure measurements, laboratory micro methods, blood gases, and pH and pulmonary function studies. Initially, space or funding for these developments was not available from the hospital, and they were located within the adjacent Department of Paediatrics, University of British Columbia, and funded by the research grants of different departmental members.

During this time, the forerunner of the Infant Transport Team (Chapter 10) was introduced to provide integrated transport by ambulance and air evacuation. This service originated during the poliomyelitis epidemic in 1958. Again, Segal, in collaboration with the Senior Medical Officer of the Royal Canadian Air Force Reserve in British Columbia (who was also the Provincial Health Officer at the time and is co-editor of this book), arranged for the Royal Canadian Air Force Air-Sea Rescue Unit to transport poliomyelitis patients with respiratory problems to Vancouver. This included preparation of the patient for flight and medical services during the flight. Positive pressure ventilation replaced cuirass respiratory support, and endotracheal tubes replaced pre-flight tracheotomy. Subsequently this service was also used to evacuate injured persons and, more importantly for this book's purposes, to provide an integrated ambulance and air evacuation service for pregnant women and sick newborn infants. It also provided intensive care en route, using a battery-operated incubator to maintain body temperature and adequate oxygen levels. Portholes were also provided for the attendants to examine and handle the neonate. Subsequently, a modification of the Bird respirator made it possible to ventilate the baby manually. At that time, the hospital residents were not authorized to work off the grounds of the Vancouver General Hospital, and, for many years, Segal or his associate, Dr. Gordon Pirie, accompanied sick newborns from remote areas of British Columbia to Vancouver.

In 1974, when the Emergency Health Services Commission in British Columbia was established, these transport services became the responsibility of the Ministry of Health, and a well-organized road and air evacuation service developed to move high risk mothers and newborns (Chapter 10). The Committee on the Foetus and Newborn of the Canadian Paediatric Society recognized the need for information on the safe transport of the neonate and published a manual describing problems of transport of high-risk newborn infants (3).

A further step was the appointment in 1974 of Dr. Margaret Pendray to the full-time position of clinical director of the Neonatal Intensive Care Nursery at the Vancouver General Hospital, with the responsibility of establishing standards of care and a teaching program for medical students and residents. At this time, she was also appointed medical director of the Infant Transport Team, a position she has held to the present time. In 1975, the Ministry of Health recognized the Neonatal Intensive Care Nursery at the Vancouver General Hospital as the tertiary care centre for the province, a move which represented the beginning of the regionalization of neonatal care. In 1976, a new Neonatal Intensive Care Nursery (thirty-five bassinets) in the Vancouver General Hospital was planned and opened, and a realistic staffing plan was developed to ensure appropriate nursing and medical coverage.

The remarkable progress in the care of the low birthweight infant and sick newborn resulted in increased referrals to the Neonatal Intensive Care Nursery in 1975 and 1976 and placed great stress on neonatal nurses and neonatologists. Pendray was determined to develop a budget that guaranteed appropriate professional care and reasonable lifestyles for staff members and gradually achieved this goal. The lessons learned in the new intensive care nursery, as regards both physical facility and staffing patterns, were applied to the Special Care Nursery (sixty bassinets) at the British Columbia Children's–Grace Hospital Complex, which opened in 1982.

Population-based Neonatal Care

Perinatal Programme of British Columbia: In 1965, the Perinatal Morbidity and Mortality Study (4) was undertaken by the former physician in charge of the newborn nursery at the Vancouver General Hospital. It represented a deliberate attempt to bring modern obstetrical and neonatal care to the population at risk in British Columbia. The chief activity was the promotion of perinatal review committees in hospitals providing maternity care in British Columbia. Space and secretarial services were provided by the British Columbia College of Physicians and Surgeons. The focus of the committee work was educational, including written material describing the value of perinatal review and presentations at local hospitals. The principal benefit was an increase in interest and awareness of local hospitals in problems of neonatal care. An important by-product was the development and supply of standard prenatal forms to physicians' offices and the improvement in medical records. In 1969, federal grant funding of the study was terminated, and the British Columbia Perinatal Society was formed to raise private money to continue the work. The Health Branch of the Department of Health Services and Hospital Insurance also contributed to the operating costs, but their support was discontinued in 1971. In a review of the study (5), Hardyment stated that the main reason for the termination was that the community, as represented by the provincial government, was not ready to accept responsibility for prenatal preventive health care. In a subsequent paper (6), he emphasized the need for the efficient organization of maternal and newborn services for the population. "We have devoted little thought, time or money to the study of these factors in this province. We provide obstetric and newborn care with patterns essentially unchanged from that of 50 years ago." The same author (7), discussing perinatal mortality in Canada (in which British Columbia had the lowest rate in 1968), commented that further reduction in perinatal mortality was dependent on the prevention of preterm birth.

In 1974, Hardyment's outstanding efforts were rewarded with the announcement of the formation of the Perinatal Programme of British Columbia, and the appointment of a Continuing Advisory Sub-Committee (CASC) on Perinatal Care of the Medical Advisory Committee of the Hospital Programs[2] (8, 9, 10). The program was funded by the provincial Ministry of Health, and two consultants were appointed to travel and promote the perinatal review committees. The objectives were to define the cause of perinatal morbidity and mortality in British Columbia, to improve data collection and analysis, and to encourage formation of hospital review committees as a means of continuing education.

New prenatal record forms for physicians were developed (11) to provide a standard record of perinatal care and provide data for future studies. The forms were sent to physicians without charge on request from hospitals. The first two copies of the form were sent to the hospital of birth at thirty-six to thirty-eight weeks gestation, one for mother's chart and the other for the newborn's chart, and the third copy remained with the physician's record.

In December 1979, the format for collection of perinatal data for British Columbia was distributed by the Ministry of Health (12). This included live births by health unit of mother, residence for selected birthweight groups (1,500 grams or less, 2,500 grams or less, and 3,000 grams or less), and selected statistics relating to the newborn by health unit of residence of mother in British Columbia (live births, stillbirths, early neonatal deaths, perinatal deaths, infant deaths, and post-neonatal deaths).

---

2 Formerly the Hospital Insurance Service.

In 1980, the functions of the CASC on Perinatal Care were redefined as follows: to assess perinatal statistics and evaluate effectiveness of perinatal care; to publish an annual perinatal report with the Division of Vital Statistics; to assist the Ministry of Health to ensure that standards of perinatal care were maintained; to assist in improving perinatal care by uniform perinatal forms (Prenatal, Labour and Delivery Summary, and Newborn Records) distributed throughout the province, by expert review of difficult cases, by improving the relationship between the medical profession and the community health programs, and by approving documents from various sources making recommendations on perinatal health; and to act as a co-ordinating body for professionals and others interested in perinatal health in British Columbia (13).

In 1982, the CASC on Perinatal Care introduced a revised package of perinatal forms (Prenatal Record, Labour Summary and Delivery Record, and Newborn Record) and undertook to implement them as widely as possible throughout the province. They also undertook to complete the work of the CASC on Maternal and Neonatal Intensive Care relating to regionalization of perinatal and neonatal services, to provide continuing advice on a variety of other issues, including mortality and morbidity statistics, rhesus isoimmunization prophylaxis, and hepatitis B vaccination, and to collaborate with the Division of Public Health Nursing of the Ministry of Health in the publication of *Baby's Best Chance* (14), dealing with prenatal and post-natal issues.

The prevention of Rh immunization was introduced in the 1960s and involved the passive immunization of Rh negative non-immunized women shortly after delivery of an Rh positive infant. Immune anti-D, either in plasma or as gamma globulin, was obtained from women with strong anti-D and was the immunizing agent. The Rh gamma globulin program was extended to all British Columbia hospitals in June 1968 and is provided free of charge by the Canadian Red Cross Blood Transfusion Service to all at-risk mothers.

The guidelines prepared by the Perinatal Programme of British Columbia (15, 16) for the post-partum use of Rh anti-D immune globulin recommended that Rh negative unsensitized women receive Rh immune globulin within seventy-two hours of delivery, if they have delivered a stillborn fetus or a liveborn Rh positive infant, when they undergo spontaneous or therapeutic abortion or have an ectopic pregnancy, when foetal maternal bleeding is suspected (abruptio placenta), and when they receive diagnostic amniocentesis.

Antepartum treatment, started in 1984, recommended that all Rh negative unsensitized women receive 240–300 μg Rh immune globulin at twenty-six weeks gestation (17). Details of management of affected pregnancies are also provided.

Perinatal transmission of hepatitis B can occur when mothers are hepatitis B surface antigen (HBsAg) positive and can result in a chronic carrier state in the infants. The carrier state can give rise to liver disease and cirrhosis in the second and third decades and to liver cancer in the fifth decade. Accordingly, all pregnant women should be tested for HBsAg, and infants of mothers with positive tests should be vaccinated. The vaccination of infants of HBsAg positive mothers should be part of routine newborn care (18). Pregnant women who are at risk of positive results are women of Asian descent, intravenous drug users, and certain health care personnel exposed to accidental needle stick.

In 1987, *Baby's Best Chance* (14) was published, co-sponsored by the Ministry of Health and Pharmasave Stores. A complimentary copy was provided to each physician, together with special prescription pads to provide a copy free of charge to pregnant couples from Pharmasave stores. In addition, a *Baby's Best Chance Instructional Guide* was published for all perinatal instructors. The Handbook provides comprehensive advice to parents about prenatal issues, childbirth, and early postnatal development and problems.

A related population-based approach concerned the regionalization of perinatal care. A joint committee of the Canadian Society of Obstetricians and Gynaecologists and the Canadian Paediatric Society was formed in 1970 to address the advantages of the regional approach to perinatal care (19). The committee report described the needs and justification for regional care and commented on the requirements for implementation. As a result, a second CASC on Maternal and Neonatal Intensive Care was appointed in British Columbia to assess the regionalization of maternal and neonatal care. It was recognized that the geography, climate, and population density in British Columbia presented some unique problems. The report recommended the establishment of regional referral centres, with transportation of high-risk pregnancies and neonates by the Emergency Health Services Program (20). It included a description of a neonatal transport program and emphasized the importance of skilled personnel being located throughout the province. It also noted that good prenatal care detects 60–70 percent of high-risk pregnancies before labour, and for these patients transfer to a referral centre is essential. In the remaining 30–40 percent, transfer of the mother before labour is impossible, and hence a neonatal transport program is also required. This report was accepted by the Hospital Programs, and regionalization of perinatal and newborn care was introduced in British Columbia in 1978 (21).

The objective of this program was to upgrade professional skills in normal and high-risk maternity and neonatal care and to reduce neonatal morbidity and mortality. The Emergency Health Services Commission was authorized to provide emergency transportation for patients at risk on request from a designated referral centre. The hospitals in four communities were designated as regional obstetrical and neonatal units, to complement the provincial Tertiary Care Centre at the Vancouver General Hospital. The roles of three levels of hospital services were defined as community (Level I), regional (Level II), and provincial (Level III). The appropriate referral hospitals for initial consultation were also defined for all community hospitals.

In 1986, the CASC on Perinatal Care expressed concern that the quality of perinatal care was deteriorating and that past standards of care were not being met. A recommendation was sent to the Ministry of Health that a task force be formed to review perinatal statistics and current resources and needs, and to improve the regionalization of care.

British Columbia Maternal and Neonatal Care Programme: The opening of the new British Columbia Children's Hospital–Salvation Army Grace Maternity complex in Vancouver resulted in an increase in both obstetric and neonatal referrals to Vancouver, often by-passing the referral resource recommended in the 1978 memorandum. Over 80 percent of the under 1,000 gram infants born in British Columbia were admitted to the Special Care Nursery at British Columbia Children's Hospital. This resulted in the overloading of the tertiary resource and even referral of neonates to the neighbouring province of Alberta. A chairman, Dr. David Boyes, of the CASC on Perinatal Care, was appointed, and a delegation of perinatal experts was brought from Nova Scotia to assess the program. As a result, the CASC recommended strengthening the existing secondary resources with staff training and education of the medical professionals in their role in the regional network. Two small (six to ten bed) tertiary care units (Level III) were recommended in 1988 to cope with the immediate workload, but this recommendation has not been implemented to date.

The Ministry of Health provided a budget to implement the plan, giving highest priority to the development of protocols consisting of guidelines dealing with appropriate referral patterns. Finally, the CASC proposed a name change to the British Columbia Maternal and Neonatal Programme (from the Perinatal Care Programme of British Columbia), with wide representation of government, hospitals, universities, and the medical and nursing professions. In addition, it proposed an action group (British Columbia Reproductive Care Programme) to address operations, including establishing standards, reviewing relevant statistical data, fostering education, and enhancing liaison and role development between hospitals and referral guidelines between institutions providing different levels of care. The British Columbia Reproductive Care Programme liaises with the British Columbia Maternal and Neonatal Care Programme and makes recommendations to Hospital Programs, Ministry of Health.

Vancouver Perinatal Health Project: Another population-based prenatal project, initiated in Vancouver, followed a report by a committee of the

British Columbia Medical Association (22) in 1973, that emphasized the importance of nutrition in pregnancy, particularly in high-risk mothers. This resulted in the Vancouver Perinatal Health Project in 1974, funded by the city of Vancouver and the Provincial Department of Health. It comprised two programs, Parents' Choice (23) and Healthiest Babies Possible (24, 25). The former was a model program of the team approach to prenatal care. It was a collaborative effort between the Vancouver Health Department, twenty-five participating physicians, the obstetrical department of St. Paul's Hospital in Vancouver, and the clients themselves. Financial support was withdrawn in 1983 and the project was terminated. The latter program, an outreach prenatal nutrition education service, was designed for pregnant women of many different ethnic backgrounds. This program is still functioning in Vancouver and is currently funded by a grant from Community and Family Services, Ministry of Health. The Registered Nursing Association of British Columbia passed a resolution urging the Ministry of Health to implement the above prenatal programs on a province-wide basis. In 1988, approximately fifteen years later, eight pregnancy outreach programs (26) were funded by the Ministries of Health and Labour and Consumer Affairs (Chapter 17). These prenatal programs are designed to improve nutrition, reduce smoking and the use of alcohol and drugs, and provide emotional support to the mothers throughout pregnancy.

THE PRESENT SERVICES

Population-based Programs

The British Columbia Maternal and Neonatal Care Programme has supported a population-based approach to reduce perinatal and neonatal morbidity. The current activities include the regionalization of obstetrical and neonatal services and facilities, the prevention and management of haemolytic disease of the newborn, the vaccination of newborn infants exposed to maternal hepatitis B, and the production of *Baby's Best Chance Parents' Handbook* in collaboration with the Ministry of Health. In addition, the British Columbia Reproductive Care Programme plays a vital role in addressing concerns identified by physicians and nurses in community hospitals and provides decentralized staff education in maternal and neonatal care.

Regionalization of Care: The regionalization of obstetrical and neonatal services ensure the twenty-four hour availability of support for physicians, nurses, and other hospital personnel providing maternal and newborn services. The basic pattern of referral from Level I to Level II and from Level II to Level III has been defined by the Ministry of Health. This system is not infallible in that it is possible to bypass the appropriate referral centre if the latter is lacking an available bed. As noted above, additional regional Level III facilities are planned. The important role of the Infant Transport Team (ITT) is described in Chapter 10.

Prevention and Management of Haemolytic Disease of the Newborn: The effectiveness of this preventive program of Rh isoimmunization is measured by the reduced incidence of Rh immunization during pregnancy and of haemolytic disease of the newborn. The combination of antenatal treatment and post-abortion and postpartum prophylaxis has provided a protection rate of 98.6 percent among primigravida at-risk women (17). The continuing presence of anti-D immunization in Rh negative women can be accounted for by ectopic pregnancies, untreated abortions, previous pregnancy failures of Rh isoimmunization (especially in immigrant women and Jehovah's Witnesses) prior to the administration at twenty-six weeks, and receipt of Rh positive blood transfusion in early childhood.

Hepatitis B Vaccination: The present treatment of infants of mothers with positive tests consists of hepatitis B immune globulin (HBIG) at birth and hepatitis B vaccine at birth and at one and six months of age. The baby is tested at six and twelve months of age. The HBIG is distributed to hospitals by the Canadian Red Cross. The hepatitis B vaccine is provided free of charge by the provincial Ministry of Health.

Baby's Best Chance: This comprehensive handbook dealing with prenatal and post-natal issues is distributed to all pregnant couples in British Columbia free of charge. When it is determined that a woman is pregnant, her physician gives her a prescription for the handbook, which she takes to the local Pharmasave store or to the local health department.

EVALUATION

The British Columbia Maternal and Neonatal Programme is one of the few services for which therapeutic outcome measures can be determined. Before describing the perinatal and infant mortality rates in British Columbia, the relationship between low birthweight and infant mortality is emphasized. First, the small number of very low birthweight (<1,500 grams) infants per year is displayed in Table 7, and, second, the enormous differences in mortality rates (or survival rates) in the <2,500 and ≥2,500 gram birthweight groups is shown in Table 8. Third, the high mortality in the first week and month of life is also apparent in Table 8. Nearly half (15 + 38 + 96 = 149) of all deaths (149/316) in the first year in 1987 occurred in the low birthweight group (<2,500 grams), of which two-thirds (96 of 149) were in the 0–7 day and over 75 percent (111 of 149) in the 0–27 day groups.

TABLE 7. BIRTHS BY BIRTHWEIGHT GROUPS: BRITISH COLUMBIA 1981–87

	1981			1982			1983			1984		
	Live Births	Still births	Total	Live Births	Still births	Total	Live Births	Still births	Total	Live Births	Still births	Total
<1,000 g	140	60	200	166	54	220	134	68	202	167	70	237
<1,500 g	343	106	449	366	91	457	332	99	431	377	97	474
<2,500 g	2,112	174	2,286	2,218	147	2,365	2,116	157	2,272	2,204	158	2,362
≥2,500 g	39,531	106	39,637	40,700	102	40,802	40,905	81	40,986	41,804	79	41,883
≥ 500 g	41,643	280	41,923	42,918	249	43,167	43,020	238	43,258	44,008	237	44,245

	1985			1986			1987			1988		
	Live Births	Still births	Total	Live Births	Still births	Total	Live Births	Still births	Total	Live Births	Still births	Total
<1,000 g	150	64	214	138	64	202	151	60	211	178	157	335
<1,500 g	366	106	472	337	98	435	356	83	439	353	191	544
<2,500 g	2,056	169	2,225	1,935	142	2,077	2,084	134	2,218	2123	245	2368
≥2,500 g	40,658	81	40,739	39,837	81	39,918	39,472	71	39,543	40609	78	40687
≥ 500 g	42,714	250	42,964	41,772	223	41,995	41,556	205	41,761	42693	218	42911

Examination of the mortality rates by birthweight specific groups in Table 8 shows that there has been a decline in the stillbirth numbers and rates in the <2,500 and ≥2,500 grams birthweight groups. In 1987, two-thirds of the stillbirths were in the <2,500 gram group and 60 percent of these were in the <1,500 gram group. There has also been a continuing fall in early neonatal numbers and rates in the <2,500 grams and ≥2,500 grams birthweight groups, and particularly in the <1,000 and <1,500 gram groups. In 1987, 75 percent of early neonatal deaths were in the <2,500 gram group (96/129), and 74 percent of these were in the <1,500 gram weight group (71/96).

The numbers are much smaller for the late neonatal rates and hence less reliable, but there is a trend to an increase in mortality in the <2,500 gram birthweight groups in 1986 and 1987. The post-neonatal mortality rates in the <1,500 grams birthweight groups show a similar pattern. A downward trend in perinatal mortality in British Columbia (27) has also been reported.

The number of "saved" infant lives each year can be determined by calculating the difference in mortality rates per 1,000 births for weight-specific groups in a given time period (e.g., 1981–82) and then multiplying the difference in rate by the population (number of births) in 1982. Thus the "saved" lives in 1982 equals the (mortality rate per 1,000 live births in 1981) – (mortality rate per 1,000 live births in 1982) × the number of births in 1982. The separate "saved" lives in the stillborn, early, late and post-neonatal subgroups for different birthweight specific groups were calculated each year from 1981 to 1987 and are displayed in Table 9 for the <2,500 and ≥2,500 grams birthweight groups. The table records

TABLE 8. MORTALITY NUMBERS AND RATES PER 1,000 BIRTHS IN BIRTHWEIGHT SPECIFIC GROUPS: BRITISH COLUMBIA 1981–87

	1981		1982		1983		1984		1985		1986		1987	
	No.	Rate	No.	Rate	No.	Rate	No.	Rate	No.	Rate	No.	Rate	No.	Rate
A. Stillbirths														
<1,000 g	60	300.00	54	245.45	68	336.63	70	295.36	64	299.07	64	316.83	60	284.36
<1,500 g	106	236.08	91	199.12	99	229.70	97	204.64	106	224.58	98	225.29	83	189.07
<2,500 g	174	76.12	147	62.16	157	69.10	158	66.89	169	75.96	142	68.37	134	60.41
≥2,500 g	106	2.67	102	2.50	81	1.98	79	1.89	81	1.99	81	2.03	71	1.80
Total (500 g+)	280	6.68	249	5.77	238	5.50	237	5.36	250	5.82	223	5.31	205	4.91
B. Early Neonatal														
<1,000 g	84	600.00	92	544.22	68	507.46	84	502.99	73	486.67	60	434.78	53	350.99
<1,500 g	107	311.95	111	303.28	91	274.10	98	259.95	94	256.83	77	228.49	71	199.44
<2,500 g	143	67.71	145	65.37	115	54.37	118	53.54	122	59.34	104	53.75	96	46.07
≥2,500 g	62	1.57	53	1.30	59	1.44	41	0.98	36	0.89	30	0.75	33	0.84
Total (500 g+)	205	4.92	198	4.61	174	4.04	159	3.61	158	3.70	134	3.21	129	3.10
C. Late Neonatal														
<1,000 g	6	42.86	3	18.07	1	7.46	3	17.96	5	33.33	9	65.22	4	26.49
<1,500 g	7	20.41	4	10.93	4	12.05	5	13.26	6	16.39	13	38.58	9	25.28
<2,500 g	12	5.68	10	4.51	8	3.78	10	4.54	9	4.38	15	7.75	15	7.20
≥2,500 g	14	0.35	24	0.59	11	0.27	10	0.24	9	0.22	13	0.33	21	0.53
Total (500 g+)	26	0.62	34	0.79	19	0.44	20	0.45	18	0422	28	0.67	36	0.87
D. Post-Neonatal														
<1,000 g	6	42.86	11	66.27	2	14.93	5	29.94	6	40.00	7	50.72	16	105.96
<1,500 g	14	40.82	11	30.05	11	33.13	12	31.83	12	32.79	15	44.51	22	61.80
<2,500 g	35	16.57	33	14.88	24	11.35	39	17.70	41	19.94	41	21.19	38	18.23
≥2,500 g	105	2.66	117	2.87	121	2.96	111	2.66	87	2.14	98	2.46	113	2.86
Total (500 g+)	140	3.36	150	3.50	145	3.37	150	3.41	128	3.00	139	3.33	151	3.63

TABLE 9. "SAVED" LIVES BY YEAR AND BIRTHWEIGHT GROUP

	1982	1983	1984	1985	1986	1987	Total
A. Stillbirths							
<1,000 g	12	−18	10	−1	−4	7	6
<1,500 g	17	−13	12	−9	−1	16	22
<2,500 g	33	−16	5	−20	16	18	36
≥2,500 g	7	22	4	−4	−2	9	36
Total (500 g+)	39	12	7	−20	21	17	76
B. Early Neonatal							
<1,000 g	8	6	1	2	7	13	37
<1,500 g	3	10	5	1	10	10	39
<2,500 g	5	23	2	−12	11	16	45
≥2,500 g	11	−6	19	4	5	−3	30
Total (500 g+)	13	25	19	−4	21	4	78
C. Late Neonatal							
<1,000 g	4	1	−2	−2	−4	6	3
<1,500 g	3	0	−1	−1	−7	5	−1
<2,500 g	3	2	−2	0	−7	1	−3
≥2,500 g	−10	13	1	1	−4	−8	−7
Total (500 g+)	−7	15	−1	1	−10	−8	−10
D. Post-Neonatal							
<1,000 g	−4	7	−3	−2	−1	−8	−11
<1,500 g	4	−1	0	0	−4	−6	−7
<2,500 g	4	7	−14	−5	−2	6	−4
≥2,500 g	−9	−3	13	21	−13	−16	−7
Total (500 g+)	−6	6	−2	18	−14	−13	−11

the numbers of "saved" lives per birthweight group for each year (e.g., 1981–82) across the 1981–87 time period. The aggregate "saved" stillbirths from 1981–87 were divided equally between the two weight groups (e.g., 36 + 36), but more early neonatal lives were saved in the <2,500 grams group than in the ≥2,500 grams birthweight group (45 + 30). Furthermore, there were more stillbirths (22 of 36) and early neonatal (39 of 45) "saved" lives in the very low birthweight groups (<1,500 grams). These same calculations in the late and post-neonatal periods show there was a small increase in deaths (lost lives) in both the <2,500 gram and ≥2,500 gram birthweight groups. This could be interpreted to mean that some neonatal deaths were shifted from early to late neonatal and post-neonatal life.

Follow-up studies of infants weighing 800 grams or less have been reported (28). Thirty-three children were examined and three were unable to complete the test battery because of mental handicap (two were also blind and one deaf). The surviving children who were free of major handicaps had a high incidence of identifiable intellectual and behavioural risk factors for educational disability. Finally, there is good evidence of the success of the post-partum prevention and prenatal treatment programs for haemolytic disease of newborn.

COMMENT

Twenty-five years ago, a few individuals identified the need for a population-based approach to obstetrical and neonatal care, but ten years elapsed before Hospital Programs responded and funded the Perinatal Care Programme of British Columbia to study perinatal morbidity and mortality and to make recommendations about improving perinatal health. After another fifteen years, the British Columbia Maternal and Neonatal Care Programme began to provide outreach staff education in maternal and neonatal care. So much for the effectiveness of the continuing advisory subcommittee system as a means of implementing policy!

The resistance within the Department of Health Services and Hospital Insurance to promoting population-based prenatal care was probably influenced by the absence of federal-provincial cost-sharing in preventive health issues. Conversely, cost-sharing applied to the hospital-based neonatal care.

In British Columbia, it will be increasingly difficult to improve neonatal survival with better medical and hospital care, but better reproductive health of women remains a reality. Birthweight, as a marker of reproductive health, is responsive to improvement in the preconceptual and prenatal lifestyle of pregnant women (29, 30), rather than neonatal care. The high technology of the Neonatal Intensive Care Nursery does not resolve this problem. It requires better prenatal care to the high-risk mothers to improve the reproductive health of the population.

The importance of an augmented program of care for women who enter pregnancy at risk, or develop medical or psychosocial risk during pregnancy, has recently been re-emphasized by the United States Public Health Service (31), which noted that treatment is generally available for medical risk, but the need for treatment for women at psychosocial risk is less available and accepted. The psychosocial risk groups included were social (low income, limited education, single, age [less than eighteen years or over thirty-five years]), psychological (inadequate personal support, abusive situation, mental illness), and adverse health behaviours (illicit drug use, alcohol abuse, poor nutrition, and excessive exercise).

It is difficult to speculate on the effect of the regionalization of care and of maternal and neonatal transport on these findings. The Division of Vital Statistics did not generate birthweight-specific mortality data until 1981, rendering trend analysis before and after the introduction of the regionalization impossible. There has been a decline, however, in stillbirth and early neonatal mortality rates since 1981, and "saved" lives have resulted in both the <2,500 and ≥2,500 gram birthweight groups. Doubtless the development of the tertiary care centre (British Columbia Children's Hospital–Grace Complex) has played a major role. To the extent that the regionalization and transport led to the greater use of the tertiary care facility, the perinatal and neonatal outcomes have improved.

The development of resuscitation techniques and technological advances for the support of the very immature newborn infant are doubtless associated with the important decline in early neonatal mortality rates, and perhaps also with the increase of the late and post-neonatal mortality rates. Neonatal morbidity rates have been examined in a previous study (32), and markedly increased rates have been reported during the past twenty years. The unreliability of these data has been subsequently reported (33).

It seems fair to conclude that, for whatever reason, the importance of population-based prenatal care (29, 30, 34) was given scant attention by the medical profession or the Ministry of Health. Although the important role of prevention of preterm birth in the further reduction of neonatal mortality and morbidity had been emphasized in the early 1970s (7), with one notable exception in Vancouver (13), a population-based program to improve the reproductive health of women and reduce preterm birth has been noticeably absent. Finally, in 1986, the CASC on Perinatal Care (27) acknowledged the importance of the promotion of preconceptual and prenatal health. While noting the dramatic improvement in survival of very low birthweight infants, the early detection and prevention of preterm birth was still described as "our largest perinatal problem," because 85 percent of normally formed babies who die in the perinatal period are born before thirty-seven weeks (27). This was the very point that Hardyment had made fifteen years previously (7), when he challenged the Department of Health Services and Hospital Insurance to get involved in this area of preventive care.

Community education programs promoting preconceptual health and improved access to prenatal care can have a major impact on perinatal mortality rates (27). Individual-based care does not reach the high-risk population of pregnant women.

REFERENCES

1. SPOHN, P. H. The adequate care of the premature infant. *Canadian Medical Association Journal* 62 (1950): 317–23.
2. HARDYMENT, A. F. personal communication, 1988.
3. SEGAL, S. (ed.). *Manual for the Transport of High-Risk Newborn Infants. Principles, Policies, Equipment, Techniques.* Canadian Paediatric Society, 1972.
4. HARDYMENT, A. F. *The Perinatal morbidity and mortality study of British Columbia.* Final Report, Maternal and Child Health Grant, 1965–1969.
5. HARDYMENT, A. F. The end of the road? *B.C. Medical Journal* 13 (1971): 97–98.
6. HARDYMENT, A. F. Perinatal mortality rates in B.C.: I. *B.C. Medical Journal* 13 (1971): 189–90.
7. HARDYMENT, A. F. Perinatal mortality rates in B.C.: II. *B.C. Medical Journal* 13 (1971): 215–18.
8. Province wide perinatal program to be launched. *B.C. Medical Journal* 16 (1974): 177.
9. Province-wide participation urged for new perinatal program. *B.C. Medical Journal* 17 (1975): 93.
10. Perinatal Program of British Columbia Memorandum, 1976. Mimeographed document.
11. B.C.'s new prenatal record. *B.C. Medical Journal* 17 (1975): 155–56.
12. BRITISH COLUMBIA. Memorandum re: Perinatal data for British Columbia. Office of the Deputy Minister, Victoria, B.C., 4 December 1979. Ministry of Health.
13. Perinatal Programme—CASC on Perinatal Care, Memorandum, May 1980.
14. WILSON, M. and MORICKY, B. I. *Baby's Best Chance: A Perinatal Manual for Parents.* Communitiy Health, Province of British Columbia, Ministry of Health, 1979.
15. Statement from the Perinatal Programme on Rhesus Iso-Immunization Prophylaxis. *B.C. Medical Journal* 22 (1980): 471.
16. Update on the prevention and management of hemolytic disease of the newborn. *B.C. Medical Journal* 26 (1984): 424–25.
17. STOUT, T., personal communication, 1988.
18. Hepatitis-B antigenemia. Statement of the CASC on Perinatal Care prepared for Perinatal Programme of British Columbia. *B.C. Medical Journal* 20 (1978): 180.
19. SWYER, P. R. and GOODWIN, J. W. (eds.). *Regional Services in Reproductive Medicine.* The Report of the Joint Committee of the Society of Obstetricians and Gynaecologists of Canada and the Canadian Paediatric Society on the Regionalization of Care in Canada, n.d.
20. Continuing Advisory Sub-committee on Maternal and Neonatal Intensive Care. *Recommendations for the Establishment of Secondary Referral Centres in British Columbia,* November 1978. Mimeographed document.
21. BRITISH COLUMBIA. Memorandum re: Provincial programme for the regionalization of obstetrical and newborn services. Hospital Programs, Victoria, B.C., 30 November 1978. Ministry of Health.

22. Nutrition in Pregnancy Committee of the Health Planning Council B.C.M.A. Nutrition in Pregnancy Committee. *B.C. Medical Journal* 15 (1973): 128–29.

23. WARNYKA, J., BRADLEY C., and ROSS, S. A team approach to perinatal health care. *B.C. Medical Journal* 21 (1977): 176–77.

24. WARNYKA, J., ROSS, S., and BRADLEY, C. Healthiest Babies Possible: The Vancouver Perinatal Health Project. *The Canadian Nurse* 75 (1979): 18–21.

25. KENDALL, P.R., CALLAWAY, R., and BELL, P. Outreach counselling in nutritionally at-risk pregnancies. *B.C. Medical Journal* 22 (1980): 538–39.

26. ASANTE, K. O. and ROBINSON, G. C. Pregnancy Outreach Program in B.C. The prevention of alcohol-related birth defects. *Canadian Journal of Public Health* 51 (1990): 76–77.

27. FISHER, M., KING, J. F., and ROWE, J. F. Perinatal mortality in British Columbia: A 10-year report. *B.C. Medical Journal* 28 (1986): 563-65.

28. GRUNAU, R.V.E., FRYER, L., MORTON, J. C., and WHITFIELD, M. F. Intellectual and behavioural characteristics of children of birthweight ≤800 grams at school age compared to controls. Paper presented at Northwest Society of Developmental Pediatrics, Vancouver, June 1988.

29. BONHAM, G. H. The measurement of birth outcome. *Canadian Journal of Public Health* 79 (1988): 385.

30. WYNN, M. and WYNN, A. *The Prevention of Preterm Birth: An Introduction to Some European Developments Aimed at the Prevention of Handicap.* London: Foundation for Education and Research in Childbearing, 1977.

31. UNITED STATES OF AMERICA. *Caring for Our Future: The Content of Prenatal Care.* A Report of the Public Health Expert Panel on the Content of Prenatal Care. Washington, D.C.: U.S. Department of Health and Human Services, Public Health Service, National Institute of Health, 1989.

32. EVANS, R. G., ROBINSON, G. C., and BARER, M. L. *Final Report. The Impact of Paediatric Hospital-based Ambulatory Care Upon Paediatric Hospital Utilization in British Columbia.* Part I. Trends in paediatric utilization in British Columbia, 1966–1982/83. Ottawa: Health and Welfare Research and Development Programs Grant No. 6610-1411-46 (unpublished), December 1987.

33. ARMSTRONG, R. W., personal communication, 1990.

34. HIGGINS, A. C., MOXLEY, J. E., PENCHARZ, P. B., MIKOLAINIS, D., and DUBOIS, S. Impact of the Higgins Nutrition Intervention Program on birth weight: A within-mother analysis. *Journal of the American Dietetic Association* 89 (1989): 1097–1103.

Part III
Population-based Community Services

13

Dental Health Program

HISTORICAL DEVELOPMENT

The Division of Preventive Dentistry[1] in the Bureau of Local Services, Health Branch, was established in 1949 and funded by one of the federal health grants (General Public Health) (1). Dr. Frank McCombie, a founding member of the Canadian Society of Public Health Dentists, was the first director of the division. Initial activities of the division included restorative and preventive care to children residing outside the cities of Vancouver and Victoria, both of whose municipal health departments operated their own dental programs. Several basic sets of equipment were designed and manufactured locally for use initially in these programs. These incorporated such items as motorcycle headlights, belt-driven handpieces for tooth preparation, and mobile dental X-ray units (2). In due course, these units were replaced by the newly developed air-driven turbine equipment, modern high-intensity lighting, and reclining chairs, all of which could be dismantled and transported in compact containers. Eventually, the transportable equipment was augmented by six recreation vehicles, fully equipped as two-chair dental offices.

In 1951, it was estimated that 81 percent of grade one children had never visited a dentist. Initially, services were provided by means of a "dental extern" program, wherein dentists, using the transportable equipment, contracted to work in rural areas for ten- or twelve-week periods, on a sessional fee basis. Funds were raised by local school districts, and matching grants were provided by the provincial Health Branch. In those areas where no practising dentists were located, older children and adults were accommodated as private patients outside the hours of normal clinic sessions.

---

1 Renamed the Division of Dental Services.

In 1953, the role of the public health dentists was shifted from provision of treatment services to activities related to the prevention of dental disease and the promotion of optimal dental health. Eventually, seven full-time dentists were employed by the division to supervise dental programs throughout the province. Their services were shared by three or more health units, and they were referred to as regional dental consultants. Those on staff were offered postgraduate training in epidemiology and health promotion services at various Schools of Public Health. By 1961, community preventive dental clinics providing education in prevention for children aged three years to grade three had been organized in sixty-six of the seventy-five school districts served by provincial health units. Treatment services were provided by the family dentists in their own offices. An increased parental awareness of dental health resulted in the 1960s, and 70 percent of five-year-old children were receiving dental care. The introduction of the "three-year-old birthday card program," initiated in the early 1960s throughout the province, further increased the attendance of preschool children for dental care (3). Cards were sent from the health unit to all children on their third birthday. These provided for an examination and the provision of preventive services, such as application of fluorides to the child's teeth, along with counselling in proper dietary and hygiene habits. The family dentists were reimbursed for these preventive services by the Health Branch, while restorative (fillings) and other services became the responsibility of the parents. With the opening of a Dental Faculty at the University of British Columbia in the early 1960s and an increased movement of dentists from other provinces to all regions of British Columbia, treatment services became more readily available. The proliferation of pre-paid dental plans also had a great influence in the increased demand for dental treatment services.

In 1964, dental hygienists were introduced in public health units and, together with dental assistants, were employed in schools under supervision of the regional dental consultants. All children in kindergarten and grade one were examined and taught home care skills, in grade three, digital skills, and, in grade four, dental flossing. A survey carried out in 1980 showed that 80 percent of children in kindergarten and grades one, three, five, and seven were attending their family dentists on a regular basis. An array of health promotion materials, including information kits, new mother's kits, posters, pamphlets, slides, and tapes, was developed by the Dental Division and the Health Education Division.

In November 1973, the Minister of Health of British Columbia appointed a special study group to research the cost of the most cost-effective system of universal dental care services for children (4). The coordinating committee submitted its report in December 1974, comprising a set of alternatives that provided dental disease preventive measures, dental health education, clinical treatment including emergency care, restorative services, surgical services, and limited specialty services for orthodontic and pedodontic treatment. The New Democratic government was defeated in 1975, and the proposed plan was never implemented.

The College of Dental Surgeons urged the government to subsidize private dental plans for the elderly, the poor, and other people ineligible for private dental insurance. In March 1979, the Dental Care Plan of British Columbia was announced, but its implementation was postponed until 1 January 1981. Four categories of persons were eligible:

1. clients of the Ministry of Human Resources;
2. recipients of Premium Assistance for the Medical Services Plan;
3. senior citizens sixty-five years and over;
4. children fourteen years of age and under.

The program was discontinued in September 1982.

In mid-1984, the regional dental consultant positions were deemed redundant, and the positions were terminated.

The Division of Preventive Dentistry, in collaboration with the Division of Vital Statistics, developed a system in 1955 to monitor dental health in the child population. Surveys of children aged five to fifteen years in provincial health units and in Vancouver and Victoria were made in a serial manner over the period 1956–80. A survey conducted in 1987 (5) counted the number of filled, decayed, and extracted teeth (FDX).[2] Each grade seven child whose age fell within eleven to fourteen years was examined at the time of the usual inspection in the school program. The results are compared with previous surveys in Figure 2 and show that the need for extractions has been almost eliminated, and that the rate of tooth decay has fallen sharply over the past thirty years. The number of filled teeth represents the level of restorative care and shows a trend downwards, as more and more tooth decay is being prevented. This suggests that most children are receiving the care they need. Furthermore, this pattern is seen in all regions of the province.

PRESENT PROGRAM

Services

The minimal program offered by all provincial health units consists of a cursory screening for children in kindergarten and dental health presentations to other grades in high-risk schools (6). When practical, this school

---

2 This is similar to the World Health Organization classification: decayed missing filled (DMF).

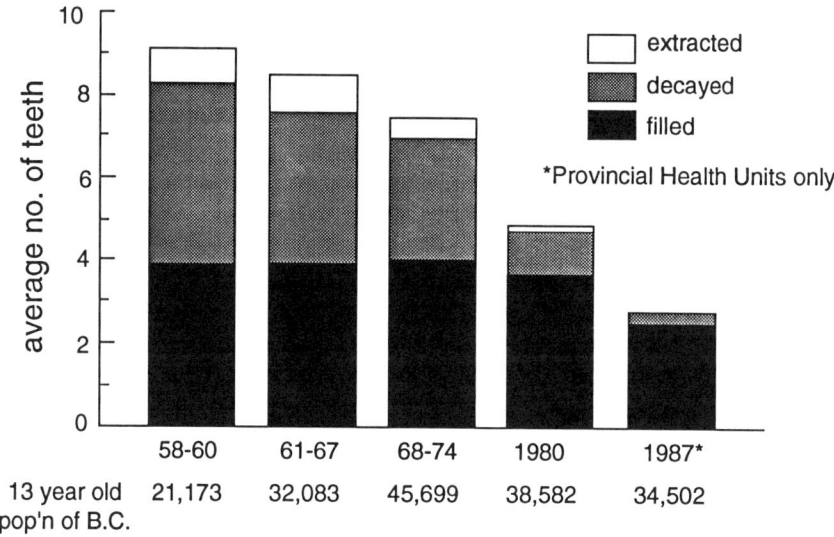

13 year old pop'n of B.C.	58-60	61-67	68-74	1980	1987*
	21,173	32,083	45,699	38,582	34,502

Figure 2 British Columbia FDX rates: thirteen-year-olds, 1958–87.

program is expanded to provide more detailed screening of grade seven children. The reduction in dental caries rates in school children has made it possible to provide preventive dental education and services, including perinatal (Pregnancy Outreach Program) and parenting (Healthiest Babies Possible) programs, preschool and day-care programs to other groups, and even to the general adult and institutionalized population. There remain, however, some pockets of high need around the province, perhaps related to the increased numbers of new immigrant children, and hence there is a continuing need for early screening programs.

The dental health program involves teaching and demonstrating proper hygiene practices. Notification cards are sent to parents if a need for treatment is evident, and a follow-up appointment is made to determine if the treatment has been carried out. It is estimated that approximately 80 percent of children are registered with private dental plans. These screening programs identify a small group of children who are in urgent need of dental care, but whose parents are unable to pay for it. In Vancouver and Burnaby, there are no- or low-cost-to-patient dental treatment centres, but in the remaining areas of the province no such facilities exist. A pilot scheme is underway to examine the feasibility of paying for private dental care services from a grant from the Ministry of Health.

The three-year-old birthday card was discontinued because of the administrative costs, but the idea has been reactivated by attaching the message to the Health Passport, which provides a record of immunization for each child. The card recommends a visit to the dentist at three years.

Dental Staff

There has been a change in the professional role related to the introduction of core programs within the health units, with the dental staff participating more actively as members of a health care team and relinquishing their position of relative isolation in the former, centrally controlled, discipline-based, program delivery system (6).

The field staff providing the services fall into two broad categories, dental hygienists and certified dental assistants, the former directing the work of the latter. They usually work in teams of one hygienist (DHI) and one assistant and are supervised by five regional dental hygienists (DHII). The supervising dental hygienists have replaced the regional dental consultants; they monitor programs and professional standards of staff and provide continuity and standardization of dental program activities across the province. The central office is comprised of one dental director, one dental hygienist (DHIII), and one secretary. The professional supervision of all positions comes from the central office and administrative control from the health units.

The certified dental assistants working in public health settings are authorized to provide dental screening for school children, either in the absence of a dental hygienist or, preferably, in conjunction with them. The cursory screening is performed yearly in kindergartens and is complemented by a more thorough examination by a dental hygienist every fifth year for research and epidemiological purposes. The dental hygienist also visits students in secondary schools to reinforce the importance of preventing periodontal disease in the late teen years and to encourage regular dental care after leaving home.

Due to geographic difficulties, staff productivity is difficult to estimate, but, in the lower mainland, a staff of one hygienist and one certified dental assistant handles the screening requirements and subsequent follow-up for at least 6,000 elementary school children in kindergarten and grades one and seven, classroom prevention presentation in grades three and six, and additional work in long-term care facilities.

EVALUATION

In grade seven, the effectiveness of the dental program is evaluated by surveying random samples of school children at five-year intervals. At the kindergarten level, one is dealing with deciduous teeth, which form the foundation for a healthy set of permanent teeth. Children in the intervening grades have mixed dentitions, some deciduous and some permanent teeth being present, until grade seven, when the focus is on the permanent teeth, which are, for the most part, fully erupted. The monitoring of dental health includes entry of the data into the computer. The relevant indices obtained are then analyzed for various age levels for each school district.

COMMENT

The provincial dental program for children is a rare example of a program initiated from within the Health Branch.

A decision was made in the early 1950s to concentrate services on very young children and to attempt to screen as many children as possible in all areas of the province. This allowed the early introduction of preventive measures, such as prophylaxis (cleaning), the application of fluoride solutions (painting), counselling in proper diet and oral hygiene, and the early correction of defects. In a period of three to four decades, the status of the dental health of the children of this province has improved very significantly. The practice of taking children to the family dentist at an early age has become a well-established social custom and is promoted by the practising dentists through their recall systems. It is interesting that recurrent screening of all children is being replaced by targeting of high-risk populations, such as recently arrived immigrant children and children living in poverty in urban centres. It is noteworthy that the screening services are provided by dental hygienists and certified dental assistants, and that all dental treatments are referred to the dentists in private practice.

The evaluation of both prevention and restorative dental care has been undertaken from 1956. The careful collection of data on each child, and the use of the computer to store the data for subsequent analysis is a valuable feature of this program. The outcome measures (extractions, fillings, etc.) are available by age and region to support the effectiveness of the program.

REFERENCES

1. McCOMBIE, F. and GRAY, A. S. Dental public health in British Columbia. *Canadian Journal of Public Health* 75 (1984): 368–69.
2. GRAY, A. S. Portable equipment for "sit-down-lie-down" dentistry. *Journal of the Canadian Dental Association* 34 (1968): 90–94.
3. GRAY, A. S. Dental birthday cards for three-year-old children. *Journal of the Canadian Dental Association* 34 (1968): 201–204.
4. BRITISH COLUMBIA. *Children's Dental Health Research Project*. Report to the Minister of Health, British Columbia and the President, the College of Dental Surgeons of British Columbia. Queen's Printer: Victoria, B.C., 1975.

5. BRITISH COLUMBIA. *A Comprehensive Review of Dental Caries Experience shown by Grade 7 Students in the Provincial Health Units of British Columbia, 1987.* Dental Health Branch, Ministry of Health, 1987.
6. WILLIAMSON, M. The Province of British Columbia's Dental Program: Issues, Concerns and Recommendations. An Interim Report, 20 December 1988. Mimeographed document.

14

Mental Health Services for Children and Youth

INTRODUCTION

The history of mental health services in British Columbia is the familiar one of geographic and administrative segregation. The mental health and public health services were initially administered by the Department of the Provincial Secretary. In 1946, public health (the Health Branch) became part of the new provincial Department of Health and Welfare, but the mental health services remained within the Department of the Provincial Secretary. In 1950, the various provincial mental health services were reorganized into the Provincial Mental Health Services (1); subsequently they were transferred to the Department of Health Services and Hospital Insurance in 1959 and were renamed the Mental Health Branch.

Mental health services, illogically by today's thinking, included the mentally handicapped and the mentally ill populations until 1974, when services for the former group were transferred to the Ministry of Human Resources. During the last forty years, there has been an almost magical turnaround for persons with mental handicaps and mental illness, characterized by a return to community living with the full expectation of a degree of integration into the community.

This chapter begins with an overview of the evolution of the provincial mental health services and then, in separate sections, describes the history and present services for the populations of mentally handicapped and mentally ill children and youth. As in all chapters, the emphasis is on the policy, planning, and allocation of services to the population of children (population medicine), as distinct from the personal care of the individual patient (personal medicine).

The origin of the mental health services in British Columbia is attributed to the population influx associated with the discovery of gold in the Cariboo in the late 1850s and early 1860s (2). Victoria, at that time a Hudson's Bay Company post, was the chief outfitting depot and point of departure for the gold fields. The occurrence of mental illness among the newcomers called for a facility to care for them, and the Royal Hospital, originally a "pest house," was converted into the first "provincial asylum" in 1872. Legislation was enacted (the *Insane Asylums Act*) to administer the service (3). In 1878, the facility became too small to cope with demands. A new building was erected in New Westminster on the site of the present Woodlands and was named the Public Hospital for the Insane (PHI), or Number 9, after the street and phone number. The *Insane Asylums Act* was amended in 1912 and renamed the *Mental Hospital Act* (4). Additional land was purchased for new buildings further up the Fraser River, and, in 1913, the Provincial Mental Hospital at Essondale was opened on a site named after the Provincial Secretary, Henry Esson Young. In 1919, a provincial jail at Colquitz on Vancouver Island was converted to house those mentally ill patients who were convicted of criminal offences. A second unit was built at Essondale in 1924 and served as a receiving centre for all patients, while the admitting service in the PHI was discontinued. A third building was added in 1930. In the early 1930s, the decision was made to convert the PHI to a training residential school for mentally handicapped children and adults (later to be named Woodlands School). Another new unit was added in 1934 to house veteran patients, and this building subsequently became the west wing of the Crease Clinic.

The reorganization of the Provincial Mental Health Services within the Department of the Provincial Secretary in 1950 coincided with the opening of a new active treatment centre for mental illness at Essondale, the Crease Clinic for Psychological Medicine, named after Dr. A. L. Crease, the Director of Mental Health Services at the time. The *Clinics for Psychological Medicine Act* (5) made provision for admission either upon the voluntary application of a patient or by medical certification of two physicians, upon application by a relative or other interested responsible person. This new facility was said to mark the change in the care of the mentally ill from paternalistic custodial care to active modern and humanitarian psychiatric care.

SERVICES FOR MENTALLY HANDICAPPED CHILDREN:[1] HISTORICAL CONSIDERATIONS

Institutional Care

The institutional model of care prevailed in Canada from the 1920s. A diagnosis of mental handicap characteristically led to an application for admission to an institution. In British Columbia, talk of returning the resi-

---

1 The term "mental handicap" has replaced "mental retardation" and, except when quoting from another source, we will follow that terminology.

dents of provincial institutions to the community prior to 1940 was rare, and only a few residents had regular visitors. "Occasionally a nurse might take a female patient out shopping. On May Day, a few children would be taken to Queen's Park and once in a while the Salvation Army band played outside the Centre Building" (6).

World War II caused many changes at the Public Hospital for the Insane. "Many staff joined the armed services and many of the more able patients returned to the community and some of these also joined the armed services" (2). In 1945, a modern school building, incorporating an auditorium–gymnasium, was opened with five teachers. Vocational training, including domestic and manual arts, was added, and a recreational therapist was employed to improve the socialization of the children. The PHI was renamed Woodlands School,[2] in recognition of its educational activity and emphasis.

The baby boom following World War II, together with the prevailing custom of admitting even mildly mentally handicapped children to institutions, resulted in a waiting list, and four more units were built on the New Westminster site, raising the capacity to 1,182 patients in 1952. The population in 1959 was 1,436, which represents the maximum number of children living there. In December 1952, children under six years of age were admitted directly to Woodlands School (2), and, in 1953, the *Schools for the Mental Defective Act* was proclaimed, allowing direct admission of all patients to Woodlands School (7). The department philosophy was "to return back to the community those who are able to carry on in tasks given to them by their employers and make satisfactory adjustment to their environment and to those with whom they come in contact" (8). In the following year, 1954, the Annual Report stated that "The families must take a more active part in providing for their assimilation in the community. There is no doubt that many of the defective children could be cared for at home with the provision of day school facilities to meet their needs" (9). In the early 1950s, a separate admission suite and service departments, including dentistry, laboratory, radiology, and dispensary, were added. In the mid-1950s, a paediatric neurologist, Dr. Henry Dunn, and, in the 1960s, a geneticist, Dr. James Miller, were appointed consultants at Woodlands School, and, together with Dr. Bluma Tischler, the director of paediatric medical services and later medical director, and her staff, provided medical services for many years.

---

2 The institution was renamed Woodlands in 1974, when the institutions were transferred to the Ministry of Social Services and Housing.

Changing Pattern of Care

It is instructive to consider the evolution of services within the broader social context of the time. Following World War II, the Civil Rights Movement was formed in the United States to establish and protect the human rights of the black population, and soon other groups, including women, children, and the disabled, joined in. Subsequently, consumers banded together to establish their rights and to challenge the consumer–provider relationship that "fostered blind faith and passivity in the consumer and bestowed magical omnipotence and paternalism on the provider" (10). This consumer advocacy movement impacted on health professionals, who were seen as fostering dependence and learned helplessness in clients. This climate gave birth to parent advocacy, which has had a profound effect upon the development of services for many groups of disabled children.

During this time, there was a rapid expansion of knowledge of child development, including the recognition of the vital role of the family and of the benefits of early stimulation and early educational opportunity for children with special needs and from poor families (11).

In 1959, the Danish government passed an Act to promote normal life experiences for mentally handicapped persons (12). This resulted in children living at home with their families, growing up with neighbourhood children, and attending regular schools. In later life, it included vocational training, employment, and the possibility of leaving the family home. The concept spread to other Scandinavian countries (13) and was introduced to the United States by Bank-Mikkelsen and Bengt Nirje in 1969 (12). Wolfensberger is credited with expanding the normalization concept, emphasizing that the mentally handicapped must not only live in a community setting but also interact freely with others (12). There have been disagreements and challenges, but normalization has become the cornerstone of programming in the United States and Canada.

In 1962, in the United States, President Kennedy's Committee on Mental Retardation was formed, and, in 1968, the federal government passed legislation to fund model preschool programs for handicapped children, such as Head Start (14). In Canada, in 1964, a federal–provincial conference on mental retardation (15) was held to "indicate practical steps that might be taken to coordinate and improve... the services for mentally retarded children." The participants stressed the need for early education, including home visiting programs by trained staff. In Canada, where, in contrast to the United States, the provincial governments are responsible for health, welfare, and education services, no uniform national programs have emerged. In 1966, however, a national Commission on Emotional and Learning Disorders in Children, sponsored by six Canadian and one international voluntary organizations, was appointed to investigate factors that affect the development of children in Canada, the present state of services to meet the needs of children with developmental disorders, and gaps in service, and to make recommendations (16). The report (the CELDIC Report) awakened awareness of the need for improved services for children with emotional and developmental delay in Canada.

In the late 1950s and 1960s, a mental health survey (17) was undertaken by the American Psychiatric Association at the request of the provincial government of British Columbia, in order to confirm trends and guide programs being developed by the provincial Mental Health Branch. The recommendations dealt largely with the mentally ill population, but included expanding institutional facilities for the mentally handicapped.

Despite the new trend to family participation and community living, institutional facilities for the mentally handicapped population were increased. The tuberculosis sanatorium at Tranquille in Kamloops was converted to house severely mentally handicapped persons in 1959. A third facility, Glendale, in Victoria, was opened in 1971.

In July 1974, the three institutions were transferred from the Department of Health Services and Hospital Insurance to the Department of Human Resources (18). The transfer came about for three reasons. First, the Department of Human Resources served many mentally handicapped persons (in foster homes, boarding and group home placements, etc.), and hence integration of services was desirable. Second, the recognition that mental handicap is not an illness and that training in social skills is the single most important issue in service delivery caused the department to undertake the responsibility for all mentally handicapped people. Third, the transfer took advantage of cost-sharing benefits under the Canada Assistance Plan. Meetings were held in 1979 to explore the transfer of community residential care of mentally handicapped persons from the Mental Health Branch, Ministry of Health, to the Ministry of Human Resources (19).

To backtrack, the government responded to the changing pattern of care for the mentally handicapped in three ways. First, community services were developed; second, the institutional routine was modified; and, third, institutional facilities were first increased, which was followed later by the policy to close them.

Development of Community-based Services

Dr. James Endicott, a family physician in Trail, founded the first branch of the Kootenay Society for Handicapped Children in 1951 (20). He was a strong believer in regional services and worked to develop a residential school in the Kootenays, which was opened in 1965 and named the Dr. W. J. Endicott Home and School. As the trend to normalization and integration evolved, the residential unit was closed, and the name was changed to the Endicott Centre.

A kindergarten class for retarded children was started by the Vancouver Richmond Chapter of the Association for Retarded Children of British Columbia[3] in 1952, and was followed by a preschool in 1959 (21). In 1965, the Department of Special Education at the University of British Columbia placed a teaching assistant in the preschool, and, in 1967, the preschool moved to a hut on the university campus (21). The preschool was funded by grants from the Vancouver School Board and the Ministry of Human Resources and by the parents.

Summer workshops were also organized for parents with children under three years of age, and these led to the Vancouver Richmond Chapter of the British Columbia Association for Community Living (BCACL) starting the first Infant Development Program in the province in 1972 (22), funded by the Ministry of Human Resources. The current preschool facility, Berwick Centre, was built in 1976 with funds raised by the Variety Club of Vancouver.

In May 1954, Dr. Donald Paterson, consulting paediatrician for the Crippled Children's Registry in Vancouver, recognizing the number of mentally handicapped children reported to the Crippled Children's Registry, called a meeting of persons interested in "the advancement of mentally retarded children" (23). In addition to government representatives, there were members of six of the seven parent groups for the mentally handicapped then in existence. As a result, the Association for Retarded Children of British Columbia was incorporated in March 1955, and was initially based in a corner of the office of the Crippled Children's Registry, with borrowed equipment and a part-time secretary.

The first executive director of the Association for Retarded Children of British Columbia, Mrs. Winnifred Goepel, was hired in 1956 (23). During the ensuing years, many more chapters of the association were formed. The chapters started private schools for children with mental handicaps, and, in 1956, the *Public Schools Act* was amended (24) to permit local school boards to pay the provincial association, for each child attending chapter schools, an amount equal to the average cost of educating a normal child. Annual summer courses for teachers were started in 1956 in collaboration with Woodlands School staff. In 1959, the *Public Schools Act* was amended (25) to permit school boards to take over

---

3 The name of the association was changed to the British Columbia Association for Mentally Retarded in 1970. In 1983, in response to the youth of the association, the name was changed again to British Columbians for Mentally Handicapped People. In 1989, in line with all other provincial associations, the name was again changed to the British Columbia Association for Community Living. The society will be referred to by the latter name throughout the text. These name changes reflect the growing societal commitment to normalization and recognition of the negative consequences of labelling.

the complete operation of classes for children with moderate handicaps. For those districts not ready to take this final step, the legislation provided for an increase of 50 percent of the grant being paid for children with mental handicaps attending chapter schools, and it also permitted boards to provide accommodation for these children.

In 1957, a resolution was submitted by the association to the University of British Columbia requesting the introduction into teacher's training of specialized teaching in mental handicaps. As a result, a new chair was created in 1959 for a Professor of Special Education to train teachers of mentally and physically handicapped children.[4] A diploma in Mental Retardation was introduced in the Faculty of Education at the university.

In the early 1960s, a foster home project for mentally handicapped children was started, in order to offer a possible alternative to the children on the waiting list for admission to Woodlands School, and to offer a more homelike placement for children who could not return to their own home (26).

In 1967, Canada's centennial year, the BCACL agreed to sponsor a professional teaching facility, the British Columbia Mental Retardation Institute, in collaboration with the universities in Vancouver and Victoria. The association negotiated and administered the federal and provincial funds that supported experts in mental retardation in the faculties of Medicine, Education, Home Economics, Social Welfare, Recreation and Physical Fitness, Psychology, and Nursing at the universities for a five-year period.

In 1968, a policy change was announced to regionalize institutions for the retarded (27). In 1970, forty-six multihandicapped children from Woodlands were moved to the Eric Martin Institute in Victoria and, in 1972, thirty-one children to Glendale in Victoria. The provision of community-based services and the policy of regional institutions caused the occupancy and waiting list at Woodlands School to fall.

A Woodlands parent group, to become the Community Living Society (CLS), was formed in 1976 (28). These parents were concerned about their children living in institutions and set about encouraging the establishment of alternative living arrangements in the community for severely and profoundly handicapped persons. A position paper was prepared, with a plan to enable people to return to the community with specific guarantees for support services. This plan was endorsed by government, and, in 1977, the Minister of Human Resources announced "the day of the massive institution for the retarded is over" (29). Shortly thereafter, the ministry announced the formation of Project Life (Living Independently For Equality), the two main components of which were the Handicapped Workshop Guild and the Community Living Board. The former

---

4 Dr. James Richardson was appointed Professor of Special Education in January 1959.

venture encountered financial difficulties and was terminated, but the above parent group organized the CLS, with its elected Community Living Board, and, in 1979, was mandated to implement its initial proposal to place adults from institutions in community facilities. The CLS promoted the concept of service brokerage. In essence, money was allocated to the individual client, along with the services of a "broker," and the decision about placement was made by the client with his or her personal network. The distinctive feature of this system is the shift in power of decision-making from the service provider system to the consumer or client. The incentives of the market are introduced to the social service system, providing the client with options (30, 31). When Tranquille was closed, the Ministry of Social Services and Housing developed its own "resource developers," who are responsible for the placement of individuals in the community. The CLS continues to operate homes and develop placement for mentally handicapped persons.

Modified Institutional Living

The British Columbia Society for Handicapped Children, a chapter of the BCACL, was formed in 1956 by the parents at Woodlands School (32) and served as an auxiliary to the school.

In 1958, the *Schools for the Mental Defective Act* was amended (33) to allow admission of children to Woodlands School for thirty days and non-resident admissions to attend day classes. The former allowed the staff a period of time to assess a child, and also gave the family relief during periods of stress or a chance to have a holiday. The non-resident day classes did not materialize for lack of funds.

Three important developments at Woodlands School were recorded in 1963 (34): first, integration of male and female staff and patients on some wards; second, a boarding home program for well socialized adult residents; and, third, the opening of the Outpatient Department (renamed the Assessment and Resource Centre), to provide a screening procedure prior to admission and a service for those caring for a mentally handicapped person in the community. In addition, in 1965, the wards at Woodlands School were grouped into three programs providing different types of service for each group of residents (35): first, the hospital unit, for patients with acute illness or with additional disabilities; second, a training unit for moderately and severely mentally handicapped residents with no physical disability; and, third, a psychiatric and rehabilitation unit for management of psychiatric illness and social admissions of mildly handicapped residents.

Closing the Institutions

In 1981, the Minister of Human Resources issued a statement concerning the phasing out of the three large institutions, Woodlands, Tranquille, and Glendale (36). It emphasized that no final decisions had been made and stressed the need to develop community-based resources before the institutions could be phased out. In 1982, a policy statement was issued that children were not to be admitted to institutions, and that managers were authorized to approve thirty-day admissions only for respite care or for assessment and planning purposes (37). From 1978 to 1988, the population at Woodlands fell from just under 900 to 600, and the population of children from over 200 to nil (38). Finally, in 1983, the plans to place Tranquille residents in the community were formally announced (39), and, in 1985, Tranquille was closed. The phasing-out of the other two institutions is in progress. The downsizing experience has been criticized because family input was limited and supportive environments for residents were not always provided (40). These lessons are helpful in the process of closing the other institutions.

The closing of the one institution has been associated with an upgrading of community living services and has been a boon to those residents who have lived in the community for many years. There has been an increase in private home operators, and there is some concern regarding quality and continuity of care. This need is recognized by the Ministry of Social Services, and a monitoring system has been developed to oversee all residents located in community settings (41).

The BCACL has worked closely with senior civil servants in planning the closure of the first institution (Tranquille) and in the development of community living support services. It emphasized the correlation between family breakdown and the severity of disability of the child, and stressed the need for adequate financial support to families with multihandicapped children. The membership of the association was expanded to include chapters or full members and affiliate members, sponsored by local associations. Other important activities have included the initiation of the Family Support Institute and legal advocacy. The Steven Dawson trial established the right of full access to medical services by mentally handicapped persons (42). In this milestone case, the Supreme Court of British Columbia ruled that Steven Dawson, a severely mentally and physically handicapped child, was entitled to a surgical procedure to relieve the blocked intra-cranial shunt, thereby reversing a prior judgment by a family court that had resulted in cancellation of surgery.

When Tranquille was closed, a group of fifty-five patients with multiple handicaps and important health care needs was identified. They were not placed in community homes but transferred to a second institution, Glendale, in Victoria. The publicity engendered by the BCACL over this unexpected development was followed by the Ministry of Health accepting the placement and maintenance costs of this group in the community and establishing the Division of Services to the Handicapped (see Chapter 19).

EPIDEMIOLOGY

Mental retardation was the second of the ten most frequent disabilities in the under nineteen years age group listed annually by the Health Surveillance Registry (Chapter 5). As noted earlier in this chapter, it was this finding that prompted Dr. Paterson to call interested government and voluntary societies together to discuss the need for services in the province, and this led to the formation of the provincial society, the BCACL.

The children were further classified by age and sex into subgroups based on the International Classification of Diseases (317–319): borderline, mild, moderate, severe, profound, and unspecified. The latter category was the most common in the under four and five to nine age group, limiting the value of the data for planning purposes.

The age-specific prevalence rates per 1,000, based on children registered by the Health Surveillance Registry, were 2.02 in the under five year age group, increasing to 6.51 and 8.76 in the six to fifteen and sixteen to twenty year age groups (43). In the United Kingdom, prevalence rates of total subnormal intelligence (IQ less than 75/80) and severely affected, respectively, were estimated to be 20 and 2.3 in the fifteen to twenty year age group per 1,000 related population (44).

As noted in Chapter 5, children with disabilities were followed up at ages seven and fourteen years to predict educational and rehabilitative needs in the community. The practice was discontinued in the early 1980s.

PRESENT SERVICES

Identification and Assessment

The Newborn Screening Program (Chapter 7) and the Developmental Screening of Infants and Preschool Children (Chapter 20) by community health nurses comprise two province-wide programs for the early identification of birth defects and children "at risk" of developmental delay. The further assessment of children identified in this way, or of children who are identified in the preschool years, is largely provided by the private medical care system in office, ambulatory, hospital-based clinics such as Medical Genetics (Chapter 18), the Clinical Investigation Facility at the

British Columbia Children's Hospital (Chapter 7), and the Child Development Diagnostic Program of Sunny Hill Hospital.

Long-term Care

The long-term care, particularly for those children with multiple disabilities and behaviour problems, requires special consideration. These children may receive long-term physio- and occupational therapy, speech and language therapy, periodic review by psychologists, and medical specialties. These services are available in different ambulatory settings, including the British Columbia Children's Hospital, the long-stay hospitals, or child development centres.

Furthermore, these children have unmet needs beyond those of other children with chronic disability. They need early stimulation, medical and dental care, special education, recreational and social opportunities to make friends, and, later, vocational training and employment.

The Ministry of Social Services operates forty-three Infant Development Programs throughout the province, serving 3,000 infants and their families. It also provides individual and group special needs day care for children with developmental problems. Some of the group day-care programs are located in the child development centres. The Ministry of Education provides for the educational needs mentally handicapped children from four years eight months of age in a variety of settings within the regular school.

Voluntary Agencies

The mentally handicapped population now includes two separate groups, a younger group, who have always lived at home, and an older group, who have experienced institutional life and have returned to live in the community. The latter group has the problem of re-entering the community, and their parents are older and are understandably concerned about long-term placement and the quality and continuity of care of their children. The current focus of the BCACL is support to families caring for their handicapped children at home. Likewise, efforts are concentrated on integrating education and eliminating segregated classrooms in schools and post-secondary educational settings. A third focus is supporting member agencies.

The provincial chapters of the BCACL are involved in the operation of sheltered workshops and recreational opportunities for the adolescent and adult mentally handicapped population. The *Guaranteed Available Income for Need (GAIN) Act* (45) provides financial aid after the eighteenth birthday for severely disabled persons.

The Family Support Institute, which began as a project of the BCACL in 1986, became a registered society in 1989. The purpose of the institute is to strengthen and support families with children and teenagers with disabilities. The institute has also been involved in the deinstitutional- ization process, training "mentor families" to support those families with a member returning to the community from an institution.

The Institute has also trained over one hundred regional resource parents in many communities in British Columbia, providing a province- wide network that assists communities to build upon and share their strengths. It acts to bring families together to address common issues, needs, and concerns, and to share solutions.

Training weekends are organized to train parents to be resource parents for their communities. They become knowledgeable in such areas as the preschool years, educational opportunities for persons with a disability, expanding employment options, and advocacy. They recognize that informed, involved, and confident parents are the most effective advocates for their sons and daughters.

SERVICES FOR CHILDREN AND YOUTH WITH MENTAL DISORDERS: HISTORICAL CONSIDERATIONS

Child Guidance Clinic

The first mental health services for children were started in Vancouver in July 1932 with the opening of the Child Guidance Clinic. Dr. Crease, a psychiatrist, was the first director, and other staff included social workers and a nurse. "The whole idea of the Clinic is that of prevention—to keep patients from being admitted to the Mental Hospital by whatever means possible, e.g., change of environment, vocational guidance, correction of poor habit formation, the incompetency of either parent to train their offspring etc." (46). The annual report mentioned that conferences were held with the referring social agency and with the parents and guardians. The children returned at stated intervals for observation of their progress and consideration of the need for further treatment. The first full-time psychologist was employed in 1938 (47). He recalled that three clinics per week were held in Vancouver; three patients were seen in the morning and two in the afternoon. On the other weekdays, visits were made to Vancouver Island and the Fraser Valley. In 1934, a clinic was started in Victoria. The patient referrals derived from private social agencies (the Children's Aid Society), boys and girls industrial schools, and the Family Welfare Bureau, included young offenders and runaways. Assessment, including psychological testing, was undertaken to provide future planning, and therapy comprised environmental management and habit training.

The Child Guidance Clinic worked closely with the social agency in charge of the problem, "the clinic assisting with the mental hygiene approach to the problems of child behaviour" (48). Review of the annual reports for the early years revealed a mixed caseload, listing unmarried mothers, adoptability of child, difficult to handle, retarded development, and delinquent tendencies, including runaway, sex difficulties, insolent and disobedient, out nights, and theft. The diagnostic classification became more sophisticated over the years, with primary behaviour disorders, mental deficiencies, and social problems (adoptions) dominating the profile (49).

The majority of the patients were preadolescent. A small number of adults were also seen. The need for an inpatient observation and treatment facility for emotionally disturbed children and the increasing volume of referrals were noted in the early 1950s. At that time, the annual report noted that the Clinic offered programs of primary and secondary prevention. The former comprised educational efforts involving parents and professional groups, and the latter encouraged early diagnosis and treatment (50). The bulk of the program was centred in the metropolitan areas, but visits to many communities throughout the province were also held. The need for adult outpatient facilities was noted in 1954 (51).

Mental Health Centres

During the 1950s, the pattern of isolating mentally ill persons in institutions began to be replaced by the development of treatment facilities in the patient's home community, as was the case for the mentally handicapped, described above (52).

The Mental Health Survey in British Columbia by the American Psychiatric Association identified needed resources (16). The recommendations included encouraging professional training and developing mental health centres, including services for children, adolescents, and adults, throughout the province. This survey was followed by the *Mental Health Act* (53), with a view to further modernizing the care of mental illness.

The first provincial mental health centre was located in Burnaby. The facility was divided into the adult and children's divisions, with the latter replacing the Child Guidance Clinic. This shift coincided with the transfer of Provincial Mental Health Services to the Department of Health Services and Hospital Insurance in 1959. The adult clinic opened in 1957 and the children's the next year (54). The children's clinic was a resource for children with behaviour problems,[5] social and scholastic difficulties, and psychosomatic complaints. A day program for preschool children in the mornings and primary school students in the afternoons was started in 1960. A travelling multidiscipline team was introduced in 1963, and in the same year, a similar clinic for children was opened in Victoria.

The function of the Mental Health Centres was to develop, in co-operation with existing community resources, a variety of services designed to meet the specific mental health needs of the area served (56). These included direct treatment services to adults and children; consultation to physicians and to health, welfare, education, and correctional agencies; educational programs, both professional and non-professional; and special programs, such as the supervision of long-term patients, preventive programs, boarding home care, special group homes, etc. The priorities for the mentally ill were divided into four overlapping programs: the care of the chronic disabled, care of the acutely ill, child and family programs, and care of adjustment problems (19).

British Columbia Youth Development Centre

The lack of psychiatric residential treatment services for children and youth with serious mental illness, gave rise to the planning and construction of the British Columbia Youth Development Centre (The Maples) in Burnaby, adjacent to the Burnaby Mental Health Centre, in 1968 (26).[6] Initially, it comprised three programs, a child and adolescent clinic, a psycho-education unit with six classrooms, and a residential unit for emotionally disturbed children (forty-five beds). In 1981, twenty-five additional secure beds were opened for the treatment of disturbed adolescents. In 1969, the child and adolescent clinic was closed, with part of the staff being transferred to the adjacent Burnaby Mental Health Centre, and the balance relocated in mental health clinics in Vancouver and Richmond and in Blenheim House, a treatment centre for preschool children, in Vancouver. These latter programs were administered by a society, the Greater Vancouver Mental Health Services, which had accepted responsibility for the delivery of mental health services to children and adults in

---

5 A mental health program for children and youth involving the public health nursing system was introduced in Metropolitan Vancouver (Vancouver, North and West Vancouver, Burnaby, and Richmond) in the late 1930s (55). This involved assessment and follow-up care. This program was gradually dismantled in the 1970s, and, currently, services to Metropolitan Vancouver are divided between agencies, including Greater Vancouver Mental Health Services, with paediatric teams servicing Vancouver and Richmond, the Burnaby Mental Health Centre, and the North Shore Health Unit.

6 The Children's Foundation, a private, non-profit society, was founded in 1957 to provide residential services to emotionally disturbed children and their families.

Vancouver and Richmond, and was funded directly by the Mental Health Branch, Department of Health Services and Hospital Insurance.

Hospital-based Services

Other recommendations of the Mental Health Survey included naming the Provincial Mental Hospital, Essondale, and the Crease Clinic, Riverview (17). More importantly, the *Mental Health Act* authorized the admission of patients on the basis of medical need (53), and the process of legal commitment was greatly curtailed. Finally, wards in certain acute hospitals were designated as observation units for mentally ill patients (57), and, shortly thereafter, the British Columbia Hospital Insurance Program authorized designated hospitals to provide outpatient services to psychiatric patients (58). The provincial *Medical Services Act* (59), in 1968, authorized payment for medical services to this population.

Subsequently, additional ambulatory and residential facilities for children were provided in acute and long-stay hospitals. These included a paediatric psychiatric inpatient unit in 1969 at the Health Centre for Children at the Vancouver General Hospital. This was replaced by a ten-bed unit at the British Columbia Children's Hospital in 1981. Also in 1969, the Child and Family Unit, an ambulatory clinic, was started on the campus of the University of British Columbia by the Department of Psychiatry. In 1981, a ten-bed adolescent unit was opened in the Vancouver General Hospital, and, in 1987, a twenty-five-bed psychiatric unit (Jack Ledger House) at the Queen Alexandra Hospital for Children in Victoria. These hospital units functioned on the referral basis of the private model of medicine. These facilities were opened both for teaching by the Department of Psychiatry at the University of British Columbia and to meet the need for regional services.

Autism

The care of autistic children has been a concern for many years. A unit for autistic children was opened in Woodlands School in 1966 (35). The Laurel House Society, incorporated in 1972, operated a residence for autistic children until 1982, when the residential program closed, and the children were integrated in regular school classes. The Pacific Association for Autistic Citizens[7] was incorporated in 1975 and has played an important role in the development of educational and vocational services for this population, including a residential facility in Greater Vancouver, called Gateway (60). More recently, a British Columbia Council on Autism has been formed to bring together parents and professionals

---

7 In 1978, the name was changed from Pacific Association for Autistic Children.

involved with this population to share resources and to improve services throughout the province.

Juvenile Services to the Courts

The mental health centres provided psychiatric assessment of juveniles before the courts for many years. The development of the Forensic Psychiatric Clinic at the Burnaby Mental Health Centre in 1966 provided evaluation and treatment of individuals with mental illness with medico-legal implications (61).[8] In 1974, the *Forensic Psychiatric Services Commission Act* was proclaimed to provide psychiatric and psychological assessment services to individuals involved in the justice system (62). In 1976, a forensic clinic was opened in Victoria to provide assessment and treatment for adults and children. The *Forensic Psychiatry Act* established the functions of the Forensic Psychiatry Commission for both adults and children (63). In 1981, amendments to the *Mental Health Act* provided immediate transfer and treatment of a mentally ill prisoner to a mental health facility, replacing the prior need for an order-in-council (64).

At the time of proclamation of the *Young Offenders Act* (65), Forensic Psychiatric Services had a centralized service delivery system through Juvenile Services to the Courts confined to Greater Vancouver and Greater Victoria. In order to develop a local response to the Youth Courts and the justice system throughout British Columbia, the Forensic Psychiatric Services Commission entered into a contract with the Mental Health Services to provide court-ordered and court-related psychological assessments and treatment for areas outside of Greater Vancouver and Greater Victoria through local mental health centres. When appropriate services were not available, access to backup services from other mental health centres or Juvenile Services to the Courts was arranged.

The British Columbia Division of the Canadian Mental Health Association

Incorporated in 1953, the association has twenty-two branches in British Columbia and has been active in promoting community awareness and acceptance and public education about mental illness, and in facilitating mental health legislation. The contrast between the social advocacy focus of this latter group and the British Columbia Association for Community Living and other voluntary societies concerned with the mentally handicapped is noteworthy, with the latter being more confrontational and

---

8 Forensic psychiatry is defined as including psychiatric consultation, assessment therapy, or treatment services provided to the courts or to other components of the administration of justice.

aggressive in their activities. The limited need for residential services for the treatment of mental illness in children may account for their focus on adult services.

Child and Youth Mental Health Services

In 1987, the provincial mental health services for children were transferred from Mental Health Services to Family Health and renamed the Child and Youth Mental Health Services. This is in contrast to Mental Health Services and Forensic Psychiatry Services, both of which are separate divisions within Community and Family Health (Chapter 3). This move is related to the advent of the care programs (see Chapter 3) within the Health Units, with the unit staff participating actively as members of the health care team.

EPIDEMIOLOGY

The diagnostic classification of mental disorders in childhood and adolescence is not easy, and underreporting has presented a major problem.

Diagnostic coding for mental illness was included in the Health Surveillance Registry from 1952. Initially, the diagnostic category "Mental, Psycho Neurotic and Personality Disorders" included psychoneurotic disorders, mental deficiency, non-organic speech disturbances, and personality disorders. Subsequently, the International Classification of Diseases–9 (ICD.9) diagnostic classification system was adopted, as was the category, "Mental Disorder," with many in-house additions, including specific delays of development, disturbance of conduct, acute stress and adjustment reaction, hyperkinetic syndrome of childhood, and disturbance of emotions specific to childhood and adolescence.

The national Commission to Investigate Emotional and Learning Disorders in Children (16) reported that one child in eight, or one million children under twenty years of age, had an emotional or learning problem.

Two important studies point to the major importance of mental disorders. First, a study in the Isle of Wight, *The Neuropsychiatric Study in Childhood* (66), documented the importance of mental versus physical disorders. The prevalence of the former was 91.5/1,000 population (five to fourteen years) compared to 87/1,000 for the latter (see Chapter 1, p. 10). The prevalence of psychiatric disorders was estimated to be 46.0 (moderate) and 22.0 (severe) per 1,000 related population (44). This study also showed that the prevalence of psychiatric disorders was much higher in children aged five to fourteen with brain disorders than in children with physical disorders (34.3 percent versus 11.6 percent). Second, the *Ontario Child Health Study* (67) of children four to sixteen years of age reported a six-month prevalence rate of 18 percent of one or more of four psychiatric disorders (conduct disorder, hyperactivity, emotional disorder, and somatization). There is little doubt that these children comprise a major component of the disability profile in children and youth.

Data describing the changing morbidity and mortality of adolescence in British Columbia ware first presented in the late 1970s, when Tonkin described a shift in the primary cause of death in the one to nineteen year age group (1951–78), with social (suicide, homicide, and accidents) replacing biological causes (68). This was associated with a marked increase in the number of deaths in the ten to nineteen year age group, particularly in males. In a subsequent monograph (69), risk-taking and violent behaviours in adolescence were shown to be a major public health problem. Violence-related mortality rates had increased in the previous decade, including motor vehicle accidents, suicide, and homicide. Misuse of the automobile and its associated mortality and morbidity dominated the profile of violence in adolescence in British Columbia. In a third monograph in the mid-1980s (70), Tonkin reported a decline in the number of deaths in adolescents, and commented on the prevalence of sexual abuse, eating disorders, especially bulimia and anorexia nervosa, use of alcohol and drugs, smoking, sexual behaviour, and teenage pregnancy.

Foundations for the Future (71), a federal publication, noted that the prevalence of all mental disorders in children in the general population ranged from 5–30 percent. These rates are higher for adolescents than for younger children, for males than for females, for those living in urban rather than in rural environments, and for those from a lower socioeconomic class than from middle or upper class backgrounds. The prevalence rates of various social problems that are correlated with mental disorders are higher among Native than non-Native children. The behavioural disorders (conduct disorder and attention deficit disorder) are more common than neurotic disorders. Conduct disorder (e.g., aggression, anti-socialization) is the most common specific childhood disorder and is much more common in boys than in girls. Attention deficit disorder is also a common form of mental disorder, often more common in boys. About one-third of all children with mental disorders show some form of neurotic disorder, and more frequently girls than boys. The prevalence of childhood psychotic disorders is more frequent in males, and is less than 0.1 percent.

The prognosis of conduct disorders is relatively poor, with 50 percent of affected children having problems in adulthood. They may also manifest depression, alcoholism, drug abuse, suicidal tendencies, and psychosis. Children with attention deficit disorder are more likely to display academic problems, alcohol and drug abuse, and contact with the legal system as they grow older. A more negative prognosis for adult mental health is also reported for children with both neurotic and psychotic disorders.

PRESENT SERVICES

The psychiatric services for children and adolescents are provided by personal medicine and a variety of ambulatory and residential services funded by the Ministry of Health. In addition, the Ministry of Social Services operates or funds a number of therapeutic group homes for children and adolescents who are wards of the Superintendent of Child Welfare. In the metropolitan areas of Greater Vancouver and Victoria, the psychiatric services are funded by the provincial government but administered and delivered either by a municipality (North Vancouver), or a voluntary society (Greater Vancouver Mental Health Services and the Jack Ledger House, operated by the Arbutus Society in Victoria).

The focus of this discussion is those psychiatric services provided by the British Columbia Ministry of Health that are organized to serve the provincial population of children and youth.

Ambulatory Services

The Child and Youth Mental Health Services: This is part of Family Health, with its own director and Director of Child Psychiatry, based in Victoria. The services are located in thirty-six mental health centres distributed in five regions (Greater Vancouver, Vancouver Island, Okanagan/Kootenay, Fraser Valley/North Shore, and the north). The staff members report to the Director of Child and Youth Mental Health Services for their program supervision and to the regional manager of Mental Health Services for administrative direction. Each regional mental health program includes up to ten mental health centres. The multidisciplinary staff includes a program co-ordinator (psychologist, social worker, or nurse) and one to five other health professionals.

The mental health centres are located within or in close proximity to other community health services, such as public health units, and other government funded services, such as Alcohol and Drug Programs. Community resources, for example, Special Needs Day Care, also receive consultation services from Child and Youth Mental Health Services.

There are long-standing problems in obtaining professional staff in some areas of the province. Recently, the Department of Psychiatry of the University of British Columbia has contracted with the Child and Youth Mental Health Services to provide consultant psychiatric outreach services involving staff psychiatrists and residents on a regular and continuing basis. This arrangement allows telephone consultations between visits with regional mental health professionals and community physicians.

Services for Autistic Children: It is probable that many autistic children are seen by specialists (paediatricians, psychologists, and psychiatrists) in private practice. In addition, the majority are seen for assessment by the Autistic Team, Child Development Diagnostic Program, at the Sunny Hill Hospital for Children in Vancouver (60). The parents are introduced to the Laurel House Society or the Pacific Association for Autistic Citizens. These two societies provide outreach consultation to families and schools throughout the province in an effort to assist families and professionals to develop special programs for the children in their own communities.

Residential Services

The British Columbia Youth Development Centre: This is a designated mental health facility for seriously mentally ill and conduct-disordered adolescents in British Columbia (72), and it is administered by Forensic Psychiatric Services. The Centre provides several residential programs. No outpatient care is provided at the Centre.

The Contained Adolescent Treatment Centre: A twenty-five-bed locked facility that is designed to assist communities throughout the province in the management of the most difficult acting-out and conduct-disordered adolescents. It is also the designated treatment facility for young offenders who are unfit to stand trial or are found not guilty by reason of insanity. A major focus of this program is to develop a community care plan, including short-term respite, short-term residential treatment, on-site training of community care-givers, and after-care support services. The services include:

- *The Response Unit*: a nine-bed facility that provides assessment of eight to thirty days duration, examines short- and long-term needs, and develops a care plan with appropriate intervention strategies to be implemented on return to the home community.
- *Residential Treatment Units*: two eight-bed residential treatment units for the short-term management and treatment of seriously conduct-disordered adolescents whose behaviour presents a danger to themselves or others. The primary objective is to stabilize their behaviour to a level that is manageable in open institutional or local community resources.
- *Psychiatric and Psychological Outreach*: this program provides consultation to regional residential resources where local services are unavailable.
- *Strengthening the Alternate Family Initiative* (see Chapter 19): this program provides pre-discharge training of alternate care-givers in

the treatment process and provides post-discharge support in implementing the care plan in the community. In the case of wards of the Superintendent, the Centre contracts with the approved placement resource prior to discharge for attendance at the Centre for training and involvement with the adolescent and for ongoing care.

Other programs at the Centre include:

- Two twelve-bed open cottages that provide residential treatment to severely disturbed, conduct-disordered adolescents.
- A twelve-bed open cottage in Burnaby provides residential treatment for adolescents throughout the province who are thought-disoriented, severely depressed, or severely neurotic.
- Community and Support Programs consists of a day program, a school-based team, social, vocational, and recreational programs, and clinical support services.

The absence of regional residential treatment centres has obliged the Centre to function as a centralized provincial resource. Residential resources in the interior and northern parts of the province are planned to decentralize the services.

The Centre has not been mandated to provide residential treatment services to conduct-disordered or thought-disordered, mentally handicapped adolescents. Current downsizing of the institutions for the mentally handicapped has not addressed the needs of those who are mentally ill. It is anticipated that the Centre will assume a greater role in the future.

Hospitals: Several hospitals provide paediatric inpatient services. These include the British Columbia Children's Hospital (ten beds), the Vancouver General Hospital (ten adolescent beds), and the Jack Ledger Unit (twenty-five beds) in Victoria.

Recently, all psychiatric referrals for admission to metropolitan hospitals have been reviewed with the staff of Child and Youth Mental Health Services in the child's home community, to determine whether the patient can be cared for in that setting. This policy has been associated with a reduction in the average length of stay of children in the various inpatient facilities in Vancouver and Victoria.

Services for children and youth with eating disorders have been developed at two general hospitals, the British Columbia Children's Hospital and St. Paul's Hospital.

Juvenile Services to the Courts

The Forensic Psychiatric Services Commission (72) is responsible for all court-ordered and court-related assessments and for outpatient treatment for young offenders consistent with the *Young Offenders Act* (65). Juvenile Services to the Courts in turn is mandated to provide court-ordered assessment and treatment of young offenders, eleven to eighteen years of age, who have broken a law under the Criminal Code of Canada and who are being tried in a Youth Court under the *Young Offenders Act*. Referrals derive from the courts, probation services, youth detention centres, and Crown counsel only.

Juvenile Services to the Courts provides court-ordered inpatient assessments, outpatient assessment and treatment, specialized treatment programs for sexual offenders, violent offenders, and offenders who are diagnosed as having a post-traumatic stress disorder related to family violence, and assessment and treatment services to young offenders incarcerated in youth detention facilities.

Juvenile Services to the Courts operates a secure nine-bed inpatient assessment unit, located in premises leased from the Willingdon Youth Detention Centre adjacent to the Burnaby Mental Health Centre. It is designated a mental health facility under the *Mental Health Act*. It also operates outpatient clinics in Burnaby, Victoria, Prince George, and Kamloops for assessment and treatment of young offenders. Psychological assessment and treatment services in areas outside of the above clinics are available from the local mental health centre.

COMMENT

Mental health services have been provided by the provincial government for over a hundred years. Initially, the prevailing strategy was to provide these services for the population in provincial institutions. Mentally handicapped and the mentally ill persons were initially admitted to the same institutions. The decision to place the two populations in separate residential settings was made in the 1930s. The private practice of medicine participated in the diagnostic process but was divorced from maintenance care. It is interesting that when the Department of Health and Welfare was created in 1946, the Health Branch was transferred from the Department of the Provincial Secretary to the new department, but the mental health services were left behind. During the 1950s and 1960s, the value of institutional placement was challenged by the normalization movement and was gradually replaced by regional community-based services. This trend, together with the advent of effective drug therapy and modern psychiatric care, probably accounted for the belated transfer of mental health services to the renamed Department of Health Services and Hospital Insurance in 1959.

Ambulatory and residential services to the mentally handicapped and mentally ill were excluded as benefits of the provincial hospital insurance plan in British Columbia in 1949 and later of the federal *Hospital Insurance and Diagnostic Services Act* (73) in 1957. The transfer of the care of the mentally handicapped from the Department of Health Services and Hospital Insurance to the Ministry of Human Resources in 1974 achieved cost sharing with the federal government Canada Assistance Plan. Gradually the provincial health insurance benefits were extended in 1968 to include patients in psychiatric units of community hospitals and day-care and outpatient services in these hospitals. A further advance, which followed the federal *Medical Care Act* (74), was the authorization of payment for medical services to patients in psychiatric hospitals. This opened the way for physicians in private practice to work part time in psychiatric hospital units and mental health centres. Therefore, it is reasonable to conclude that federal health insurance made a contribution to the development of population-based psychiatric services, albeit delayed.

Services for Mentally Handicapped Children

While the hospital insurance benefits excluded the institutional care of the mentally handicapped population, the transfer of the three institutions to the Ministry of Human Resources took advantage of the Canada Assistance Plan to transfer federal funds to the provincial budget.

Perhaps the most notable achievement in the care of this population was the role of the voluntary societies in the development of community services for the care of the mentally handicapped. The BCACL has an illustrious record in the promotion and development of community services (75). It played a major part in the closure of the institutions and the transfer of residents to community settings, and influenced the Ministry of Health to accept responsibility for the cost of care of severely multi-handicapped persons (the medically fragile) in the same community settings. In addition, it started the Family Support Institute, which created a network of community resource parents, and is currently working to integrate mentally handicapped students in various educational and vocational settings. Similarly, the CLS has made an important contribution in demonstrating that it was feasible for severely mentally handicapped adults to live in community settings. For a period of forty years, the advocacy movement has enjoyed, if not always a harmonious, then certainly a productive relationship with the various departments and ministries of government responsible for the care of the mentally handicapped population. These various departments and ministries, in turn, have been increasingly responsive to the presentations of the different voluntary societies.

The community living movement, however, has also created new responsibilities for families and society to provide services and facilities for mentally handicapped persons. Community living does not guarantee true integration in residential neighbourhoods, educational settings, or the workplace. Likewise, the medical and dental care services are often ill prepared to cope with these children and youth. The upsurge in private homes for residents discharged from institutions has created the need to monitor the quality of life and the supportive environment available to each individual.

Services for Children with Mental Disorders

The focus of the provincial mental health services has been the development of a population-based treatment service comprising ambulatory and residential programs. The services for children and youth have evolved as adjuncts to the system serving mentally ill adults, despite the very different profile of mental disorders and mental health problems in the younger age group.

The CELDIC Report (16) observed that many different professions and institutions were involved with children with emotional and learning disorders, and there was little communication between them. In addition, each specialist was likely to have his or her ideas about the nature of the child's needs and how these can be best met. The report stressed the need for greater integration of the efforts of departments of government (Education, Health, Welfare, and the Attorney General). Problems of intra and inter ministerial integration of mental health services persist. The component parts, the Child and Youth Mental Health Services and their urban counterparts in Vancouver and Victoria, the British Columbia Youth Development Centre, the hospital-based services, and the Juvenile Services to the Courts, are accountable to different administrative units in the ministry and function virtually independently of one another. To compound the complexity medical (family physicians, paediatricians, and psychiatrists) and other health professionals provide a parallel service (personal medicine) to the population.

Arguably the most significant development of services to children and youth in British Columbia was the recent transfer of Child and Youth Mental Health Services from Mental Health to Family Health (Chapter 3). This gave belated recognition to the distinctive profile of mental disorders and problems in children and youth and their relationship to family function. In addition, the Child and Youth Mental Health Services, the British Columbia Youth Development Centre, Juvenile Services to the Courts, and the hospital-based services are in the process of developing an integrated clinical psychiatric service for children and youth. This seems to have come about more because the psychiatrists who direct the different programs work well with each other, rather than from any formal policy pronouncement. There are plans to extend the collaboration with the university Department of Psychiatry in the outreach program, to decentralize the services provided by the British Columbia Youth Development Centre with regional residential units, and to bring all hospital-based services into one facility under the administrative umbrella of the British Columbia Children's Hospital.

A federal government publication, *Mental Health for Canadians* (76), introduced a broader definition of mental health to include not only mental disorders but also mental health problems. A mental disorder is defined as "a medically diagnosable illness that results in the significant impairment of an individual's cognitive, affective or relational abilities." A mental health problem is defined as "a disruption of the interactions between the individual, the group and the environment." Mental disorders may be represented by a horizontal line, from presence of at one end to freedom from psychiatric symptoms at the other end, and, similarly, mental health by a vertical line, from absence at one end to presence of conflict from individual, group, and environmental factors at the other end. The relationship between the mental health disorder and the environmental factors related to mental health can be illustrated by crossing the two lines. Absence of conflict and absence of psychiatric symptoms yield optimal mental health, while presence of psychiatric symptoms and presence of conflict yield minimal mental health. The two other combinations yield marginal mental health. Mental health problems may result from factors within the individual, e.g., physical or mental disorders or inadequate coping skills, or external factors, e.g., sociocultural or family factors. Sociocultural risk factors include poverty, minority ethnic status, low social class, parental unemployment, overcrowded housing, and residency in a delinquent neighbourhood. Family-related risk factors include parental psychopathology, deviant patterns of parent-child interactions, and marital discord and divorce.

In the *Ontario Child Health Study* (67), Offord reported that the commonest risk factors were one-parent families, families on social assistance, and families from subsidized housing. Others reported children at extremely high risk for mental problems were those in care of child welfare systems, physically abused or neglected children, victims of sexual abuse, and children from poverty-stricken and divorced families (71).

In summary, the mental health status of children and youth is influenced by two primary factors, the vulnerability to mental disorder and environmental risks. It follows that efforts to improve the mental health of children and youth must include not only services which support the prevention, treatment, and rehabilitation of mental disorders, but also those that support the promotion and protection of mental health by alleviation of causal environmental factors. *Mental Health for Canadians*, using the *Framework for Health Promotion* model (77), reviews current mental health challenges (reducing inequities, e.g., poverty), increasing prevention and enhancing coping with potential responses.

A further implication for health planners is that children with mental disorders or mental health problems are at increased risk for other morbidities, including school failure, unwanted pregnancy, chronic health problems, and substance use. There is evidence that these disorders of childhood and youth, if left untreated, can lead to criminal behaviour, alcoholism, and drug use. These morbidities lead to further implications in planning management because several ministries are involved.

This broader definition of mental health has implications for treatment and for mental health promotion. Rae-Grant et al. (78) suggest that three implications follow from the *Ontario Child Health Study*. First, the size of the problem dictates that family physicians and educators must work with the mental health services in the assessment and treatment of children with emotional and behavioural problems. Second, these specialized services should be targeted at those children and families most in need and most likely to benefit from them. Third, effective interventions of a primary prevention nature that are targeted at groups of children need to be explored. These might include groups of children known to be at risk of mental health problems, such as the offspring of families on social assistance, or living in communities of children at high risk, such as those in subsidized housing and with single parents. Poor children need programs aimed at raising their quality of life in order to improve their future life prospects. In the Ottawa study (79), an intervention study which targeted populations of children at risk of conduct disorders in an attempt to prevent anti-social behaviour, the beneficial effects of the program were confined to unobtrusive measures of anti-social behaviour, such as security reports and fire alarms, and were not reflected in school performance or home behaviour. It is reasonable to assume that community recreational programs can divert children from anti-social behaviour, and it is essential to include those children living in poverty in these programs. These children are often excluded because the family cannot afford the cost.

Foundations for the Future, the first federal government report on the state of mental health services for children and youth in Canada (71), described four basic principles essential for the planning, development, and implementation of mental health programs for children and youth.

1. The family is central to the provision of health, and health policy must strengthen the capacity of families to provide for their children.

2. The specific health needs of children and youth need to be recognized and met within the health service.
3. The institutional model must be complemented by community-based programs and initiatives with consultants available to support primary care staff (public health and social service staff, teachers, etc.).
4. Proactive programs must be available for those at risk who do not use the existing service.

The report also identified priority issues, including the need for planning and co-ordination of the children's service network, the need for integration of hospital and community mental health systems, including private practitioners and mental health centres, the need for proactive planning to develop preventive and early intervention services, and the need to develop immediate responses to different problems such as family conflict, adolescent suicide, and lifestyle issues, such as premature sexuality and alcohol and drug abuse, that are often the focus of underlying mental health concerns.

Finally, the report identified four critical issues in service provision and integrated delivery of mental services to children and youth: the importance of mental health promotion; the development of partnerships with the family and the service providers; access to services, including effective screening and appropriate referral; and innovation and excellence, including planning to provide a framework within which children's services can develop and meet changing needs.

Sixty years after the *Annual Report of the Child Guidance Clinic* stated "The whole idea of the Clinic is that of prevention" (46), the director, Dr. Crease, would be encouraged by some trends in mental health in children and youth. He would be astonished by the prevalence and content of the mortality and morbidity, but gratified by the new interest in primary prevention, and by developmental screening for infants and preschool children at social risk, followed by educational programs (Post Partum Parent Support Program and Nobody's Perfect), the introduction of health promotion strategies, and the recently announced Child Development Initiative.

REFERENCES

1. BRITISH COLUMBIA. *Annual Report for Twelve Months Ended March 31, 1951.* Department of the Provincial Secretary, Mental Health Services, 1951.
2. BRITISH COLUMBIA. *Annual Report for Twelve Months Ended March 31, 1953.* Department of the Provincial Secretary, Mental Health Services, 1953.
3. *Insane Asylums Act*, S.B.C. 1873, c. 28.
4. *Insane Asylums Amendment Act*, S.B.C. 1912, c. 13.

5. *Clinics for Psychological Medicine Act*, R.S.B.C. 1948, c. 52, s. 3.
6. ADOLPH, V. *Woodlands: 100 Years of Progress*, 1978.
7. *Schools for the Mental Defective Act*, S.B.C. 1953, c. 26.
8. BRITISH COLUMBIA. *Annual Report for the Twelve Months Ended March 31, 1953.* Department of the Provincial Secretary, Mental Health Services, 1953.
9. BRITISH COLUMBIA. *Annual Report for the Twelve Months Ended March 31, 1954.* Department of the Provincial Secretary, Mental Health Services, 1954.
10. HEIFETZ, L. J. From consumer to middleman: Emerging roles for parents in the network of services for retarded children. In *Parent Education and Intervention Handbook*, ed. R. R. Abidin. Springfield, Ill.: Charles C. Thomas, 1980, pp. 349–84.
11. TJOSSEM, T. D. Early intervention: Issues and approaches. In *Intervention Strategies for High Risk Infants and Young Children*, ed. T. D. Tjossem. Baltimore: University Park Press, 1976, pp. 3–33.
12. SCHEERENBERGER, R. C. New foundations. In *A History of Mental Retardation. A Quarter Century of Promise*. Baltimore: Paul H. Brookes, 1987, pp. 109–40.
13. PALMESTIL, G. Developments in the care of the mentally handicapped. In *The Mentally Handicapped Towards Normal Living*, ed. K. Grunewald. London: Huntington, 1978, pp. 175–85.
14. CALVERT, D., OLSHIN, G. M., DEWEERD, M. J., and BERSON, M. P. Office of Education describes model projects for young handicapped children. *Exceptional Children* 36 (1969): 229–48.
15. CANADA. *Mental Retardation in Canada*. Report of the Federal-Provincial Conference, Ottawa, October 19–22, 1964. Department of National Health and Welfare. Ottawa: Queen's Printer, 1965.
16. CELDIC STUDY COMMITTEE. *One Million Children—The CELDIC Report*. A National Study of Canadian Children with Emotional and Learning Disorders (Co-Chairmen: Denis Lazure and C.A. Roberts). Lenard Crainford, 1969.
17. ROSS, MATHEW (ed.). *Survey of Mental Health Needs and Resources of British Columbia*. Medical Director, American Psychiatric Association, 1961.
18. BRITISH COLUMBIA. *Annual Report, 1975*. Department of Human Resources.
19. BRITISH COLUMBIA. *Annual Report, 1979*. Ministry of Health, p. 145.
20. *History of the Kootenay Society for the Handicapped*. Castlegar, B.C., n.d. Mimeographed document.
21. JUSTICE, W., personal communication, 1989.
22. BRYNELSEN, D. Infant development programmes in British Columbia. In *Parents, Professionals and Mentally Handicapped People*, ed. P. Mittler. London: Croom Helm, 1983, pp. 77–90.
23. *Report of the Executive Director*. Association for Retarded Children, 1954.
24. *Public Schools Amendment Act*, S.B.C. 1956, c. 39.
25. *Public Schools Amendment Act*, S.B.C. 1959, c. 75.
26. CAMPBELL, I. J. Letter to Ms. B. Smith, Kings Regional Health and Rehabilitation Centre, Waterville, Nova Scotia, 1982.
27. BRITISH COLUMBIA. *1967/68 Annual Report*. Mental Health Branch, Department of Health Services and Hospital Insurance, 1969.
28. DICKIE, J., personal communication, 1989.
29. BRITISH COLUMBIA. Project Life (news release, 11 June 1977). Ministry of Human Resources.

30. SALISBURY, B., DICKEY, J., and CRAWFORD, C. *Service Brokerage: Individual Empowerment and Social Service Accountability.* Downsview, Ontario: G. Allan Rocher Institute, 1987.
31. RIOUX, M. and CRAWFORD, C. *Choices. The Community Living Concept is a Way of Thinking.* Vancouver: Community Living Society, 1982.
32. BRITISH COLUMBIA. *Annual Report for Twelve Months Ended March 31, 1957.* Department of the Provincial Secretary, Mental Health Services Branch, 1957.
33. *Schools for the Mental Defective Amendment Act*, S.B.C. 1958, c. 28.
34. BRITISH COLUMBIA. *1963/64 Annual Report.* Mental Health Services Branch, Department of Health Services and Hospital Insurance, 1965.
35. BRITISH COLUMBIA. *1965/66 Annual Report.* Mental Health Services Branch, Department of Health Services and Hospital Insurance, 1967.
36. BRITISH COLUMBIA. Phasing out of institutions (news release, 4 June 1981). Ministry of Human Resources.
37. BRITISH COLUMBIA. Operational Directive No. 7, 1982/83 Re: Interim Policy Regarding Admissions to Woodlands, Tranquille and Glendale. John Noble, Deputy Minister, Ministry of Human Resources, 7 May 1982.
38. TISCHLER, B., personal communication, 1989.
39. BRITISH COLUMBIA. Community placement of Tranquille residents (news release, 9 December 1983). Ministry of Human Resources.
40. LORD, J. and JEARN, C. *Return to the Community. The Process of Closing an Institution.* Kitchener, Ontario: Centre for Research and Education in Human Services, 1989.
41. POULOS, S., personal communication, 1989.
42. DICKENS, B. M. Medicine and the law: Withholding paediatric medical care. *Canadian Bar Review* 62 (1984): 196–210.
43. RENWICK, D.H.G. Estimating prevalence of certain chronic childhood conditions by use of a central registry. *Public Health Reports* 82 (1987): 261–69.
44. *Report of the Committee on Local Authority and Allied Personal Social Services*, July, 1968, Chairman: Frederick Seebohm. London: Her Majesty's Stationery Office, Appendix Q, pp. 349–51.
45. *Guaranteed Available Income for Need Act*, R.S.B.C. 1979, c. 158.
46. KILBURN, JOSEPHINE F. Report on the Child Guidance Clinic. In BRITISH COLUMBIA, Department of the Provincial Secretary, *Annual Report of the Mental Hospitals of the Province of British Columbia for the 12 Months Ended March 31, 1933*, pp. 15–16.
47. WATSON, C., personal communication, 1989.
48. BRITISH COLUMBIA. Department of the Provincial Secretary. *Annual Report of the Mental Hospitals of the Province of British Columbia for 12 Months Ended March 31, 1934.*
49. BRITISH COLUMBIA. Department of the Provincial Secretary. *Annual Report of the Mental Hospitals of the Province of British Columbia for 12 Months Ended March 31, 1949.*
50. BRITISH COLUMBIA. Department of the Provincial Secretary. *Annual Report of the Mental Health Services for 12 Months Ended March 31, 1953.*
51. BRITISH COLUMBIA. Department of the Provincial Secretary. *Annual Report of the Mental Health Services for 12 Months Ended March 31, 1956.*

52. BRITISH COLUMBIA. Department of the Provincial Secretary, Mental Health Services. *Annual Report for Twelve Months Ended March 31, 1958.*
53. *Mental Health Act,* S.B.C. 1964, c. 29.
54. BRITISH COLUMBIA. Department of the Provincial Secretary, Mental Health Services Branch. *Annual Report for 12 Months Ended March 31, 1959.*
55. MENZIES, M. A. Preventive psychiatry: The psychiatric team as consultant to the public health nurse. *Canadian Medical Association Journal* 93 (1965): 743–47.
56. BRITISH COLUMBIA. Ministry of Health. *Annual Report, 1978.*
57. BRITISH COLUMBIA. *Annual Report for Twelve Months Ended March 31, 1966.* Mental Health Services Branch, Department of Health Services and Hospital Insurance, 1967.
58. BRITISH COLUMBIA. *1968—20th Annual Report, BCHIS.* Department of Health Services and Hospital Insurance, 1968.
59. *Medical Services Act,* S.B.C. 1967, c. 24.
60. HO, H. Changing concepts in early childhood autism. *B.C. Medical Journal* 27 (1985): 326–28.
61. BRITISH COLUMBIA. *1966/67 Annual Report.* Mental Health Services Branch, Department of Health Services and Hospital Insurance, 1968.
62. *Forensic Psychiatric Services Commission Act,* S.B.C. 1974, c. 35.
63. *Forensic Psychiatry Act,* R.S.B.C. 1979, c. 139.
64. BRITISH COLUMBIA. Ministry of Health. *Annual Report, 1981.*
65. *Young Offenders Act,* R.S.C. 1985, c. 1.
66. RUTTER, M., GRAHAM, P., and YULE, W. *A Neuropsychiatric Study in Childhood* (Clinics in Developmental Medicine, Nos. 35/36). London: Spastics International Medical Publ./Heinemann Medical Books; Philadelphia: J. B. Lippincott, 1970.
67. OFFORD, D. R., BOYLE, M. H., FLEMING, J. E., BLUM, H. M., and GRANT N.I.R. Ontario child health study: Summary of selected results. *Canadian Journal of Psychiatry* 34 (1989): 483–91.
68. TONKIN, R. S. *Child Health Profile.* British Columbia, 1979.
69. TONKIN, R. S. *Child Health Profile. Violence in Adolescence.* British Columbia, 1981.
70. TONKIN, R. S. *Child Health Profile.* Youth Today, 1986.
71. CANADA. *Foundations for the Future.* A Report of the Working Group on Child and Youth Mental Health Services. Prepared for the Federal/ Provincial/Territorial Advisory Committee on Mental Health. Health and Welfare Canada, March 1990.
72. *Forensic Psychiatric Services, Youth Services.* Mimeographed document, 28 June 1989.
73. *Hospital Insurance and Diagnostic Services Act,* S.C. 1957, c. 28.
74. *Medical Care Act,* S.C. 1966–67, c. 64.
75. ETMANSKI, A. B. Attitude changes towards mentally handicapped persons. *B.C. Medical Journal* 25 (1983): 143–46.
76. CANADA. *Mental Health for Canadians. Striking a Balance.* Health and Welfare Canada, 1988, p. 8.
77. EPP, J. *Achieving Health for All: A Framework for Health Promotion.* Ottawa: Health and Welfare Canada, 1986.

78. RAE-GRANT, N., OFFORD, D. R., and MUNRO BLUM, H. Implications for clinical services, research and training. *Canadian Journal of Psychiatry* 34 (1989): 492–99.

79. JONES, M. B. and OFFORD, D. R. Reduction of anti-social behaviour in poor children by non-school skill development. *Journal of Child Psychology* 30 (1989): 737–50.

15

Services for Children with Cerebral Palsy

INTRODUCTION

Children with "cerebral palsy" share certain motor impairments, and sometimes other neurological disorders, such as developmental delay and epilepsy, that are secondary to underlying brain pathology. The need for early identification, assessment, and continuing care, together with family support and education, is an important component of care for these disabled children.

The concept of non-residential, community-based, inter-disciplinary services for the population of children with developmental disabilities, such as cerebral palsy, was unheard of until the middle of this century. Prior to that time, the Children's Hospitals provided outpatient services, often confined to a financially indigent group of families (called public as distinct from private patients), that was largely comprised of diagnostic services. During the past forty years, community-based rehabilitation[1] services have emerged to provide assessment, plus therapy, education, and vocational training for the child, and education and support for family members.

This rehabilitation movement can be attributed to several factors, including the need to provide services for seriously disabled veterans after World War II, the epidemics of poliomyelitis, and the changing pattern of disease. The combination of immunization and chemotherapy, together with an improved standard of living, has resulted in the control of many acute illnesses and the emergence of a new concern for the rehabilitation of individuals with neuromuscular disabilities and handicaps. In order to describe the ways in which chronic and progressive disorders

---

1 Also referred to as "habilitation" when applied to children, to reflect the congenital nature of the disability. The term "rehabilitation" implies habilitation, when appropriate, throughout the text.

impact on everyday life, the following sequence of events has been proposed (1):

$$Disease \rightarrow Impairment \rightarrow Disability \rightarrow Handicap$$

The impairment represents a disturbance at the system level, the disability the consequence of the impairment in terms of performance and activity, and the handicap the resulting disadvantage that limits or prevents the fulfilment of a role that may be normal for that individual. The handicap is the outcome of the social, economic, cultural, and environmental consequences that stem from the disability. Additionally, age and sex may influence the extent to which an individual experiences a handicap. Thus an impairment may or may not imply disability, and disability may or may not imply a handicap. In essence, a disability is absolute, while a handicap is variable and determined by the limitations imposed by society on daily living.

This chapter describes the gradual emergence of the provincial network of child development centres primarily established for children with cerebral palsy. It begins, however, with a description of the role of the G. F. Strong Rehabilitation Centre in the evolution of rehabilitation services for children and adults. This included the development of the first multidisciplinary treatment service for children with developmental disabilities in British Columbia.

HISTORICAL CONSIDERATIONS

G. F. Strong Rehabilitation Centre

The rehabilitation movement achieved a new status during and following World War II, and rehabilitation centres were developed across Canada for seriously disabled veterans. After the war, these services were also developed for individuals with non-service connected disabilities. The Canadian Paraplegic Association was formed in 1945, and a Western Division in British Columbia was established in the same year. Edmund Desjardins, himself a veteran with severe spinal cord injury, was active in the formation of the Western Division. At the same time, Dr. George F. Strong, a prominent Vancouver physician, whose daughter became a paraplegic in her teen years, was exploring the development of rehabilitation services for individuals with spinal cord injury. Their combined efforts resulted in the formation of the Western Society for Physical Rehabilitation in Vancouver, later to be renamed the G. F. Strong Rehabilitation Centre following the death of Dr. Strong, in 1957 (2). Desjardins was appointed manager of the Centre in 1948 and held that position with distinction until his retirement in 1979. Since his retirement, he continues to serve as a consultant to the Centre.

The Centre has played a pivotal role in the development of rehabilitation services in British Columbia. The policy of the directors was to build a single facility for children and adults to serve the needs of different disability groups, such as spinal cord injuries, polio, arthritis, amputees, and cerebral palsy. The directors planned a comprehensive facility to be built in four stages, in response to needs and as funds were raised. The site was purchased in 1947 from the Canadian Pacific Railway for $6,000 and the funds were donated by the Kinsmen Club of Vancouver. Construction of Unit 1 was started in 1948, and it opened for operation in 1949. The construction of Unit 2 began in 1949, and again was largely funded by voluntary contribution, with the addition of grants from the provincial and federal governments. Units 3 and 4 were built simultaneously and were operational in 1954, providing the Centre with a total of 53,000 square feet of floor area. The latter two units provided for an inpatient wing of twenty beds designed to accommodate children. The paediatric ward never materialized, however, because of the increasing number of individuals suitable for admission to the Centre who required a nursing care bed before they were able to occupy a self-care bed. In 1955, this twenty-bed wing was converted to a nursing unit.

The capital cost of Units 3 and 4 was shared equally between the Centre, the provincial, and the federal governments. In 1973, another major addition, three times as large as the original complex, was completed. It provided a hundred rehabilitation nursing beds and fifty self-care beds.

Grants from the Health Branch, and subsequently the Welfare Branch (as it was then known), contributed to the funding for operating costs. Federal health grants were also obtained for professional training. In the early 1960s, the Centre was licensed under the provincial *Hospital Act* as a hospital facility, and thus became eligible for operating funds through the federal–provincial fiscal arrangements. The provincial *Hospital Insurance Act* (3) was subsequently amended through the efforts of the G. F. Strong Rehabilitation Centre to make all designated rehabilitation units and hospitals eligible for these benefits. Initially, the inpatient care was funded, and subsequently, when ambulatory services were also covered by the British Columbia Hospital Insurance Service[2] (BCHIS) (4), the annual Health Branch grant was withdrawn. Prosthetic, orthotic, and assistive self-help devices were not covered by BCHIS. When Pharmacare was introduced in later years, it assumed some of these costs.

In 1951, the G. F. Strong Rehabilitation Centre rented space to the Canadian Arthritis and Rheumatism Society to develop an outpatient

---

2 Later British Columbia Hospital Programs.

clinical program for adults with arthritis (5). In addition, four inpatient beds were available for these patients. In 1960, a program for children was added (6), and this became eligible for insurance benefits from the Hospital Insurance in 1972 (7). Subsequently, a free-standing facility, the Arthritis Centre, was opened in 1969, and ambulatory services for children and adults were shifted to the new setting. While the inpatient services for adults remained at the G. F. Strong Rehabilitation Centre, the operating costs of the new facility were eligible for funding by the provincial Hospital Insurance Service. Currently, paediatric services for children with juvenile rheumatoid arthritis and other connective tissue diseases, such as dermatomyositis and scleroderma, are provided at ambulatory clinics at the Arthritis Centre and the British Columbia Children's Hospital.

The Centre was also active in encouraging the development of a variety of professional services in British Columbia. These included a School of Audiology and Speech Services and a School of Rehabilitation Medicine at the University of British Columbia, programs in prosthetics and orthotics at the British Columbia Institute of Technology, and a residency training program in physical medicine and rehabilitation for physicians in association with the Department of Medicine, Faculty of Medicine, at the University of British Columbia.

Regional Treatment Centres (Child Development Centres)

Services for children with cerebral palsy were initially developed at the Children's Hospital in Vancouver in 1948, when a day-school unit for the treatment, training, and education of these children was opened. The school was operated by the Vancouver School Board, and classes were held through to grade six (8).

In 1944, the Vancouver School Board employed a teacher to provide home teaching for disabled children, the majority of whom had cerebral palsy (9). This remarkable primary teacher, Miss Mary Pack, who was later to organize the Canadian Arthritis and Rheumatism Society (CARS), urged the parents to form the Spastic Paralysis Society of British Columbia.[3] A centrally located store served as a schoolroom and home visits were made to those children who were unable to travel. In 1949, an outpatient program for children with neuromuscular disabilities was started at the G. F. Strong Rehabilitation Centre, and the schoolroom was

---

3 The Spastic Paralysis Society of British Columbia was incorporated under the *Societies Act* in 1945. It was renamed the Cerebral Palsy Association of British Columbia in January 1952, then the Cerebral Palsy Association of Greater Vancouver in November 1953, and finally the Children's Rehabilitation and Cerebral Palsy Association in April 1964 (10).

relocated at the Centre to take advantage of the clinical services. This arrangement continued until 1968, when the Children's Rehabilitation and Cerebral Palsy Association relocated their clinical program at the Vancouver Neurological Centre (11). Outpatient services for children were continued at the G. F. Strong Rehabilitation Centre (12).

The Cerebral Palsy Association of Lower Vancouver Island opened a clinic in the Royal Jubilee Hospital in Victoria in 1953. The Fraser Valley Cerebral Palsy Association, also formed in 1953, initially concentrated on providing transportation for local children to access services in Vancouver. Subsequently, a Children's Treatment Centre was opened in Surrey in September 1961. These programs were operated by non-profit societies, and were funded by parents, donations, and federal health grants.

The board of directors of the Cerebral Palsy Association of British Columbia conceived the idea of a parents conference, in order to promote treatment services in other parts of the province (13). The conference was held in May 1952 at the Western Society for Physical Rehabilitation, and Dr. G. F. Strong gave a talk on rehabilitation. Dr. Donald Paterson was chairman of a panel on the medical aspects of cerebral palsy, and other panel discussions were on the child and education, the child and the community, and the child and the family.

The conference elected a committee to explore the best means of expanding the operation of the Cerebral Palsy Association of British Columbia throughout the province. A medical advisory committee was also formed, with Dr. J. F. McCreary appointed chairman. Finally, plans were made for another conference next year, which was held in May 1953. The Cerebral Palsy Association of British Columbia was incorporated in February 1954 (10), and, at the first annual meeting in May 1954, a provincial board of directors was elected, with Dr. Donald Paterson as president. Representatives came from the Vancouver Association for the Advancement of Retarded Children, the Cerebral Palsy Association of Lower Vancouver Island, the Cerebral Palsy Association of Greater Vancouver, the Children's Hospital, Vancouver, the Kootenay Society for Handicapped Children, the Lower Fraser Valley Cerebral Palsy Association, the Powell River Society for the Handicapped, and the Upper Fraser Valley Society for Handicapped Children.

The minutes of the founding meeting noted that the association was dedicated to "fighting the greatest single crippling condition of children" with a strong provincial association and the extension of services throughout British Columbia (13, 14).

After incorporation, the association maintained a central office with an executive director. The original objectives of the association were to promote research, diagnosis, treatment, education, and welfare for individuals handicapped with cerebral palsy, to promote public awareness of the problems of cerebral palsy, and to distribute to organizations and institutions experience and information to provide an appropriate environment for individuals with cerebral palsy.

The membership initially included four categories: first, member groups, i.e., societies that sponsored regional treatment centres throughout the province and received funds from the association; second, affiliates, i.e., organizations and clubs that provided care for individuals with cerebral palsy but did not receive funds from the association; third, individual members who paid annual dues; and fourth, honorary members appointed by the board (15). In addition, a professional advisory committee of medical and allied health professionals from metropolitan Vancouver advised the board on matters of treatment program, education, etc.

The medical advisory committee recommended, first, that the development of many centres for the treatment of cerebral palsy in British Columbia be discouraged, and, second, that the existing clinics at the Children's Hospital, the Western Society for Physical Rehabilitation in Vancouver, and the Clinic in Victoria be enlarged to serve children in the two metropolitan areas and to establish more extensive home programs for children from other areas.

Mrs. Frances Lamont, who was appointed executive secretary of the society in 1959, recalled that Dr. Paterson tried to bring about an amalgamation between the Cerebral Palsy Association and the Association for Retarded Children of British Columbia, and that his motion was soundly defeated at the annual general meeting. She added that "He was so annoyed that he resigned and would have nothing to do with the Cerebral Palsy Association for several years." A newsletter, *The Cerebral Palsy News*, was launched in 1961.

Unlike the G. F. Strong Rehabilitation Centre, the regional treatment centres were not designated as chronic hospitals under the *Hospital Act*[4] (16) and hence were ineligible for benefits from the provincial *Hospital Insurance Act*. No provincial Act authorized their activity, and the acquisition of operating funds was a constant concern to the provincial association and the member groups. The provincial association was also involved in planning and developing the regional treatment centres throughout the province, and provided support and advice to different communities to assist them in planning and operating centres. It also published a newsletter and arranged training and refresher courses for staff.

The Development Centre for Handicapped Children in Prince George was started in 1968, and was renamed the Child Development Centre

---

4 One exception is the G. R. Pearkes Centre in Victoria, which is under the administration of the Queen Alexandra Hospital for Children, and, like the G. F. Strong Rehabilitation Centre, receives funding from Hospital Programs.

when a new facility was opened in 1973. The term "child development centres" has been unofficially adopted to refer to regional treatment centres, though often the name includes the donor who built and equipped the facility as well (17). There were six centres in 1972 and twenty in 1990.

Centres developed as a result of local initiative, in a random fashion and in the absence of a regional plan. Each centre served a large area and many clients attended infrequently because of distance and extreme climatic conditions in winter. When a number of children were identified in a centre's referral area, the centre endeavoured to provide outreach services, usually physiotherapy, to communities within easy reach, until they developed their own services. This usually involved sending a staff physiotherapist to the community and, in some instances, a local special needs pre-school was set up. It has also been possible for some centres to utilize the services of therapists employed by other agencies to work with children in their home communities, with the direction and support of the centre staff.

In 1956, concern was expressed by the provincial association over the lack of services and vocational opportunities for adolescents (13). The Happy Club was formed in 1957, introducing a program of rehabilitation for adults with cerebral palsy, and then a society for the rehabilitation of adults with cerebral palsy was formed in 1959.

In 1964, the provincial government delegated authority to the provincial association to apportion government granted funds to member bodies. The individual centres prepared their budgets and the association submitted them to the government, which in turn returned the grant to the association and on to the members' association.

The Cerebral Palsy Association of British Columbia was a charter member of the national body of the cerebral palsy section of the Canadian Council for Crippled Children and Adults, formed in 1958.

Over the years, the group members became increasingly dissatisfied with their membership in the association. In contrast to the British Columbia Association for Community Living (Chapter 14), there was a lack of parental involvement in the organization. Doubtless the fact that the budget for the office and staff of the Cerebral Palsy Association of British Columbia was provided by the government accounted for the lack of social advocacy by the association on behalf of their constituency.

The Ministry of Health decided to fund the centres directly in 1982 (15, 18), and government funding to the provincial association was terminated. The Cerebral Palsy Association of British Columbia undertook an organizational review in the early 1980s, and recommendations were accepted by the board of directors. They included the development of a standards manual by a group of executive directors to guide the operations of the child development centres (19). The manual acknowledged that the centres were autonomous, each operated by local incorporated societies, and therefore each individually responsible for the quality of its own programs.

In 1986, the board requested the resignation of the executive director, and, the following year, at an extraordinary meeting, requested the resignation of the entire board (17), with a caretaker board appointed to carry on business. The office of the association was closed. The decision was made to continue operations under a new constitution and an office was reopened in 1988. A position of provincial co-ordinator was established, and the office was funded by donations, memberships, and fund raising. The provincial association changed its mandate, withdrawing from service- and centre-related operations and focusing on public education programs.

The new mandate is to act as an advocate and consultative resource for persons affected by cerebral palsy and other developmental disorders, to increase public awareness of the causes and consequences of cerebral palsy and other developmental disorders, and to solicit, and to co-ordinate the solicitation of, financial aid for the purposes of the society.

There is now only one class of membership. The provincial office distributes a number of information kits, operates a lending library, publishes a newsletter for members and donors, and co-ordinates Cerebral Palsy Week in British Columbia. The provincial association also serves as an advocate on behalf of people with cerebral palsy, particularly adults, and establishes and maintains liaison with other provincial disabled consumer groups.

Each child development centre now negotiates its own budget with government. Recently, the parents at some centres have employed consumer power to inform elected representatives of their service needs, and this initiative has resulted in significant budgetary increases. In collaboration with the Ministry of Health, the parents have also organized an annual meeting, called Family Focus, which is held in different regions of the province. These meetings address family-related issues, strategies, and tactics that have been tried in different communities.

The Canadian Cerebral Palsy Association was founded in 1969 as a national voluntary charitable organization with a two-fold mission, to improve the quality of life for Canadians with cerebral palsy and their families, and to reduce the incidence of the disorder. The association accomplishes its mission through education and awareness programs, public policy advocacy research, and information exchanges and co-ordination. These activities support and complement those of the provincial and regional associations across Canada.

EPIDEMIOLOGY

The Health Surveillance Registry provided annual data for cerebral palsy, based on the International Classification of Diseases (ICD) (343.1–343.9),[5] plus special codes in order to identify conditions for which no code exists or to adapt an existing ICD-9 code to specify a disability (20). In addition, it provided the population by age group, so that age- and sex-related prevalence rates could be calculated (21). This information was available on a regional basis defined by Health Unit boundaries and was invaluable in planning services.

PRESENT SERVICES

Policy

A child development centre is a non-residential facility providing a range of rehabilitation services for children with a developmental delay or neuromuscular disability or handicap. Each centre is operated by an incorporated non-profit voluntary society. The governing body is responsible for the operation of the centre and for appointing an executive director, who is responsible for the day-to-day management of the centre and its community relationships. The individual centres, for the most part, adopt and implement the standards as described in the *Standards Manual* (19), and each has a quality assurance program. The scope of the service varies between the individual centres, but all include assessment and planning, therapy, and the education of the child and of the family in connection with the child's problems. The parents are members of the planning team. Access to the centre is by parent or referral by a health professional, educator, or social worker. The age range varies, but the principal focus is on the under-six-year-old age group and on older children with neurological problems.

The *Standards Manual* recommends that each centre provide:

1. a written mission statement (geographic area, population, services provided, objectives, etc.);
2. a description of the organization delineating lines of communication inside and outside the centre, by-laws, and meetings;
3. a statement of existing programs and support services;

---

5 Individual diagnostic categories are assigned a code number to encourage uniformity of diagnostic classification and to allow comparisons from one region to another. The codes are compiled in the *International Classification of Diseases* (ICD-9).

4. adequate space, facilities, equipment, and supplies to meet the professional, educational, and administration needs of the centre;
5. written policies and procedures to provide all staff with the scope and limitations of their responsibilities;
6. educational programs for staff including orientation and in-service education;
7. preparation of regular reports of the quality assurance program to the governing body.

The manual also addresses environmental safety requirements, including safety against fire, infection, and accidental injury to children, staff, and visitors, and the provision of a safe sanitary environment and written plan for evacuation of the building in the case of emergency.

The admission procedure receives special attention because first impressions are so important in shaping future relationships. This is usually done at the centre, but may be arranged at the child's home. It involves registration of the child, supplying information to the parents about services and policies, collection of prior assessments elsewhere, and the initial assessment by selected members of the rehabilitation team, perhaps including professionals from outside agencies. Initial assessment impressions are interpreted to the parents by the most appropriate member of the team, together with recommendations for future management.

The documentation of the patient visit in a client record system is defined, including basic content and storage retrieval. The Ministry of Health has authorized use of a problem-oriented record for children attending the centres.

Unlike hospitals, the child development centres have no health record department and hence routine diagnostic classification is not practical. A problem oriented record, which includes diagnostic information, is used, and some centres report children to the Health Surveillance Registry. Considerable thought has been given by some centres to evaluation and follow-up, but, as in other health settings, including hospitals, these remain unsolved problems.

Services

The professional staff includes a paediatrician or general practitioner, usually for a limited number of hours per week, who is paid a sessional fee by the Medical Service Commission. The physician is involved in the assessment, program planning, and discharge of patients.

The rehabilitation therapy services include the on-site services of physiotherapy, usually occupational and speech therapy, and access to audiology, psychology, prosthetics, orthotics, seating devices, and family counselling. Travel-related difficulties are compounded for parents whose children require specialized services not available in the referral area. These special problems were recognized by the Ministry of Health in 1987, and additional outreach services were initiated, including a seating clinic, psychological assessment, and other consultant services. Family support services are available, and the scope varies with the size, location, and function of the centre. These services respond to the requirements of children and parents, enabling them to access information, locate resources, find a listening ear, and obtain support from peer groups. Parents are helped to build on family strengths to empower them to be as independent as possible of professionals and to cope with the responsibilities of rearing their child. The family support services also include advocacy and community education.

Volunteers play an important part in fund raising, special projects, the maintenance of buildings and grounds, making equipment, preparing materials (therapy aids), and working with children under supervision. Some other roles of the centres are operating group homes for persons with disabilities, assisting with vocational training and employment, and operating respite care.

Under the title Children's Early Intervention Program, the Ministry of Health provides the salaries for approved positions in therapy and family support for children aged under six years of age. In order to serve the total case load, centres must raise funds to cover administrative costs and additional health costs to meet the needs of children of school age. Some of the centres have had their services purchased by the local school board. In the larger centres, the family support position is filled by a full-time social worker, but, in the majority, the family worker is employed part time.

In all the centres, approximately one-third of the budget is derived from non-government sources and is collected by patient fees, membership fees, the United Way, fund raising, and donations. This one-third of the budget funds administrative and residual professional costs. Three of the centres are unionized.

The child development centres all include a special needs preschool aimed at providing each child with the skills to minimize the effect of the disability and maximize independent functioning. The programs may or may not be integrated. The Ministry of Social Services and Housing funds the preschool.

Some infant development programs, which are also operated by the Ministry of Social Services and Housing, are based in the centres. This latter program provides a home-based service for the under three years of age child with developmental delay.

COMMENT

The history of the G. F. Strong Rehabilitation Centre and the child development centres illustrate again the key role played by a few citizens, many of whom were parents, in the initiation of community health services. They responded to the need for a rehabilitation centre (G. F. Strong Rehabilitation Centre) and for regional rehabilitation services for children (child development centres). Neither the private practice of medicine nor the public health service provided a leadership role in meeting new service needs for children. Universal health insurance provided acute hospital and medical care for individual children with chronic disabilities (personal medicine), but the organization of community rehabilitation services for this population of children was not provided. It was left to voluntary societies to patch together these services. As a result, many of the children with these conditions were poorly served. The Cerebral Palsy Association of British Columbia assumed the responsibility for the development and operation of a network of services across the province for children with cerebral palsy.

Their achievements were impressive in the early years, though they were less successful in influencing government policy to fund rehabilitation services for children than was the British Columbia Association for Community Living (Chapter 14). This has been attributed to the smaller number of children with cerebral palsy, the greater demands placed by these children on their parents, and, in part, the dependent relationship of the provincial office on the government. This conflict of interest was resolved when the funding of the provincial office was cut off. It was illogical, however, that the inpatient services at the G. F. Strong Rehabilitation Centre were eligible for benefits under the provincial *Hospital Insurance Act* in 1960, but the regional treatment centres, providing ambulatory services to a comparable population of disabled children, were not eligible for funding. The federal health grants, funds derived from Health and Welfare Branches, and private fund raising were the source of funding for professional services of the regional treatment centres. In contrast, in 1967, the provincial *Medical Services Act* (22) authorized the payment of physicians working in the regional centres, subject to the approval of the Medical Service Commission.

The Ministry of Health formally accepted responsibility for the health component of the operating costs in the regional rehabilitation centres in 1982. Currently, the funding for the health component of the child development centres derives from the Services for the Handicapped, within Community and Family Health.

The commitment of government funding of child development centres, including a family support worker in each of the centres, served as belated recognition by government of the exceptional responsibilities and great stresses that occur in families of children with these chronic disabilities. Furthermore, the traditional medical model, often driven by professional concerns, has been replaced by a family-centred one that asks, "What needs do this child and family have?" and "What can be done to meet them?" This shift is reminiscent of the changes occurring in the British National Health Service (23), where patients have been transformed from passive recipients of treatment into consumers who scrutinize what is available. Decision-making is transferred from the service system to the patient and/or parent.

REFERENCES

1. WORLD HEALTH ORGANIZATION. *International Classification of Impairments, Disabilities and Handicaps. A Manual of Classification relating to the Consequences of Disease.* Geneva: WHO, 1980.
2. DESJARDINS, E. J. *The Inception and Development of the G. F. Strong Rehabilitation Centre. A Brief Historical Review.* Vancouver: Evergreen Press, 1983.
3. *Hospital Insurance Act*, S.B.C. 1948, c. 28.
4. BRITISH COLUMBIA. Order-in-Council 3771, 1970.
5. PACK, M. *Never Surrender.* Vancouver: Mitchell Press, 1974, Chapter 6, pp. 62–77.
6. WALKER, P. F. and HILL, R. H. Children's arthritis programme. *Journal of the Canadian Physiotherapy Association* 20 (1968): 1–3.
7. BRITISH COLUMBIA. Order in Council 4110, 1972.
8. Children's Hospital, Board of Directors Minutes, 1947–48, Administrator's Report, 24 February 1948.
9. PACK, M., personal communication, 1988.
10. BRITISH COLUMBIA. Society Section, Corporate Central and Mobile Home Registry, Ministry of Finance and Corporate Relations.
11. VANCOUVER NEUROLOGICAL CENTRE. Association Structure for the Future. Mimeographed document, 1986.
12. ANDREWS L. G. G. F. Strong Rehabilitation Centre. The Children's Rehabilitation Service and Cerebral Palsy Clinic. *B.C. Medical Journal* 13 (1971): 136.
13. *Cerebral Palsy News.* Vancouver: Cerebral Palsy Association of British Columbia, 1978. Mimeographed document.
14. SHERRITT, D. Early History of Cerebral Palsy in B.C., Vancouver and the Fraser Valley. Mimeographed document.
15. LAKE, G. and MARTIN, A. *Provincial Association.* Vancouver: Cerebral Palsy Association of British Columbia, 1985. Mimeographed document.
16. *Hospital Act*, S.B.C. 1911, c. 102.
17. MARTIN, A., personal communication, 1989.
18. GEE, B., Ministry of Health, personal communication, 1989.
19. KUMBA, M., LAKE, G., RICE, K., THOMSON, D., WOLSEY, D. and MARTIN, A. *Standards Manual for Child Development Centres.* Cerebral Palsy Association of British Columbia, 1987.

20. BRITISH COLUMBIA. *Health Surveillance Registry Annual Report, 1981*. HSR No. 6. Chronic Disabilities—Congenital Anomalies Genetic Defects. Division of Vital Statistics.
21. RENWICK, D.H.G. Estimating prevalence of certain chronic childhood conditions by use of a central registry. *Public Health Reports* 82 (1967): 261–69.
22. *Medical Services Act*, S.B.C. 1967, c. 24.
23. LISTER, J. Proposal for reform of the British National Health Service. *New English Journal of Medicine* 320 (1989): 877–80.

16

Speech and Hearing Services

HISTORICAL CONSIDERATIONS

Hospital-based Services

This chapter provides an overview of the evolution of services for the population of children with hearing disorders and with speech and language disorders. The emphasis is on the organization of services to the population of children, as distinct from care of the individual child.

The first speech and hearing services in British Columbia developed in hospital settings, the G. F. Strong Rehabilitation Centre and the Health Centre for Children of the Vancouver General Hospital, in the early 1950s.

Mr. A. B. Clemons, formerly the director of the Speech and Hearing Clinic at the University of Witswatersrand, was employed as a speech therapist at the G. F. Strong Rehabilitation Centre in Vancouver in 1953. He and his wife, M. E. Clemons, also a speech therapist, organized the British Columbia Speech and Hearing Association[1] in 1957, thereby giving professional credibility to those with professional training in speech pathology and audiology, and including those both with American and British qualifications (1). The latter organization and individual members contributed briefs to the Royal Commission on Education in British Columbia, addressing planning, training, and service needs (2, 3).

In the pre-medicare era, hospital outpatient services were provided only for those families with an income below an arbitrary limit. In 1955, an exception to this arrangement was negotiated in the case of hearing impairment in infants and young preschool children. This policy change was triggered by the new importance placed on the early recognition of

---

1 Renamed the British Columbia Association of Speech/Language Pathologists and Audiologists.

hearing impairment and the early introduction of amplification and auditory training (4) in infants and preschool children. A Speech and Hearing Clinic in the outpatient department of the Health Centre for Children of the Vancouver General Hospital developed programs[2] for preschool children with hearing impairment (5) and other communication disorders (6). The children were carefully reviewed by practitioners in several disciplines, including audiology, speech pathology, otology, paediatrics, psychology, and medical genetics, and the assessment process concluded with a team conference chaired by the otologist, Dr. K. G. Cambon, in the case of the hearing program, and a paediatrician, Dr. James Hingston, in the communication disorders program. Dr. David Kendall, a psychologist who had audiological training and experience in assessing deaf children, was appointed director of the Speech and Hearing Clinic at the Health Centre for Children in 1958. The medical and speech and hearing staff were funded by a federal health grant (General Public Health Grant) and grants provided by the British Columbia Foundation for Poliomyelitis Rehabilitation and Child Care.[3]

These outpatient services were expanded in 1959 to provide ongoing preschool services for the burgeoning case load. A preschool therapy unit for children with hearing impairment was started in an adjacent old house by Ms. Hilda Gregory, a teacher of the deaf and of early childhood education. In 1963, the preschool was moved to the grounds of the Sunny Hill Hospital for Children in Vancouver. For one year, the teacher spent the mornings at the preschool and the afternoons at the therapy unit, conducting a home training program with children under two years old and their parents (7). The next year, the facilities at Sunny Hill Hospital were expanded to include a kindergarten class, and the home training program was also transferred to the hospital site. Initially, the salary of the teacher was provided by the British Columbia Foundation for Poliomyelitis Rehabilitation and Child Care, until a parents' group, the Society for Children with a Hearing Handicap, assumed this responsibility. The preschool, kindergarten, and home training program became the Vancouver Oral Centre for Deaf Children, with Ms. Gregory as principal. A school-age program was introduced, and classroom facilities in existing hard of hearing facilities in Greater Vancouver were made available by the Vancouver School Board. In 1972, the school program moved to an attractive, former parochial school, where it remains to this day. All newly enrolled students are referred for assessment at the Hearing Disorder Program at the British Columbia Children's Hospital.

The preschool therapy unit was converted into an observation unit for children with communication disorders not due to hearing loss, and

---

2 These programs continue to operate at the British Columbia Children's Hospital.

3 Renamed the Kinsmen Rehabilitation Foundation of British Columbia.

has subsequently became a free-standing, special needs preschool, named Small Talk, for children with language delay.

In 1959, a joint planning committee, chaired by Dr. Gordon Francis, Professor of Otolaryngology, Faculty of Medicine, University of British Columbia, was formed to oversee the further development of a provincial speech and hearing program. Two subcommittees were organized in 1960, one to oversee the hospital-based assessment and therapy services (central clinics), and the other to develop the provincial services (field services). The director of the Speech and Hearing Clinic at the Health Centre for Children assumed professional direction of both the hospital-based and the field services. Speech therapists, as they were called then, involved in the latter program were employed by the Kinsmen Rehabilitation Foundation of British Columbia. A mobile van equipped with a soundproof room and other audiology equipment was purchased, but, after a hazardous trip associated with winter travel problems, the staff put an end to this venture.

The Director of Speech and Hearing resigned in 1961 and the chairmen of subcommittees assumed responsibility for the two programs, reporting regularly to the joint planning committee. Dr. John Gilbert was appointed director of the Speech and Hearing Clinic in the Health Centre for Children in 1966. The hospital-based speech and hearing programs were transferred to the new British Columbia Children's Hospital in 1982.

In 1975, the Counselling and Home Training Program for Deaf Children and their Families was started at the Vancouver Children's Hospital (8). In 1978, the program added a day-care preschool and, in 1979, the first Annual Summer Parent–Deaf Child Learning Vacation Experience. The Learning Vacation Experience is offered to families from British Columbia who have a deaf child under five years of age. When the new British Columbia Children's Hospital was opened in 1982, the Deaf Children's Society of British Columbia was formed, and the facility was moved to the grounds of the Sunny Hill Hospital for Children. The society advocates a total communication approach to assist families and their deaf children to acquire effective communicative competence, and the program is funded by the Ministries of Education and Social Services and Housing. An early intervention program is provided for the hearing parents, to help them understand the cause and implications of hearing loss, together with information about the probable future educational course of their child. A Parent–Infant Home Training Program is also provided, whereby a teacher of the deaf visits families of deaf children from birth to three years of age to help them with amplification, sign language, oral language, attending skills, mime, and early childhood development. Other services include a Preschool Program for children aged three to five years, five full days per week, and group sessions with families to discuss relevant issues, sign communication, home instruction, and a sign communication training program. The staff have written a book, *Can't Your Child Hear?*, which has also been published in Danish and Dutch (9).

Provincial Speech Therapy Services

In the interior of the province and on Vancouver Island, private speech therapists worked in co-operation with local public health units to meet service needs, again with financial assistance from the British Columbia Foundation for Poliomyelitis Rehabilitation and Child Care.

A speech therapist, Ms. Elizabeth McMahon, was employed to conduct a three-year (1961–64) survey of speech and hearing needs in British Columbia. This position was funded by a federal health grant and by the Kinsmen Rehabilitation Foundation of British Columbia. Prevalence data of speech and hearing problems were collected in collaboration with the Division of Vital Statistics, Ministry of Health. The final report described the needs of the provincial speech and hearing program (10), and recommended that the administration and funding be assumed by the Department of Health. The Health Branch accepted the report and assumed responsibility for operating the speech program in 1966. Ms. Patience Towler was appointed in 1968 as Director of Speech Therapy Services, Special Health Services Division, Health Branch. Five positions for regional speech therapists were also approved.

Division of Speech and Hearing Services

In 1972, a lobby by a group of old age pensioners to obtain government subsidy for hearing aids resulted in the *Hearing-aid Regulation Act* (11) and the British Columbia Hearing Aid Program. The Act required the licensing of hearing aid dealers, following a prescribed training program at the British Columbia Institute of Technology. The Act also specified the appointment of a director of the Division of Speech and Hearing Services within the Department of Health Services and Hospital Insurance to supervise the new program. In 1973, the Division of Speech and Hearing was established within the Bureau of Local Health Services, Health Branch.[4]

In 1973, the Minister of Health appointed a committee, chaired by Dr. John Gilbert, head of the division of Audiology and Speech Sciences, Department of Paediatrics, Faculty of Medicine, University of British Columbia, to examine services for the communicatively impaired (12), and in the following year, a six-man task force was appointed to advise on the best approach towards the implementation of the report (13). The

---

4 Currently these programs are in Family Health.

report recommended a regional approach, with a central tertiary unit in Vancouver, five regional districts, and an advisory council, with both lay and professional representation from the central and regional districts. Finally, it was proposed that each district establish a plan to provide information and co-ordinate services "for the handicapped persons within each community."

In 1974, the Hearing Aid Program, which provided hearing aids at cost, was started, and four of five pilot audiology clinics in health units were operating by the end of 1974.

There was a major expansion of speech pathology services in 1974, with a speech pathologist added to each of the pilot audiology clinics (14). The audiology and speech/language pathology programs have developed independently.

In 1975, the Hearing Impaired Infant Identification Program was introduced in collaboration with the newborn nurseries of the main hospitals in each health unit (15), and currently all hospitals in the provincial health units are included, plus the city of Victoria, Burnaby, and Richmond. A high-risk hearing registry was started in each health unit, consisting of a checklist completed on all newborn infants. The checklist includes five questions, history of hereditary hearing loss, maternal rubella, hyperbilirubanaemia, low birthweight, and presence of congenital anomalies of the ear. These questions have been incorporated in the questionnaire for the risk assessment for infants and children (Chapter 20). All babies with positive responses are followed up by a public health nurse home visit, and initial audiological tests are performed at six months. Appropriate assessment and habilitation treatment follows, and all at-risk children are reviewed in kindergarten and grade one. The unknown aetiology group of children, which accounted for approximately half the cases of congenital sensorineural hearing loss (16), are presumably identified during the preschool years.

In 1976, the Ministry of Education requested the Division of Speech and Hearing Services to provide speech pathology services to local school districts on a contractual basis. This arrangement continued until 1984, but differing expectations between the school districts and the Speech and Hearing Services Division resulted in a termination of the contracts in that year. The Ministry of Education appointed a Provincial Co-ordinator for Programs of Speech and Language, who is responsible for the speech and language disorders program throughout the school districts. The speech programs of the Division of Speech and Hearing Services, Ministry of Health, concentrate on preschool children and on school-aged children who are not attending regular school.

In 1977, the Speech and Hearing Services Division began a ten-clinic expansion of the audiology programs, and, by the end of 1978, the Hearing Aid Program was providing services to fourteen rural districts and three urban areas. Throughout the development of this program, the Benevolent Protective Order of Elks made significant contributions to the cost of audiological equipment. The Division of Speech and Hearing staff grew from four speech therapists in 1972 to thirty-five speech pathologists and eighteen audiologists by the end of 1978.

School of Audiology and Speech Sciences

A proposal for a speech therapy training program at the University of British Columbia was first developed by a joint committee of the British Columbia Speech and Hearing Association and the university. A proposal for a M.Sc. degree in audiology and speech sciences was approved by the Senate in 1968, and the program started in 1969 (17). Initially, the Division of Audiology and Speech Sciences was in the Department of Paediatrics. It became the School of Audiology and Speech Sciences, Faculty of Medicine, in 1981, and Dr. J.H.V. Gilbert was appointed director. In 1985, the school was authorized to offer a Ph.D. degree.

PRESENT SERVICES

Audiology and speech services for a defined population of children are provided by the Ministries of Health and Education.

Ministry of Health

There are currently twenty-two audiology and speech clinics, which are operated by the Division of Speech and Hearing Services, and these services are available in all provincial health units. The majority of health units in the two metropolitan areas purchase services as well.

The audiology clinics give priority to the assessment of young children and to the more difficult problems in adults. Appropriate assessment and rehabilitation of children with disorders of hearing are undertaken in collaboration with the local medical profession. The clinics conduct the province-wide Hearing Impaired Infant Identification Program and maintain the High Risk Hearing Register. In addition, they provide auditory rehabilitation, including hearing-aid evaluation, selection, the fitting and maintenance of hearing aids, auditory training, speech reading, and speech therapy on physician referral. Hearing instruments meeting government standards are provided to patients at cost plus carrying charges.

Assessment services for infants and preschool children with hearing impairment continue to be provided by the Hearing Disorder Program at the British Columbia Children's Hospital, and are available on referral by the family physician. The services include a multidisciplinary assessment, involving audiology, otology, paediatrics, nursing, social work, and psychology, as needed. The Medical Services Plan funds the medical services, and Hospital Programs funds the remainder of the assessment team. All new students to the Vancouver Oral Centre for Deaf Children are assessed by this team. There is no formal association between the programs at the British Columbia Children's Hospital and the Division of Speech and Hearing Services of the Ministry of Health.

The provincial speech clinics provide assessment and treatment. The caseload is approximately 60 percent preschool children, 20 percent school-age children not in school, and 20 percent adults. Only severe cases are taken into therapy. Preschool children with speech and language delay are assessed by the Child Development Diagnostic Program at the Sunny Hill Hospital for Children.

Ministry of Education

The Program for Speech and Language disorders is provided to school-age children whose problems have a significant effect on their educational and/or social progress within the educational system (18).

These speech services are available in sixty-six of seventy-five school districts. It is noteworthy that in small communities in which school populations do not warrant a full-time speech pathologist, arrangements have been worked out to share a position with the Ministry of Health.

The Provincial Education Review Committee reviews every deaf preschool child prior to school entry and is available to review hearing impaired children of school age.

Other Services

In addition to the above clinical services, members of the British Columbia Association of Speech/Language Pathologists and Audiologists conduct private practices and offer alternatives to services given through hospital clinics, health units, and schools.

COMMENT

Professional lobby groups, based in hospital settings, stimulated the development of clinical services, first, for the assessment of hearing impaired infants, and, subsequently, for children with speech and language disorders. They wrote briefs and made forays to the Legislative Assembly to present the need for services to the Premier and the Ministers of Education and Health. Their efforts resulted in the development of hospital-based assessment and treatment services and, later, the provincial speech therapy services.

The Kinsmen Rehabilitation Foundation of British Columbia, the Health Branch of the Department of Health Services, and Hospital Insurance provided the financial support to develop the speech and hearing services in the 1950s and 1960s. The appointment of a Director of Speech Therapy Services in the Health Branch in 1966 was a major advance, but it was the *Hearing-aid Regulation Act* in 1972 that resulted in the formation of the Division of Speech and Hearing Services, followed by the introduction of audiology and speech services in health units. The introduction of national health insurance had no immediate impact on the development of audiology and speech programs. The *Established Programs Financing Act* (19), and the per capita grant that followed, probably contributed to the development of community audiology and speech services.

REFERENCES

1. CLEMONS, M. E., personal communication, 1988.
2. BRITISH COLUMBIA SPEECH AND HEARING ASSOCIATION. Brief to Royal Commission on Education, Province of British Columbia, 1959.
3. CLEMONS, M. E. Brief to Royal Commission on Education, Province of British Columbia, 1959.
4. EWING, A.W.G. *Educational Guidance and the Deaf Child*. Manchester: Manchester University Press, 1957, p. 303.
5. ROBINSON, G. C., KENDALL, D. C., and CAMBON, K. G. Hearing loss in infants and preschool children. The development of a provincial preschool hearing program and some preliminary results. *Pediatrics* 32 (1963): 103–14.
6. ROBINSON, G. C. and HINGSTON, J. The evaluation and management of communication disorders in preschool children in British Columbia. *Journal of Pediatrics* 62 (1963): 279–80.
7. GREGORY, H., personal communication, 1988.
8. CARBIN, C. F. A total communication approach. A new program for deaf infants and children and their families. *B.C. Medical Journal* 18 (1976): 141–42.
9. FREEMAN, R. D., CARBIN, C. F., and BOESE, R. J. *Can't Your Child Hear? A Guide for Those Who Care About Deaf Children*. Baltimore: University Park Press, 1981.
10. MCMAHON, E. M. *Report on a Three-Year Survey to Assess Speech and Hearing Needs in the Province of British Columbia*. Vancouver, 1964.
11. *Hearing-aid Regulation Act*, S.B.C. 1971, c. 24. Proclaimed effective July 1972.
12. GILBERT, J.H.V. *Recommendations on Services for the Communicatively Impaired in British Columbia, October, 1973*. Vancouver.
13. GILBERT, J.H.V. *Report of the Committee to Examine Services for the Communicatively Impaired of British Columbia, June, 1974*. Vancouver.
14. BRITISH COLUMBIA. Ministry of Health. Memorandum, 1982.
15. FITZZALLAND, R. E. Identification of hearing loss in newborns. Results of eight years experience with a high risk register. *Volta Review* 87 (May 1985): 195–203.

16. BUDDEN, S. S., ROBINSON, G. C., MACLEAN, C. D., and CAMBON, K. G. Deafness in infants and preschool children. An analysis of etiology and associated handicaps. *American Annals of the Deaf* 119 (1974): 387–95.

17. GILBERT, J.H.V. Audiology and speech services. *B.C. Medical Journal* 29 (1987): 101.

18. BRITISH COLUMBIA. Ministry of Education. *A Manual of Policies, Procedures and Guidelines*. Special Programs, 1985.

19. *Federal–Provincial Fiscal Arrangements and Established Programs Financing Act*, S.C. 1976–77, c. 10.

17

Alcohol and Drug Programs

INTRODUCTION

The excessive use of alcohol has been a social concern throughout the world for many centuries. Public efforts to control the production and distribution of alcohol have waxed and waned during the past two hundred years. During the nineteenth century and up to the first decades of the current century, "the notion took hold that alcohol was addicting and that this addiction was capable of corrupting the mind and body. With this concept, alcohol became the focus of concern" (1). By 1850, the temperance movement had set out to abolish the sale of alcohol, and eventually succeeded in the introduction of prohibition in the United States and Canada. This resulted in a reduced rate of alcohol consumption, reduced mortality rates from cirrhosis of the liver and alcohol-induced psychoses, fewer arrests for public drunkenness and disorderly conduct, and a decline in alcohol-related family problems. Drinkers, willing to pay exorbitant prices, gave rise to the development of a black market in booze, and the enforcement of the legislation proved impractical. After a few years, prohibition was abandoned.

In the 1930s, the concept emerged that alcoholism was a chronic disease, with alcoholics having a special vulnerability to alcohol for which abstinence is the only cure. This represents the professional viewpoint of the "alcoholism movement" and its protagonist, Alcoholics Anonymous. This organization, founded in the United States in 1936, introduced a non-judgmental, long-term, mutual support approach that has helped many people to return to sobriety. During the same period, the public health concept, which had its roots in the repeal of prohibition, attributed alcohol-related problems to social causes, and advocated the resolution of these causes, rather than the treatment of their results.

Blume has emphasized that the drinking patterns of women have changed since World War II in the direction of increased consumption (2). While women drink less, and have lower rates of alcohol problems than men, alcoholism in women is an important problem. The highest rates of alcohol-related problems, such as driving offences and inter-personal conflict, and alcohol-dependence symptoms, such as memory lapses and morning drinking, are found in the twenty-one to thirty-four year age group, and the highest proportion of heavy drinkers in the thirty-five to forty-nine year age group. It is noteworthy that women purchase a significant proportion of the alcohol sold. As a result, they are targeted by advertising and the cultural norms that have served to protect women are in danger of vanishing.

Current programs focus on abstinence during pregnancy in order to prevent alcohol-related birth defects. Blume stresses that this is only part of the problem, and that further effort must be directed toward public policy issues, such as the marketing of alcoholic beverages directed at young women and the impact on child custody, abuse and neglect laws, and highway safety policy.

Narcotic drugs have been used in British Columbia since the late nineteenth century. The *Opium Act* (3), now the *Narcotic Control Act* (4), was designed to control the supply and sale of the drugs, but this offered no help to the user.

In the mid-1960s, a changing pattern of drug use emerged, with soft drugs, such as marijuana and hashish, amphetamines, and barbiturates (5), becoming increasingly available and the age of use of non-narcotic drugs falling. In 1969, the Dean of Law at Osgoode Hall in Toronto, Gerald Le Dain, was appointed to lead a national Commission of Inquiry into the Non-Medical Use of Drugs (6). The commission recommended the decriminalization of simple cannabis, lighter sentences for the posses-sion of opiates and hallucinogens, compulsory treatment of heroin addicts, and advertised warnings of the dangers to health of alcohol and nicotine.

In the early 1970s, the effects of the use of licit and illicit drugs upon the foetus during pregnancy became of increasing concern. Two syn-dromes were described, the foetal alcohol syndrome (FAS) (7) and the neonatal abstinence syndrome (8), resulting from the effects of maternal use of alcohol and narcotics upon the developing foetus. More recently, the effects of cocaine have been described (9).

HISTORICAL CONSIDERATIONS

Provincial Responses

Prohibition was introduced in British Columbia in 1917, and alcohol was legally available only for medicinal, sacramental, scientific, or manufac-turing purposes (10). Liquor remained available, however, from boot-leggers and home brew, and it has been suggested that the government was obliged to enact legislation to combat the excessive use of alcohol! In 1921, the *Government Liquor Act* (11) authorized the sale of liquor at government liquor stores, and the government became the province's primary liquor distributor. The Act also created the Liquor Control Board to supervise the administration and enforcement of the Act.[1] Seventeen government liquor stores were opened in the province and currently there are 216 stores. Finally, the Act repealed the *British Columbia Prohibition Act*.

In June 1952, at the time of the provincial election, a plebiscite asked the question: "Are you in favour of the sale of spirituous liquor and wine by the glass in establishments licensed for that purpose?" The majority voted yes (12). In 1952, the British Columbia Liquor Inquiry Commission was appointed, under the chairmanship of the Honourable H. H. Stevens. The recommendations addressed administration by the Liquor Control Board, enforcement, permits, and licences (13). In October 1953, a new *Government Liquor Act* was introduced (14), and the sale of "spirituous liquors, vinous and malt liquor by the glass with meals" in a number of outlets (hotels, public houses, clubs, restaurants, night clubs, resorts, vessels, and trains) came into being. Prior to that time, only beer was available in beer parlours, which were divided into areas euphemistically labelled "Gentlemen" and "Ladies and Escorts."

In 1947, the social costs of alcoholism, together with the success of Alcoholics Anonymous, led the government of British Columbia to establish a Division of Alcohol Education in the Department of Education (15). The division prepared an integrated course of studies on alcohol for schools and the *Manual of Reference for Alcohol Education* as a teacher's guide. Teacher workshops were provided, but this practice was discontinued after a few years.

Three unrelated non-profit organizations concerned with alcohol and drug addiction emerged in British Columbia after World War II. These were the Alcohol–Drug Education Service, the Alcoholism Foundation of British Columbia, and the Narcotic Addiction Foundation of British Columbia.

The Alcohol–Drug Education Service: This organization, originally called the Alcohol Research and Education Council, was established by the Council of Christian Churches in 1952, and its goal was to introduce education regarding alcohol into the school system. Its origin reflected the public concern for the recent liberalization of the sale of distilled spirits.

---

1 In 1973, the Liquor Control Board became the Liquor Administration Branch, and, two years later, the licensing and distribution functions were split, with the establishment of the British Columbia Liquor Distribution Branch and the British Columbia Liquor Control and Licensing Branch.

The original office was located in a church basement in Vancouver, and the organization was dependent on private fundraising until 1959, when the provincial government agreed to contribute funds on a matching basis. Professional staff were hired to develop teaching materials and teaching programs for use throughout local school districts and to a variety of public groups.

Unlike the other two organizations involved in substance use prevention, the Alcohol–Drug Education Service was not taken under the umbrella of the Alcohol and Drug Commission after the New Democratic Party was elected in 1972. In fact, government funding was discontinued and the staff were terminated. The executive director, however, continued the work on a voluntary basis in a basement suite donated by a society member, and started the Alcohol and Drug Education Service (ADES) newsletter, later renamed *Update* (16). This continues to be published four times a year; it provides a forum for the Alcohol–Drug Education Service to dispense educational information and serves in an advocacy role, commenting on relevant policies and issues. When the New Democratic Party was defeated in 1975, a new executive director rebuilt the society until his retirement in 1984 (17).

During the late 1970s, the staff, in collaboration with the Faculty of Education of the University of British Columbia and the Vancouver School Board, developed a teachers' manual for grade six, called *Making Decisions* (18), and, in the 1980s, *Making Decisions* for grade seven (19). *Making Decisions 1* and *2* inservice handbooks for teachers, together with videos, have also been produced. A further manual, *Mission D.A.D. (Decisions about Drugs)* has also been produced for grade four students (20). These educational services are optional, and approximately four hundred schools in British Columbia take advantage of the teacher training sessions. A recent project involved the production of print and video materials to train trainers in four ethnic communities (Chinese, Latin American, Indo-Canadian, and Vietnamese) in British Columbia.

The Alcohol–Drug Education Service sponsors an annual meeting, the Pacific Institute on Addictive Studies, in collaboration with their counterpart organization in Ontario (CONCERNS). *Prevention Network* is a quarterly newsletter recently introduced "to strengthen and expand British Columbia's self reliant mutually supportive network of community substance abuse prevention task forces" (21).

The British Columbia Prevention Resource Centre is an Alcohol and Drug Program initiative, operated by the Alcohol–Drug Education Service, that provides toll-free telephone advice concerning local services, a video lending service, and a reference collection of resource material. It publishes *Frontline* on a quarterly basis, dealing with specific topics and with information on videos, pamphlets, posters, and booklets.

Alcoholism Foundation of British Columbia: Community groups interested in treatment and rehabilitation facilities for alcoholics developed the constitution of the Alcoholism Foundation of British Columbia, and the organization was incorporated under the *Societies Act* in 1953 (15). The program was initially funded by the Department of the Attorney General, and, subsequently, by the Department of the Provincial Secretary, until the early 1970s.

In 1954, the first executive director, E. D. McRae, was appointed, and was temporarily located in an office donated by the Health Branch of the provincial Department of Health and Welfare. The executive director attended the Yale Summer School of Alcohol Studies, visited many alcoholism programs in Canada and the United States, and presented a report recommending an outpatient treatment clinic, a rehabilitation program, and an educational and research program.

An outpatient clinic and administrative centre was opened in February 1955. Dr. B. B. Moscovich was appointed clinical director, a position he held for twenty years, and P. J. Fogarty was appointed the first full-time counsellor. The clinic offered active treatment "to those alcoholics who wish to do something about their drinking," and counselling services to those friends and relatives who wished to understand alcoholism better.

Rehabilitation services had as their objective "the restoration of the individual so that he/she might assume a productive place in society and manage the problems of life in such a manner that he/she may no longer need the sedative crutch of alcohol" (15).

In April 1954, the Foundation assumed responsibility for a rehabilitation centre that had previously been developed by the Alcohol Committee of the John Howard Society. "By canvassing local businessmen, the sum of $400 in cash was raised and a number of blankets, beds, pots and pans etc. were donated to the Committee which then rented space in downtown Vancouver which previously had been occupied as a cigar counter." The object of the centre was to provide a sober environment for alcoholics while they were away from alcohol, and to provide a space where they might live under "Alcoholics Anonymous therapy," until they secured employment. There was accommodation for six men.

The Foundation published a monthly newsletter, *Alcoholism Review*, directed to a professional audience. Jack Scott, a well-known Vancouver journalist, wrote a column in 1960 that was quoted in the newsletter, in which he noted that "interest in the problem of drinking women is growing" (22). He referred to a survey by the Yale Centre on Alcohol Studies that noted that the "respectable woman drinker is even more vulnerable to the perils of booze than the equivalent male."

During the period 1955 to 1973, the Foundation continued to offer outpatient treatment and rehabilitation services. In Vancouver, the core clinic staff increased, and psychological and psychiatric services were added. The need for hospital inpatient facilities for withdrawal therapy was met by arranging for the use of two beds for males at the Vancouver General Hospital and for women at the Edith Cavell Private Hospital. In 1960/61, travelling clinics to Kamloops and the Okanagan were started in health unit facilities, and in 1964/65 the first branch clinic was started in Victoria.

The educational program was instituted in 1957/58 (23), and the community information program was very popular. Research studies were commissioned by the Foundation and a part-time director of research was appointed in 1964 (24).

The New Democratic Party was elected in a provincial election in 1972, and the *Community Resources Board Act* (25) was enacted in 1974 to provide integration of social services at the local level (26). The administration and staff of the Alcohol Foundation program was transferred to a newly established Vancouver Resources Board in 1974. The name of the Foundation was changed to the Alcohol Drug Dependency Society of British Columbia (ADDIX) in 1975. This society was initiated to develop personnel policies in connection with the use of alcohol and was dissolved in 1988.

Narcotic Addiction Foundation of British Columbia: In 1952, a growing public concern about narcotic addiction led to a preliminary study by the Vancouver Community Chest and Council, followed by a more comprehensive study, *Drug Addiction in British Columbia—A Research Survey*, a seven hundred page report published after thirty-two months of study (27).

The Narcotic Addiction Foundation of British Columbia was established by the Vancouver Community Chest and Council in 1955 (28). The program was initially funded by the Department of the Attorney General and then by the Department of the Provincial Secretary. The original executive director resigned after one year, and Dr. R. Halliday, a psychiatrist, carried the dual responsibility of executive and clinical director until 1964/65, when Mr. H. F. Hoskin was appointed to the former position. There was initial public opposition to the development of a treatment facility for narcotic addiction, but a clinic was started in Vancouver in 1958. The Foundation instituted a fourfold program of education, treatment, rehabilitation, and research.

Inpatient services for withdrawal treatment were not covered by the Hospital Insurance Program, and the request for inpatient withdrawal treatment beds at the Vancouver General Hospital was unsuccessful (29). Psychiatric nurses were employed, and withdrawal outpatient treatment was started at the Foundation treatment and administration unit. The annual report also mentioned that the age of addiction was falling, and that there was need for withdrawal treatment for women (30). During this time, there were discussions with the federal government regarding the planning of a treatment unit for convicted addicts and follow-up care of parolees.

A full-time research associate was appointed in 1964 (5). An outpatient drop-in centre was opened in the Vancouver downtown east side area, where many addicts lived (30). Concern was expressed for pregnant addicts and their offspring, and for the need for a separate detoxification unit for these women. The use of soft drugs was also described as an enormous problem (31). The executive director was invited to Ottawa for discussions about the treatment of narcotic addicts in British Columbia. A second Vancouver residence was added in 1968/69, with facilities for sixteen patients (32).

The Narcotic Foundation of British Columbia pioneered the controversial voluntary methadone treatment plan. Federal funding for the methadone program and laboratory was provided in 1967/68, and the program began to attract widespread interest. Despite the advent of soft drugs, the main focus of the Narcotic Addiction Foundation remained heroin addiction and outpatient methadone treatment.

In 1970, the changing pattern of drug use led to the Addiction Prevention Project in the second residence, renamed "The House" (33). The new project was designed to provide an immediate response to the young multidrug user not yet using heroin, and the residential function was largely eliminated. This program, later renamed "Youth and Family Counselling Services," provided family and individual counselling, short-term social and clinical intervention services, including three beds, drop-in contacts and recreational facilities, liaison contacts with other agencies, and outreach services that put workers "on the street."

In 1971/72, regional treatment units were started in Nanaimo, Prince George, and Victoria (34). The Narcotic Addiction Foundation was accredited as a chronic hospital by the British Columbia Hospital Insurance Service (BCHIS) and became eligible for benefits, while grants from the Health Branch assisted the regional units. The increase in non-narcotic soft drugs was again emphasized. Full-time medical services were provided at The House. In the following years, two more regional units in Trail and Coquitlam were added to cope with the spread of narcotic drugs (35), and BCHIS extended hospital insurance coverage to the regional centres for treatment with methadone, including laboratory and pharmacy costs (36).

The Foundation moved to new facilities in 1972. During this year, the federal government placed controls on the use of methadone by physicians because of the increase in addiction associated with an illicit methadone market. The methadone treatment program was described as "winding down" (35).

After the New Democratic Party was elected in 1972, the administration of the Narcotic Addiction Foundation of British Columbia was also transferred to the Vancouver Resources Board in 1974 (37), and the Foundation was struck off the Register in 1976.

When the two Foundations were dissolved, the employees became provincial civil servants, and were transferred to the Vancouver Resource Board, under the direction of the Alcohol and Drug Commission.

Alcohol and Drug Commission: The provincial *Alcohol and Drug Commission Act* (38) was enacted in April 1973, and the commission was appointed in 1974 (39). It assumed responsibility for the administration of all monies directed to alcohol and drugs by five provincial and two federal departments and for the co-ordination of all provincial decision-making in the alcohol and drug field. The commission placed initial emphasis on staff training and the development of treatment programs throughout the province. Subsequently, the Alcohol and Drug Commission was empowered to operate programs for alcoholics and drug users (40). The Alcoholism Foundation of British Columbia, the Narcotic Foundation of British Columbia, and Youth and Family Counselling Services, including staff, were subsequently transferred from the Vancouver Resources Board to the commission. The first chairman of the commission, Mr. Peter Stein, a member of the Le Dain Commission of Inquiry into the Non-Medical Use of Drugs, reported directly to the Minister of Human Resources. In 1976 (41), the commission was transferred from the Department of Human Resources to the Department of Health, and H. F. Hoskin, formerly executive director of the Narcotic Addiction Foundation of British Columbia, was appointed chairman. He retained the position until 1980. Planning emphasized the regionalization of a system of care for the treatment of alcoholics and the methadone treatment program for narcotic addicts (42). The components of care comprised counselling, detoxification services, residential treatment, and supportive recovery houses (43).

The control of narcotic addiction was a major concern of the commission. The options were control of the supply, a federal responsibility, and reduction of the demand by treatment and rehabilitation, including commitment for treatment. One of the recommendations of the Le Dain Commission was the compulsory treatment and rehabilitation of narcotic addicts (6). In order to implement the rehabilitation program, the *Heroin Treatment Act* of British Columbia was enacted in 1978 (44), and the Ministry of Health initiated a Health Entry Plan (45). A residential treatment and rehabilitation centre at Brannen Lake was provided both for addicts who were committed by the courts and for voluntary admissions. The program immediately encountered legal difficulties concerning the constitutionality of the *Heroin Treatment Act* (46). The case was ultimately heard by the Supreme Court of Canada, and the Act was found to be legal, but, in the interim, the enthusiasm for the Methadone Maintenance Program had subsided, and the Act was never enforced. The chairman of the commission resigned in 1980, and Brannen Lake was closed. The last outpatient receiving methadone treatment in a government clinic was discharged in 1987. The *Heroin Treatment Act* was repealed in 1989 (47), but private physicians can prescribe methadone to patients in accordance with the federal *Narcotic Control Act*.

In 1981, the role of the Alcohol and Drug Commission was changed to an advisory function co-ordinating the alcohol and drug services that had developed over the prior eight years with other government bodies (48). The commission was disbanded in 1983.

Alcohol and Drug Programs: The services were reorganized and named "Alcohol and Drug Programs" within the Community Care Services of the Ministry of Health with their own executive director (49). The mission was defined as the promotion "of the well being of people affected by, or at risk of developing, alcohol and other drug related difficulties," and "respects the integrity of each human being and believes that each person has the ability to change and to accept personal responsibilities for physical, emotional, social and spiritual health" (50).

Three independent provincial initiatives occurred in the eighties. In 1985, the Kaiser Substance Abuse Foundation was formed in British Columbia with a goal of preventing substance abuse in youth. The Foundation organized a major conference (*Potential 1988*) and started a number of initiatives in the province, one of which is the annual publication, prepared in collaboration with the Ministry of Health, of a *Directory of Substance Abuse Services in British Columbia*. The government appointed a Liquor Policy Review, which reported in 1987 (51). In 1986, the Task Force on Alcohol and Drug Abuse in the Workplace was appointed under the joint sponsorship of the Ministry of Health and the Workers Compensation Board, and submitted a report in 1987 (52). In the same year, the federal study *"Booze, Pills and Dope," Reducing Substance Abuse in Canada* was published (53).

There has been a significant reorganization of services since the mid-1980s with the province divided into five regions of service delivery. In April 1988, the British Columbia government transferred Alcohol and Drug Programs to the Ministry of Labour and Consumer Services, to co-ordinate substance abuse programs within the ministry responsible for the central licensing and distribution of liquor, divorcing them from the Ministry of Health. In September 1988, the Ministry of Labour and Consumer Services announced a new three-year Community Awareness and Action Plan to address alcohol and drug abuse that included treatment, a special emphasis on prevention, community action, and evaluation and research (54). The goal was to change public attitudes to the problem and to encourage behaviour change. It stressed that the problems are self-imposed and are largely preventable. The new program provided funds to enable communities to introduce prevention programs that addressed local alcohol and drug problems. Approval for funding was obtained from the regional offices of the Alcohol and Drug Programs, and projects could be prevention- or treatment-oriented. Successful programs were shared with other communities and regions.

In 1989, the TRY (The Responsibility is Yours) program was introduced in British Columbia. A handbook emphasized that British Columbia has the highest rate of alcohol and drug abuse in Canada (55). It discussed intervention tactics and community preventive strategies, and itemized alcohol and drug services available in the five regions. A twenty-four hour confidential toll free information and referral telephone service (1-800-663-1441) was provided.

In 1989, a new hospital program, the Chemical Dependency Resource Team (CDRT), was introduced in a number of hospitals in an attempt to identify the underlying, but usually neglected, alcohol-related causes[2] of many hospital admissions (56). The CDRT was a multidiscipline team, skilled in chemical drug dependencies, which focused on intervention, patient and family education, staff education, and liaison with community resources. The lack of formal training in chemical dependencies by health professionals in British Columbia was recognized, as was the continuing need for training within the health care system.

The British Columbia Liquor Distribution Branch, the Ministry of Labour, and Consumer Services participated in various preventive initiatives, including the TRY program, the Counter Attack drinking driving awareness campaign, and Serving It Right, a service training program that is mandatory for all who sell or serve alcohol. Recently, signs warning about the danger of drinking during pregnancy were installed in all British Columbia liquor stores.

In 1991, the provincial New Democratic Party was elected, and Alcohol and Drug was transferred back to the Ministry of Health.

The Office of Health Promotion, through its various programs, such as Healthy Schools and Healthy Communities (Chapter 3), has been concerned with fostering the healthy development of young people. It has also collaborated in the production of a new curriculum, *Learning for Living*, which has been developed for kindergarten to grade three students, and will be further developed for other grades by the Ministry of Education and other ministries. A chapter on substance abuse prevention is included.

Federal Responses

National Native Alcohol and Drug Abuse Program (NNADAP): One of the most serious social problems in British Columbia is due to the unresolved

---

2 A study in a British Columbia hospital revealed that 27 percent of patients had an alcohol dependency problem. The funding was terminated in 1991.

settlements of aboriginal lands occupied by European colonists, compounded by subsequent paternalistic policies of the colonial government. These included the settlement of the aboriginal people on reservation lands, a disregard for their former ways of living and their culture, the imposition of foreign religions and educational systems in their place, and their disenfranchisement until recent times. The basic living conditions and nutrition of Native people are often substandard, and unemployment is common. These issues, of course, contribute to poor health. Only about one-third of Native students completes high school education, and many enter the circle of poverty. The impact of such regressive policies upon the aboriginal society has been devastating, and one coping mechanism has been the use of alcohol. Alcoholism remains a major burden for aboriginal people living on and off reserves, and has significantly influenced morbidity and mortality statistics. The British Columbia Royal Commission on Health Care and Costs (Chapter 3) recommended alcohol and drug programs for Native youth (57).

Total prohibition of the use of alcohol by Indians, except for medicinal purposes, was included in the *Indian Act* (58). The initial purpose was to protect the Indians from unscrupulous traders who might take advantage of them. In 1951, the Act was amended to allow Native Indians to drink in public places, if the provincial government wished to extend this privilege to its Native population. British Columbia was the first province to apply, and this privilege came into force on 15 December 1951 (59). In 1953, the *Government Liquor Act* was amended, legalizing the sale of alcoholic beverages in establishments serving meals (14). In 1956, federal legislation granted full liquor rights to Indians in accordance with provincial law. These rights were granted in British Columbia in 1961 (60), and Indians of the province could purchase and consume intoxicants off Indian reserves in the same way as other citizens.[3] However, Indians are only allowed to take liquor to their home on the reserve if the band has voted in favour of permitting liquor on reserve.

The Medical Services Branch, Health and Welfare Canada, provides health services to registered Indians and Inuit through the Indian and Northern Health Services Directorate (Chapter 2). One of the programs of the latter, the National Native Alcohol and Drug Abuse Program (NNADAP), was introduced in 1982, to support community-based prevention programs and treatment centres.

National Drug Strategy: The National Drug Strategy, "Action on Drug Abuse," was announced by the Minister of National Health and Welfare in 1987 (62), and involved extensive collaboration over a five-year period

---

3 The principal of the school at Alkali Lake, an Indian reservation in central British Columbia, a child at the time, recalled that a wagon loaded with alcoholic beverages arrived on reserve from Williams Lake the day the new law came into effect (62).

between the federal, provincial, and territorial governments, non-governmental organizations, and addiction experts. The objective was to reduce the harmful effects of substance abuse on individuals, families, and communities by addressing the supply and demand sides of the problem. Several government departments are involved in the National Drug Strategy, Health and Welfare, Solicitor General, External Affairs and International Trade, Justice, National Defence, Employment and Immigration, Treasury Board, and Fitness and Amateur Sport. Within Health and Welfare Canada, the NNADAP, the Bureau of Dangerous Drugs, the Policy, Communications, and Information Branch, and the Health Promotion Directorate are actively involved. Six strategic components form the framework of the National Drug Strategy, Education and Prevention (32 percent),[4] Treatment and Rehabilitation (38 percent), Enforcement and Control (20 percent), International Co-operation (3 percent), Information and Research (6 percent), and National Focus (1 percent). The National Drug Strategy has been extended for a second five-year period. The renewed strategy brings the Driving While Impaired Strategy into Canada's Drug Strategy.

Community-based prevention/treatment initiatives, called Community Support Programs, provide financial assistance for local groups to undertake community-based activities dealing with alcohol and drug problems. They are administered by the designated addictions agency in each province or territory and by the Department of National Health and Welfare. NNADAP co-ordinates the aboriginal component of the National Drug Strategy.

Canadian Centre on Substance Abuse: During the consultations preceding the National Drug Strategy, Canadian addiction specialists emphasized the need for a national addictions focus that would tap existing provincial expertise for national purposes. As a result, the Canadian Centre on Substance Abuse, a semi-autonomous national agency, was created by an Act of Parliament in 1988 to form a national focus for efforts concerned with the abuse of licit and illicit drugs (63).

EPIDEMIOLOGY

A 1987 province-wide survey of self-reported drug use by adolescents in British Columbia in grades eight to twelve revealed that alcohol was used by the sample population more than any other drug, but substantial rates of use were also observed for cannabis, tobacco, hallucinogens, and prescription depressants (64). There were no gender differences in terms of the percentages of males and females using alcohol, though males

---

4 The percentage of five-year expenditures.

were heavier drinkers than females and were more likely to have associated behavioural problems.

Substantial differences by grade were found with the percentage of users, the amount consumed increasing with grade. Alcohol was the easiest drug to obtain, even for grade eight students. In addition to the considerable use of alcohol by adolescents, the survey showed that a significant proportion have personal and social difficulties due to alcohol. Almost one-quarter had been drunk at least once in the previous four weeks and almost one-third stated that they had had five or more drinks on at least one occasion during this period. More than one in five adolescents had gone on a weekend drinking binge three or more times in their lives. Eighteen and a half percent had demonstrated aggressive or destructive behaviour due to alcohol, and 12 percent had been involved with police.

The use of prescription drugs was relatively high in the sample, but no gender, grade, or regional differences were noted. More than 15 percent had used tranquillizers or barbiturates during the past year with a prescription. The use of crack was reported by 1.6 percent, though one in ten grade twelve adolescents reported that they had used cocaine during the previous year.

These findings were compared with similar studies in Ontario and New Brunswick. Alcohol, cannabis, and tobacco had the highest utilization rates. British Columbia had the highest percentage of alcohol and cannabis users, and New Brunswick had the highest percentage of smokers.

When the survey was repeated during the 1989–90 school year (65), there had been a decline in drug use in all but five (prescription, barbiturates, heroin, crack, PCP, and LSD) of eighteen substances. Approximately one quarter of public high school students were considered in a high risk category for substance abuse. The most uniform pattern of decrease was found in grade eight students. Similar studies, conducted in 1989 in Ontario and New Brunswick, showed that alcohol, cannabis, and tobacco were the most commonly used substances. The Ontario and New Brunswick studies included grade seven students, and, because younger adolescents report less use of alcohol and drugs, this will lower prevalence rates. New Brunswick had the highest percentage of smokers and Ontario the lowest. British Columbia had the highest percentage of drinkers and cannabis users, followed by New Brunswick in both instances.

No reliable data is available from the Health Surveillance Registry for alcohol and drug problems in children and youth. Children with FAS are reported, but the data are considered unreliable.

PRESENT SERVICES

A province-wide population-based alcohol and drug service has developed in British Columbia for all age groups and is operated by Alcohol and Drug Programs, Ministry of Health.

Organization of Alcohol and Drug Programs

Regional Structure: The province is divided into five regions[5], Vancouver Island, Greater Vancouver, the North, Fraser Valley, and Central. Each region is further divided into usually three areas, each of which is responsible for clinical programs.

Alcohol and Drug Programs is managed by an executive director. There is a Director of Preventive Services, and each region has a regional director, area managers, and preventive, financial, and standards officers. There is also a part-time provincial medical adviser, and each region has part-time medical advisers and part-time consultants, paid on a sessional basis.

The executive director, the Director of Preventive Services, the regional directors, and the provincial medical adviser comprise the Central Management Committee, and the regional and area managers and other officers a Regional Management Team.

Interministerial Structure: The interministerial Committee on Substance Abuse Policy includes membership from those ministries that include any aspect of substance abuse, plus Crown Corporations (Workers Compensation Board and Insurance Corporation of British Columbia), the Premier's Office, and the Treasury Board. This group meets six times yearly to monitor the Community Awareness and Action Plan.

An Advisory Committee on Substance Abuse Policy, comprised of twenty-three members (education, health, vintners, brewers and distillers, police, United Way, etc.) also meets regularly to monitor the alcohol and drug program.

Clinical and Other Services: The clinical services include the outpatient, residential, detoxification, and supportive treatment services, and are provided free of charge to all age groups by addiction counsellors and other professionals located within each area and region. The services are administered by a mixture of direct government and non-profit agencies, and the latter contract with the government to provide services. The contracts dictate the policy and service to be provided by the various

---

5 Two of the regions include the municipalities of Vancouver and Victoria.

agencies. It is estimated that 90 percent of services are delivered through contracts with autonomous societies (57).

Services for Children and Youth

In 1992, a school-based primary prevention model was introduced in British Columbia in collaboration with staff and students (grades eight to twelve) in a large number of secondary schools. This three-year project will culminate in an evaluation process. Previously, the primary prevention programs were provided by the Alcohol Drug Education Service and, more recently, the Learning for Living Curriculum.

The secondary and tertiary services for children and youth and for pregnant women (and their unborn children) are provided by the addiction counsellors. Every alcohol and drug program has a youth counsellor. Individual regions, in turn, have additional special programs to meet local needs, and some of these are described below.

In the greater Vancouver region, School Prevention Services were introduced three years ago.[6] A staff of five addiction counsellors, based in high schools, concerned with prevention and early intervention, offers individual and group counselling to children and youth from families with alcohol and drug problems. They also offer parent education nights, train teachers on professional development days, and participate with the school counselling departments in discussions with students in grades eight, nine, and ten. The need for a population-based primary prevention program for all school attenders, including Native children and youth, has been recognized and a three-year multischool-based (grades eight to twelve) pilot study has been introduced.

A residential treatment centre, Peak House, for children and youth was started in Vancouver in 1988. The centre, which has an Adolescent Treatment Program, is operated by a voluntary society, Pacific Youth and Family Addiction Services Society. The unit has eight beds and the treatment programs last fifty-six days. The programs start at 7 a.m. and end at 11 p.m. Referrals (ages thirteen to eighteen) are accepted from across the province, but only from accredited addiction counsellors. All admissions require prior active family involvement during admission and after discharge. Follow-up care is managed by the referring agency. Three beds are set aside for youth in the Police Detoxification Centre in Vancouver.

Two-day programs, named "Odyssey 1 & 2," in Vancouver and Burnaby, offer intensive day-treatment programs, and evening and weekend programs in drug-free environments. The Nexus Program is a street program in Vancouver in which counsellors contact street kids and link them with services. These programs are funded by Alcohol and Drug

---

6 Previously the Youth and Family Counselling Services.

Programs, but operated by Boys and Girls Clubs of Greater Vancouver. A similar street program is available in Victoria.

The name "Odyssey" reflects a "journey of growth and exploration," comparable to adolescence and to the process of growing and maturing in dealing with issues like substance use. The philosophy of the program is, first, that the best way to prevent further substance abuse is to understand how current drug use helps each client cope with his or her life, and, second, to learn new and healthier ways to cope with the problems. The program is designed for youth (twelve to nineteen years) and families where substance use is a problem. Some teens come to get off drugs, or to control drug use, and some, who are no longer using drugs, want support to stay off. No referral is necessary, though many derive from local schools. The program is open Monday through Friday evenings and all day Saturday. Regular scheduled events occur throughout the week, and a gym and games room are always available. Particular attention is given to teaching refusal skills by interactive video presentations, i.e., Target Interaction Program (TIP) and Drug Alcohol Responsibility for Teens (DART). Parent involvement is encouraged.

Services for Native People

All alcohol and drug programs on reserves are operated by voluntary non-profit societies under contract to NNADAP. There are 124 treatment beds for Native Indians in British Columbia located in nine regional treatment centres. Community health representatives and NNADAP workers are trained together in community development strategies in an effort to reduce the impact of the underlying social causes of alcohol addiction.

Services off reserve include those described above for the general population and vary with the regional needs. There are also alcohol and drug counsellors in every Friendship Centre except the Vancouver region. The centres are funded by the Ministry of the Secretary of State and the alcohol and drug counsellors by Alcohol and Drug Programs. In Vancouver, the Hey-Way'-Noqu' Healing Circle for Addictions Society has been formed for Native families with alcohol and drug problems. The latter society has a contract with Alcohol and Drug Programs to provide a day-treatment program for urban Native and Métis people of all ages who are ready to make a commitment to sobriety for two years. The program is designed to help individuals to restructure "their lifestyles to their maximum levels of functioning, in a culturally relevant way that enhances individuality, independence and uniqueness."

Alkali Lake, an Indian community in central British Columbia, has gained international recognition during the 1980s for achieving almost total sobriety, attributed to a combination of spiritual and contemporary alcoholism treatment strategies and the leadership of the chief and his wife (66).

Perinatal Drug Dependency Services

Prenatal care of heroin addicts and mothers on maintenance methadone is provided by the Department of Obstetrics of two general hospitals in Vancouver. A postnatal program for addicted neonates of heroin addicts, of mothers on a methadone maintenance program, and of mothers using cocaine during pregnancy, is provided by a multidiscipline team at Sunny Hill Hospital in Vancouver (67). This team includes a paediatrician, a community health nurse, and a social worker. Special foster home placements and a support group for foster mothers are arranged by the social worker in collaboration with local Infant Development Program consultants.

One of the recommendations of the provincial Community Awareness and Action Plan was a Perinatal Awareness Program. In October 1988, a Pregnancy Outreach Program (POP) was instituted, consisting of eight community outreach projects for pregnant women at risk of having a poor pregnancy outcome (68). The goal of this program was to promote positive health practices in at-risk pregnant women, particularly Native women, through outreach education and support. As in the case of mothers of infants with neonatal abstinence syndrome, these mothers may also lack parenting skills, and ongoing support and monitoring of the family unit is important. The objectives were, first, to reduce at-risk behaviours associated with poor pregnancy outcome, that is, to decrease the use of alcohol, drugs, and cigarettes, to improve food intake, to ensure consistent emotional support, and to encourage breast feeding, and, second, to educate physicians and other health workers about the effects of alcohol and drugs on pregnancy outcome. The early identification of drinking by pregnant women, followed by early intervention, was designed to prevent the fetal alcohol syndrome (FAS) and the serious residual damage to the nervous system of the offspring. Evaluation studies of the pregnancy outreach programs have revealed that the programs were effectively reducing maternal drinking, and six additional programs were introduced in 1991 and 1992. Unfortunately, there is reluctance or genuine difficulty to establish a firm diagnosis of FAS in the newborn period and during the first year or two of life, thereby denying the family much needed support and the infant the benefit of early infant stimulation. A recent study in Alaska has estimated that the lifetime cost per FAS birth is $1,400,000 (69), thereby underlining the importance of prevention programs.

EVALUATION

The need for ongoing evaluation of the program is well accepted. It is difficult to document changes in drinking behaviours, and evaluation is based on measures that include evidence of community involvement, the increasing number of clients seeking treatment, the expansion of treatment capacity, and the use of the toll-free help line. The self-report studies of students in grades eight to twelve have been described.

COMMENT

The introduction of the provincial, and later the national, hospital and medical insurance services had no immediate impact upon the development of clinical services for these problems. Gradually, the increasing use of alcohol and drugs by both sexes, and the declining age of the users, became more widely recognized, and, in 1974, during the tenure of the New Democratic Party, the programs operated by the Alcoholism and the Narcotic Addiction Foundations were transferred to an Alcohol and Drug Commission within, first, the provincial Department of Human Resources and, subsequently, the Department of Health. This initiative effectively, if inadvertently, eliminated the two organized advocacy groups that had been such a positive force in developing public attitudes and promoting the development of clinical services. Furthermore, the current trend to provide local community alcohol and drug services administered by non-profit societies, which are funded by, and therefore dependent on, government for future income, further discouraged social advocacy. The recent British Columbia Royal Commission on Health Care and Costs noted that this approach leads to a variable regional response to program development and service delivery (57). The commission assumed the task of developing clinical services, including outpatient clinics, detoxification services, residential treatment, and supportive recovery services, and the infrastructure for a population-based service evolved in British Columbia.

Since 1987, there have been major federal and provincial efforts to address the alcohol and drug problem. An expert panel (70) has endorsed three prevention policies, first, by regulating the supply through licensing, limited prohibitions (by age group and location), and taxation, second, by influencing the drinking practices of the consumers (by law and education), and, third, by environmental intervention to avoid the consequences of drinking (e.g., passive restraint technology for drinking drivers and by Serving It Right, The Responsible Beverage Service Program). These approaches have been utilized on a province-wide basis. Primary prevention programs, designed to discourage experimentation and regular drug use, are usually targeted at late childhood or early adolescence (71). The common model relies on learning skills to resist youth peer pressure. The British Columbia Royal Commission on Health Care and Costs recommended that the priority for prevention, planning, program development, and services must be in order of importance, i.e., children and youth for tobacco and alcohol, Natives for alcohol and drugs, and seniors for prescription drugs and alcohol (57).

Making it Fit, a manual jointly funded by Alcohol and Drug Programs and the British Columbia School Trustees Association, and designed to assist schools and communities to develop substance abuse prevention programs, has emphasized that abuse starts in childhood and adolescence, and hence that prevention must begin early (72). It stresses the frequency of substance abuse and the sequelae (e.g., suicide, criminal activity, and the emotional scars in the children of alcoholics), and the need for health promotion strategies to achieve a healthy community environment for our youth. Six generic strategies for prevention and ten community attributes that influence the choice of strategy are discussed. The implementation strategies include school-based education, community/adult education, social marketing/mass media campaigns, social planning exemplified by the Healthy Communities Project (see Chapter 3), social action, and community mobilization/empowerment. A table that outlines the generic strategies to consider, based on community attributes, is presented. In the third section, school-based curriculum models and the issues associated with the selection of substance abuse prevention programs are reviewed. In the fourth section, the need for broad community involvement is reiterated.

A recent publication by the Ontario Ministry of Health presents a framework within which communities can plan and implement programs, services, and policies to reduce the frequency and severity of problems associated with the use of alcohol and other drugs (73). It is lucid, comprehensive, practical, and population-based. It is also notes that the available evidence suggests that most people with illicit drug and inhalant problems can be served by the same programs and services that address alcohol problems. In fact, many clients suffer from combined alcohol and illicit drug problems.

Another recent publication described youth-oriented prevention programs in five European countries (74). In Norway and Sweden, there was widespread concern, led by non-government organizations, for prevention in children. This concern was lacking in Finland. The liberal views on substance use in Holland, which allow addicts to be visible in the community, has a powerful effect upon the young, and contributes to the decision not to use illegal drugs. Teacher training is emphasized as an effective prevention strategy. In Great Britain, alcohol use is tolerated, whereas illicit drug use is viewed with strong disfavour. This double standard is changing with mandated drug education, regional consultants, and specific teacher training in drug education.

Foetal alcohol syndrome has recently been the subject of a standing committee in Ottawa that presented twenty-one recommendations, addressing various aspects of prevention and the management of these children (75). Until recently, the age-related needs of children and youth have taken a back seat to those of adults. This is about to change.

REFERENCES

1. GERSTEIN, D. R. Alcohol use and its consequences. In *Alcohol and Public Policy: Beyond the Shadow of Prohibition*, ed. M. H. Moore and D. R. Gerstein, Washington D.C.: National Academy Press, 1981, pp. 182–224.

2. BLUME, S. B. Women and alcohol, A review. *Journal of the American Medical Association* 256 (1986): 1467–70.

3. *Opium Act*, S.C. 1908, c. 50.

4. *Narcotic Control Act*, R.S.C. 1985, c. N-1.

5. Narcotic Addiction Foundation of British Columbia, *Ninth Annual Report, 1964–65.*

6. *Final Report of the Commission of Inquiry into the Non-Medical Use of Drugs to the Ministry of National Health and Welfare.* Information Canada, 1973.

7. JONES, K. L., SMITH, D. W., ULLELAND, C. N., and STREISSGUTH, A. P. Pattern of malformation in offspring of chronic alcoholic mothers. *Lancet* (1973): 1267–71.

8. FINNEGAN, L. P., CONNAUGHTON J. F., KRON, R. E., and EMICH, J. P. Neonatal abstinence syndrome: Assessment and management. *Addictive Diseases, an International Journal* 2:1 (1975): 141–58.

9. DOERING, P. L., DAVIDSON, C. L., LAFAUCE, L., and WILLIAMS, C. A. Effects of cocaine on the human fetus: A review of clinical studies. *Drug and Poison Information Centre* 23 (1989): 639–45.

10. *British Columbia Prohibition Act*, S.B.C. 1916, c. 49.

11. *Government Liquor Act*, S.B.C. 1921, c. 30.

12. BRITISH COLUMBIA. Liquor Control Board. *Thirty-second Annual Report, April 1, 1952 to March 31, 1953.*

13. BRITISH COLUMBIA. *Report of the British Columbia Liquor Inquiry Commission, 1952.*

14. *Government Liquor Act*, S.B.C. 1953, c. 14.

15. *The First Annual Report of the Alcoholism Foundation of British Columbia for the year ending March 31, 1955.* Vancouver, 1955. Mimeographed document.

16. GREEN, L., personal communication.

17. STEINMANN, A., personal communication.

18. ALCOHOL-DRUG EDUCATION SERVICE. *Making Decisions, An Approach to Prevention, Teachers Manual. A Grade 6 Unit.* Vancouver: Alcohol-Drug Education Service, 1983.

19. ALCOHOL-DRUG EDUCATION SERVICE. *Making Decisions, Choosing a Drug-Free Lifestyle, Teachers Manual. A Grade 7 Unit.* Vancouver: Alcohol-Drug Education Service, 1988.

20. ALCOHOL-DRUG EDUCATION SERVICE. *Mission D.A.D.: Decision About Drugs.* Vancouver: Alcohol-Drug Education Service, 1987.

21. ALCOHOL-DRUG EDUCATION SERVICE. *Prevention Newsletter. A Newsletter for Substance Abuse Task Forces* 1:1 (1989).

22. SCOTT, JACK. *Vancouver Sun*, 30 August 1960.

23. ALCOHOLISM FOUNDATION OF BRITISH COLUMBIA. *Fourth Annual Report, 1957–58*, Vancouver, 1958.

24. ALCOHOLISM FOUNDATION OF BRITISH COLUMBIA. *Eleventh Annual Report, 1963–64*, Vancouver, 1964.

25. *Community Resources Board Act*, R.S.B.C. 1979, c. 58.

26. BRITISH COLUMBIA. *Services for People.* Report of the Department of Human Resources, 1975.

27. STEVENSON, G. H., LINGLEY, L.R.A., TRASOV, G. E., and STANSFIELD, H. *Drug Addiction in British Columbia—A Research Survey.* 1955. Mimeographed document.

28. Narcotic Addiction Foundation of British Columbia, *First Annual Report, 1956–57*.

29. Narcotic Addiction Foundation of British Columbia, *Fourth Annual Report, 1959–60*.

30. Narcotic Addiction Foundation of British Columbia, *Tenth Annual Report, 1965–66*.

31. Narcotic Addiction Foundation of British Columbia, *Eleventh Annual Report, 1966–67*.

32. Narcotic Addiction Foundation of British Columbia, *Thirteenth Annual Report, 1968–69*.

33. Narcotic Addiction Foundation of British Columbia, *Fifteenth Annual Report, 1970–71*.

34. Narcotic Addiction Foundation of British Columbia, *Sixteenth Annual Report, 1971–72*.

35. Narcotic Addiction Foundation of British Columbia, *Seventeenth Annual Report, 1972–73*.

36. BRITISH COLUMBIA. *Twenty-fourth Annual Report*, British Columbia Hospital Insurance Service, January 1 to December 31, 1972.

37. BRITISH COLUMBIA. Alcohol and Drug Commission. *Annual Report, 1975.* Department of Human Resources.

38. *Alcohol and Drug Commission Act*, S.B.C. 1973, c. 3.

39. *Special Report to the Legislature of the B.C. Alcohol and Drug Commission*, 15 March 1974.

40. *Annual Report to the Legislature of the Alcohol and Drug Commission*, January 1–December 31, 1974, Department of Human Resources.

41. BRITISH COLUMBIA. Department of Health, *Annual Report, 1976.*

42. BRITISH COLUMBIA. *Annual Report to the Legislature of the Alcohol and Drug Commission, 1976–77.* Ministry of Health.

43. BRITISH COLUMBIA. Alcohol and Drug Commission. *Annual Report, 1977–78*, Ministry of Health.

44. *Heroin Treatment Act*, S.B.C. 1978, c. 24.

45. BRITISH COLUMBIA. Ministry of Health, *Annual Report, 1978*.
46. BRITISH COLUMBIA. Ministry of Health, *Annual Report, 1979*.
47. *Heroin Treatment Amendment Act*, S.B.C. 1989, c. 14, s. 1(b).
48. BRITISH COLUMBIA. Ministry of Health, *Annual Report, 1981*.
49. BRITISH COLUMBIA. Ministry of Health, *Annual Report, 1982*.
50. BRITISH COLUMBIA. *Memorandum*, Alcohol and Drug Programs, Ministry of Labour and Consumer Affairs, n.d.
51. BRITISH COLUMBIA. Liquor Policy Review, Liquor Policies for British Columbians, June 1987.
52. BRITISH COLUMBIA. *Report of the Task Force on Alcohol and Drugs in the Workplace*. Ministry of Health and Ministry of Labour and Consumer Services, September 1987.
53. CANADA. *Booze, Pills and Dope: Reducing Substance Abuse in Canada*. National Health and Welfare Canada, 1986–87.
54. BRITISH COLUMBIA. *British Columbia's New Community Awareness and Action Plan*. Ministry of Labour and Consumer Services, Alcohol and Drug Programs, Alcohol and Drug Abuse, 1988.
55. BRITISH COLUMBIA. *The TRY Book, Alcohol and Drug Programs*. Ministry of Labour and Consumer Services, 1989.
56. BRITISH COLUMBIA. *Innovative Hospital and Community Response*. Chemical Dependency Response Team, Alcohol and Drug Programs, Ministry of Labour and Consumer Services, 1989.
57. BRITISH COLUMBIA. *Closer to Home*. The Report of the British Columbia Royal Commission on Health Care and Costs, 1991.
58. *Indian Act*, S.C. 1876, c. 18.
59. Records of the Indian Advisory Committee. R. J. McInnes, Director, *Indian Advisory Act*, S.B.C. 1957, c. 28.
60. *Statute Law Amendment Act*, S.B.C. 1961, c. 59, s. 12.
61. JOHNSON, F., personal communication, 1987.
62. CANADA. *Action on Drug Abuse: Making a Difference*. Ministry of Supply and Services Canada, 1988.
63. *Canadian Centre on Substance Abuse Act*, R.C.S. 1985, c. 49 (4th Suppl.).
64. BRITISH COLUMBIA. *The British Columbia Alcohol and Drug Programs, Adolescent Survey. Preliminary Report, 1987*. Ministry of Health, Alcohol and Drug Program, 1987.
65. BRITISH COLUMBIA. *1990 British Columbia Student Drug Use Survey: Summary Report*. Alcohol and Drug Programs, B.C. Ministry of Health and Minister Responsible for Seniors.
66. *The Honour of All* (video). Phil Lucas Productions, Santa Fe, New Mexico.
67. SEGAL, S., personal communication.
68. ASANTE, K. O. and ROBINSON, G. C. Pregnancy Outreach Program in B.C. The Prevention of Alcohol-Related Birth Defects. *Canadian Journal of Public Health* 81 (1990): 76–77.
69. WEEKS, M. *Economic Impact of Fetal Alcohol Syndrome in Alaska*. Senate Advisory Council for Senator John Burkley, Alaska State Senate, February 1989. Mimeographed document.
70. Report of the panel. Summary. In *Alcohol and Public Policy Beyond the Shadow of Prohibition*, ed. M. H. Moore and D. R. Gerstein. Washington, D.C.: National Academy Press, 1981, pp. 112–16.

71. JOHNSON, C. A., PENTZ, M. A., WEBER, M. D., DWYER, J. H., BAER, N., MACKINNON, D. P., HAWSEN, W. B., and FRAY, B. R. Relative effectiveness of comprehensive community programming for drug abuse prevention with high risk and low risk adolescents. *Journal of Consulting and Clinical Psychology* 58 (1990): 447–56.

72. VERTINSKY, P. A. and MANGHAM, C. *Making it Fit. Matching Substance-Abuse Prevention Strategies.* Vancouver: B.C. School Trustees Association, 1991.

73. ONTARIO. *A Framework for the Response to Alcohol and Drug Problems in Ontario, 1988.* Ministry of Health, E. Caplan, Minister, 1988.

74. BURDEN, K.N. *An Overview of Youth-Oriented Prevention Programmes in Five European Countries. A Report of a Ten-Week Study Tour.* Ottawa: The Canadian Centre on Substance Abuse, 1990.

75. *Foetal Alcohol Syndrome: A Preventable Tragedy.* Report of the Standing Committee on Health and Welfare, Social Affairs, Seniors and the Status of Women. B. Green, M.P., Chair, S. Wilbee, M.P., Chair. Sub-committee on Health Issues, June 1992.

18

Medical Genetic Services

HISTORICAL CONSIDERATIONS

Introduction

James R. Miller, the first head of Medical Genetics at the University of British Columbia, arrived in Vancouver in 1958 to take up a job in mouse genetics in the Kinsmen Laboratory for Neurological Research. He has commented that this move was an accident of sorts (1). Professor W. C. Gibson, head of the Kinsmen Laboratory at the University of British Columbia, wrote to Dr. Clarke Fraser, Professor of Genetics at McGill University and head of Medical Genetic Services at the Montreal Children's Hospital (and incidentally chairman of Miller's doctoral committee), for a supportive reference about someone he was about to hire. Fraser, thinking he was writing to his old McGill classmate, W. M. Gibson, replied that, though he had nothing against the person, he had a student about to obtain a Ph.D. degree who would do a far better job. During the ensuing negotiations, Fraser came to realize that he was dealing with W. C. and not W. M. Gibson, but this did not influence the outcome. Suffice to say, Miller began his distinguished academic career with the mouse studies in muscular dystrophy in the Kinsmen Laboratory.

During graduate studies, he had extensive clinical training with Dr. Norma Ford Walker at the Hospital for Sick Children in Toronto and with Dr. Clarke Fraser at the Montreal Children's Hospital, and hence was well prepared for clinical work and the teaching of medical genetics. Shortly after his arrival, he was introduced to Dr. John F. McCreary, professor and head of Paediatrics, and soon to be the Dean of Medicine, and expressed an interest in starting a program in medical genetics. This led to involvement in clinical work and teaching in the outpatient department of the Health Centre for Children, initially in the Preschool Hearing Program (Chapter 16). An introduction to Miss A. E. (Nancy) Scott and

Dr. Donald Paterson in the Crippled Children's Registry (Chapter 5) soon followed, and a long and productive professional association was thereby initiated. Miller wrote about this pair, "He and Nancy Scott made what at first seemed an improbable pair and, at times, coming upon them during their policy discussions, I had the strong impression that they were about to come to blows. However, they were simply two strong— very strong—personalities coming to an agreement in their own way" (1). In 1961, he was appointed genetic consultant to the Registry and retained that position until 1980. The Registry was adjacent to the office of the Assistant Deputy Minister of Health (then G.R.F. Elliot), and this association led to collaboration with the provincial health units and the introduction of the Outreach Program.

In 1966, stimulated by his association with Paterson and Scott, Miller wrote that the changing pattern of disease in most industrialized societies, characterized by an increase in prevalence of chronic long-term illnesses, many of which are genetically determined, had implications for public health programs (2). He noted that these chronic illnesses have profound significance for the individuals afflicted, for their families, and for society as a whole in terms of the cost of health and other resources of a community. He stressed the importance of measuring the incidence and prevalence of genetic and non-genetic disorders by means of a registry (see Chapter 5). He emphasized the value of genetic counselling as a preventive measure, adding that "We must concern ourselves with the study of populations as a whole and of course this is the domain of public health."

In 1959, Dr. Bruce Graham was appointed head of the Department of Paediatrics at the University of British Columbia, and, in the following year, invited Miller to join the Department of Paediatrics. He was assigned a base, including a conference room and laboratory, in the Health Centre for Children, and he was invited to teach genetics in the first year and to introduce some clinical material in the second year of medicine.

In the early 1960s, Miller initiated chromosomal studies in embryos and foetuses from spontaneous abortions (3). At this time, human embryology was described as almost a moribund science (4), though Miller predicted the forthcoming union of genetics and embryology and the important role this would play in studies of infertility and in counselling. The development of embryo pathology (0–9 weeks) and foetal pathology (nine weeks to term) testifies to the accuracy of this prediction (5).

Brian Lowry joined the Department of Paediatrics in 1965 (and subsequently the Division of Medical Genetics), and was appointed medical consultant to the Registry in the same year.

In 1967, Medical Genetics was established as a division within the Department of Paediatrics, and Miller was appointed professor and head.

He had the distinction of being the only non-medically qualified, full-time professor in a clinical department of a medical faculty in Canada. There was a rapid expansion of knowledge in clinical genetics and genetic counselling in the 1960s and 1970s. Dr. Victor McKusick established an annual meeting addressing birth defects that served to bring clinical genetics into the mainstream of medicine, and, coincidentally, to make the geneticists in Vancouver very busy. Finally the Department of Medical Genetics was established in the Faculty of Medicine in 1973, and a new department base was established.

Miller was succeeded by Patricia A. Baird in 1979. During the following decade, she supervised the expansion of the university department, with a twelvefold increase in research funding, a doubling in academic courses offered (from six to twelve) and of the clinical program (nearly a ten-fold increase in the number of families seen) (6). Baird had replaced Lowry in 1976 as medical consultant with the Registry, and continued until this position was terminated in 1989 (see Chapter 5). In 1990, she resigned as department head and served as chairperson on the Royal Commission on New Reproductive Techniques. Dr. Judith Hall joined the Department in 1981 as director of the Clinical Program and supervisor of the Clinical Fellowship Program. She has overseen the expansion of diagnostic and genetic counselling services and prenatal diagnosis services in the major teaching hospitals.

Medical genetics services in Montreal, Toronto, Winnipeg, Edmonton, and Vancouver were initiated by university faculty with the scientific (Ph.D.)[1] rather than the medical (M.D.) background. When universal medical insurance was introduced in 1968, the Medical Services Insurance Plans were not authorized to pay for services provided by non-medical doctors, and hence an important source of medical funding was denied to these departments. Likewise, the Royal College of Physicians of Canada did not recognize the specialty of medical genetics, and hence medical geneticists, many of whom were not M.D.s, decided to form the Canadian College of Medical Geneticists in 1975. Once the clinical relevance of medical genetics in modern medicine was more widely recognized, more physicians entered the specialty, and insurance funding became available to fund these departmental members.

As a result of this dilemma during the pre-medicare days of the department, the University of British Columbia and the Health Branch, not the Hospital Insurance Service of the Department of Health Services and Hospital Insurance, provided the operating funds for clinical services. In 1980, the Community Health Services, Ministry of Health, provided a grant to the Department of Medical Genetics at the University of British Columbia.

---

1 Fraser subsequently obtained a medical degree.

Development of Clinical Services

Genetic Counselling Clinic: In 1962, a genetic counselling clinic was quietly introduced in the Department of Paediatrics, then located in the Health Centre for Children of the Vancouver General Hospital. The services included outpatient and inpatient consultation. The value of genetic counselling (7) and the indications for and availability of chromosomal analysis were described (8). When the division achieved departmental status, new faculty were added, and the department moved to new facilities that included clinical examination facilities. A separate department unit with facilities for basic research was located at the University of British Columbia. The clinical unit moved to the new British Columbia Children's Hospital–Grace Maternity Hospital, which was opened in 1982.

Prenatal Diagnosis Program: In 1971, the Prenatal Diagnosis Program was started by the Division of Medical Genetics, and the indications for and the results were described (9). A subsequent paper reviewed the indications for amniocentesis and developments in ultrasonography and foetoscopy (10). The age limit for amniocentesis was lowered from thirty-eight and over to thirty-five years at the expected date of delivery in 1982 (11).

Two new advances, chorionic villae sampling (CVS) and realtime ultrasound guidance (12) allowed, earlier and more accurate prenatal diagnosis. CVS involves the transcervical (or transabdominal) aspiration of placental tissue at nine to eleven weeks gestation. Ultrasound is used to identify pregnancy viability, gestational age, and placental implantation site. CVS allows earlier (first trimester) diagnosis of chromosomal and biochemical disorders, but it cannot screen for neural tube or other anatomical defects. Diagnostic ultrasound, using realtime scanning technique, has greatly increased the ability to identify congenital malformations in the foetus. Depending on the type of malformation, the ultrasound scan is recommended between sixteen and nineteen weeks gestation.

Outreach Program: A scheduled outreach program was started in 1979. These regular pre-planned visits followed from intermittent follow-up visits involving research studies by departmental members, Brian Lowry and Patrick McLeod. Regular genetics clinics were introduced in Victoria and the Thompson–Okanagan region (13, 14). An advisory board of local physicians in each area was formed to assist in planning, and clinics were held in the local health units. This service has been very popular, and Baird has stated that they "hope to achieve a truly province-wide service" (13, 14).

PRESENT SERVICES

Diagnosis and Counselling Services

These services include:

1. Routine consultation in an outpatient department or ward relating to congenital malformations and genetic defects.
2. Counselling after recurrent early loss (less than twenty weeks) and loss of stillbirth (over twenty weeks) or neonatal death. This is provided by obstetricians who are members of the Department of Medical Genetics. This program works closely with the Embryo Foetal Pathology laboratory in the British Columbia Children's Hospital in establishing an aetiological diagnosis for recurrent spontaneous abortions by means of morphological, cytogenetic, biochemical, and bacterial/viral studies. The results provide a basis for appropriate counselling and have important preventive implications.
3. Consultation services to the multidiscipline programs of the British Columbia Children's Hospital, including cleft palate, cystic fibrosis, and muscle disease, and to the biochemical disease clinic (Chapter 9).
4. Attending the Lipid Clinic of the University Hospital and assessing children in affected families.
5. Co-ordination of a multidiscipline program to assess and manage infants and children with gender abnormalities.
6. An in-depth assessment of the pregnancy and family history of all children placed for adoption by the Ministry of Social Services and Housing. The service is not provided to private adoptions. Infants placed for adoption not infrequently are the offspring of young single mothers, who may have drug addiction problems or other medical problems with potential implications for the future functioning of their offspring.
7. Adult genetic clinics at the University Hospital and consultation to the multiple sclerosis and Alzheimer clinics at that hospital.

Prenatal Diagnosis Program

For many years, genetic evaluation and counselling were provided to all patients referred for genetic prenatal diagnosis by the Department of Medical Genetics. In 1989, a new mechanism was introduced to share this responsibility with the referring physician. Responsibility for counselling of all referrals dealing with advanced maternal age (thirty-five years or older at the expected date of delivery) was given to the physician providing the patient's general prenatal care. A physician's packet and a patient information packet, which included a screening questionnaire, were prepared by the Department of Medical Genetics and provided to all referring physicians in British Columbia.

The physician's packet includes the indications for genetic prenatal diagnosis, and for the risks by age for total chromosome abnormality and Down syndrome, a note on screening at-risk populations (Tay Sachs disease and thalassaemia), and management of unsensitized Rh negative women who receive amniocentesis or CVS. The patient information packet contains the prenatal genetic counselling screening questionnaire, information sheets describing and illustrating the procedures (amniocentesis, CVS, and ultrasound), risks, and limitations, and the informed consent letter that the patient signs before a procedure.

When a procedure is found to be indicated (amniocentesis or CVS), it is performed at the Grace Hospital in Vancouver and occasionally, in the case of amniocentesis, in Victoria General Hospital. The results of the fetal cytogenetic studies on the foetal cells and alpha-foetoprotein determinations are sent to the referring physician by the laboratory. If any of the tests are abnormal, the Department of Medical Genetics is also notified immediately, and contacts and discusses the abnormal results with the family physician. Evaluation and counselling are provided as required by the department to any patient found to have an abnormal result in prenatal testing.

Genetic evaluation and counselling are provided to all referred patients with problems, other than advanced maternal age, that increase their risk of having a baby with congenital abnormalities. All diagnostic procedures are performed at the Grace or Victoria General Hospitals.

It is estimated that 70 percent of the prenatal counselling work has been shifted to the family physicians, leaving 30 percent to the Department of Medical Genetics, and that, appropriately, being referrals with more complex problems than simply older age.

Outreach Program

Clinics are conducted in the Thompson–Okanagan region, and one community is visited about every two weeks. A regional genetic counselling clinic is conducted by a member of Medical Genetics in Victoria every two weeks. These clinics are conducted in the local health unit offices. Approximately two-thirds of referrals are children. There have been requests from other health units for this service, but current funding is not available to support this.

COMMENT

The development of medical genetic services began within the Department of Paediatrics at the University of British Columbia, and the paediatric services were expanded to include prenatal obstetrical and adult care. The potential for the prevention of genetic disease and congenital malformations was early recognized by the Health Branch, as was the need for a population approach to prevent these disorders. The prenatal diagnosis program and outreach services followed, together with a consultant role in the Health Surveillance Registry (Chapter 5).

Initially, funding of the service was difficult because non-medical faculty were not able to bill the Medical Services Plan for outpatient or inpatient consultations. This left the planning and growth of the range and standard of clinical services up to the university department staff, a bonus not always enjoyed by other specialties, and resulted in a first class clinical program. It meant that the ideal blend of academic and service components could occur, so essential in a rapidly expanding field of knowledge. It also meant that researchers worked side by side with clinical geneticists to bring about early application to families of the insights learned from research. While university staff were routinely involved in virtually all the different programs described in this book, the control of the Department of Medical Genetics in shaping the provincial clinical services, for the reasons noted above, is unique.

REFERENCES

1. MILLER, J. R. The early development of medical genetics at the University of British Columbia. In *Medical Genetics in Canada: Evolution of a Hybrid Discipline*, ed. H. C. Soltan, London, Ontario: University of Western Ontario, Graphic Services, 1991, Chapter 7, p. 111.
2. MILLER, J. R. Human genetics in public health research and programming. *Canadian Journal of Public Health* 57 (1966): 7.
3. POLAND, B. J. and LOWRY, R. B. The rise of spontaneous abortions and still-births in genetic counselling. *American Journal of Obstetrics and Gynecology* 118 (1974): 322–26.
4. MILLER, J. R. Some recent advances in human genetics and cytology. *Manitoba Medical Review* 42 (1962): 528–31.
5. KALOUSEK, D. K., FITCH, N., and PARADISE, B. *Pathology of the Human Embryo and Previable Fetus, An Atlas.* New York: Springer-Verlag, 1990.
6. UNIVERSITY OF BRITISH COLUMBIA, Department of Medical Genetics. *Annual Report, 1988–89.*
7. MILLER, J. R. Genetic counselling and chromosome service. *B.C. Medical Journal* 12 (1970): 171.

8. LOWRY, R. B. and DILL, F. J. Chromosomal analysis in British Columbia. *B.C. Medical Journal* 16 (1974): 200–201.
9. POLAND, B. and SUDERMAN, L. Genetic amniocentesis program in B.C. *B.C. Medical Journal* 20 (1978): 243–45.
10. MCGILLIVRAY, B., SHAW, D., and SUDERMAN, L. Genetic prenatal diagnosis in British Columbia. *B.C. Medical Journal* 22 (1980): 497–99.
11. Ministry of Health. *B.C. Medical Journal* 24 (1982): 547.
12. WILSON, R. D. and WITTMANN, B. K. New developments in prenatal diagnosis: Chorionic villi sampling and real time ultrasound. *B.C. Medical Journal* 28 (1986): 739–44.
13. BAIRD, P. A. The Medical Genetics Program at U.B.C. *B.C. Medical Journal* 22 (1980): 527.
14. BAIRD, P. A. The Medical Genetics Services in B.C. *B.C. Medical Journal* 29 (1987): 88–91.

19

Services to the Handicapped

The suffering of handicapped children is matched only by the suffering of their parents. . . . Families with handicapped children need every support from relations, friends, neighbours and from community services.(1)

HISTORICAL CONSIDERATIONS

One of the most profound changes in child care during the post-war years has been the shift from institutional to community care of children with multiple disabilities. The virtual elimination of paediatric admissions to the institutions for the mentally handicapped population is recognition of the vulnerability of children to separation from family and of the primacy of the family as a nurturing and support system for its members. While the need for this shift was acknowledged in British Columbia in the early 1950s (2), the provision of the range of community-based services was a gradual process. It involved planning services, not only for those who were residents of institutions and would return to their own homes or to another community-based home, but also for the younger children who would remain with their families in their own homes. The British Columbia Association for Community Living (BCACL) was in the forefront of this movement, and, in collaboration with the Ministry of Education, initiated the development of regional, community-based, special needs preschool and school programs. The Ministry of Social Services and Housing moved beyond its traditional role of protection and child welfare services, and introduced supportive services to families with children with mental disabilities, enabling them to live at home in their own communities. These services included the Infant Development Program, special needs day care, special services to children and homemakers, and some respite care. These changes in mandate called for new client and interministerial relationships, and introduced legal liabilities involving service providers in community settings.

The transfer of children from long-stay hospitals and institutions to the community began in the 1970s (Chapter 14). The first group home for children with severe disabilities was developed in 1975 by the Sunny Hill Hospital and was funded by the Ministry of Social Services and Housing (3).

The transfer of the major institutions (Woodlands, Tranquille, and Glendale) from the Ministry of Health to Social Services and Housing took place in 1974, and, in 1983, government deinstitutionalization policy was formally proclaimed in the Throne Speech. This culminated in the closure of Tranquille in Kamloops in 1985. This first phase of deinstitutionalization identified fifty-five adult residents who were "medically fragile," and they were transferred to Glendale, in Victoria. This move resulted in media coverage of the blockade of the road from Tranquille to the airport to obstruct the transfer. The move went ahead, but subsequent meetings between the Ministry of Health and the BCACL resulted in the Ministry of Health accepting the responsibility for community placement of the fifty-five residents. This was both a moral victory for the mentally handicapped and the advocacy movement and the cue for the Ministry of Health to develop community-based services for persons with multiple disabilities. The closing of the institutions, incidently, separated parents into two groups, those whose children have always lived at home and those whose children have returned from an institution to live at home or near home. The latter group of parents are older, with different concerns, including the well-being of their offspring when they can no longer oversee the care.

In addition to the children with chronic disability associated with the nervous system pathology, there is another group with other chronic physical illnesses, including congenital anomalies (cardiac, pulmonary, renal, and spina bifida), genetic diseases (haemophilia, cystic fibrosis), inflammatory bowel disease, cancer, and others. Some of these children are technology dependent, and require the routine use of a specific medical device to compensate for the loss of a life-sustaining body function. The most common group are the very low birthweight infants with bronchopulmonary dysplasia, requiring continuous oxygen. Others include children who are ventilator-dependent, who have tracheotomies and require intermittent suctioning, who are on renal dialysis, or who require total parenteral nutrition, or nasal or gastrotomy feeds. These children place heavy demands on their families, necessitating regular nursing respite. They need access to preschools and day care, but early education is often denied because of potential legal liabilities involved. They need help with the costs of the children's equipment and ongoing supplies, such as ventilators and tracheotomy care, which are not covered by Pharmacare (Chapter 3). These families also faced the paradox that foster parents are paid to care for such children, while natural parents are not. Many parents care for their children at the price of great financial hardship. Finally, some of these children have chronic disabilities that require long-term care for life.

It is not surprising that, in many instances, the family functioning is seriously disrupted and sometimes dissolved. The societal trends of modern life, in particular the loss of the extended family, single parent families, and the increase in working mothers, further complicate the home care of these children with disabilities and the lives of other family members. Suffice to say that the closing of the institutions, the need to care for the subgroup with chronic medical problems and for those who are technology dependent imposes many new responsibilities on the Ministry of Health. In 1986, a Resource Line was established by the Ministry of Health to provide a centre within the provincial government where issues relating to chronic disability could be addressed. In 1986, a philosophy statement was published by the Ministry of Health to introduce the new Services to the Handicapped Division, which could guide service development to persons with a disability or handicap and to their families (4). It noted that the commitment of services to the handicapped is to the individual, the family, and the community. The importance of the family, natural or alternate, was recognized as the key resource and support for the development and care of the person with a handicap. In May 1986, Services to the Handicapped Division officially commenced operations within the Community Care Division (now Community and Family Health) of the Ministry of Health. Its mandate included promoting the empowerment of parents and individuals and developing a partnership based on working together for a common goal.

PRESENT SERVICES

Organization

Services to the Handicapped is a branch within the Family Health Division, which in turn is part of Community and Family Health. The Family Health Division is responsible for the programs below.

Programs

Resource Line: A toll-free line functions as a type of ombudsman. Since 1986, it has helped to identify service gaps, which led to the development of the Nursing Respite Program (see below) and of services to persons with head injuries.

Community Placement (Adults): A service which places and supports persons who previously lived in institutions (Glendale, Woodlands, and young adults at the Sunny Hill Hospital and Queen Alexandra Hospital for Children) in suitable community settings. Services also include day programs and respite for parents whose adult children remain at home.

Children's Early Intervention Program: The salaries are provided for approved positions in therapy and family support of the Children's Early Intervention Program in child development centres (Chapter 15). Additional funds for the centres derive from the Ministry of Social Services and Housing and from fund raising.

Associate Family Program: This program was introduced in 1987 to allow children with multiple disabilities, with the support of their natural families, to live in the community with "associate families" (5). The associate families care for and nurture the children and treat them as though they were members of their own families. Children residing in institutions or long-stay hospitals are eligible for the program. The associate families receive training at the two long-stay hospitals for children and, in some cases, local hospitals or child development centres.

In all cases, the parents or guardians of each child agree to explore a family-based alternative to hospital care, and their permission to proceed with planning and the eventual placement is first obtained. At the time of placement, an Individual Program Plan (IPP) sets out in detail the care and services a child is to receive and the goals for the child's progress. The care and services include physical development and health, sensorimotor development and skills, communication and social skills, emotional and spiritual development, educational and vocational skills, and recreation and leisure.

The Ministry of Health views the parents or legal guardians as the ideal caregivers for all children and, when they are unable to do so, as in this program, it encourages parents to play an active role in the planning and provision of care for their child. They are encouraged to contribute and to participate in their child's care by regular visiting, attending regular review of the child's IPP, providing respite care to the associate family, and participating in all major decisions regarding their child.

All the associate families are paid a fixed daily amount for the services they provide under contract. The monitoring of the performance of the various caregivers and the progress of the children is a regular part of associate family care, and involves assessing the care and progress of the child against the goals and standards set in the IPP. A liaison worker is also responsible for monitoring and co-ordinating various other assessments made by other team members. The process provides an opportunity to discuss and resolve problems and to plan for the improvement of care, including modifying the IPP.

Nursing Respite Program: This program was introduced on a pilot basis in 1988 and is now available throughout the province. Children eligible for this program have complex medical care needs and require special services and some form of medical support for survival. Care may include tracheotomy care, ventilator support, total parenteral nutrition, home dialysis, cardiac monitoring, complex seizure disorder management, and palliative care.

The program is intended to support the family in their primary caregiving role by providing respite or relief on a planned or unanticipated basis for twelve to four hundred hours per month. It is provided in home and/or out of home by qualified and trained, licensed practical nurses and/or registered nurses at no cost to the family.

At Home Program (AHP): This program, introduced in October 1989, is a joint venture of the Ministries of Health and Social Services and Housing (6). The responsibility of the Ministry of Health in the AHP is to process applications, determine eligibility, admit eligible children, and process appeals. The Ministry of Social Services is responsible for the administration of the program in the provision of supports and services. The program was designed to meet several goals.

These goals included assisting families in their role as primary caregivers of children with severe disabilities, providing support and services to children with severe disabilities, relieving the financial burden placed on families caring for their children at home, and preventing institutional and foster care placement. The program defines a severe disability as either total dependence on a caregiver for the daily functional self-care activities of eating, toileting, dressing, and washing, or the requirement for nursing respite care.

Children are eligible if they are under eighteen years of age, have a legal right to live in Canada, and are living in the family home or moving home from a health care institution, foster home, or associate family home. The assessment process used to determine the severity of a child's disability comprises a review of the child's dependency on a caregiver for the activities of daily living (eating, toileting, washing, and dressing). Children admitted to the Nursing Respite Program automatically qualify for admission to the AHP. These children are usually medically fragile, technology dependent, or terminally ill.

The Ministry of Health provides facilitators in each region to screen potential clients for the AHP, in co-operation with health professionals in hospitals and in the community, and, with parents and other caregivers, assesses the degree of the child's disability. There are ten regional committees, one in each of the ten regions of the Ministry of Social Services and Housing in British Columbia, which recommend acceptance, and a central advisory board in Victoria, which decides on admissions.

Successful applicants receive benefits that include Medical Service Plan premium coverage, complete Pharmacare coverage, supplies for health care needs, medically essential equipment and its maintenance and repair, medical transportation and ambulance, special required therapies, dental care coverage, orthotics and prosthetics, and respite care. While the program provides a wide range of benefits, it does not seek to duplicate supports and services available through other resources and will not provide communication aids, dialysis equipment, household items or renovations, vans or van lifts or conversions, vision devices, clothing, and food.

If a child is not eligible for the AHP, but the parents are, or if they will incur extraordinary costs in providing for health-related care needs of the child, the parents are offered the Medical Benefits Package of the program. Alternatively, the child may not qualify for the AHP but be offered the respite benefits.

COMMENT

Services to the Handicapped represents a major addition to the child care services in British Columbia, and serves to illustrate the need for both personal and population medicine in the care of children with severe and multiple disabilities. It is obvious that the policy and planning of these services are outside the area of responsibility of private medicine and traditional public health.

This service was initiated by the Ministry of Health to place adults with severe multiple disabilities in community-based settings and, in collaboration with the Ministry of Social Services, has since been expanded to provide other innovative programs for children in need of long-term care. These programs are a good advertisement for health insurance, and became feasible after the *Established Programs Financing Act* (7) (1977), when programs were no longer tied to legislation, offering the provinces greater flexibility in program development.

These various new programs also represent welcome, though long overdue, acceptance by the government of the special needs of children, and the role of the family in providing for their psychosocial needs, in addition to the medical treatment of disease and injury. The emotional and financial burdens of caring for children with severe disabilities at home has been carried for years by many devoted families in the absence of a long-term care program for children. The resultant psychological and economic load has often disrupted family functioning. Furthermore, the practice of paying foster parents of children with disabilities extra financial aid, while denying it to the natural parents, has long been a contentious issue. These programs are in their infancy, but they represent a significant commitment by the government to provide quality care for all children.

REFERENCES

1. WYNN, M. and WYNN, A. Prevention of handicap, the spirit of our age. In *Prevention of Handicap and the Health of Women*. London: Routledge and Kegan Paul, 1979.
2. BRITISH COLUMBIA. *Annual Report for the Twelve Months Ended March 31, 1954*. Department of the Provincial Secretary, Mental Health Services 1955.
3. MACNAUGHTON, D., personal communication, 1989.
4. BRITISH COLUMBIA. *Philosophy Statement, Services to Handicapped*. Ministry of Health, 1986.
5. BRITISH COLUMBIA. *The Associate Family Program—Community-based Care in Family Homes for Multiply Handicapped Children*. Services to the Handicapped Division, Ministry of Health, 8 June 1987.
6. BRITISH COLUMBIA. *At Home Program for Children with Severe Disabilities*. Policy and procedure guidelines for eligibility and acceptance to the program, 3 October 1989. Mimeographed document.
7. *Federal-Provincial Fiscal Arrangements and Established Programs Financing Act*, S.C. 1976–77, c. 10.

20

Developmental Screening of Infants and Preschool Children

HISTORICAL CONSIDERATIONS

The concept of early identification of disability, followed by the institution of appropriate intervention, has long been accepted for biochemical diseases, sensory handicaps (hearing and vision), and cerebral palsy. In addition to children with these known disabilities, there has also been a concern for the development and well-being of two other groups of infants and preschool children, namely, those reared in socially deprived environments and those with a biological risk factor in their history, e.g., maternal rubella in pregnancy or very low birthweight. These children are at risk of development delay and the resultant consequences.

There have been two principal approaches to developmental screening for the early identification of these at-risk children. The first of these is total surveillance, whereby virtually all children are screened regularly from birth through to school age. This approach has been followed in some countries with national health services, such as England, Scotland, Sweden, and Cuba. The second approach, selective screening, focuses on the progress of infants who are vulnerable to the effects of one or more possible disorders, such as genetic disease or pathological insult occurring in prenatal, perinatal, or post-natal life. Experience has shown that, while a high percentage of infants are at risk of disability, only a small percentage develop a clinical problem. Furthermore, a significant proportion of disabilities arise in infants who are not at risk. The effectiveness of this approach is limited by the degree of co-operation of the parents, who may or may not seek primary care for their children. As a result, the children of socially disadvantaged families, who are at risk of developmental delay, may escape assessment and follow-up care. For these various reasons, the risk registry concept has fallen into disrepute.

Köhler reminds us that screening methods are not diagnostic; they should discover the sick, i.e., have high sensitivity, but not at the expense of many well infants being classified as being sick, so they should have high specificity (1). Low sensitivity misses cases, and low specificity taxes resources and causes needless worry.

In the early 1980s, Parkyn and his colleagues, while seeking to define the functions of their public health nursing practice, singled out the importance of nursing assessment in the identification and follow-up of at-risk infants and preschool children (2). This led to the development of a tool for risk assessment by public health nurses. They recognized that the use of factors in an unweighted fashion (with equal weight given to an infant 1,000 grams at birth and to one with a family history of congenital heart disease) was flawed, and adapted a model used in perinatal medicine (3, 4), in which a scoring system was used to identify obstetric patients at special risk of adverse outcomes. The latter model grouped abnormal conditions into eight categories (maternal age, race and marital status, parity, post-obstetric history, medical obstetric disorders and nutrition, generative tract disorders, emotional, and socioeconomic), each of which was assigned a score (0–30). The relative weight of each adverse factor was based on the estimate of the degree of insult with respect to perinatal outcome. All scores were computed at the initial perinatal visit. The index score represented the numerical value resulting from the sum of all such penalties subtracted from a perfect score of 100. In this way, high risk (scores less than 70), moderate risk (70–84), and low risk (85 and over) groups were identified. This approach identified the 30 percent of patients at high risk who accounted for 60 percent of all pathologic outcomes.

In this way, Parkyn (2) produced a comparable, semi-objective weighted, multiple factor questionnaire (Figure 3), which screens for three groups of children:

A. children with known handicap.
B. developmental risk factors (low birthweight, bilirubin over 20 mg%, etc.)
C. family interaction/social risk factors.

There are a total of seventeen questions and each has a score of 1 to 9. The total score distinguishes low risk (3–5), moderate risk (6–8), and high risk (9+). The instrument has been validated by a panel of experts (5), and tested for inter-rater reliability by nurses with varying degrees of experience. It is currently in use in health units in all provinces.

The questionnaire also contains the data for the High Risk Hearing Registry (see Chapter 16), but these responses are separate from the risk assessment.

PRESENT SERVICES

The questionnaire for the risk assessment for infants and preschool children is routinely initiated in the hospital of birth in all provincial health units, and is completed either by the public health liaison nurse or the hospital staff nurse. All infants with a score of 6+ (moderate risk) or at risk of a hearing loss receive a home visit by the public health nurse for further assessment. Experience has shown that more satisfactory answers, particularly in regard to financial position, are obtained at this time. The infant's name is placed on a risk assessment follow-up index card, and, as well, a problem-oriented record is started. The family physician is advised by letter and by phone when relevant issues need to be discussed during follow-up. For example, the public health nurse may suggest the developmental testing of a child and then make the appointment for testing for the family.

The follow-up varies with the three categories, known handicap(s), developmental/risk factors, and social and/or family interaction factors. The follow-up also will be influenced by the extent of the disability and availability of resources in the community, including the community health nurse. The public health nursing role may involve facilitating the follow-up of medical recommendations, co-ordinating referrals to community agencies for assessment, teaching and support, regular developmental screening, intervention to prevent neglect or abuse, and early intervention as a result of known neglect or abuse. In the latter situation, the Ministry of Social Services and Housing is advised.

When the progress of the infant is judged to be satisfactory, the family physician is advised by letter that the infant has been discharged and is no longer being followed by the public health nursing. If an infant moves away the records are sent to the new health unit.

COMMENT

The objective of the risk assessment instrument is to screen the target population in order to facilitate early intervention and/or correction of disability in children. The target population includes all newborns, plus those infants and preschool children that are seen by health unit staff. In this way, the total newborn population is screened, using a semi-objective weighted multifactorial tool to identify an at-risk group of infants. In contrast to the total surveillance approach, only the at-risk group is followed up. The scoring system identifies the 5–6 percent at high risk, and the 5–12 percent at moderate risk. The socioeconomic status of the community will influence the rates. The thrust is to replace crisis intervention with preventive strategies. The identification of the developmental and

Province of British Columbia — Ministry of Health

PRIORITY ASSESSMENT FOR INFANTS AND PRESCHOOL CHILDREN

CHILD'S NAME (FAMILY NAME)	GIVEN NAMES	SEX	BIRTHDATE YY MM DD
		☐ M ☐ F	

I. DISCHARGE NOTES

DELIVERY:		BIRTH WEIGHT _____ gms.						YES	NO
☐ VERTEX	☐ BREECH	GESTATION AGE _____				PRIMIP		☐	☐
☐ SPONTANEOUS	☐ FORCEPS	SINGLE	TWIN		TRIPLET	ICN - 24 hrs OR MORE		☐	☐
CAESARIAN SECTION	☐ 1'ST	☐ 1	☐ 1 ☐ 2	☐ 1 ☐ 2 ☐ 3		PKU DONE		☐	☐
	☐ 2 PLUS					FEEDING - Breast		☐	☐
☐ ELECTIVE		APGAR 1 MIN. _____				FEEDING - Formula		☐	☐
☐ EMERGENCY		APGAR 5 MIN. _____				PRENATAL EDUCATION		☐	☐
DISCHARGE DATE		YY	MM	DD		DISCHARGE WEIGHT			GM

COMMENTS

II. HIGH PRIORITY HEARING REGISTRY

		YES	NO
A.	Birth weight below 1500gm — If yes, score item 3a) at right.	☐	☐
B.	Bilirubin level greater than or equal to 20gm/100ml OR 340umol/l — If yes, score item 4 at right.	☐	☐
C.	Any defect of the ear(s), nose, throat, mouth, palate or eye(s)? — If yes, score item 1b) at right. Describe:	☐	☐
D.	Clinical or serological evidence of maternal rubella during pregnancy? — If yes, score item 5a) at right.	☐	☐
E.	Is there anyone in the parents' families, (first cousin or closer) with hearing impairment, with onset prior to age 20 years?	☐	☐

RELATIONSHIP OF HEARING IMPAIRED INDIVIDUAL TO INFANT	WAS THE LOSS PERMANENT?			AGE THE LOSS DIAGNOSED/ POSSIBLE CAUSE OF LOSS.	TYPE OF LOSS IN THIS INDIVIDUAL.		
	YES	NO	UN-KNOWN		CON-DUCTIVE	SENSORI-NEURAL	UN-KNOWN
(1) _____	☐	☐	☐	_____	☐	☐	☐
(2) _____	☐	☐	☐	_____	☐	☐	☐

MARK ITEM 7 IN SECTION III PART B AT RIGHT, IF RELEVANT.

COMMENTS _____

DATE _____   NAME OF PERSON COMPLETING PART I&II _____

HEALTH UNIT USE ONLY	FULL ASSESSMENT COMPLETED	DATE
	SIGNATURE, H.U. STAFF	

HLTH 184 REV 90/01

MOTHER'S NAME (IF NOT STAMPED AT RIGHT)
AGE

FATHER'S NAME (FAMILY/FIRST)

ADDRESS   PHONE No.

NAME OF HOSPITAL (IF NOT ON STAMP)

PHYSICIAN'S NAME

MOTHER'S HOSPITAL STAMP

III. NURSING PRIORITY ASSESSMENT

IF YES
CIRCLE

A. CHILDREN WITH KNOWN HANDICAP

1. Congenital anomaly
   a) Major (probability of permanent disability) eg: Down's Syndrome 9
   b) Moderate (correction may be possible) eg: Cleft palate 6
2. a) Major handicap acquired during first 5 years of life (probability of permanent disability)
      eg: Cerebral Palsy, severe brain damage 9
   b) Moderate handicap acquired during first 5 years of life (correction may be possible)
      eg: loss of limb 6

B. DEVELOPMENTAL RISK FACTORS

3. Low birth weight   a) 0-1499 gm 9
                        b) 1500-1999 gm 8
                        c) 2000-2499 gm 6
4. Bilirubin level over 20 gm or 340 umol/L 8
5. Complications of pregnancy
   a) Infections that can be transmitted in utero and may damage the fetus (eg: rubella) 9
   b) Drugs — eg: alcohol abuse diagnosed in mother 9
6. Complications of labour and delivery
   a) Labour requiring mid and high forceps including breech delivery with forceps 4
   b) Infant trauma or illness (eg: convulsions, respiratory distress syndrome) 6
   c) Apgar at 5 minutes only if less than 7. Deduct apgar score at 5 minutes from 10 points ...... ____
7. Family history of a handicap not detectable at birth that could affect development
   eg: deafness, mental retardation 4
8. Developmental concerns not already covered in any above catgory
   a) Acquired risk of developmental delay due to illness or trauma in first 5 years 6
   b) Delayed developmental assessment in first 5 years 9

C. FAMILY INTERACTION RISK FACTORS

9. Age of mother   a) 15 and under 9
                     b) 16 or 17 8
                     c) 18 or 19 5
10. Social Situation
    a) Father of infant not resident but other support available 2
    b) Father not resident and no support 7
    c) Father resident and supportive but no other social support,
       or severe isolation by language or geography 4
11. On social assistance or financial difficulties 3
12. No prenatal care before sixth month 4
13. Mental illness or retardation in mother and/or father
    a) Schizophrenia or manic depression 7
    b) Post-partum depression 9
    c) Mental retardation of parent 6
14. Prolonged post-partum maternal separation (5 days or more)
    a) With frequent infant contacts (visits or phone as feasible) 2
    b) Little or no contact 6
15. Assessed lack of bonding eg: Eye contact, touching, etc. minimal 6
16. 3+ hospitalizations in a year in absence of known handicap or chronic illness 7
17. Other — eg: marital distress, low education status, failure to thrive,
    difficulty raising an older child, etc. (score 0 to 9) .... ____
    Specify reason:

PRIORITY SCORE	9 AND OVER = HIGH PRIORITY	6 TO 8 = MODERATE PRIORITY
	3 TO 5 = LOW PRIORITY	0 TO 2 = MINIMAL PRIORITY

TOTAL
PRIORITY
SCORE

Figure 3 Priority Assessment for Infants and Preschool Children questionnaire.

family interaction groups is a reflection of the importance of social pathology in contemporary child health.

This screening program was conceived and implemented by a few members of the public health nursing staff during the early 1980s, and was introduced throughout the provincial health units in 1988. It represents one of the few examples of a response emanating from inside the health system. The follow-up is done in collaboration with the practising physician.

REFERENCES

1. KÖHLER, L. and JAKOBSSON, G. Measuring health in children. In *Children's Health and Well Being in the Nordic Countries*. Oxford: Blackwell Scientific, 1987, pp. 16–22.

2. PARKYN, J. H. Identification of at risk infants and preschool children. In *Early Identification of Children at Risk*, ed. W. K. Frankenburg, R. N. Emde, and J. W. Sullivan. New York: Plenum Press, pp. 203–209.

3. AUBRY R. and PENNINGTON J. Identification and evaluation of high-risk pregnancy: The perinatal concept. *Clinical Obstetrics and Gynecology* 16:1 (1973): 3–27.

4. NESBITT R. E. and AUBRY R. High risk obstetrics: Value of semi-objective grading system in identifying the vulnerable group. *American Journal of Obstetrics and Gynecology* 103 (1969): 972–85.

5. PARKYN J. H., BLAIR F. R., McLAREN M. I., PARKES C. C., and WILSON J. Testing the reliability and validity of a weighted multifactor assessment form in identification by Public Health Nurses of infants and preschool children at risk (unpublished).

Part IV
Population-based Services for Children and Youth

21

The Evolution and Scope
of Population Medicine
in British Columbia

INTRODUCTION

In Chapter 1, a movement was described that focused on the health care needs of all people in the community, not just those who seek medical care. This movement was called population medicine, to distinguish it from the traditional medical model of practice (personal medicine). In Parts II and III, the development and scope of a variety of population-based services that have evolved in institutional and community settings in the past forty years were described. During this period, Canada introduced legislation providing universal hospital and medical insurance. In this chapter, we examine the influence of this legislation and politics, together with other factors, upon population medicine.

THE INFLUENCE OF LEGISLATION AND POLITICS

The year of origin of each program in the institutional and community subgroups is displayed in Figure 4. In over half the programs, the source of funding changed from other source (e.g., another ministry, federal health grant, or voluntary society, shown by black bars) to permanent funding by the Ministry of Health (white bars). The program development in each of four time periods is then reviewed. The four time periods are Phase I: 1948–57—federal health grants;[1] Phase II: 1958–67—the federal *Hospital Insurance and Diagnostic Services Act* (1957) (1) resulted in cost sharing of hospital services in British Columbia; Phase III: 1968–77—The federal *Medical Care Act* (1966) (2) extended cost sharing to include payment to physicians involved in direct medical care; Phase IV: 1978–90—the *Established Programs Financing (EPF) Act* (1977) (3) substituted block funding for cost sharing and provided a per capita grant

---

1 The federal health grants continued until 1972.

to the provinces to serve as an incentive to adopt lower cost alternatives, including long-term and ambulatory care.

Institutional Programs for Children

Figure 4A shows the years that programs for children were initiated and the years they were accepted for funding by institutional services of the Ministry of Health.

Phase I: 1948–57: The provincial *Hospital Insurance Act* (1948) (4) was followed by the introduction of the British Columbia Hospital Insurance Service in 1949 and funding of the acute care hospital system. Federal health grants funded planning studies of bed needs, emergency services, etc., and contributed to construction costs.

The majority of public general hospitals provided paediatric inpatient hospital care. Paediatric outpatient services were started by Dr. Donald Paterson in an old building near the Vancouver General Hospital, named the Health Centre for Children, and provided care to children of financially indigent families (public patients) (5). The Faculty of Medicine of the University of British Columbia was started in 1951 and Dr. J. F. McCreary was appointed professor and head of Paediatrics. A renovated inpatient facility at the Vancouver General Hospital, renamed the Health Centre for Children (HCC), was opened in 1954, and the outpatient program was transferred from the old building to the ground floor of the new facility (6). The HCC became the base for the new Department of Paediatrics at the University of British Columbia, rather than the smaller autonomous Children's Hospital in Vancouver. The two private long-stay hospitals for children, the Preventorium in Vancouver and the Queen Alexandra Solarium on Vancouver Island, were not eligible for benefits from the provincial hospital insurance program. The need for paediatric services in rural British Columbia was partly met by the travelling clinic of the Children's Hospital, which sent medical and surgical specialists to many communities (7).

There was close collaboration between the Health Branch of the provincial Department of Health and Welfare and the Department of Paediatrics at the University of British Columbia. The need for improved perinatal statistics was recognized, and the notification of birth form was modified to include birthweight, gestational age, and maternal and neonatal morbidity. Likewise, the need for prevalence data of disability in children led to the creation of the Registry for Crippled Children, a branch of the Division of Vital Statistics.

Phase II: 1958–67: The federal *Hospital Insurance and Diagnostic Services Act* initiated cost sharing of acute care hospital costs between the two levels of government on 1 July 1958. In British Columbia, the insurance benefits that applied to inpatients and outpatient services, with rare

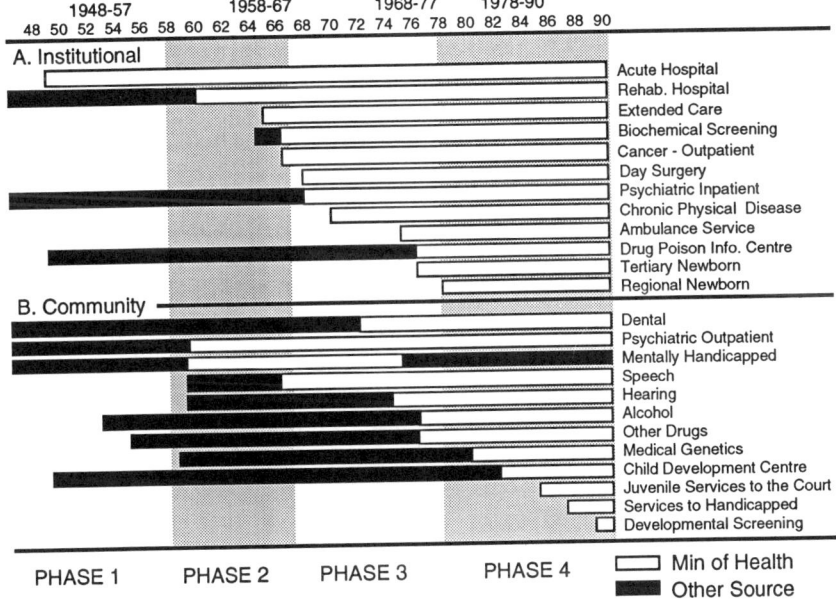

Figure 4 Sources of funding for the institutional and community programs. White bars indicate years in which permanent funding derived from the Ministry of Health. Black bars indicate other sources of funding.

exceptions (e.g., outpatient cancer therapy in designated settings [8]), continued to be available only to the indigent group of families. Additional benefits included funding of PKU screening of all newborns (9).

In 1960, the *Hospital Insurance Act* defined "rehabilitation, chronic and convalescent hospital" to mean a hospital, the prime function of which is "to provide facilities for the active treatment of persons requiring rehabilitative procedures or for persons suffering from a chronic illness or disability" (10). As a result of this amendment, insurance benefits became available for the two long-stay hospitals for children, the Preventorium (renamed Sunny Hill Hospital for Children) and the Queen Alexandra Solarium (renamed Queen Alexandra Hospital for Children). In 1965, the *Hospital Insurance Act* was amended to distinguish "rehabilitation hospital" ("active treatment of persons requiring rehabilitative care and services") and "chronic and convalescent hospital" ("for persons who require skilled nursing care and continuing medical supervision") (11). The term "extended care hospital" replaced "chronic and convalescent hospital" in 1974 (12).

The federal *Hospital Insurance Diagnostic Services Act* excluded residents in mental institutions. The Mental Health Services, including the institutions for mentally handicapped (Woodlands School) and mentally ill persons (no such facility existed for children), were administered by a branch of the Department of the Provincial Secretary. These were transferred to the Mental Health Branch of the renamed Department of Health Services and Health Insurance in 1959. In 1966, certain acute hospitals provided wards designated as observation units for mentally ill patients (13).

Phase III: 1968–77: The federal *Medical Care Act* (1966) and the provincial *Medical Services Act* (1967) (14) resulted in medical insurance to all residents in British Columbia in 1968, and the distinction between private and public patients was eliminated.

The first residential service for children and adolescents with psychiatric disorders (The Maples) was opened in 1968. Outpatient psychiatric services became eligible for insurance benefits in 1968 (15), and a psychiatric ward in the HCC was opened in 1969. Medical staff employed in acute and psychiatric hospitals, including psychiatric wards of general hospitals, mental health centres, and institutions for the mentally handicapped, were funded, either on a sessional or a salaried basis, by the Medical Services Plan.

Day-care surgery became an insurance benefit in 1968 (16), followed by hospital-based ambulatory programs for children with arthritis and rheumatism (17), diabetic day care (18), and outpatient dialysis treatment for chronic renal failure (19). Multidiscipline programs for children with congenital malformations (spina bifida and cleft palate) and chronic disease (fibrocystic disease and endocrine and metabolic diseases) were started in the late 1960s and early 1970s, and medical staff were funded by the Medical Services Plan on either a sessional or a salaried basis.

The marked progress in neonatal technology and care was reflected in the development of neonatal intensive care, and the Vancouver General Hospital was named the provincial tertiary care centre in 1975.

Additional insurance benefits included the establishment of the Emergency Health Services in 1974, later reduced to the British Columbia Ambulance Service. The Drug and Poison Information Centre was moved in 1975 to St. Paul's Hospital in Vancouver, and designated as a hospital facility eligible for hospital insurance benefits (20).

Phase IV: 1978–90: In the mid-1970s, the rising cost of health care was a major concern of the federal government because its contributions were tied to provincial expenditures. The *EPF Act* rectified this by substituting block funding for cost sharing. A per capita grant to the provinces that followed shortly after served as an incentive to the provinces to adopt lower cost alternatives, including long-term and ambulatory care. This led to the introduction of the Long-Term Care Program (Chapter 3) in January 1978. Children under eighteen years were not eligible for this benefit in British Columbia. There was an expansion of the multidiscipline clinics for children with chronic physical disease.

A regional obstetrical and neonatal service, which included the pre-existing maternal and infant transport system and the provincial neonatal tertiary care centre at the Vancouver General Hospital, was introduced in 1978.

In summary, eleven of the twelve institution-based programs were introduced by the end of the third time period. The children's component was added on to the adult program in eight of the programs.

Community Programs for Children

The Health Branch of the Department of Health and Welfare and the Health Departments of Greater Victoria and Greater Vancouver provided well child care, including immunization clinics and school health services, during the 1940s. These population-based public health services preceded the introduction of health insurance and are excluded from this review.

Figure 4B shows the years that programs for children were initiated and the years they were accepted for funding by Community Services of the Ministry of Health. More of these programs had prior funding from other sources than the institution-based group.

Phase I: 1948–57: A provincial dental program was initially funded by a federal health grant and, when these terminated, by the Health Branch. The shift to community-based mental health centres began in 1957, when the first centre was opened for adults in Burnaby.

Phase II: 1958–67: The child guidance clinics were started in 1932 by the Department of the Provincial Secretary, and became the children's service of the Mental Health Centres. The first children's clinic was started in the Burnaby Mental Health Centre in 1958. Foster placements and boarding homes for residents were explored by the staff at Woodlands School. Services for the mentally handicapped were funded by the Department of Health Services and Hospital Insurance from 1959–74.

Phase III: 1968–77: The Canada Assistance Plan (CAP) was introduced in 1974 to provide federal–provincial cost sharing in other legislative areas not covered by the federal health Acts. Mentally handicapped residents in mental institutions operated by the Ministry of Health were ineligible for provincial hospital insurance; however, by transferring the institutions to the Ministry of Human Resources, they became eligible for CAP funding. In 1974, the three institutions, Woodlands School, Tranquille, and Glendale, were transferred to the Ministry of Human Resources. The process of returning children in Woodlands to live at home was initiated. The provincial mental health centres expanded and initiated regional services for children.

Funding of speech (1966) and hearing (1973) programs was assumed by the Health Branch of the (renamed) Department of Health Services and Hospital Insurance. The Alcoholism and Narcotic Addiction Foundations were terminated, and their programs were transferred to the provincial Alcohol and Drug Commission, administered by the Ministry of Human Resources (21). In 1976, the Commission was transferred to the Ministry of Health.

Phase IV: 1978–90: After the *EPF Act*, the per capita grant was initially used to develop long-term care, but, subsequently, was used for other purposes deemed appropriate.

The Medical Genetics Program was funded by Community Services of the (renamed) Ministry of Health in 1980. The community-based services for children with cerebral palsy (child development centres) were started in Vancouver (1947), Fraser Valley (1953), and Victoria (1953), but were not eligible for funding by the provincial Hospital Insurance Service and were dependent on annual fund appeals by voluntary agencies, provincial grants, and federal health grants. In 1982, the health component of this program was assumed by Community Services, Ministry of Health.

The *Forensic Psychiatry Act* established the functions of the Forensic Psychiatric Services Commission for both adults and young persons (22). The commission is responsible for all court-ordered and court-related assessment and outpatient treatment for young offenders through Juvenile Services to the Courts.

The Ministry of Social Services and Housing introduced regional institutional facilities for the mentally handicapped population, followed by the policy of deinstitutionalization and return to community living. Aside from thirty-day admissions for respite care, admissions of children to institutions were eliminated. The transfer, in 1985, of mentally handicapped persons from institutional to community-based services was followed, in 1986, by the formation of the Division of Services to the Handicapped within the Community Care Division (now Community and Family Health).

In 1987, the Child/Youth Mental Health Service replaced the children's mental health services and moved from the Mental Health Services to Family Services.

A new service, the developmental screening of infants and preschool children, was introduced throughout the public health units in 1988.

In summary, twelve community-based programs were identified, and Figure 4B shows their extensive dependence for financial support from outside the Ministry of Health from 1948–77, with a shift to greater ministerial support during the end of the third and fourth time periods. Again, the children's services are additions to adult services in eight programs.

Legislation-based Programs

Tables 10A and 10B show which of the programs were based on legislation or amendments to the latter, e.g., the *Hospital Insurance Act*, the *Mental Health Act*, the *Emergency Health Services Act*, the *Alcohol and Drug Commission Act*, the *Forensic Psychiatry Act*, etc. The legislation-based programs demand adherence to the Regulations in the Act. The institutional programs are largely based on amendments to the *Hospital Insurance Act*. Conversely, the majority of programs in the community-based group are not legislation-based, reflecting the lack of funding for non-hospital care. Non-legislation-based programs can be discontinued or changed readily, and allow policy to be more flexible and to follow the policy direction of government.

Political Influence

The federal Department of Health and Welfare has had a profound influence upon the evolution of the provincial health services, beginning with the federal health grants in 1948. It was a hotbed of new ideas and new policies during the 1970s and 1980s. Today, the government is preoccupied with deficit reduction and fiscal restraint. Mention has been made of the amendments to the *EPF Act* (Chapter 2) and of reduced cash transfers to the provinces for health and education. There has also been a change in social policy, with elimination of universal family allowances and replacement by child benefits to low and middle income families. The national child care program has been cancelled and replaced by the child development initiative (Chapter 2). The provinces, in addition to public health services, have assumed responsibility for the administration of personal and population medicine. The provinces are also concerned with the rising health care costs and ways to control them, and there is a possibility that less affluent provinces will not be able to maintain social programs, including medicare.

An important political role is making decisions concerning the service needs of the population, and, in that sense, all of the programs described in this book are political decisions. The possibility exists, of course, that some policies are shaped by self-interest, and, while this was noticeably lacking, the creation of the Long-Term Care Program (children excluded) was a blatant example. It is noteworthy that the concept of a child health service was never considered. Two-thirds of the programs for children and youth were additions to adult programs. Children do not vote.

TABLE 10A. LEGISLATION-BASED:
INSTITUTIONAL PROGRAMS

Acute Hospital	yes
Rehabilitation Hospital	yes
Extended Care Unit/Hospital	yes
Neonatal Biochemical Screening Program	no
Cancer Outpatient	yes
Day-care Surgery	yes
Psychiatric Inpatient	yes
Chronic Physical Disease	yes
Ambulance Service	yes
Drug and Poison Information Centre	yes
Tertiary Newborn	no
Regional Perinatal and Newborn	no

TABLE 10B. LEGISLATION-BASED:
COMMUNITY PROGRAMS

Dental	no
Psychiatry Outpatient	yes
Mentally Handicapped	no
Speech Problem	no
Hearing Disorders	no
Alcohol	yes
Other Drug	yes
Medical Genetics	no
Child Development Centres	no
Juvenile Services to Courts	yes
Services to Handicapped	no
Development Screening of Infants/Preschool Children	no

THE INTERVENING FACTORS

The progress in health care services was not solely the result of legislation and politics. There were other important influencing forces that moulded health care services for children. Before describing these other influences, three intervening factors are reviewed because they also influenced policy decisions during the period of the evolution of the new health care system.

Demographic Changes

Two demographic factors influenced the content of health programs in Canada in the 1960s and 1970s. The first was the drop in the number of children, due to a fall in the birth rate that followed the baby boom (1946–62). From 1962 to 1985, the proportion of children under fifteen years of age in the total population in Canada fell by 12.4 percent (from 33.9 percent to 21.5 percent). The second was the increase in elderly people—the seniors boom. The proportion of people over sixty-five years of age in the total population increased by 2.8 percent between 1962 and 1985 (from 7.6 percent to 10.4 percent).

Societal Changes

During this time frame (1948–90), many important changes were taking place in our society. Some of these were of a general nature, and others were specifically related to health. Among the general issues were the urbanization of the population and the loss of the extended family, the liberation of women and their return to the workplace, the increase in family breakdowns and of single parent families, birth control and the reduction in family size, the rise in the standard of living, and the higher expectations of the public. Some of the health-related issues were associated with new knowledge of child development and family function. These included the psychological effects of separation of the child from its family, the importance of the integration into the community of persons with disabilities, and the value of early educational opportunity for disadvantaged children and of early identification and rehabilitation of children with disability. Finally, the consumer movement challenged the health system to replace a paternalistic medical model with a user-friendly model that responded to the needs of the individual and the family.

The changes in family structure have important effects upon its dependent members, the young and the elderly. The loss of the extended family and the economic aftermath of family breakdown and single parent families have created many problems in child development and child care. The health insurance programs assumed a greater degree of responsibility for the elderly, protecting them from the changes in family structure. This is exemplified by improved health services and long-term care in the community for the elderly. Comparable benefits are only just developing to support the young family (see Brighter Futures, in Chapter 2).

Changing Pattern of Disease

The old morbidity, characterized by nutritional disorders and acute and chronic infections, is seldom seen today. The new morbidity, the sociogenic problems, including developmental and behavioural disorders, alcohol and drug problems, accidents, homicide and suicide, and chronic disorders and diseases, outnumber the biogenic problems and present quite different challenges in prevention and treatment. More recently, the newer morbidity, AIDS, and problems such as technology-dependent children are assuming a new importance. This changing pattern of disease has consistently challenged the emerging system to adapt to the changing needs of children.

THE INFLUENCE OF OTHER FACTORS

Unlike the influence of legislation, the other factors which moulded the new health care programs were not tied to any time phase. Sometimes working alone, or in combination with others, they affected different age groups and populations. They exerted their effects either from outside (extrinsic) or inside (intrinsic) the health care system.

Extrinsic

Advocacy Groups: The principal outside influence was the advocacy group, characterized by the voluntary non-profit societies that championed the cause of a particular disability and initiated community-based facilities and services. The Cerebral Palsy Association of British Columbia, the Canadian Arthritis and Rheumatism Society, the British Columbia Association for Community Living, and the Alcoholism and Narcotic Addiction Foundations are a few examples of advocacy groups that achieved major successes in support of population-based programs for the disabled. These societies were instrumental in shaping public attitudes and government policy, and played a major role in initiating population-based health care programs. They were involved in initiating three and seven of the twelve institution-based and twelve community-based programs described.

The British Columbia Medical Association was active in lobbying for improved medical care. The British Columbia Cancer Institute, formed in response to the recommendations of the British Columbia Medical Association, resulted in improved diagnostic and treatment services. Thirty years later, the formation of the British Columbia Cancer Agency was stimulated by the British Columbia Medical Association; the Cancer Agency further improved clinical services and introduced preventive strategies. In a similar way, the Medical Association was involved in the initiation and implementation of the Newborn Screening Program, the Emergency Health Services, and the British Columbia Maternal and Neonatal Care Program. Other professional societies played similar roles, e.g., the British Columbia Speech and Hearing Association in the development of Hearing and Speech Services and the School of Audiology and Speech Sciences at the University of British Columbia. The Faculty of Medicine at the University of British Columbia, including the Departments of Medicine, Obstetrics, Paediatrics, Psychiatry, Health Care, and Epidemiology, acting alone or as a member of an advocacy group was also involved in the development of health care programs.

Finally, the service clubs provided financial support to different clinical programs. The Knights of Pythias supported cerebral palsy, the Kinsmen Rehabilitation Foundation of British Columbia the speech and hearing program, the Elks the hearing impaired, the Lions Club transportation and temporary housing, and the Variety Club many important ventures. More recently, Ronald MacDonald House has provided lodging for families with children attending hospital clinics. These organizations have provided support to many people, and collectively have made an enormous contribution to the health services for children. In effect, the service clubs have provided development funds that have served to demonstrate the feasibility of new programs of care.

It is important to emphasize that much ingenuity was displayed by the Health Branch of the provincial government in working with these non-profit societies before programs received permanent financial support from hospital or medical insurance. Thus treatment programs, including ambulatory services for children with cerebral palsy, speech and hearing disorders, and alcohol and drug problems, received partial support from provincial health grants to supplement their annual budget.

Intrinsic

The forces from within that shape health care systems can act at different levels of the health hierarchy, from the minister's office to the hospital ward or community program. The magnitude of the resultant effect, for example, to implement or obstruct change, will vary with the level of involvement. Thus a ministerial policy to regionalize mental health services will exert a system-wide impact. Conversely, the decision by one hospital to introduce a new operative procedure on a day surgical basis, for example, tonsillectomy, will have a relatively small impact on the system.

Organizational Design: The significant role of organizational design upon the development of services has been illustrated in British Columbia. The Department of Health and Welfare was introduced in 1946, with two deputy ministers reporting to the minister. A third branch, the Hospital Insurance Service, with another deputy minister called a commissioner, was added in 1949. This system continued until 1959, when the Department of Health Services and Hospital Insurance was formed, and the Welfare Branch became a separate department. The Mental Health Services were transferred from the Department of the Provincial Secretary to the new health department, which now had separate Deputy Ministers of the Health Branch, Hospital Insurance Service, and Mental Health Branch. The introduction of the provincial *Medical Services Act* in 1967 saw the addition of the Medical Services Commission and another deputy minister. Throughout the period from 1946 to 1959, each branch published its own separate annual report and each functioned as an autonomous unit, thereby contributing to fragmented and poorly integrated systems of care.

The period from the 1950s to the mid-1970s was one of increasing expansion of the health services. The asymmetrical nature of the expansion, engendered by the federal–provincial cost-sharing arrangements, benefitted the hospital and medical services, but not community services comprising public and mental health. Again, the organizational design tended to promote empire building. This is exemplified by the failure to develop a single statistical data base. Both the Hospital Insurance Service and the Medical Services Commission developed their own statistical units for their own immediate purposes, essentially measures of throughput largely concerned with fiscal data, whereas the Health Branch continued to work closely with the Division of Vital Statistics and the Health Surveillance Registry. As a result, it was not possible to examine the patterns of hospital, community health, and medical utilization for different age and diagnostic groups for policy, planning, and evaluation purposes. This dilemma has been remedied with the establishment of the Centre for Health Services and Policy Research (Chapter 3).

The department was reorganized in 1975 and named the Department of Health, and, in 1977, renamed the Ministry of Health with one deputy minister reporting to the minister and two main divisions, Institutions and Medical Services and Prevention and Community Services, each with its own deputy minister. For the first time, in 1975, a single departmental annual report appeared. This reorganization coincided with a new concern for prevention and community services. The opportunities provided by the federal *EPF Act* and the per capita grant to develop alternatives to inpatient care were quickly implemented. There was a noticeable shift from services dictated by existing legislation, especially the *Hospital Insurance Act*, to a more flexible planning process related to the needs of the population. An office of Health Promotion was opened in 1989, reflecting the new direction of the federal government (23, 24).

Economic Influences: The forces of the market place have also influenced program development. In the Canadian hospital industry, the costs (expenditures × the number of patients) equal the sales revenue (or the incomes of the participants involved in the industry). It is a fact that the introduction of a new technology that increases hospital throughput, and therefore yields economic incentives to hospitals and health professionals, is well accepted, while one that mainly benefits the patients and perhaps reduces hospital throughput is resisted. This irrationality has been explained by dividing innovations into product and process technologies (25). The product innovations (intensive care and selected transplant procedures) offer new outcomes, including therapeutic effects not previously possible and requiring more resources. The process innovations (alternatives to inpatient care and psychosocial issues) offer cheaper and less stressful ways of achieving current outcomes. The response of the system is related to the product/process distinction. The product innovations benefit the patient and the providers of care. They generate more expenditures and add to the income of the system. The process innovations, on the other hand, benefit the patient in terms of satisfaction, but may reduce expenditures, and thus the incomes of the participants. Process innovations may or may not meet resistance to their expansion, depending on whether they can be converted into increased hospital expenditures and income to the hospital. Day-care surgery is a process innovation that has expanded costs and incomes thereby generated. The Care By Parent Unit is a process innovation that has not increased costs, and therefore sales, and has met resistance to its acceptance.

With this response to innovation in the health care system in mind, it is reasonable to ask whether the successful uptake of some programs described in this book may be related to these underlying forces. The neonatal tertiary care centre, the Biochemical Disease Program, and a number of medical (oncology and endocrine) programs utilize product technologies and have enjoyed expansion. Day surgery, the Prenatal Diagnosis Program, and some multidiscipline clinics for children with different disabilities (e.g., speech and hearing disorders) are examples of process technologies that have potential for cost expansion and have been accepted. The developmental screening of infants and preschool children and child development centres are process innovations that have less or nil potential for cost expansion and have met resistance to development.

Sociological Influences: A number of sociological factors have been described that can influence the acceptance or rejection of a new technology. Like the previous economic influences, these tend to work at the micro level of the hospital. The slow implementation in the United Kingdom of the Platt Report (26), which advocated unlimited visiting by parents and the admission of parents with children, was attributed to inadequate consideration of the effects of changes on the staff who were to make the new policies work (27). The mothers did not know what was expected of them and were bewildered or bored. The nurses tended to withdraw from the interaction and received little support. The entry of new participants (parents) into the hospital social system created new forms of personal interactions for the staff, and, without careful and planned support at all levels of the organization, their resistance to these pressures was not overcome. Jacobs emphasized that the social structure of the hospital itself—hierarchical organizational design, specialization, and fragmentation of care—serves effectively to control measures to address the psychological needs of the child and family (28).

In summary, the extrinsic factors, represented by social advocacy groups, played a significant role in the initiation of population-based programs for different groups of disabled children. Other more subtle and silent intrinsic factors, e.g., management, economic, and sociological, also had considerable influence in policy development. It took a generation for the health care system to move from the traditional hospital pattern to a regional and community-based system.

EVALUATION

One of the guidelines recommended by the Royal Commission on Health Care and Costs was the measurement of outcomes and the funding only of those services shown to improve health care (29). This is a laudable goal but the identification of reliable outcome measures is a problem. The outcomes attempt to measure the value of the intervention to the recipient. One can invite the consumers to comment on their perception of a health care encounter. The therapeutic value of the health care encounter can be measured by follow-up and observation of patients. In other patients, utilization trends before and after the introduction of a new technology can be measured. We reviewed the population-based programs for evidence of use of three outcome measures, psychological (measured by tests of behaviour, anxiety, satisfaction, etc.), therapeutic (measured by mortality and morbidity rates), and economic (measured by utilization rates, i.e., cases and days/1,000 population and work units per time period. The results are recorded in Tables 11A and 11B. There is a marked difference in the two subgroups, with one of the three measures available in all institutional programs but only in one of the community programs.

TABLE 11A. EVALUATION MEASURES: INSTITUTIONAL PROGRAMS

Program	Health Care Strategy: Prevention		
	Psychological	Therapeutic	Economic
1. Acute Hospital	−	−	+
2. Rehabilitation Hospital	−	−	+
3. Extended Care Unit/Hospital	−	−	+
4. Neonatal Screening Biochemical Disease	−	+	−
5. Cancer Outpatient	−	+	−
6. Day-care Surgery	−	−	+
7. Psychiatric Inpatient	−	−	+
8. Chronic Physical Disease	−	−	+
9. Ambulance Service	−	+	−
10. Drug and Poison Information Service	−	+	−
11. Tertiary Newborn	−	+	+
12. Regional Perinatal and Newborn	−	+	+

TABLE 11B. EVALUATION MEASURES: COMMUNITY PROGRAMS

Program	Health Care Strategy: Prevention		
	Psychological	Therapeutic	Economic
1. Dental	−	−	+
2. Psychiatric Outpatient	−	−	−
3. Mentally Handicapped	−	−	−
4. Speech Problems	−	−	−
5. Hearing Disorders	−	−	−
6. Alcohol	−	−	−
7. Other Drug	−	−	+
8. Medical Genetics	−	−	−
9. Child Development Centre	−	−	−
10. Juvenile Services to Courts	−	−	−
11. Services to Handicapped	−	−	−
12. Developmental Screening Infants/ Preschool Children	−	−	−

COMMENT

The notion of a national health insurance system is deceptive if it is perceived that all health problems of the population are addressed. When health insurance was introduced in Canada, the provincial governments were obliged to develop health care systems within the limits defined by the related federal and provincial legislation. As a result, in British Columbia, a population-based, inpatient hospital service for the treatment of acute illness dominated the health care marketplace in the 1950s, followed by prepaid medical care in the late 1960s. Gradually, other programs emerged, either by amending the *Hospital Insurance Act* (e.g., rehabilitation and extended care, outpatient cancer therapy, day-care surgery, psychiatric outpatient, inpatient, and day-care services in selected hospitals, chronic disease programs, and the Drug and Poison Information Centre, or by new legislation (e.g., *Alcohol and Drug Commission Act* [30], the *Emergency Health Services Act* [31], the *Mental Health Act* (1964) [32], and the *Forensic Psychiatric Services Commission Act* [33]). In addition, a number of non-legislation-based programs were introduced, particularly in the community group. The introduction of medical care insurance in 1968 largely benefitted personal medicine, but the availability of sessional fees and part-time salaries to physicians and surgeons fostered the development of outpatient hospital services for various populations of children with developmental problems and chronic physical diseases.

The drive to produce community-based programs for children was provided by advocacy groups long before they were funded by the Ministry of Health. The need for legislation to finance these services was resolved in the late 1970s, following the *EPF Act*, when the per capita grant to the provinces encouraged less costly alternatives to inpatient care. It led to greater flexibility in program development and needs-related policy-making in the late 1970s.

The national health insurance system has greatly expanded the responsibilities of the Ministry of Health, which, in turn, has responded to the health care needs of both individuals (personal medicine) and aggregate and target populations (population medicine). The answer to the question posed in Chapter 1, "Does national health insurance accommodate population medicine?" is yes, and to the second question, "Are its benefits confined to personal medicine?" is obviously no. Undoubtedly, personal medicine was the initial beneficiary of the medical insurance legislation before various population-based programs were accepted as health insurance benefits.

REFERENCES

1. *Hospital Insurance and Diagnostic Services Act*, S.C. 1957, c. 28.
2. *Medical Care Act*, S.C. 1966–67, c. 64.
3. *Federal–Provincial Fiscal Arrangements and Established Programs Financing Act*, S.C. 1966–67, c. 10.
4. *Hospital Insurance Act*, S.B.C. 1948, c. 28.
5. PATERSON, D. Children, health centres and their uses. *Canadian Medical Association Journal* 62 (1950): 39.
6. ROBINSON, G. C. and MACLENNAN, J. M. The Vancouver Health Centre for Children: Evolution of the outpatient department during a ten-year period. *Canadian Medical Association Journal* 85 (1961): 1–6.
7. SHAH, C. P. The Delivery of specialist services to remote areas. Experience of a travelling clinic in British Columbia. *B.C. Medical Journal* 14:2 (1972): 25–27.
8. BRITISH COLUMBIA. Order-in-Council 2298, 1966.
9. BRITISH COLUMBIA. *Eighteenth Annual Report of B.C. Hospital Insurance Service. January 1–December 31, 1966.*
10. BRITISH COLUMBIA. Order-in-Council 315, 1961.
11. BRITISH COLUMBIA. Order-in-Council 3315, 1965.
12. BRITISH COLUMBIA. Order-in-Council 448, 1974.
13. BRITISH COLUMBIA. *Annual Report for the Twelve Months Ended March 31, 1966.* Mental Health Services Branch, Department of Health Services and Hospital Insurance, 1967.
14. *Medical Services Act*, S.B.C. 1967, c. 24.
15. BRITISH COLUMBIA. Order-in Council 4019, 1968.
16. BRITISH COLUMBIA. Order-in-Council 552, 1968.
17. BRITISH COLUMBIA. Order-in-Council 4110, 1972.
18. BRITISH COLUMBIA. Order-in-Council 224, 1975.
19. BRITISH COLUMBIA. Order-in-Council 2932, 1978.
20. BRITISH COLUMBIA. Order-in-Council 2358, 1975.
21. *Alcohol and Drug Commission Act*, S.B.C. 1973, c. 3.
22. *Forensic Psychiatry Act*, R.S.B.C. 1979, c. 139.
23. LALONDE, M. *A New Perspective on the Health of Canadians: A Working Document.* Ottawa: Health and Welfare Canada, 1974.
24. EPP, J. *Achieving Health for All: A Framework for Health Promotion.* Ottawa: Health and Welfare Canada, 1986.
25. EVANS, R. G. The perverse economics of alternatives to inpatient care. In *Ambulatory Care of the Sick Child*, ed. R. M. Issenman. McMaster University Press, 1985, pp. 123–36.
26. UNITED HEALTH SERVICES COUNCIL. *The Welfare of Children in Hospital.* Report of the Committee, Ministry of Health (Chairman: H. Platt). London: H.M.S.O., 1959.
27. STACEY, M. Practical recommendations. In *Hospitals, Children and Their Families: The Report of a Pilot Study*, ed. M. Stacey, K. Dearden, R. Pill, and D. Robinson. London: Routledge and Kegan Paul, 1970, pp. 149–57.

28. JACOBS, R. The meaning of hospital: Denial of emotions. In *Beyond Separation: Further Studies of Children in Hospital*, ed. D. Hall and M. Stacey. London: Routledge and Kegan Paul, 1979, pp. 82–108.
29. BRITISH COLUMBIA. *Closer to Home*. The Report of the British Columbia Royal Commission on Health Care and Costs, 1991.
30. *Alcohol and Drug Commission Act*, S.B.C. 1973, c. 3.
31. *Emergency Health Services Act*, R.S.B.C. 1979, c. 254.
32. *Mental Health Act*, S.B.C. 1964, c. 29.
33. *Forensic Psychiatric Services Commission Act*, S.B.C. 1974, c. 35.

22

Health Services for Children and Youth

"THE WAY IS LIKE A BOAT THAT DRIFTS"

The above quotation rather aptly applies to the development of health services in British Columbia since the introduction of national health insurance. The services developed in response to different pressures, rather than following any master planning process. In spite of this, a network of personal and population-based health care services has emerged to complement the pre-existing traditional public health services. This chapter comments further on the evolution of population-based programs for children and youth in institutional and community-based settings.

THE SPECIAL NEEDS OF CHILDREN AND YOUTH

A brief review of the dates of recognition of some of the age-related health needs of children and youth is presented here, followed by the responses of the provincial government.

During the late 1940s and early 1950s, the needs of children were acknowledged to be separate from those of other age groups. In the health field, there was recognition of the age-related mortality and morbidity of infants, children, and youth, and the study of specific subpopulations, e.g., newborns and adolescents, was emerging. The importance of the family in child development, and the psychological vulnerability of young children to separation from the family, was acknowledged, together with the important implications for hospitals, and, of course, other institutions where children lived (1, 2, 3, 4). Over half the paediatric inpatient population was under six years of age, emphasizing the need for family-centred care and age-appropriate developmental and psychological support systems. The vulnerability of children to physical abuse was first reported in 1946 by a paediatric radiologist (5), and, in 1962, the various aspects of the battered child syndrome were described by Dr.

Henry Kempe and his associates (6). The importance of perinatal morbidity and mortality was emphasized during the 1960s (7). The importance of early identification of physical, mental, and sensory disabilities, and, likewise, the early introduction of appropriate interventions, was recognized in the 1950s and 1960s (8, 9, 10). The principle of normalization of the disabled population followed (11), with the implication that the disabled person had the same rights and obligations as other people. Special education for the disabled, initially in segregated schools and later in special classes in ordinary schools, was also introduced in the 1950s.

These fundamental concepts have important policy implications for planning child health services, and the provincial responses to them are briefly examined. *A Survey of Health Services and Facilities in British Columbia in existence on December 31, 1948* (12) stated that "Children are our seed corn,"[1] and that public health programs have always emphasized child health. It went on to suggest that, in developing plans for health insurance, "consideration be given to the introduction of a comprehensive health insurance plan to cover medical services of children." While provincial hospital insurance was in effect in British Columbia when the survey was published (1952), medical care insurance did not materialize until sixteen years later. Nevertheless, this message indicated a positive attitude toward child health.

The introduction of the Faculty of Medicine at the University of British Columbia in 1950 gave rise to collaboration between the Division of Vital Statistics, the Health Branch of the provincial Department of Health and Welfare, and the paediatric community, beginning in the 1950s, and resulted in improved neonatal statistical data (Chapter 4) and the development of the Crippled Children's Registry, now the Health Surveillance Registry, in 1952 (Chapter 5).

The institution-based services for children were expanded in the 1960s by amendments to the provincial *Hospital Insurance Act* (13), providing rehabilitation and extended-care hospital units, and ambulatory services for cancer therapy, day surgery, psychiatry, and selected chronic physical diseases. The support of the provincial Biochemical Disease Program in 1966 indicated a concern for the early diagnosis and treatment of mental handicaps. The *Mental Health Act* (1964) (14) led to the development of mental health centres and psychiatric services in general hospitals, expanding the services for children and youth with mental health problems. The development of the British Columbia Ambulance Service, including the Infant Transport Team, and the neonatal tertiary care centre occurred in the mid-1970s.

---

1 This quotation is attributed to Ms. Grace Abbott, former Chief of the Children's Bureau, Washington, D.C. We have been unable to confirm the source.

During the tenure of the New Democratic Party (1972–75), a survey of health care in British Columbia (15) was undertaken (Chapter 3). In a separate section on primary prevention in mental health, there was a revealing comment by Sidney Israels, then professor and head of Paediatrics at the University of British Columbia. "This is the first time—and I have been a professor of Paediatrics for ten years—that I was ever invited by a government group to bring my people here to talk about preventive services for children." This indicated that the collaboration between the renamed Department of Health Services and Hospital Insurance and the paediatric community had deteriorated during the 1960s and early 1970s.

The development of community services for the children with mental handicaps and with cerebral palsy was initiated by non-profit, voluntary societies in the 1950s. The admission of children with mental handicap to institutions was terminated in the 1970s, and followed by the policy of normalization, with the closing of the institutions in the 1980s. The development of special services for children with physical disabilities, e.g., cleft palate and spina bifida, and chronic diseases, e.g., fibrocystic disease and chronic gastrointestinal disease, was initiated in the late 1960s and early 1970s. In general, there was a considerable time gap between the recognition of need and the acceptance by government of financial support for ambulatory and community-based services for children and youth with mental and physical disabilities. This contributed to the breakdown in communication between the Department of Health Services and Hospital Insurance and the paediatric community in the 1960s and 1970s.

Following the *Established Programs Financing (EPF) Act* (16), the Extended Health Care Services (Chapter 2) provided funding for a number of non-legislation-based programs, including the regional Obstetrical and Neonatal Care Program, medical genetic clinics, child development centres, Services for the Handicapped, and Developmental Screening of Infants and Preschool Children, in the late 1970s and 1980s. These programs fostered the prevention of handicaps that begin before birth, the early identification and assessment of disabled children, and the encouragement of normalization and home-based management for technology-dependent and severely mentally handicapped children. The special assessment and treatment needs of young offenders were assumed by Juvenile Services to the Courts in the mid-1980s.

An unsolicited but significant contribution to child health, *The Child Health Profile* (17), was introduced in the late 1970s by Dr. Roger Tonkin (Chapter 1). The purpose of the project was to develop a data base on the status of children in the province by gathering, co-ordinating, and analyzing relevant data from the Ministries of Health, Education, Human Resources, etc. As noted in the previous chapter, the concept of a statistical workshop for public health (Chapter 4) was not extended to the new components of the health care system. Regrettably, the Hospital Insurance Division, and later the Medical Services Plan, both developed their own independent data bases, and linkage of information between the branches of the Department of Health Services and Hospital Insurance was not feasible.

The Provincial Study of Severely Handicapped Children (18) was commissioned in 1979 (Chapter 3), and reflected the new concern for services for children and youth, possibly created by reaction to the 1978 decision to exclude children under eighteen years from the new Long-Term Care Program.

In summary, the provincial government's response to the special health care needs of children was impressive in the 1950s and early 1960s, but then declined until the late 1970s. Initially, the services for children and youth were legislation-based and confined to a hospital setting, while community programs were not funded. There has, however, been a major change within the past fifteen years that began during the tenure of the New Democratic Party (1972–75)[2] with the reorganization of the Ministry of Health in 1975, and the creation of two main divisions, Medical and Hospital Programs and Community Health Programs (and the subsequent variations on that theme), and was aided by the *EPF Act* in 1977, with a shift from legislation-dependent to needs-related policy making. There was an accompanying addition of compassionate and informed senior civil servants, representing different health disciplines. This has given new hope to the myriad community child care workers involved in the day-to-day care of the disabled population.

WHY POPULATION MEDICINE?

In Chapter 1, this question was answered by explaining that certain health care problems required a population-based approach, and hence were outside the limits of competence both of the private practice of medicine and of traditional public health practice. This point is illustrated by the twenty-four population-based programs described, ten of which serve the aggregate provincial population and fourteen a target or subpopulation. In the first category are hospital-based services for illness, disability, surgery, the Obstetrical and Neonatal Program (renamed the British Columbia Maternal and Neonatal Care Program in 1988), two screening programs, a dental program, an ambulance service, and a drug and poison information service. In the second category are services for specific target populations, such as those concerned with sick newborns, chronic physical disease, mental handicap and mental disorder, alcohol

---

2 Dennis G. Cocke, Minister of Health.

and drug use, speech and hearing disorder, and medical genetics. In this section, two important related issues are addressed, the integration of community services and the interdigitation of personal medicine, population medicine, and public health.

Integration of Community Services

The individual care of the disabled child usually begins with the family physician or public health unit, and may involve private consultants, followed by referral to one or more of the regional health and social services (Mental Health Centre, Audiology and Speech Clinic, child development centre, acute or long-stay hospital, Alcohol and Drug Program, Infant Development Program, or special needs day care). Referral may also originate from the school system or the justice system with referral to one of the population-based programs. The availability of the services, early access to them by the family, and the ensuing collaboration between family and professionals are important determinants of the effectiveness of care for the individual child and family.

It is easy to understand the complexity of organizing throughout the province a network of population-based programs that provide prenatal care, early case finding, appropriate assessment and reassessment, various therapies, family support, child protection services, and appropriate educational opportunity. It is not difficult to imagine the task of the health professional trying to match the needs of a disabled child with the available services, and the frustrations and discouragement when these are lacking. The problems of children do not follow the boundaries of ministries, and there is also a need for integrating the provision of services both within the Ministry of Health and with other ministries.

The need for improved integration within and between ministries and with personal medicine has been emphasized many times, but it took the tragic death of a fifteen-year-old youth, a ward of the Ministry of Social Services and Housing, in a privately operated youth care facility, and an ensuing investigation by the provincial Ombudsman in 1990 to institute change. The Ombudsman's report reinforced existing concerns about the need for improved integration and accountability of ministry and non-ministry services provided to children, youth, and their families (19). It also revealed that the Inter-Ministry Children's Committees (IMCCs), established in 1977, no longer served as a province-wide co-ordinating system (Chapter 3). The report listed seventeen recommendations, the first of which was the creation of a single authority within government to ensure uniform, integrated, and client-centred approaches to policy setting, planning, and administration of publicly funded services to children, youth, and their families. As a result, a new British Columbia Child and Youth Secretariat was established (Chapter 3) to co-ordinate and implement interministry policies and programs for children and youth for a three-year period (20). Four ministries that are the major service providers to children and youth, Education, Health, Social Services and Housing, and Solicitor General, are represented. In June 1991, a Children's Policy for the Province of British Columbia was announced (21). The secretariat will, it is hoped, mould a new child health policy for children and youth in British Columbia.

Interdigitation of Personal and Population Medicine and Public Health

In the main, personal medicine (the private practice of medicine), population medicine, and traditional public health function independently of one another. Personal medicine has the privilege of utilizing population-based services, as represented by acute and long-stay hospitals, maternal and neonatal care services, the ambulance service, mental health services, cancer clinics, etc., for the individual patient. Personal medicine, usually represented by a specialist employed on a sessional basis, is also an integral part of many population-based programs. There are physicians in practice who resent the competition offered by community-based programs, much as a prior generation resented immunization clinics when they were first introduced fifty years ago. It is true that some of the population-based programs compete with personal medicine, and there have been criticisms of unfair advantage from the ranks. These usually reflect the critic's limited understanding either of the purpose of the program or of the natural history of chronic disability. Such criticisms are not heard from the specialists involved in sessional work with a population-based program. Some consultant paediatricians (and other consultants) hold the view that they can cope with a child and family with a chronic disease as well as a multidiscipline team can, and there are doubtless examples where this is true. There are also situations where personal and population medicine duplicate services. This is exemplified in child psychiatry, where the choice exists for referral to a private psychiatrist, or paediatrician, or to the Child and Youth Mental Health Service in mental health centres (or their metropolitan counterparts). Because of the multidisciplinary nature of the latter, the more disturbed children and dysfunctional families tend to gravitate to the Child and Youth Mental Health Service, much to the resentment of their professional staff and, doubtless the relief of the solo psychiatrists. There is also duplication of the services in other diagnostic categories (alcohol and drugs, speech and hearing, chronic physical disabilities, and medical genetics).

It is difficult for personal medicine to keep informed of the population-based programs for different clinical problems. The usual pattern of practice is for the child to be referred to a specialist, who is likely to be more aware of services such as population-based programs, and more able to decide the need to refer the child on to the program. This results in some reduplication of work, but it serves to screen out inappropriate referrals.

Just as there are limitations to personal medicine, so there are to population-based medicine. The Maternal and Neonatal Care Program (Chapter 12) illustrates an effective response by the community physicians, obstetricians, and neonatologists to reduce neonatal mortality rates. In contrast, the Vancouver Perinatal Health Project (Chapter 12) attempted to provide a population-based approach to prenatal care, but was discontinued. The Canadian model of private medical practice is not compatible with population-based approaches to improve the reproductive health of women, thereby reducing the rate of low birthweight infants and birth defects. It is difficult to persuade high-risk pregnant women to seek early prenatal care (Chapter 12) and to become involved in the augmented prenatal care programs (22). Easy access to care does not equate with obtaining care.

There have also been problems with neonatal referrals to the hospital with the appropriate level of care, as recommended by the Maternal and Neonatal Care Program. There remain too the time-honoured problems of communication between personal medicine and public health, as evidenced by the fact that the prenatal forms provided to physicians by the Ministry of Health are not shared with the public health nurses who are involved in prenatal and postnatal care.

THE LIMITS OF HEALTH CARE AND HEALTH PROMOTION

Health Care

The health care strategies constitute primary, secondary, and tertiary prevention (Chapter 1). Table 12A displays the strategies for each of the institutional programs. The acute hospital, the Biochemical Screening Program, the Ambulance Service (prevention of shock), the Drug and Poison Information Centre (prevention of absorption of drug or poison), the neonatal tertiary care centre (resuscitation), and the British Columbia Maternal and Neonatal Care Program (prevention of preterm birth) provide secondary prevention. Eleven of twelve programs provide tertiary prevention.

Table 12B displays the strategies for each of the community programs. The Dental Program (brushing, flossing, and fluoride) and Medical Genetics (counselling service) provide primary prevention. The Mentally Handicapped Program (early stimulation), the Hearing Impaired Infant Identification Program (early auditory training), Medical Genetics (prenatal diagnostic program), the child development centres and the De-

TABLE 12A. HEALTH CARE STRATEGIES: INSTITUTIONAL PROGRAMS

Program	Health Care Strategy: Prevention		
	Primary	Secondary	Tertiary
1. Acute Hospital	–	+	+
2. Rehabilitation Hospital	–	–	+
3. Extended Care Unit/Hospital	–	–	+
4. Neonatal Screening Biochemical Disease	–	+	+
5. Cancer Outpatient	–	–	+
6. Day-care Surgery	–	–	+
7. Psychiatric Inpatient	–	–	+
8. Chronic Physical Diseases	–	–	+
9. Ambulance Service	–	+	+
10. Drug and Poison Information Centre	–	+	–
11. Tertiary Newborn	–	+	+
12. Regional Perinatal and Newborn	–	+	+

TABLE 12B. HEALTH CARE STRATEGIES: COMMUNITY PROGRAMS

Program	Health Care Strategy: Prevention		
	Primary	Secondary	Tertiary
1. Dental	+	+	–
2. Psychiatry Outpatient	–	+	+
3. Mentally Handicapped	–	+	+
4. Speech Problems	–	–	+
5. Hearing Disorders	–	+	+
6. Alcohol	–	+	+
7. Other Drug	–	+	+
8. Medical Genetics	+	+	–
9. Child Development Centre	–	+	+
10. Juvenile Services to Courts	–	–	+
11. Services to the Handicapped	–	–	+
12. Developmental Screening Infants/ Preschool Children	–	+	–

velopmental Screening Program for Infants and Preschool Children (early intervention) provide secondary prevention. Nine programs offer tertiary prevention.

The institutional and community population-based programs play a very limited role in primary prevention. In contrast, fourteen and twenty-one programs provide secondary and tertiary prevention. This restricted role of health care in the primary prevention of contemporary pathology in children and youth is partly explained by the importance of psycho-social factors. Many of the major health problems in children and youth are multicausal and rooted in the social and physical environment, as illustrated by the developmental and behavioural disorders associated with disadvantage, the neglect and abuse of children living in dysfunctional families, alcohol and drug use, and the adverse sequelae of women who enter pregnancy at psychosocial risk.

The determinants of health, both of populations and individuals, go far beyond health care. Evans has rightly emphasized that these observations do not denigrate the importance of health care (23). The capacity of health care to contribute to health has greatly increased in the last century, as evidenced by major advances in the prevention of disease (immunization against infectious diseases and the control of phenylketonuria), the treatment of others (including cure with antibiotics), the alleviation of symptoms of chronic physical diseases, the repair of damage from injury, and the rehabilitation of individuals with disabilities. These advances, however, have been associated with a dramatic increase in allocation of national resources spent on health care, and the inference has been fostered that the maintenance or restoration of health is primarily a question of ensuring the availability of appropriate forms of health care. As the limits of health care are recognized, the scope for improvement from other determinants (physical and social, environmental, and genetic) is being explored.

Health Promotion

The emergence of the concept of health promotion, defined as a process that enables people to increase their control over and to improve their own health, and its translation into service programs, is breaking new ground. After an initial emphasis on personal responsibility for healthy lifestyles, the focus has shifted to population health. The potential for extending primary prevention to psychosocial problems is a real and exciting possibility (Chapter 2). A main strategy involves the creation of healthy communities in which the social and physical environment supports health.

The four priority areas for action in children and youth in British Columbia have been identified as the special needs group (Native, poor, and disabled), the prevention of low birthweight and prematurity, the prevention of injury and poisoning, and the promotion of mental health and family functioning (24), and it is proposed that the Office of Health Promotion focus its programming for children and youth on these four areas (Chapter 3). There is evidence of a decline in accidental deaths due to automobiles, in the rates of adolescent pregnancy (25), and in the use of alcohol and drugs (26). The ultimate goal of health promotion is to empower society to eradicate the inequities.

There are substantial barriers obstructing the reduction of the prevalence of family violence, physical and sexual abuse, and developmental and mental health problems, the most obvious of which is socioeconomic disadvantage.

The Role of Poverty

Birch and Gussow have written of the environmental relationships between poverty and educational failure (27), and conclude that "The children growing up in poverty and deprivation today will not be easily rescued". *Born to Fail?*, the apt and sad title of the Report of the National Child Development study, which followed the progress from birth to maturity of all the children in England, Scotland, and Wales who were born (10,504 children) in the week of 3–9 March 1958 (28), showed vast differences between the way of life of the disadvantaged and ordinary children. One in sixteen children were judged to live a life of social disadvantage, defined by large numbers of children in the family (five or more) or only one parent-figure, low income, and poor housing. It is no surprise that many of these children fail to behave, fail to learn, and fail to succeed.

The *Black Report* (29) in the United Kingdom examined why the differences in health status among social classes persisted after removal of financial barriers to health care, and concluded that "class differences in mortality are a constant feature of the entire human life span. They are found at birth, during the first year life, in childhood, adolescence and in adult life . . . in general, they are more marked at the start of life." The Report also noted that "Early childhood is the period of life at which intervention could most hopefully break the continuing association between health and social class." The beneficial effects of an early enrichment opportunity are well documented (30, 31).

It has also been shown that reproductive health improves step by step from Social Class V to Social Class I (32). The step-by-step improvement from Social Class V to Social Class I is a step-by-step improvement in the health of women.

Mustard has recently spoken out in favour of supporting child development, and decried the expenditure of resources to extend the life of "dying seniors" (33). He also notes that "healthy cultures" tend to be those that allow women to play a key role in society, education, and child development. Furthermore, they often make arrangements for working mothers to continue to exercise significant control over the development of their children.

Shah et al. have recently emphasized that childhood poverty in Canada affects nearly 20 percent of children under sixteen years of age (34). It is highest amongst children of single mothers, unemployed parents, Canadian aboriginal people, and recent immigrants, particularly refugees. The poverty is reflected in higher infant mortality rates, deaths from infectious disease, and accidents. Other problems are anaemia, dental caries, chronic ear infections, mental retardation, learning disabilities and poor school performance, and suicide rates. A related social concern is the changing family structure and the rise in the number of poor mother/child units. Nearly half of one parent families in Canada live below the poverty line, and it is not uncommon for the children to manifest developmental delay, learning difficulties, poor school achievement, and increased suicide rates. Eisenberg (35) has stressed that the change in the American family structure (one in four children under eighteen years living with one parent), demography, and economics is placing children at higher risk. It is all too clear that health care cannot resolve these problems. To what extent will health promotion strategies, by improving material circumstances, reduce the gap between the social classes?

It is relevant that the Committee on Child Welfare of the Ontario Medical Association (36), noting that poverty is correlated with higher mortality and higher morbidity rates, has emphasized that the solutions are not medical. "What poor children need is decent housing, recreational facilities, better nutrition, and greater support to achieve education potentials." It made two recommendations, first, that consideration be given to the potential impact on the physical and mental health of children when new government policies and programs are formulated, and, second, that existing public policies and programs should be monitored to assess their impact on the physical and mental health of children. Recommendations to accomplish these goals include communication between senior government staff and non-government agencies to explore and identify which health problems would benefit from changes in public policy.

COMMENT

This review of the evolution of child/youth services in British Columbia yields several conclusions. The first, captured by the epigram of this chapter ("The Way is Like a Boat that Drifts"), is the absence of a health policy and plan. The second is the indifference to the unique and changing needs of children and youth. The third is the vulnerability of children and youth to political decisions. It has been a disadvantage to be young (and have no vote). We have seen that prenatal programs to prevent handicaps were not implemented, that patterns of care that respected the needs of children were ignored, that there was a gap of many years between recognition of need and the implementation of programs for disabled children and youth, and that adult programs took preference over children's programs for reasons of political expediency. "We live in an adult world, designed for adults by adults" (37). The fourth conclusion is that socioeconomic factors continue to play an important role in the production of health. It is both humane and cost effective to reduce the impact of poverty in families with children, for instance by increased support to high-risk pregnant women, post-natal mother and child support, infant and child development programs, recreational opportunities, day care, and homemakers. The recent federal child development initiative (Chapter 2) appears to be designed with the above concept in mind.

What else can be done to rectify these shortcomings? The late John Law, formerly executive director of the Hospital for Sick Children in Toronto and founder of the Canadian Institute of Child Health, was an advocate of a national child health policy. In an address to the Association of Canadian Paediatric Hospitals, he defined the constituency of the children's hospital as all children in the province, not just those who are treated at the hospital, and its role as a child health centre concerned with all aspects of child health (38). He recommended that children's hospitals assume a leadership role to set standards, systems, programs, and procedures for all hospitals in the province to raise the quality of care. "Particularly important is the need for child health centres to seek rapprochement with public health agencies and school health programmes." There is not much evidence that children's hospitals have been preparing for this role. As the work of the children's hospital becomes increasingly specialized, the hospital becomes distanced from many concerns in child health that are not hospital dependent. Children's hospitals play a very important but limited role in contemporary child health.

Dr. Barry Pless, a distinguished investigator in child health, when chairman of the Canadian Institute of Child Health, also called for a national child health policy (39). "Such a public policy document would serve as more than a road map. It must say not only where we want to go, but also indicate the best routes to get there. It should state specific goals, list target figures and timetables and spell out the strategies to achieve the goals listed."

In our view, there is a role for the federal government. The vision that inspired a department to produce *A New Perspective on the Health of Canadians* and *Achieving Health for All* has much to contribute to child health. This role would be a continuation of the occasional projects concerning the welfare of children and youth, such as Foundations for the Future and Nobody's Perfect. In addition, periodic reports on health services research would be helpful. There is much to learn from regional comparisons with other provinces (health and vital statistics), innovative approaches to health issues (e.g., technology, evaluation, etc.), and economic studies. At present, it is extremely difficult to obtain an overview of child/youth programs in the other provinces and territories. Regional comparisons with other countries would also be profitable. It will be interesting to observe whether the Children's Bureau accepts such a leadership role, or whether it confines its role to housekeeping activities.

The role of the provincial government entails a more direct involvement concerning needs, policy, planning, allocation of resources, and evaluation of programs for children and youth. The British Columbia Child and Youth Secretariat (Chapter 3) has been assigned the task of coordinating and implementing programs for children and youth for a three-year period. This function should be ongoing, because the needs of children and youth change over time, and public policies need to be altered and adapted to provide appropriate responses to current problems. There is also much to be gained by involving the paediatric community and non-governmental organizations concerned with child and family issues (40). The role of the Continuing Advisory Sub Committee (CASC) has not been a model of success.

In conclusion, we reiterate what one of us (GRFE) suggested forty years ago: "Children are our seed corn" (12). There is good evidence that prenatal and early life experiences play a key part in shaping the development of children and youth. There is evidence that the reproductive health of women can be improved by population-based prenatal care. It will be of great interest to follow the effectiveness of the British Columbia Maternal and Neonatal Care Program. When early experiences are negative, school failure, unemployment, and inappropriate behaviour are common outcomes. There is also evidence that these latter outcomes can be reversed by the introduction of appropriate replacement strategies. If Canada's Child Development Initiative can serve this need, it would be an enormous help to many people. Such an investment in children is both rational and just, and is the key to the building of healthy communities.

REFERENCES

1. SPITZ, R. A. Hospitalism: An inquiry into the genesis of psychiatric conditions in early childhood. *Psychoanal. Study Child* (1944) 1: 53.
2. BOWLBY, J. *Maternal Care and Mental Health.* World Health Organization. Monograph Series, No. 2. Geneva: WHO, 1952.
3. SPENCE, J. The purpose of the family. In *The Purpose and Practice of Medicine.* London: Oxford University Press, 1960, pp. 174–203.
4. ROBERTSON, J. *Young Children in Hospital.* London: Tavistock, 1958.

5. CAFFEY, J. Multiple fractures in the long bones of infants suffering from chronic subdural hematoma. *American Journal of Roentgenology* 56 (1946): 163–73.

6. KEMPE, C. H., SILVERMAN, F. N., STEELE, B. F., DROEGEMUELLER, W., and SILVER, H. K. The battered child syndrome. *Journal of American Medical Association* 181 (1962): 17.

7. NIXON, W.C.W. Preface. In *Perinatal Mortality*, ed. N. R. Butler and D. G. Bonham. London: Livingstone, 1963.

8. WILSON, J. L., moderator. Scope of Services Needed by the Handicapped Child and his Family. In *Development of Community Health Services for Children with Congenital Anomalies*. Ann Arbor, MI, 1964.

9. EWING, A.W.G. *Educational Guidance and the Deaf Child*. Manchester: Manchester University Press, 1957.

10. ELONAN, A. S. and ZWARENSTEYN, S. B. Appraisal of developmental lag in certain blind children. *Journal of Pediatrics* 65 (1964): 599.

11. SCHEERENBERGER, R. C. *A History of Mental Retardation, A Quarter Century of Promise*. Baltimore: Paul H. Brookes, 1987, pp. 116–21.

12. ELLIOT, G.R.F. *Survey of Health Services and Facilities in British Columbia in Existence on December 31, 1948*. Health Branch, Department of Health and Welfare, British Columbia, 1952.

13. *Hospital Insurance Act*, S.B.C. 1948, c. 28.

14. *Mental Health Act*, S.B.C. 1964, c. 29.

15. FOULKES, R. G. *Health Security for British Columbians*. Report to the Minister of Health, British Columbia. Victoria, B.C.: Queen's Printer, December 1974.

16. *Federal-Provincial Fiscal Arrangements and Established Programs Financing Act*, S.C. 1976–77, c. 10.

17. TONKIN, R. S. *Child Health Profile*. British Columbia, 1979.

18. TALBOT, J., DUNBAR, P. B., STULL, S., and SHEPS, S. Provincial Study of Severely Handicapped Children, 1981 (unpublished).

19. BRITISH COLUMBIA. *Public Services to Children, Youth and their Families in British Columbia: The Need for Integration*. Office of the Ombudsman. Public Report No. 22, November 1990.

20. BRITISH COLUMBIA. Interministry services to children and youth enhanced (news release, 9 November 1990). Ministry of Social Services and Housing.

21. BRITISH COLUMBIA. A children's policy for the province of British Columbia (news release, 3 June 1991). Office of the Premier and Ministry of Social Services and Housing.

22. UNITED STATES OF AMERICA. *Caring for Our Future: The Content of Prenatal Care*. A Report of the Public Health Service Expert Panel on the Content of Prenatal Care. Washington, D.C. U.S. Department of Health and Human Services. Public Health Service, National Institute of Health, 1989.

23. EVANS, R. G. *The Health of Populations and the Program in Population Health*. Canadian Institute for Advanced Research. CIAR Population Health Publ. No. 1, January 1989.

24. BEARPARK, S. The Health of Children and Youth in British Columbia: Issues for Health Promotion. Discussion Paper. The Office of Health Promotion, B.C. Ministry of Health, 1 April 1990. Mimeographed document.

25. TONKIN, R. S. *Child Health Profile: Youth Today*. British Columbia, 1986.

26. BRITISH COLUMBIA. *1990 British Columbia Student Drug Use Survey. Summary Report.* Alcohol and Drug Programs, B.C. Ministry of Health and Ministry Responsible for Seniors, 1992.

27. BIRCH, H. G. and GUSSOW, J. D. *Disadvantaged Children: Health, Nutrition and School Failure.* New York: Grune and Stratton, 1970.

28. WEDGE, P. and PROSSER, H. *Born to Fail?* London: Arrow Books, 1973.

29. BLACK, D., MORRIS, J. N., SMITH, C., and TOWNSEND, P. The Black Report. In *Inequalities in Health,* ed. P. TOWNSEND and N. DAVIDSON. London: Penguin, 1982.

30. BERRUETA-CLEMENT, J. R., SCHWEINHART, L. J., BARNETT, W. S., EPSTEIN, A. S., and WEIKART, D. P. *Changed Lives. The Effects of the Perry Preschool on Youth Through Age 19.* Monograph of the High/Scope Educational Research Foundation, No. 8. Ypsilanti, Michigan: High/Scope Press, 1984.

31. JORDAN, T. J., GRALLO, R., DEUTSCH, M., and DEUTSCH, C. P. Long-term effects of early enrichment: A twenty-year perspective on persistence and change. *American Journal of Community Psychology* 13 (1985): 393–415.

32. WYNN, M. and WYNN, A. *Prevention of Handicap and the Health of Women.* London: Routledge and Kegan Paul, 1979, p. 81.

33. HELWIG, D. Stop wasting health care dollars on dying seniors, physicians say: In health care. *Canadian Medical Journal* 143 (1990): 653–54.

34. SHAH, C. P., KAHAN, M., and KRAUSES, J. The health of children of low-income families. *Canadian Medical Journal* 137 (1987): 485–90.

35. EISENBERG, L. The social context of behavioural pediatrics. *Developmental and Behavioural Pediatrics* 9 (1988): 382–87.

36. Committee on Child Welfare, Ontario Medical Association Editorial. Public policies and the health of children. *Canadian Medical Association Journal* 137 (1987): 181–82.

37. BERFENSTAM, R. The work of the Swedish Joint Committee for Childhood Accident Prevention. In *Children the Environment and Accidents,* ed. H. Jackson. Tunbridge, Kent: Pitman Medical Publ., 1977, pp. 133–53.

38. LAW, J. T. Children's hospitals should be child health centres. Paper presented at the Association of Canadian Paediatric Hospitals Tenth Annual Conference, Banff, Alberta, October 4–7, 1977.

39. AVARD, D. and HARVEY, L. Message from the Chairperson. In *The Health of Canada's Children: A CICH Profile.* Canadian Institute of Child Health, Ottawa, 1989.

40. ROBINSON, G. C. John T. Law lecture. Interrelationships and organization of child health care. In *Redesigning Relationships in Child Health Care,* ed. R. S. Tonkin and J. R. Wright. B.C. Children's Hospital, Canada, 1987.

Index